INSIGHT GUIDES

SHANGHAI

Discovery
CHANNEL

APA PUBLICATIONS
Part of the Langenscheidt Publishing Group

ABOUT THIS BOOK

INSIGHT GUIDE
SHANGHAI

Editorial

Project Editor
Francis Dorai
Editorial Director
Brian Bell

Distribution

UK & Ireland
GeoCenter International Ltd
The Viables Centre, Harrow Way
Basingstoke, Hants RG22 4BJ
Fax: (44) 1256 817988

United States
Langenscheidt Publishers, Inc.
46–35 54th Road, Maspeth, NY 11378
Fax: (1 718) 784 0640

Canada
Thomas Allen & Son Ltd
390 Steelcase Road East
Markham, Ontario L3R 1G2
Fax: (1 905) 475 6747

Australia
Universal Publishers
1 Waterloo Road
Macquarie Park, NSW 2113
Fax: (61 2) 9888 9074

New Zealand
Hema Maps New Zealand Ltd (HNZ)
Unit D, 24 Ra ORA Drive
East Tamaki, Auckland
Fax: (64 9) 273 6479

Worldwide
Apa Publications GmbH & Co.
Verlag KG (Singapore branch)
38 Joo Koon Road, Singapore 628990
Tel: (65) 6865 1600. Fax: (65) 6861 6438

Printing

Insight Print Services (Pte) Ltd
38 Joo Koon Road, Singapore 628990
Tel: (65) 6865 1600. Fax: (65) 6861 6438

©2003 Apa Publications GmbH & Co.
Verlag KG (Singapore branch)
All Rights Reserved

First Edition 2003

This guidebook combines the interests and enthusiasms of two of
the world's best-known information
providers: Insight Guides, whose titles
have set the standard for visual travel
guides since 1970, and Discovery
Channel, the world's premier source
of nonfiction television programming.

The editors of Insight Guides
provide both practical advice and
general understanding about a destination's history, culture and people.
Discovery Channel and its website,
www.discovery.com, help millions of
viewers explore the world from the
comfort of their homes, and encourage them to explore it firsthand.

Insight Guide: Shanghai has been
carefully structured to convey a keen
understanding of this cutting-edge
city, its surroundings and its people
as well as to guide readers through
its wealth of sights and activities.

◆ The **Features** section, indicated by
a yellow bar at the top of each page,
covers the history and culture of the
city in a series of informative essays.

◆ The main **Places** section, indicated
by a blue bar, is a complete guide to
all the sights and areas worth visiting.
Places of special interest are coordinated by number with the maps.

◆ The **Travel Tips** section, with an
orange bar, provides a handy point of
reference for information on travel,
hotels, shops, restaurants, and more.

The contributors

This book was produced by **Francis
Dorai**, Insight Guides' Singapore-
based managing editor. One of his
first tasks was to assemble a stellar
team of writers – virtually all of whom
either live (or have lived in the recent

past) in Shanghai or are intimately connected with this city in some way. The fact that almost everyone on the team speaks fluent Mandarin was an added bonus.

Encapsulating Shanghai's turbulent history into three readable chapters was **Andrew Field**. A university lecturer on modern Chinese and East Asian history, Field's PhD dissertation at Columbia University was on the somewhat unusual subject of Shanghai nightlife in the 1920s–30s.

As former chairman of Shanghai's American Chamber of Commerce, **Wm Patrick Cranley** was the perfect choice for the Business & Economy chapter. Cranley currently runs Asia Media Group, a strategic communications firm in Shanghai. His role as co-founder of the Shanghai Historic House Association also made him

the ideal candidate to write the chapter on Architecture.

Graham Earnshaw, who wrote the Shanghainese chapter, also had his work cut out for him: Earnshaw was the former Beijing-based bureau chief of Reuters and has lived in Shanghai since 1995, where he runs his own publishing firm. Lending her expertise to the Performing and Visual Arts chapters was writer **Sheila Melvin**. This former Shanghai resident, who has written on the Chinese arts scene for the *International Herald Tribune* and *New York Times*, currently divides her time between Beijing and the US.

Combining the rare ability to sniff out a bargain and to write succinctly is **Ceil Bouchet**, who contributed the chapter on Shopping. **Lisa Movius**, who has written on topics as divergent as Chinese rock music and business from her Shanghai base for a string of international publications, contributed the Shanghai Nights and Events & Festivals chapters.

Anchoring the book was Shanghai-based **Tina Kanagaratnam**. On top of running her own editorial consultancy, this inveterate writer and editor found time to comb the length and breadth of Shanghai and its environs to write the Places and Travel Tips sections (plus act as invaluable resource person). As author of a guidebook to Shanghai restaurants, she was also a natural choice for the Cuisine chapter.

The striking images in this book were mainly sourced from Shanghai-based photo agencies **Imaginechina** and **Document China**, with added picture contributions from **Bill Wassman**, **Blaine Harrington** and **David Henley**, among others.

Map Legend

— ‧ —	International Boundary
— — — —	Province Boundary
‧	National Park/Reserve
— — — —	Ferry Route
Ⓜ	Metro
✈ ✈	Airport: International/Regional
🚌	Bus Station
ℹ	Tourist Information
✉	Post Office
† ✝	Church/Ruins
†	Monastery
☾	Mosque
✡	Synagogue
🏰	Castle/Ruins
🏠	Mansion/Stately home
∴	Archaeological Site
∩	Cave
🗿	Statue/Monument
★	Place of Interest

The main places of interest in the Places section are coordinated by number with a full-colour map (e.g. ❶), and a symbol at the top of every right-hand page tells you where to find the map.

INSIGHT GUIDE
Shanghai

CONTENTS

The magnificent Bund – a stark reminder of Shanghai's treaty port history – is best viewed when it's all lit up at night

Travel Tips

◆ **Full Travel Tips index is on page 273**

Information panels

Places

CHINA'S FUTUREWORLD

Bold and brash Shanghai is where the faded glory of China's treaty port history and its visions for the future meld into one

Aldous Huxley wrote of old Shanghai: "Nothing more intensely living can be imagined". Decades later, the experience of Shanghai is no less intense. Modern Shanghai surprises, no, shocks with a futuristic face that is almost space age. Walk out of gleaming Pudong airport and the world's fastest train harnesses electro-magnetic levitation technology to whisk you to downtown Pudong in eight minutes flat. The same 30-km (19-mile) journey by car would take you an interminable 45 minutes. In the city, neon-glowing elevated highways seem to fly through the air and the rocketship-like Oriental Pearl Tower pierces the sky against the canyon of sky-scrapers framing Lujiazui district in Pudong. This is where the world's tallest building, the Shanghai World Financial Centre, is under construction, a glass ferris wheel planned for its 101st-storey pinnacle.

At ground level, art galleries are blossoming, cigar bars are every-where and café society is back. Shanghai restaurants, declare the international magazines, are among the best on the planet. Fusion is chic, designer is big, mobile phones are small.

The people of this city, they say, are the smartest, savviest, coolest, most progressive citizens in all of China. When asked how it was that Shanghai people came to be so smart, a former mayor famously replied, "It's not that Shanghai people are smart. It's that smart people come to Shanghai." They go against the grain of human nature by embracing change, seeking it out, and expertly steering this time-travelling machine that is their city. It is not surprising, then, that Chinese from elsewhere perceive the Shanghainese to be arrogant and self-centred.

This sense of cocky self-confidence stems in part from the city's early exposure to the West. Shanghai first rose to the world's attention in 1842 when China suffered defeat at the hands of the British in the First Opium War. Transformed into a booming treaty port, everyone came: fat-cat foreign companies and their taipans, small-time businessmen from surrounding provinces, and hungry peasants with burning dreams. Shanghai quickly became known as the region's most advanced city in the 1920s, boasting the tallest buildings and the most fashionable women – earning the sobriquet "Paris of the East" in the process.

The Shanghai of today in fact is little different from its former self – only things are more sharply defined. Parts of old Shanghai are still very evident in the Chinese quarter of Nanshi, in the neo-classical buildings of the Bund, in the architectural imprints left behind in the old Concessions, and in the tenement housing of old *longtang* (lane) neigh-bourhoods. The city may dazzle with its newness at first blush, but there are rewards aplenty for those seeking out slivers of its old. ❏

PRECEDING PAGES: bored brides and their grooms waiting to pose for their wedding pictures; Yu Garden Bazaar takes on a festive air during the annual Spring Festival (Chunjie); hot summer weekend at Dino water park in Shanghai's suburbs.
LEFT: flashy Shanghainese couple along Nanjing Road, where commerce is king.

Decisive Dates

1074 Shanghai progresses from a humble fishing village (*hudu*) to a commercial town (*zhen*).

1159 Shanghai's status is further elevated to that of a market town (*shi*).

1292 New county is created with Shanghai as its capital seat (*xian*).

1404 Ming dynasty engineers build a channel in Huangpu River to keep it from silting and re-route the Songjiang to exit into the Yangzi River. Huangpu becomes the main watercourse for Shanghai.

1554 Following successive attacks by pirates, the

citizens of Shanghai petition the government to build a wall around the administrative district.

1684 Kangxi Emperor sanctions maritime trade. Shanghai becomes a major distribution centre for both maritime and Yangzi river trade.

1732 Shanghai becomes headquarters of the Jiangsu customs office.

1760 The Pan family auctions off Yu Garden (Yuyuan) to the public. Yu Garden is combined with the Temple of the Town God (Chenghuang Miao) to become Shanghai's largest public space. The Qianlong Emperor restricts all foreign trade to Canton.

1826 When the Grand Canal linking the Yellow and Yangzi rivers is blocked, the Qing imperial government relies on Shanghai shipping merchants to transport tribute rice from the Lower Yangzi region by sea to Peking (Beijing).

1839 The British launch the first Opium War, and proceed to take China's coastal cities by force.

1842 The British attack and capture the walled city of Shanghai. The Qing government is forced to sign the Treaty of Nanjing to end the first Opium War. The treaty designates that five ports open to foreign trade and residence, including Shanghai.

1843 The British establish a settlement in Shanghai near confluence of Huangpu River and Suzhou Creek.

1849 The French establish their own settlement along Huangpu River, just south of British settlement.

1853 Small Swords uprising by groups of local rebels put down by settlement forces. The Taipings, another rebel faction and led by Hong Xiuquan, set up their "heavenly capital" in Nanjing.

1854 Land Regulations instituted, allowing foreigners to lease land "in perpetuity" from Chinese, and provides basis for establishment of Shanghai Municipal Council, governing body of the International Settlement. Americans claim a settlement in Hongkou just north of Suzhou Creek. Shanghai Volunteer Corps is formed, with branches comprising various nationalities, to protect the city.

1859 Imperial Maritime Customs in Shanghai is placed under the charge of British agent, Sir Robert Hart.

1861 Chinese official Li Hongzhang takes control of Shanghai customs and uses revenue gained from it to fund the Huai Army.

1863 British and American settlements merge to form the International Settlement.

1864 Taiping Rebellion is quelled by Qing forces.

1872 Englishman Ernest Major establishes China's first modern newspaper, the *Shenbao*, published in Shanghai's International Settlement. The *Shenbao* continues to run until 1949.

1895 Following China's defeat in Sino-Japanese war, the Treaty of Shimonoseki allows Japanese to set up factories in Shanghai and other treaty port cities. Other foreign powers follow suit.

1912 A weak and battered Qing dynasty gives way to a fledgling Republic.

1917 Opium is declared illegal by international agreement. Shanghai becomes a smuggler's paradise.

1919 On June 5, workers launch several strikes in Shanghai, shutting down the city's industries.

1921 Chinese Communist Party (CCP) holds first general meeting in Shanghai, with goal of establishing trade unions in China's most proletarian city.

1922 Sun Yat-sen, leader of the Nationalist, or Kuomintang (KMT), party in Canton, meets with Communist International (Comintern) agents in Shanghai and agrees to allow CCP to join the Kuomintang revolutionary movement.

1924 Du Yuesheng becomes head of the Green Gang, taking power from Huang Jinrong following an incident at an opera house.

1925 May 30th Movement begins in Shanghai when students march to the Shanghai Municipal Police headquarters, only to be shot at by police. Death of 12 students leads to nationwide demonstrations against imperialism.

1927 On 12 April, Kuomintang, under its new leader Chiang Kai-shek, teams up with Shanghai Green Gang to enforce violent purge of CCP members in Shanghai. Kuomintang establishes Greater Shanghai Municipality, and attempts over next 10 years to clean up the city and rid it of Communist influence.

1932 War is fought in Zhabei district between the Japanese military and Cantonese 19th Route Army. Japan wins but is forced to evacuate area under international pressure.

1934 Kuomintang launches New Life Movement to clean up Shanghai and other cities, part of broader initiative to rid cities of decadent Western influences.

1937 Japan invades China; attacks Shanghai in August, but leaves concessions untouched. Kuomintang government retreats to Chinese interior.

1940 In June, Vichy government of France gives up French Concession to Japanese military control.

1941 Following the attack on Pearl Harbour, Japan takes over Shanghai's International Settlement and begins to round up Allied nationals.

1943 Agreements between Allied powers and China end extraterritoriality in Shanghai and other treaty ports; Shanghai's concessions given up to Chinese sovereignty, ending 100 years of "semi-colonial" rule.

1945 Japan surrenders. US forces occupy Shanghai and other Chinese port cities.

1946 Chiang Kai-shek's Kuomintang returns to Nanjing.

1949 CCP's People's Liberation Army (PLA) defeats Kuomintang forces, who flee to Taiwan and set up the renegade Republic of China (ROC). Shanghai is "liberated" in May. On 1 October, Mao Zedong announces establishment of People's Republic of China (PRC).

1949–54 CCP shuts down vice industries in Shanghai, including gambling dens, brothels and dance halls.

1950 Beginning of campaign to "resist America and assist Korea"; foreigners expelled from Shanghai.

1958 Mao Zedong launches the Great Leap Forward.

1966–76 Cultural Revolution period marks the rise

of the Gang of Four, who take over Shanghai's propaganda apparatus.

1976 Cultural Revolution ends with death of Mao, Gang of Four is arrested and brought to trial.

1979 Deng Xiaoping launches "opening and reforms" (*gaige kaifang*) era.

1985 Jiang Zemin is named mayor of Shanghai.

1988 Jiang is succeeded by Zhu Rongji.

1989 Tiananmen crisis rocks Beijing; Jiang and Zhu maintain stability in Shanghai. Jiang becomes the Communist Party Secretary.

1990 Pudong area is designated as special development zone. Shanghai becomes "dragon head" of economic development in China.

1992 Deng takes his "southern tour", and encourages foreign investment and growth in Shanghai. Municipal revenues are used to build up Shanghai's infrastructure.

1993 The 468-metre (1,535-ft) tall iconic Oriental Pearl Tower is opened and becomes the symbol of new Shanghai.

1999 Pudong international airport opens in time for Fortune 500 Global Economic Forum. Work on the elevated highway system is also completed.

2001 Shanghai hosts the APEC conference.

2002 Despite strong competition, Shanghai wins bid to host World Expo in 2010.

2003 In September, the high-speed Maglev train starts operations, connecting Pudong airport to the city. ❏

LEFT: fishing boats along the harbour in old Shanghai.
RIGHT: Jiang Zemin, a former mayor of Shanghai, was China's president from 1993 to 2003.

A RIVER RUNS THROUGH IT

*Location had a key role to play in Shanghai's metamorphosis from
a sleepy backwater to a bustling maritime trading centre*

In late imperial times, travelling by boat was the only way to get anywhere in China's Yangzi Delta region. For a few copper coins, a merchant from Nanjing, the imperial capital in early Ming times, could hop onto a ferry and head down the Yangzi River to the Grand Canal. From the dock, he could walk a short distance through town and catch a connecting boat down the Grand Canal to the ancient walled city of Suzhou, with its splendid gardens, canals and pagodas. If the old Song capital of Hangzhou was his final destination, a night ferry could transport the merchant there, where he could stroll along the bridges crisscrossing the picturesque West Lake and catch the glowing sunset over the hills beyond. Otherwise, for a small fee, he could jump on a sand boat headed east along the Songjiang River to Shanghai, the "city on the sea".

At one point, the town of Shanghai lived up to its name, but over the centuries, silt from the Yangzi pushed the swampy Delta lands further eastward. In ancient times, Shanghai was a coastal backwater. By late imperial times, however, it had become a bustling port of trade.

Geographical advantages

Shanghai had distinct geographical advantages over other Chinese coastal cities. Situated at the centre of China's vast eastern coastline, Shanghai was conveniently located near the mouth of its most populous and productive river system, the Yangzi.

Moreover, as a result of careful planning and engineering, an intricate network of canals crisscrossed the region. These provided a water transport network for the hundreds of market towns that dotted the Lower Yangzi.

Shanghai's history as a port of trade begins in the Song dynasty (960–1279). The Song was a period of rapid urbanisation for China, particularly in the south. Loosened from the restrictions in trade and commerce that Confucian officialdom had imposed on the merchant classes, Song cities were able to shed their identities as political centres and re-emerged as centres of commerce and trade.

Meanwhile, local elites organised projects to promote agriculture and industry in their home-

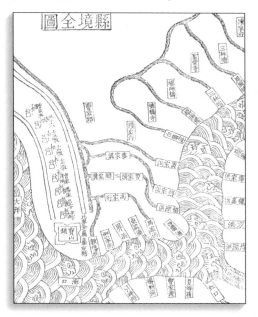

towns and native villages. These talented and enterprising men supervised the construction of canals, dykes and dams, and the draining of new areas for cultivation in the swampy Yangzi Delta, making it both habitable and productive. By the late Song period, educated men throughout the realm could consult a wide variety of illustrated manuals describing in detail the latest techniques to dredge, drain and channel waterways for irrigation and transport.

The official history of Shanghai during the late Song and early Yuan dynasty (1279–1368) reflects its rising fortunes. In 1074, the provincial bureaucracy promoted Shanghai in status from a fishing village (*hudu*) to a commercial

---

LEFT: in imperial China, boat travel was the only means of transport around the Yangzi Delta region.
RIGHT: Huangpu River running its course in old Shanghai.

town (*zhen*). In 1159, officials raised Shanghai's status to that of a market town (*shi*). By 1292, the population of the region surrounding Shanghai had grown so rapidly that officials created a new county (*xian*) with Shanghai as its capital. From then on, Shanghai served as a seat of government and eventually became one of the most productive counties in China.

One major factor that contributed to the commercial growth of Shanghai during the 10th to 14th centuries was the dredging and dyking of the Huangpu River. Originally, the main river running through the region was not the Huangpu, but the Songjiang, which ran west to

east carrying goods and people to and from larger and more important towns further inland. However, the Songjiang required a great deal of maintenance to keep it navigable.

The Huangpu was merely a stream at the time, but gradual efforts to widen it over the years had turned it into a tributary of the Songjiang. In 1404, government officials built a channel to keep the Huangpu from silting and re-routed the flow of the Songjiang into the Huangpu, contributing to its stability as a navigable waterway until modern times. From the 15th century onwards, the Huangpu gradually widened and deepened to become Shanghai's main river. The neglected Songjiang meanwhile

withered to its present proportions as Suzhou Creek. With its main river now flowing directly into the Yangzi River estuary and out to the sea beyond, Shanghai's fortunes soared.

Cotton farming

Key to Shanghai's growth during the Ming dynasty (1368–1644) was the cotton industry. Cotton originated in India but spread into China from the 13th century onwards. The warm and fertile Jiangnan region provided an ideal climate and environment for growing cotton. Cotton was cheaper to grow and to spin into cloth than silk, and more comfortable to wear than hemp. Cotton thus became the most popular fabric for making clothing for commoners. It was also easy to grow in drier areas, as opposed to rice, which required heavy irrigation. By the Ming period, over 70 percent of arable land in Shanghai county was used to grow cotton.

Cotton spinning and weaving techniques were perfected during the 13th century, and were based largely on the principles of silk weaving. By the 1300s, cotton growers in Shanghai county were also aided by the invention of the cotton gin, which used rollers mounted on a frame equipped with metal teeth. This device saved time in picking out seeds from cotton balls. Nothing, however, went to waste, since the seeds were pressed into oil.

Cotton cloth manufacture became a major cottage industry for villagers and tenant farmers throughout the Jiangnan region. Men planted, while women spun and wove. In the region surrounding Shanghai, most people either grew cotton or made cotton cloth for sale. By late Ming times, merchants imported raw cotton from other areas to spin and weave into cloth, which they then exported to other regions throughout China.

By the Qing dynasty (1644–1912), many other industries had grown around cotton production. These included the cultivation of indigo for producing *nankeen* (blue cotton cloth), and soybean cake for use as fertiliser in cotton fields. Soybeans grown in north China were brought to Shanghai, where merchants distributed them to the hinterlands. In 1749, the imperial government sanctioned maritime trade. Soon there-

LEFT: in the 14th century, cotton growing and weaving was an important industry in Shanghai.
RIGHT: Xu Guangqi was an early Christian convert.

after merchant ships carried beans, grain and other supplies up and down the China coast. As a result, Shanghai became a major distribution centre for both maritime and river trade.

The rise of shipping

Key to the system of river and ocean transport in late imperial China were shipping merchants. These men arranged to ship, unload and store supplies in local warehouses, and served as middlemen for buyers and sellers. Shipping merchants owned or controlled large fleets of ships that could transport goods within the country or to markets outside China. By Qing times, Shanghai shipping merchants were among the most powerful in the realm. When the Grand Canal was blocked in 1826, the Qing imperial government relied on the shipping merchants of Shanghai to transport tribute rice from the Lower Yangzi region by sea to Peking.

During Qing times, merchants and traders came from all over China to Shanghai to engage in trade and commerce. Community guilds (*huiguan*) dominated transport and trade functions in the city, serving as economic and social units of organisation for merchants and traders. These guilds also became important entities in local politics. By the Qing period, guilds in

CHRISTIAN INFLUENCE IN EARLY SHANGHAI

Western influence in Shanghai predates the treaty port era by nearly 250 years. Matteo Ricci (1552–1610), an astronomer for the Ming court, was one of several Italian Jesuit missionaries who lived in China during the late Ming period. The Jesuits succeeded in converting many educated Chinese, including a Shanghai-born official named Xu Guangqi (1562–1633) to Christianity.

During a trip to Beijing, Xu met Ricci, who exposed the bright young scholar to Western scientific knowledge. Over the next few decades, with the aid of Jesuit missionaries, "Paul" Xu promoted Christianity and Western learning in his hometown. Known for his broad-minded views, Xu

attracted many local scholars into his intellectual circle, with whom he published a number of volumes of Chinese and Western books, including studies of agriculture, astronomy, religion and philosophy.

With the aid of cannons and guns imported from Macau, Xu was also instrumental in building up military defences against banditry and rebellions in the Jiangnan region. The imprint of Paul Xu and his Jesuit friends on Shanghai may be seen today in the Xujiahui (Xu family residence) district, where the double-spired St Ignatius Cathedral, more popularly known as Xujiahui Cathedral *(see page 199)*, stands tall and proud.

Shanghai served many quasi-governmental functions in areas such as public works projects and the building of schools and temples.

All this while Japanese and Chinese pirates continually preyed upon coastal towns, and Shanghai was no exception. In the 1550s, the citizens of Shanghai petitioned the Board of Works to build a wall around the administrative district of the city. When the Board failed to respond, however, local elites financed and supervised the construction of a high wall to protect the city,

REFUGE WITHIN WALLS

During pirate attacks, guards would sound the alarm and people would flock through one of six gates to enter and seek refuge within the high walls of the city.

walk along the banks of the Huangpu. And adding to the colour, alongside the many merchant and trading ships, sampans and barges, were "flower boats" or floating brothels carrying girls from Suzhou and other nearby towns.

On shore, merchants and sailors could choose from a variety of inns, teahouses and brothels to while away their evening hours. For wealthier merchants and officials, elaborate courtesan houses offered women trained in the arts of poetry, music and seduction.

along with a moat surrounding the wall. Over the years, the wall grew in size and strength. The money to build and maintain the wall was raised by the merchants themselves.

Bustling centre of trade

In 1684, the Qing emperor lifted restrictions on ocean transport. Although the effect was not immediate, by the mid-1700s Shanghai had become a bustling centre of maritime trade. With thousands of dockworkers towing boxes and bundles off the docks to be stored in nearby warehouses, and local restaurant owners and street vendors hawking their wares to hungry travellers, it must have been quite a sight to

Most of Shanghai's residents lived outside the city walls. Wealthy families, however, tended to build their homes inside the walled city, and surrounded them with luxurious gardens. Within the walled city were several Buddhist and Taoist temples, as well as county government offices, charity halls, guildhalls and private academies where members of the wealthier families could study for the Confucian examinations.

Although periodic Japanese pirate attacks on Shanghai were a problem, the unification of Japan under the Tokugawa Shogunate in 1600 helped to ease the situation. After that, the wall remained but began a long, slow decline through lack of maintenance.

Yu Garden and Town Temple

At the heart of the old walled city were the Yu Garden or Yu Yuan and the Temple of the Town God, or Chenghuang Miao *(see page 151)*. In the 15th century, a temple was built at this site by the Ming emperor. Called Jinshan Miao, it was reconstructed in 1726 as the Temple of the Town God and dedicated to the spirit of Huo Guang, a famous Ming general. The temple served as a locus for worship for the inhabitants of Shanghai, who believed that their town god possessed the power to ward off pirates, bandits and other marauders.

Local residents held numerous ceremonies, rituals and festivals, both official and unofficial, at the temple. Attached to the temple was the Yu Yuan or "Pleasure Garden", originally owned by a local member of the powerful Pan family who built it in honour of his aging father. In the 1700s, during a wave of prosperity at the height of the Qing dynasty, the Temple of the Town God expanded. In 1760, the Pan family, having fallen on hard times, auctioned off the Yu Garden. A group of Shanghai shipping merchants bought the garden and donated it to the city.

The Yu Garden and the temple grounds became a major social centre for the city's wealthiest merchants. These men socialised in guildhalls and teahouses in the old walled city, including the so-called Mid-Lake Pavilion Teahouse *(see page 152)*, which sat in the middle of a fishpond and was accessible by the twisting Bridge of Nine Turnings.

Rise of the opium trade

During the Qing period, Chinese merchants in various port cities also became involved in trade with Europeans. Dominating the trade with China was the British East India Company, which swapped Mexican silver for Chinese tea.

In 1760, the Qing emperor restricted all foreign trade to the port of Canton (Guangzhou), south of Shanghai. By 1800, the British were importing into Canton opium, grown and processed in Bengal. The British exchanged opium with the Chinese for silver, some of which they used to buy Chinese tea. In 1796, realising the folly of this trade, the import of opium was banned by the Qing emperor. But

it came too late – by the early 1800s, millions of Chinese had become opium addicts, and silver flowed out of China by the tonnes. In 1839, a Chinese official declared a ban on opium and destroyed the British opium supply in Canton, heralding the start of the First Opium War.

Over the next three years, the British Navy decimated Qing defences along the coast, attacking and occupying several port cities including Shanghai. The British also forced China to open these cities to international trade, heralding the start of a new era in Shanghai's history. Over the next 100 years foreigners took control of the city and built it into a centre of international trade. ❏

TEMPLE OF THE TOWN GOD

During Ming and Qing times, Shanghai's Temple of the Town God (Chenghuang Miao) was a focal point for public gatherings. A motley group of acrobats, storytellers, itinerant monks and opera singers would entertain the crowds that gathered at the temple grounds, while the cries of trinket sellers and food vendors filled the air. The scent of incense wafting from nearby temples would intersperse with the pungent aroma of fried tofu and other local treats to give the air a heady aroma. Camphor and magnolia trees rose majestically to form a natural canopy against the hot summer sun, and in their branches, according to Shanghai poet Fei Jiajiong, "bulbuls chided the noisy crowds below".

LEFT: a high wall and a moat was built around old Shanghai in the 1550s to protect the city from pirates.
RIGHT: Yu Garden's Mid-Lake Pavilion Teahouse.

TREATY PORT SHANGHAI

Westerners brought wealth and a certain savoire faire to Shanghai,
but this was no match for the military might of the Japanese

In 1842, the Qing government signed a treaty with the British to end the First Opium War. Among other things, the Treaty of Nanjing designated five "treaty ports" – including Shanghai – where British nationals could reside and conduct trade with the Chinese. Later, beginning with the Americans in 1843, a "most favoured nation" clause in subsequent treaties with Western powers ensured that each would be granted the same advantages that others won. During the late 19th century, as treaty piled upon treaty, the privileges and powers of Western nations in China expanded and the number of treaty ports grew to around two dozen. The Treaty of Nanjing formed the legal basis for the foreign settlements that arose in Shanghai, where foreign nationals built and ran their own businesses, schools, hospitals, churches and courts of law.

Foreigners take over

The original British settlement was located at the confluence of the Huangpu River and Suzhou Creek. The French settled just south of the British along the Huangpu. In 1854, the Americans occupied lands north of Suzhou Creek. By driving timber piles deep into the mud and floating concrete rafts upon them, the Westerners built the foundations for a grand façade of colonial buildings lining the river. Eventually these structures included a consulate, a customs house, several banks, hotels and private clubs. Using the Hindustani word for "embankment," a borrowing from British colonialism in India, they called this stretch of river bank the Bund.

Over the next 50 years, the British and French settlements expanded westward to encompass several square miles of choice real estate south of Suzhou Creek. With its hands tied by treaties and internal rebellions, the Qing was helpless to prevent this gradual expansion of foreign control over Shanghai and other treaty port cities.

In 1863, the British and American settlements merged to form an enclave called the International Settlement. Both the International Settlement and the French Concession were run by their own municipal governments.

A safe haven

The Taiping Rebellion of 1850–64 boosted the population of Shanghai, while contributing to

its growing reputation as a haven during times of war. Led by a rebel called Hong Xiuquan, who claimed to be the younger brother of Christ, the Taipings appeared to the Westerners as a somewhat enlightened group of rebels. This illusion, however, disappeared as soon as they threatened the treaty ports.

In order to protect Shanghai from bandits and rebels, the settlements joined forces to form the Shanghai Volunteer Corps in 1854, a volunteer army composed of various nationals. British and American soldiers also trained armies of Chinese in modern tactics and weaponry. These armies kept the Taipings and other rebels at bay and gave Shanghai a reputation as a safety zone.

LEFT: opium caused China's downfall in 1842.
RIGHT: Western architecture along the Bund, circa 1920.

Meanwhile, in 1859, the lucrative Shanghai Customs was put under the control of the incorruptible British agent Sir Robert Hart. In the 1860s, revenue from the Customs supported the Huai army based in Anhui Province, which helped to defeat the Taipings.

Lane housing

With thousands of Chinese families streaming into the city to seek refuge from the Taiping Rebellion, the foreign settlements gave up their monopoly on land sales and made land and property available to the Chinese.

Soon blocks of houses known as *shikumen* (stone gate) or *longtang* (alley or lane) housing sprang up in the settlements, displaying a mixture of Western and Chinese architectural forms. In later years, these spacious lane houses became smaller and closer in order to accommodate the growing population of sojourners from other parts of China.

The *longtang* housing had an enormous impact on the structure of daily life in Shanghai. People could find everything they needed right inside their neighbourhood compounds, including stores, barbershops, dentists, newspaper kiosks, as well as roving merchants who sold everything from cakes to noodle soup.

> **CRAMPED QUARTERS**
>
> A lane house that housed one Shanghai family in the late 1860s was likely to hold four families by the turn of that century.

Families who lived on the second floor of lane houses had an ingenious system of transporting goods: vendors could place their goods on a platform on the ground floor, which was then raised up to their floor by means of a pulley system. However, most of these houses were tiny and lacked basic amenities like toilets and sinks. People in lane houses used chamber pots and were forced to share communal sinks and kitchens with their neighbours.

Even so, the city as a whole did not lack in modern amenities. By the early 20th century, the foreign settlements had paved roads, streetlamps, running water, a sewage system, electricity and tall buildings built along Western architectural lines. Chinese visitors coming to Shanghai from other places gaped at the technological marvels of the city, or as one famous Chinese author put it, the "light, heat and power" that Shanghai produced.

The first trolley cars introduced in the early 1900s dramatically transformed Shanghai's urban landscape, bringing the commercial centre of the city into closer contact with its suburbs. Wealthy foreigners and Chinese who lived in mansions on the outskirts of the city commuted to work by motorcar.

Shanghai prospers

The plethora of job opportunities in Shanghai attracted millions of Chinese from neighbouring provinces, as well as thousands of foreign nationals from all over the world who settled there permanently. In the span of 50 years, Shanghai's population grew 10-fold, making it one of the world's fastest growing cities.

By 1930, the total population of Shanghai was around 3 million, placing it among the top five most populous cities. Most of the city's residents lived in lane houses but wealthy Chinese and Westerners lived in grand mansions in the French Concession, surrounded by high walls enclosing private gardens. By the 1930s, many affluent citizens also lived in posh art deco apartment buildings located close to the city's entertainment districts.

Given such a concentration of wealth, entertainment of all sorts thrived in Shanghai. The Shanghai Racecourse, built during the 1850s, was the fulcrum around which the entertainment and commercial districts arose. Thousands gathered there seasonally to watch foreign jockeys race Mongolian ponies.

By the early 20th century, the area surrounding the racecourse on Nanjing and Tibet roads had grown into a major commercial district. By the 1930s, the district offered a unique mixture of traditional and modern entertainment, including department stores, opera houses, bathhouses, massage parlours, restaurants, hotels, dance halls and cinemas *(see page 33)*. Shanghai was also Asia's most fashion-oriented city. Women walking down the city's main thoroughfares wore the latest fashions, which melded influences from China and abroad.

night for pitiful wages in the foreign-owned cotton and silk textile factories lining Suzhou Creek. For many Chinese intellectuals, these workers were the most visible sign of the exploitation of China by foreign imperialists.

It was during this time that Shanghai became a centre for political intrigue as various political factions, warlords and gangsters attempted to recruit the city's labourers for their power schemes. In 1912, the ailing Qing dynasty gave way to a fledging Republic, which soon fell to rapacious warlords. The leading figure in the revolutionary movement to depose the Manchus was Sun Yat-sen, but the presidency was given to

A cauldron of revolution

In 1895, following a naval war over the protectorship of Korea, the defeated Qing government signed a treaty allowing the Japanese to build and run factories on Chinese soil. The "most favoured nation" clause also ensured that other nations enjoyed the same privilege.

By the early 20th century, Shanghai was a major manufacturing centre for the textile industry. Hundreds of thousands of Chinese men, women and children laboured day and

LEFT: entrance leading into a *longtang*, or lane, in old-style Shanghai homes. **ABOVE:** Shanghai Racecourse was where the taipans gathered on weekends.

the country's most powerful general instead, Yuan Shikai. In 1913, the power-hungry Yuan ousted Sun and his followers from Peking (Beijing). Sun formed the Nationalist Party or Kuomintang (KMT) and moved its headquarters to the southern city of Canton. Attracted by the safety the foreign settlements in Shanghai offered, Sun kept a house in the French Concession, which he shared with his young bride Soong Ching Ling, the youngest of three daughters from a wealthy and influential Chinese family.

In 1919, the Treaty of Versailles ceded German colonial territory on the Shandong peninsula to the Japanese. The warlord government that controlled Peking was heavily dependent on Japanese bank loans, and signed the treaty. On 4 May 1919, several thousand Chinese students and merchants in Peking staged a mass protest against foreign imperialism. Inspired by this, students and merchants in Shanghai led a series of workers' strikes and boycotts against foreign goods in the first open exhibition of Chinese mass nationalism.

Communism takes root

The politics of anti-imperialism fanned the flames of the Communist movement in China. Chinese Marxism was born in Peking but nurtured in the concessions of Shanghai. The city, with its large worker and student population, was the perfect breeding ground for a Communist revolution. In 1921, the Chinese Communist Party (CCP) held its first meeting in Shanghai's French Concession. And in 1922, Sun Yat-sen met with a Soviet representative from the Comintern, who persuaded him to allow CCP members into his party in exchange for Soviet aid.

In 1925, the opportunity presented itself: a Japanese foreman shot a striking Chinese worker in a Japanese textile mill in Shanghai, causing groups of university students to take to the streets to protest against foreign imperialism. Fearing mob rule and anarchy, Settlement police arrested

"NO DOGS OR CHINESE ALLOWED"

During the 1920s, enraged Chinese complained that Shanghai's Huangpu Park *(see page 136)* had a sign at the gates stating, "No dogs or Chinese allowed." In actual fact, no such sign existed, although entrance rules at the park did forbid dogs and unaccompanied Chinese from entering, save for Chinese nannies entrusted with European children. The Westerners retorted that the Chinese masses lacked public consciousness; many felt that the Chinese would spoil the park with their tendency to spit and litter. Following the Kuomintang revolution of 1926–7, under pressure from the new government, the International Settlement authorities lifted the ban.

a number of protestors. On 30 May 1925, a mob of angry Chinese students swarmed the Settlement and surrounded the headquarters of the Shanghai Municipal Police, hoping to free the students who were locked up inside. Upon orders given by their captain, police shot directly into the crowd, creating 12 more martyrs for the cause of Chinese nationalism.

The May 30th Movement that ensued led to further waves of strikes in Shanghai and other Chinese cities. The mass nationalism and antiforeign attitude of the mid-1920s provided a popular support base for the Kuomintang revolution led by its new leader Chiang Kai-shek. Chiang, head of the Kuomintang army in Canton, had taken over the Kuomintang government by force following the death of Sun Yat-sen in 1925. In 1926, declaring his intention to unite China and rid the country of warlords and imperialists, Chiang led his army northward out of Canton on the Northern Expedition. Through the agency of the Green Gang, Shanghai played a decisive and macabre role in the Kuomintang revolution of 1926–7.

Shanghai Green Gang

In 1917, an international agreement made opium illegal worldwide. Overnight, Shanghai became a smuggler's paradise. With its com-

seller in Pudong, his birthplace. The restless youth soon became involved in Shanghai's prostitution and gambling rackets, first as a messenger, then as a thug, finally as an assassin. Over the years, Du worked his way up in the rackets until he gained the notice of Huang. Another key member of the gang was Zhang Xiaolin, the "playboy gangster" whose close connections with the Zhejiang warlord Lu Yongxiang helped to secure the gang's control of the opium trade.

In 1924, "Pockmarked" Huang made the mistake of ordering his men to attack Lu's son after the young man booed Huang's favourite opera singer. Lu sent his men to capture Huang,

mand over the vast network of waterways in the Yangzi Delta, the former boatmen's association known as the Green Gang came to dominate the city's opium trade. Its leaders included two of the most notorious figures in the history of crime: Huang Jinrong and Du Yuesheng.

"Pockmarked" Huang was a police detective in the French Concession. Through contacts with the city's gangsters, Huang developed a vast network of informers and became a powerful crime boss. "Big Ears" Du began his career as a fruit

LEFT: Shanghai street scene in 1906.
ABOVE: 1930s Chinese actress Ruan Lingyu.
RIGHT: infamous Shanghai mob boss Du Yuesheng.

THE MOSQUITO PRESS

In 1900, a Shanghai newspaperman discovered that he could sell more papers by including gossip from the city's brothels. Since Shanghai was full of sojourners from all over China, one of the best places to gather or dispense news was at a local courtesan house. News from the brothels gave rise to the institution of the Chinese tabloid or *xiaobao*. Known in English as the "mosquito press", these papers covered the private lives of the city's famous prostitutes. By the 1920s, *xiaobao* reporters had turned to the lives of Shanghai film stars. In 1934, a famous actress named Ruan Lingyu committed suicide as a result of scandalous information printed about her in a local paper.

and Zhang and Du were sent to negotiate for Huang's release. As a result of this incident, Huang lost most of his power and prestige and Du emerged as the gang's *primus inter pares*. In a bathhouse conversation with a police detective named Xue Gengxin, Huang confessed that Du had stopped calling him "uncle" and now referred to him merely as "elder brother".

Huang and Zhang were old-style gangsters, who favoured Chinese opera and courtesans. The younger Du was a modern gangster who frequented the city's nightclubs, dated dancing girls, and recognised the potential of the heroin racket. Over the next decade, with the aid of the corrupt settlement authorities, regional warlords and the Kuomintang government, Du forged the most powerful and lucrative drug monopoly China ever saw.

The White Terror

In 1927, Chiang Kai-shek's Northern Expedition made it to Shanghai. The fledgling Chinese Communist Party (CCP), an ally of Chiang till now, paved the way for the Kuomintang by organising a citywide strike. Yet Chiang had other plans. After sending delegates to meet with Du Yuesheng, Chiang ordered a purge of the Communists in Shanghai. On 12 April

RUSSIAN AND JEWISH DIASPORAS

During the 1930s, Shanghai was home to refugees from all over the world. Two of the largest streams from abroad were White Russians and European Jews. With some 30,000 refugees from Russia and Eastern Europe, and 20,000 Jewish refugees from Nazi-occupied Europe, they far outnumbered all other foreign nationals put together, save for the Japanese.

Thousands of White Russians who opposed the Bolshevik Revolution of 1917 made the perilous journey across frozen Siberia to China. Those who made it to Shanghai brought few possessions and no money. Most men took menial jobs as servants, bodyguards and entertainers for the wealthy classes, while those who could do so served as doctors or lawyers for their own communities. Despite their notorious reputation as femmes fatales in the local cabarets, most Russian women raised families by running small businesses such as dressmaking shops.

During World War II, thousands of Jewish refugees settled in Shanghai's Hongkou area *(see pages 208 and 213)*, where they set up communities complete with stores, synagogues, schools, newspapers and cafés. Although privileged Westerners viewed them with disdain, these refugees from war-torn Europe brought vitality to the city through their culture, cuisine, religion, music and tragic tales.

1927, in an episode known afterward as the White Terror, Green Gang members and Kuomintang soldiers rounded up and executed thousands of Communists and strike organisers operating in Shanghai.

Chiang's purge of the CCP was part of a bid to gain the support of the wealthy classes in Shanghai, who ran the city's factories and enterprises. Chiang headquartered his government in Nanjing and set about consolidating his power over the country. Over the next several years, Chiang organised four extermination campaigns designed to wipe out the Communists. In Shanghai, the CCP continued to operate, but moved deep underground.

Meanwhile, Shanghai bankers and industrialists proved reluctant to support Chiang, believing him to be just another power-hungry warlord. It took the aid of the Green Gang to ensure that these men contributed to the Kuomintang cause. Over the next decade, the number of kidnappings in Shanghai skyrocketed, and money poured into the coffers of the Kuomintang government.

The Green Gang was also instrumental in helping the Kuomintang to ferret out the underground Communist elements. Joining forces with the Shanghai Municipal Police, Kuomintang police and Green Gang members arrested several key CCP operatives, who led them to others. Soon, however, Settlement police were unearthing the bodies of family members of the turncoats.

Meanwhile, relations between the Green Gang and the French Concession began to sour. In 1932, the French authorities forced Du and his heroin factories out of their concession. As a gesture to show that he was not insulted, Du held a farewell banquet for the French officials. Within the following month, several officials who attended Du's dinner died of mysterious causes. Some alleged that Du had served up a batch of poisoned mushrooms.

During the 1930s, Du made an attempt to become a model citizen by serving on the board of several major companies and organising philanthropic projects to help the Chinese poor. When the Kuomintang government organised an Opium Suppression Bureau, in an ironic twist that only Shanghai could produce, Du was appointed its chairman.

LEFT: in the 1930s, Shanghai was home to a refugee community of White Russians, like these chorus-line girls.
RIGHT: Shanghainese fleeing the Japanese attack, 1937.

World War II Shanghai

Beginning with the takeover of Manchuria in 1931, Japan launched an aggressive military campaign that was aimed at taking control of China. In 1932, the Japanese provoked a war in the Zhabei district of Shanghai, just north of Suzhou Creek. Foreigners living in the untouchable settlements watched bemusedly from their hotel rooftops as Japanese planes bombed this manufacturing and residential district to shreds. Although the Cantonese 19th Route Army staged an impressive defence, they were no match for imperial Japan.

Although international pressure forced the

Japanese out of Zhabei, they continued to mount an aggressive campaign in north China.

Chiang Kai-shek preferred to annihilate the Communists before dealing with the more powerful Japanese. This led many Chinese, including Shi Liangcai, the chief editor of China's most influential newspaper, the *Shenbao*, to accuse him of appeasement. Since the paper was printed in Shanghai's International Settlement, Chiang couldn't attack it directly. In 1934, Shi was returning by car from Hangzhou to Shanghai when he was stopped and killed by four gunmen.

In 1937 Japan finally launched a full-scale invasion of China from its power base in

Manchuria. Chiang sent his most powerful troops to protect Shanghai while Green Gang members dug trenches and fought valiantly along the shores of the Huangpu. But, these motley troops were no match for the Japanese, who had mastered the art of coordinating air, land and sea attacks.

Forced to flee Nanjing and retreat into the Chinese interior, Chiang Kai-shek and his Kuomintang forces eventually settled in the city of Chongqing in Sichuan Province, where they remained for the duration of the war. Even so, Chiang's head of secret police, Dai Li, left several key lieutenants in Shanghai to fight a

and anti-Japanese factions, but many people remained neutral in the war, preferring instead to wait it out.

Japanese seize control

Following the attack on Pearl Harbour on 7 December 1941, the Japanese military quickly seized control of the International Settlement area. Foreigners who were suspected of treason were interrogated and tortured in prisons by the Japanese military. Allied nationals living in Shanghai were forced to wear armbands designating their national status: "A" for Americans, "B" for British, and so forth. In 1943, the

vicious underground war of attrition against the Japanese and their Chinese collaborators. Over the next four years, Dai Li's men conducted a vigorous campaign against the pro-Japanese factions in the city.

The years 1937–41 marked what is known as the "lone island" era, when Shanghai was ruled by the Japanese but the foreign concessions were still under control of foreigners.

Fearful of engaging the Western powers in a war, the Japanese military decided to leave the settlements alone. Even so, Shanghai quickly became an arena for deadly battles between the pro-Chongqing and pro-Japanese terrorists. Almost overnight, the city was divided into pro-

Japanese rounded up Allied nationals in Shanghai and incarcerated them in prison camps.

That same year, the Allied powers signed a treaty with the Kuomintang government in Chongqing, finally agreeing to end the policy of extraterritoriality. At the same time, Shanghai's concessions were returned to Chinese sovereignty under the aegis of the Japanese. In the flick of a pen and the flash of a sword, some 100 years of "semi-colonialism" in treaty port Shanghai came to a sudden crashing end. ❑

ABOVE: US Marines bid farewell at the Bund in December 1941, after Japanese seize the International Settlement.

The Rollicking 1930s

Dubbed the "Paris of the Orient", Shanghai was once world famous for its thriving nightlife scene. By the 1930s, Shanghai had over 30 licensed cabarets or "dance saloons" and hundreds of unlicenced ones, mostly in the guise of "dance academies". These establishments offered dining, drinking and dancing to a live orchestra, as well as pretty female dance partners for the thousands of single men who lived in or visited the city.

High-class dance palaces included the Paramount ballroom on Yuyuan Road, and Ciro's night club on Bubbling Well Road. At these nightspots, the city's wealthiest residents could be spotted, dressed to the nines. The men in tuxedos and the women in evening gowns, decked out with their finest jewellery, would arrive in chauffeured cars at elegant dance halls. From the polished bars serving fancy cocktails to the sprung wooden dance floors and the African-American orchestras playing the latest jazz tunes, these establishments offered luxuries on a par with the finest ballrooms in London and New York.

In the middle of the cabaret spectrum were dozens of cavernous, albeit lower-class dance halls such as the Casanova on Avenue Edward VII and the Majestic Ballroom on Bubbling Well Road.

During the late 1920s, such dance halls catered to an elite crowd of Chinese bohemians at a time when most Chinese considered embracing in public to be a vulgar activity. By the 1930s, through the cultural influence of Hollywood films, Chinese society in Shanghai came to accept Western practices of dancing, kissing and other forms of public intimacy.

Meanwhile, forced by the economic fall-out from the depression and war, exclusive Shanghai ballrooms began opening their doors to a wider public. In the heat of competition, new dance halls sprang up "like bamboo shoots in spring rain", according to one Chinese hack.

Chinese managers staffed these dance halls with pretty hostesses from the countryside. These women, whose ages ranged from 15 to 25, danced, drank and flirted with Chinese male customers in exchange for tickets, which they then traded with management for cash. They used most of the money they earned to keep up with the latest fashions in manicures, hairstyles, dresses and high heels. Although municipal rules forbade prostitution, many of these women engaged in private relations with patrons outside the dance hall, which considerably boosted their incomes.

At the low end of the nightlife scene were the cheap dives that lined the so-called Blood Alley near the Bund, and the Trenches in Hongkou. These rowdy halls catered to thousands of soldiers and sailors temporarily stationed in Shanghai from countries all over the world. In joints such as the Venus, Mumm's and the Frisco, the lonely sailor could find a girl of almost any nationality he desired. For a modest fee he could spend an energetic evening with her dancing the Lindy Hop, fol-

lowed by an equally enervating night in bed. The following morning he might wake up with a nasty hangover and a case of the clap, his girl gone and his week's earnings scattered to the wind.

From 1937 until 1941, when the foreign settlements were operating as neutral zones, Shanghai's residents threw themselves even deeper into the city's hedonistic nightlife. Cabarets, nightclubs and casinos prospered and flourished as never before. While patrons cavorted on the dance floor, Chinese staffers and dance hostesses worked behind the scenes to squeeze precious information from drunken Axis officers for the sake of the resistance movement. Underneath a thin veil of respectability, Shanghai's cabarets bubbled with war-time political intrigue. ❏

RIGHT: Shanghainese calendar girl typified the glamour of cosmopolitan Shanghai in the 1930s.

A LIBERATED CITY

*Having survived the war, communism and the Cultural Revolution, Shanghai
is again poised to take its place as East Asia's leading city*

During the war years, Shanghai's industries suffered from a combination of neglect, abuse and over-taxation by the Japanese Occupation government. The Japanese took over many of the city's factories and milked them dry to fund their war machine. By the end of the war, supplies of coal and cotton had dwindled to a mere trickle. Hundreds of thousands of factory workers had lost their jobs, and factories had been looted for their metal and machinery. Banks pumped out worthless currencies on newspaper print, while prices spiralled in a runaway inflation as currency speculation rose. A black market flourished in basic commodities such as sugar, oil and rice.

Yet indomitable Shanghai would not be kept down. After the Japanese surrendered in August 1945, former residents rushed back to rebuild the city and rekindle its glorious legacy as Asia's leading metropolis. Under the protection of US Marines, many foreigners returned to their old stomping grounds, and the dusty hotel lobbies and nightclubs buzzed with entrepreneurs seeking to introduce the latest industries to the Chinese market.

The taming of Shanghai

In May 1946, Chiang Kai-shek returned to Nanjing. Since the concessions no longer existed, the Kuomintang (KMT) or Nationalists had full control over Shanghai. Orders went out from Nanjing to clean up Shanghai and regulate its notorious vices.

In an epic campaign, the Kuomintang police set out to catalogue and categorise the thousands of brothels, prostitutes, gambling halls and opium dens operating in the city, with the eventual goal of driving them out of business. Thousands of war-weary soldiers and civilians intent on enjoying their return to Shanghai to the fullest did not make it any easier for the Kuomintang to do their job.

LEFT: the Communist People's Liberation Army marches down the Bund after seizing Shanghai in 1949.
RIGHT: a young Chiang Kai-shek.

While the Kuomintang fought to tame the city and control its vice industries, a series of worker strikes spurred on by the Communist underground movement added to the woes of the municipal government. Rampant post-war inflation and currency speculation, along with the policy of allowing collaborationists –

Chinese officials who worked for the Japanese Occupation government – to remain in their official posts after the war, did little to contribute to the popularity of the Kuomintang in Shanghai and other cities. Instead of dismantling the institutions of regulation and control set up by the Japanese, the Kuomintang enhanced them.

Arise the Communists

Another legacy of the war years was the dramatic growth of the Chinese Communist Party (CCP). Between 1937 and 1945, the CCP greatly expanded in size and extended its occupation of north China. In 1945, the Soviet Union entered the Pacific theatre and occupied Manchuria. It conveniently left stockpiles of Japanese weapons for the CCP, who then entrenched themselves in Manchuria.

In 1949, following a bitter four-year civil war fought mostly in the northeast, the Communist's People's Liberation Army (PLA) marched southward, taking China's coastal cities. Chiang and his cohorts fled to Taiwan, vowing to return. But they never did; Chiang set up the Republic of China (ROC) with Taipei as its capital.

In May 1949, the PLA "liberated" Shanghai, and, on 1 October, Mao Zedong triumphantly declared the foundation of the People's Repub-

lic of China (PRC). Thus began the saga of the "two Chinas", the PRC and the ROC, which continues till today.

Between 1949 and 1954, in a sweeping campaign, the CCP made great efforts to clean up the opium, gambling, prostitution and other rackets that had made Shanghai the most notorious city in the world. The new government sent those who resisted its cleanup efforts to so-called "re-education camps", a euphemism for labour camps located in remote places like Hainan Island and Inner Mongolia. Over the next three decades, millions more would join them from Shanghai and other cities. The revolution had just begun.

Communism takes root

After its "liberation" by the CCP, Shanghai continued to play a leading role in rebuilding the nation. Despite the exodus of many of the city's most talented business managers to Hong Kong and Taiwan, Shanghai still had the greatest concentration of technical know-how, the most diverse and effective educational system, and the most productive workers in China.

For the fledgling CCP, as for the Kuomintang and Japanese occupiers who had preceded them, Shanghai provided the industrial and tax support base for building a new and stronger China. Over the next four decades, the central government in Peking milked Shanghai, siphoning off the city's fiscal revenues to build up other parts of the country.

True to its legacy as a cauldron of revolution, Shanghai also remained at the forefront of the revolutionary forces that were shaping the new China. During the campaign to "Resist America and Aid Korea" in 1950, nearly all of Shanghai's foreign nationals were either expelled or driven from the city. The subsequent Three Antis campaign in 1951 and the Five Antis campaign in 1952, organised by the CCP, targeted corrupt bureaucrats and tax evaders. While workers gained greater control over their jobs and lives through unions formed during this period, the state also extended its control over private industry.

Private life was also not spared: the CCP strictly prohibited dancing, gambling, fashion and other forms of leisure that had made Shanghai the "Paris of the Orient". In 1954, the last dance halls either closed down or converted their establishments into proletarian culture palaces. During the anti-rightist campaign of 1957, private dance parties were outlawed. Women traded in their colourful dresses and high heels for drab workers' uniforms. Perms and skirts slowly gave way to the ascetic hairstyles and unisex clothing of the Mao years.

The Great Leap Forward

During the Great Leap Forward of 1958 – Mao's campaign to increase rural productivity through the formation of communes under government control – party cadres were encouraged by the central government policy to misreport yields. The result was widespread famine. Between 1959 and 1961, the countryside faced mass starvation in epidemic proportions and millions died. The workers of Shanghai were fed and protected from the famine, but were encouraged to work longer hours to bolster the country's sagging economy.

The Great Leap Forward also helped fuel the puritanical asceticism that had descended upon Shanghai like a dark shadow. Any sort of eccentricity, from the way one combed one's hair to the cultivation of hobbies such as fishing or chess, was noticed by neighbourhood or company spies and immediately reported to one's work unit or *danwei*.

> **REVOLUTION CREDO**
>
> The Cultural Revolution which lasted from 1966–76 was aimed at ridding China of four "olds": old customs, old habits, old culture and old thinking.

ning of the Cultural Revolution, a campaign designed to weed out party members and social leaders who did not follow the Maoist line.

During this period, Shanghai's student and worker population exploded into violent revolutionary activity. Militant Maoist youth groups known as Red Guards took to the streets, distributing leaflets, putting up posters and giving lectures on Maoist thought to passersby.

Zealous youths attacked all vestiges of bourgeois culture, harassing people with Western

The new regime encouraged a culture of mutual hostility and suspicion, which reached a frenzied peak during the Cultural Revolution years.

The Cultural Revolution

In 1966, in an attempt to deepen the revolution and to shore up his own power against his "revisionist" enemies, Mao called upon China's youthful students and workers to "bombard the headquarters" and take the country's political institutions by force. This marked the begin-

clothing or hairstyles, and destroying symbols of foreign domination in the city. Shanghai lost important buildings, monuments and books as well as a lifetime's worth of precious art and music. The spires of Xujiahui Cathedral were lopped off, Jing An Temple was destroyed and the Bund was renamed Revolution Boulevard. Thankfully, although they were raided and plundered, many of the city's churches and other foreign concession buildings remained intact.

Shanghai's workers took advantage of the revolution to air their grievances. Under the economic policies of the 1960s, many jobs in Shanghai's industries were given to contract labourers who worked for lower wages and did

LEFT: Communist flag atop a Shanghai government building. **ABOVE:** Mao Zedong visiting workers at a Shanghai factory.

not ask for costly benefits. In December 1966, however, 500,000 Scarlet Red Guards – a Shanghai-based organisation composed mainly of workers – demanded higher wages, permanent contracts and better working conditions.

As the Cultural Revolution heated up, incidents of political violence rose. In September 1966 alone, student violence led to 704 suicides and 354 murders in Shanghai. The influx into the city of several hundred thousand student Red Guards from Beijing exacerbated the tense political situation in Shanghai. By December, battles waged between student and worker Red Guard factions and a defunct municipal government had paralyzed the entire city, disrupting its shipping, railways and factory production.

In January 1967, the central party leadership in Beijing appointed Zhang Chunqiao, Shanghai's Director of Propaganda, to restore order with the aid of the army. A member of the notorious "Gang of Four" *(see box below)*, Zhang had risen to power in the party by toeing the Maoist line during his years in Shanghai. Under Zhang's leadership, the army wrested control of the city's key production and transportation facilities from the hands of militant student and worker groups, forcing them to give up their radical goals and return to work.

THE GANG OF FOUR

During the Cultural Revolution years (1966–76), Shanghai became the power base for a group of party leaders dubbed the Gang of Four after their fall. Its members were Zhang Chunqiao, Jiang Qing (Mao's wife), Yao Wenyuan, and Wang Hongwen. They secured their power on the national stage by supporting Mao's radical policies, using the city's newspapers to push their views and to denounce their "revisionist" enemies. Following the death of Mao Zedong in 1976, the Gang of Four was arrested and brought to trial on a long string of charges. Over the years, through their manipulation of local politics, they had earned the deep hatred of Shanghai's citizens.

A rising consumer haven

The Cultural Revolution lost its steam with the death of Mao in 1976 and the subsequent fall of the Gang of Four. In 1978, Deng Xiaoping became China's paramount leader, and he launched a new era of "reform and opening up" (*gaige kaifang*) in 1979.

Under his leadership, China sought foreign investment, education and technological assistance from the West, particularly the US. Deng promoted a series of market reforms and allowed for the formation of four "special economic zones" in southern China to encourage foreign investment. As a result of the CCP's new economic policies, China emerged from relative political and economic isolation to become one of the fastest growing economies in the world.

Certainly the effects of new government policies were felt in the rise of material standards in Shanghai. By the early 1980s, families in Shanghai were buying television sets, refrigerators and other appliances that were once off limits to all but high-level party cadres.

Shanghai's financial success, however, was a double-edged sword. Between 1949 and 1988, over 80 percent of the city's fiscal revenues were channeled to the central government in Beijing. This led to a stagnation in Shanghai's infrastructure development. In 1988, the tallest

the long process of removing the shackles of a planned economy. With the opening of Shanghai to foreign investment in the early 1990s, the stage was set for an economic and infrastructural boom whose proportions are perhaps unprecedented in world history.

The dragon rises

Thanks in part to the efforts of Jiang Zemin and Zhu Rongi *(see box below)*, both former mayors of Shanghai, the CCP allowed Shanghai's government to use its fiscal revenues to build up the city's long-neglected infrastructure. Jiang, who assumed China's leadership in 1993,

building in town was the Park Hotel, built in 1934. Most people living in the city were crowded into the old lane (*longtang*) houses or socialist blockhouses built for factory workers. People rode bicycles down narrow streets, or piled like sardines into public buses.

Under a planned economy, the city's industries were harnessed for the greater good of building China. In 1992, following the vindication of economic reforms in Shanghai and other cities in southern China, the CCP began

LEFT: Shanghai workers celebrating the fall of the dreaded Gang of Four. **ABOVE:** an economic boom in the early 1980s saw rising affluence in Shanghai.

GROOMED FOR LEADERSHIP

Many people associate the 1990s Shanghai boom with two of the city's former mayors, Jiang Zemin and Zhu Rongji. Jiang was appointed mayor in 1985, Zhu in 1988. Zhu weathered Beijing's Tiananmen crisis in 1989 by keeping order in Shanghai without resorting to martial law. As the Communist Party secretary, Jiang also scored brownie points by shutting down a Shanghai newspaper that supported the student movement. Their achievements were noticed by Deng Xiaoping, who elevated Jiang and Zhu to the Standing Committee of the Politburo, the most powerful body in the CCP. After Deng's retirement in 1993, Jiang assumed China's leadership; Zhu became premier in 1998.

continued to uphold the economic reforms introduced by Deng.

In 1990, Shanghai's Pudong district *(see page 215)* was set up as a Special Economic Zone (SEZ), and became the showcase for the city's modernisation scheme. Through tax incentives, lowered tariffs and other benefits, the municipal government encouraged foreign enterprises and banks to move into Pudong.

In 1997, the gleaming new Shanghai Stock Exchange Building opened in Pudong's Lujiazui financial zone, the new "Shanghai Wall Street". The municipal government has also encouraged real estate companies to build new

futuristic Pudong International Airport. In September 2003, the Maglev, the world's fastest train started operations, zipping passengers from the Pudong airport to the city in minutes.

Two new icons arose in Pudong to dominate the skyline: the Oriental Pearl Tower in 1993, and the Jin Mao Tower, the world's third tallest building and housing the swanky Grand Hyatt hotel, in 1998. Both tower menacingly over the colonial edifices along the Bund across the river.

All over the city, state-owned department stores and street markets have given way to glitzy supermarkets and shopping malls. Thousands of overseas Chinese, Japanese, Koreans,

housing complexes and offices in Pudong since the mid-1990s, and has successfully lured many city residents and businesses to move across the Huangpu River.

State-of-the-art infrastructure

Meanwhile, city planners and engineers have started to build a new transportation infrastructure for the 21st century. Over the decade of the 1990s, the city government constructed an elevated highway system to ease urban traffic, built four suspension bridges spanning the Huangpu River, expanded many of the city's clogged streets, dug a subway line running north–south and another east–west, and constructed the

and Westerners have settled in Shanghai to operate businesses and to take advantage of the city's entrepreneurial spirit.

Since the 1990s, Shanghai also experienced a renaissance in urban real estate, not seen since the boom years of the 1920s. Overcrowded and dilapidated tenements are being knocked down to make way for new skyscrapers. In the span of a few years, Shanghai has rapidly changed from a horizontal maze of *longtang* (alley or lane) neighbourhoods to a vertical city of highrises. Housing conditions have improved remarkably but the downside is that to make way for urban development, tens of thousands of residents have been forcibly relocated from their old *shikumen* (stone gate) houses to the suburbs with little compensation.

By revamping the infrastructure, city planners have temporarily solved some of the pressing over-crowding problems that the city faced during the early 1990s. The city government's plan to build a "green city" of public parks and gardens, which by 2005 will afford 7 sq metres (75 sq ft) of green space per capita, is already making a difference in the quality of life for residents in many parts of the crowded city.

> **GREENING THE CITY**
>
> The Shanghai Gardening Administration Bureau promises that by 2005, 30 percent of the city's public lands will have been converted to parks and gardens.

The downside

Despite these positive changes, the city's rapid transformation in recent years has brought a new set of social problems for Shanghai's residents, which they share in common with many of China's other cities.

The growing number of cars and motorbikes has raised air pollution levels, despite efforts to green the city. With the easing of restrictions on mobility during Shanghai's construction boom, hundreds of thousands of migrant workers have moved into the city;

Preservation schemes have assured that some of the city's historic neighbourhoods and buildings will survive the recent construction frenzy, giving the city a sense of historical continuity that it might not otherwise have. In particular, the former French Concession has remained relatively unchanged. In certain neighbourhoods, one can still stroll along quiet streets under a canopy of trees past old mansions and art deco apartments and get a sense of what the city was like during the pre-Liberation era.

LEFT: Nanpu Bridge spanning the Huangpu River.
ABOVE: whimsical bronze statues at Huaihai Park, part of the local government's efforts to beautify the city.

many do the work that modern Shanghainese shun, and often lack access to basic amenities such as housing and education. Brothels, often thinly disguised as massage parlors, karaoke halls or hair salons, employing young women from neighbouring provinces, have sprung up in many areas.

For those who have successfully navigated the transition to a market-oriented economy, life in Shanghai offers a greater variety of amenities and pleasures than any time since its decadent heyday of the 1930s. But for the beggar rattling his tin of coins outside the sparkling shopping malls of Huaihai Road, the future is somewhat less certain. ❏

BUSINESS AND ECONOMY

The city is expected to steamroll China's growth in the 21st century,
possibly eclipsing its counterpart Hong Kong within the next decade

From the incessant clatter of construction that fills the gleaming metropolis of Pudong and the old downtown in Puxi to the clink of glasses toasting a steady stream of closed deals in conference rooms and restaurants all over the city, Shanghai is abuzz with a high-voltage energy that spells, no – screams – economic development.

Shanghai's citizens are the wealthiest in China: their GDP per capita reached that of middle-income countries in 2000, and with expected annual growth rates of between 8 and 10 percent, Shanghainese will enjoy purchasing power equal to or exceeding that of Australians and Italians by 2010. It is little wonder that manufacturing and service companies are beating a path to the city, or that real estate developers are rushing to build shopping malls, office complexes and apartments that seem to materialise here as quickly as they can be conceived.

It is hard to overstate the importance of Shanghai to the national economy. With only one percent of the country's population, Shanghai generates 5 percent of the nation's output, and 25 percent of its total trade. China's annual economic growth has averaged between 5 and 8 percent in recent years (depending on whose statistics you consult), but Shanghai's growth has averaged an astounding 10 percent per annum during the same period – and the pace shows no sign of slackening.

Shanghai's thriving retail sector is evidence that the service sector now accounts for more than 50 percent of Shanghai's GDP. *Shanghairen* (or Shanghainese) are indubitably the most style-conscious of Chinese, which explains the city's packed clothing shops, screaming billboards and sidewalks that can sometimes look more like catwalks. Visitors may wish to purchase Chinese silk or porcelain as gifts for family and friends, but they can just as easily opt for Burberry on Nanjing Road or Versace on Huaihai Road.

LEFT: computer chip manufacturing plant in Shanghai.
RIGHT: making money is Shanghai's new *raison d'être*.

Loosening the shackles

Shanghai has not always been a great place in which to invest. In 1949, the very qualities that had made the city a business mecca suddenly turned into an industrialist's nightmare when Shanghai was seized by the Communists. Shanghai's business elite either fled the country or suf-

fered the iniquity of watching their factories nationalised and their personal assets seized. By the late 1950s, Shanghai's business intelligensia had been driven to the brink of extinction.

During the first 10 years of its rule, the Communist Party tore apart the laissez-faire capitalism of pre-1949 China and instituted in its place a textbook example of centrally-planned economics. All production was set by the state and distributed by the state. In return for his labour and loyalty, a citizen's needs were provided from cradle to grave by the government. Once assigned to a *danwei* (work unit), it was generally impossible to transfer to another.

In the early years of the People's Republic,

central planners soaked up tax revenues from Shanghai and starved the city of resources, in part out of fear that Shanghai's capitalist reflexes could undermine the Communist experiment. This policy was maintained even as Deng Xiaoping's administration began dismantling parts of the state apparatus under the "reform and opening up" *(gaige kaifang)* drive in the 1980s.

After former Shanghai mayors Jiang Zemin and Zhu Rongji assumed top positions in Beijing, they became lobbyists for Shanghai's economic development. When Deng agreed to loosen Shanghai's reins after 1990, the city reacted like an orchard exposed to warmth after a long winter. Forty years was not long enough to extinguish Shanghai's commercial instincts: the stage was set for the intensive development that began in the 1990s and continues today.

Economic pillars

While services now account for more than 50 percent of Shanghai's economy, the foundation of the city's economic power is manufacturing, both light and heavy. Shanghai-made products have maintained their pre-1949 reputation as the best-made in the country, and most nationally recognised brand names originated in Shanghai. Bao Shan Steel is one of the largest

COMMERCIAL CULTURE

The intangible factor in the city's economic success is the confident, urbane and commercial-minded character of the typical Shanghainese. The forefathers of most of today's Shanghainese moved to the city decades ago from nearby provinces to seek their fortunes. They were mostly brave (some would say foolhardy) Chinese with an appetite for risk and the brains to make the best of opportunity. To this day, Shanghai is the lodestone that attracts the brightest Chinese from all corners of the country. Shanghainese may refer derisively to newcomers as *waidiren* (outsiders), but as long as they are intelligent and ambitious, they quickly integrate into Shanghai society.

steel producers in the world and a symbol of Chinese industrial might. Shanghai Automotive Industry Corp (SAIC) is the largest producer of cars in China, and operates joint ventures with both Volkswagen and General Motors.

But with wage levels rising, Shanghai manufacturers have moved up the technology curve. With the encouragement of both the municipal and central governments, Shanghai has become a production centre for high-tech items like semiconductors and telecommunications equipment. These industries rely on educated workers with good language skills, and this is where Shanghai excels – it trails only Beijing in the level of education of its population, and no other Chinese city is as cosmopolitan. In addition, Shanghai is the world's third busiest port (after Rotterdam and Singapore). Growth in annual volume is expected to continue at between 20 and 30 percent, and when Shanghai's new deep-water port is completed in 2020, throughput may make another big jump.

Shanghai also serves as the logistics centre for the inland provinces located along the longest river in China, the Yangzi. A network of modern highways link industrial centres in the Yangzi River Delta, so lorry transport between Suzhou, Wuxi, Yangzhou, Hangzhou, Nanjing and Shanghai is fast, reliable and inexpensive. Naturally, Shanghai is also a major node along the nation's rail network. Shanghai has two airports, one for domestic flights (Hongqiao Airport) and another for international traffic (Pudong International Airport) that is brand-new and has plenty of room to grow.

> **INVITATION TO INVEST**
>
> Check out the Shanghai government's business website at www.investment.gov.cn. The government is very supportive of business, both local and foreign.

Will Shanghai displace Hong Kong?

Shanghai's renaissance as the financial centre of China is another driver in the city's economic miracle. China's rapid move toward a market-oriented economy over the past two decades has required the development of modern financial institutions. Pudong's Lujiazui district *(see page 216)* is home to China's most powerful banks and insurance companies, as well as the Shanghai Stock Exchange.

But despite what the pundits say, it will be years before Shanghai is in a position to challenge Hong Kong as Asia's financial centre. China's state-owned banks are financially weak; capital markets are in their infancy when compared to those in Hong Kong; and it is likely that the Chinese yuan (RMB) will not be made convertible on the capital account until the financial system is more mature.

Nevertheless, Shanghai is increasingly displacing Hong Kong as the preferred location for multinational corporate headquarters in Asia. Shanghai's strategy includes showcasing the city by hosting international conferences and competitions, like the 2001 APEC forum,

and the 2010 World Expo. It's clear that Shanghai does not require an elaborate public relations strategy to sell itself: the city's outstanding physical, financial, communications, logistical and human infrastructure speak volumes and are winning over more and more investors every month.

It is no surprise that Shanghai attracts a great deal of foreign direct investment (FDI) too – some 10 percent of the tens of billions of dollars that pour into China every year go to Shanghai. Today, more than half of Shanghai's

exports are produced by foreign-invested companies, exceeding, in terms of value, exports by Chinese state-owned enterprises. Foreign-invested companies employ hundreds of thousands of Shanghainese workers, who seek out foreign employers not only for higher wages but for the exposure to cutting-edge technology and the management thinking that they provide. The symbiosis between foreign business and Shanghai is evident everywhere in the city.

Shanghai is a challenging place to do business. Language differences play a role, certainly, as does the unfamiliarity of Chinese business culture – especially those aspects that arise from the mainland's decades of Commu-

LEFT: Shanghai's new white collar set will drive the city's growth in the coming years. **RIGHT:** Bao Shan Steel represents China's industrial might.

nist rule. The process of replacing aspects of a centrally planned economy with more market-oriented policies has produced a business environment that is both unique and challenging. Foreign investors may find it confusing to deal with a Mandarin-speaking Communist Party member in the morning and a young Chinese entrepreneur who speaks in fluent English about IPOs and basis points like a New York investment banker in the afternoon.

China presents serious business challenges found in many other developing economies as well. Experts say that most Chinese companies file false financial reports in order to reduce taxes or to deceive investors. Even Chinese officials admit that a significant proportion of business contracts signed in China are fraudulent in some way. Enforcement of intellectual property rights is poor, and no industry or product category is immune to large-scale counterfeiting. The government has promulgated many pro-business laws over the past 20 years, but recourse to Chinese courts remains so fraught with difficulties that most disputes are settled out of court or simply written off.

To be fair, these business challenges are faced by all businesses operating in China, whether foreign-invested or Chinese-owned. China

NEW BUSINESS ETIQUETTE

The traditional and old-fashioned formality of Chinese business meetings is changing rapidly in China, and nowhere as quickly as in Shanghai, where the idea that "time is money" is well understood. Still, it's important to recognise the classic patterns of an old-style meeting; pack some modest gifts (a bottle of wine or a pen) in case you are presented with one yourself, and remember that it helps open doors if you are introduced through a trusted friend. But more and more these days, it is likely that your Chinese business counterparts – at least in Shanghai – will want to get down to dollars and cents and sign on the dotted line as quickly as you do.

experts emphasise that most legal and economic changes are headed in the right direction. And ultimately, the market reveals the attitude of business toward the risks and rewards found in China – the PRC is second only to the US as a destination for foreign direct investment (FDI).

Investors who accept the unique risks presented by the Chinese environment are betting that its rapidly growing economy will bring them profits on a scale not possible in smaller and more mature markets. Only time will tell if they have read the tea leaves correctly. ❏

ABOVE: even Shanghai's elderly keep watch on the Chinese stock market's ups and downs.

China's Trade Wars

After 15 years of stormy negotiations, China joined the World Trade Organisation in December 2001. What this means for China – and for the rest of the world – is both very complex and immensely important.

The WTO provides the legal ground-rules for international commerce. Its rules cover trade in goods and services, the treatment of intellectual property rights and dispute resolution. WTO members grant other economies the same rights in their own jurisdictions that other countries grant to them – what is known in WTO-speak as "national treatment."

For China, the WTO is a double-edged sword: the country's membership means unfettered access for Chinese goods in overseas markets, but it will also expose domestic firms to international competition that may drive some out of business. On balance, China calculates that benefits to the Chinese economy of adhering to WTO standards outweigh the costs. As a low-cost manufacturing base with a huge capacity and room for growth, China expects a long-term export boom as a result of its entry into the WTO.

The wild card for China is the effect of the WTO accession on unemployment. Millions of workers at over-staffed and under-competitive state-owned enterprises risk losing their jobs, and many don't have the skills to land new ones in the modern Chinese economy. Post-WTO food imports from countries with mechanised and highly efficient farming industries are likely to have severe repercussions on Chinese agriculture and result in the displacement of millions of farmers. Sporadic labour unrest is already common in China, some observers worry that increased unemployment may create problems that will affect social stability.

For more developed economies, China's accession to the WTO will mean increased access to Chinese markets, and a Chinese business environment that abides by international norms – in WTO jargon, "rules-based, non-discriminatory market access." The price China's trading partners will pay for access to China's markets depends on the complementarities of their economies. Those economies which produce goods and services that China does not produce stand to gain; others may have industries that will be hurt by increased trade with China.

New WTO members can bargain for extended implementation of certain rules, and China took

advantage of the opportunity. Some changes took effect immediately upon China's accession, while others will be implemented over the next few years. All of China's WTO obligations must be fulfilled within five years of accession, or by December 2006.

Meeting WTO's obligations requires a complete overhaul of Chinese commercial and investment laws and regulations – a task that involves comparing existing Chinese laws with WTO standards, drafting new laws, and getting them approved by the appropriate legislative bodies. Following that Herculean task is the no less arduous one of training Chinese and foreign businesses, lawyers and judges in the application of the new rules. It will

take years and a lot of legal resolution before the system will work effectively.

In the meantime, both the WTO and China are working to ensure that China's entry into the multilateral trading system is as smooth as possible. WTO Affairs Consulting Centres have been set up in a number of Chinese cities, with Shanghai taking the lead: Pudong will serve as the test site for the country's WTO implementation programmes. China's progress is also subject to annual scrutiny within the purview of a WTO "Transitional Review Mechanism" until 2011. After 25 years of reforms and 15 years of negotiations, China's full participation in the world economy is no longer in question – it is finally a reality. ❑

RIGHT: China's entry into WTO took 15 years to engineer.

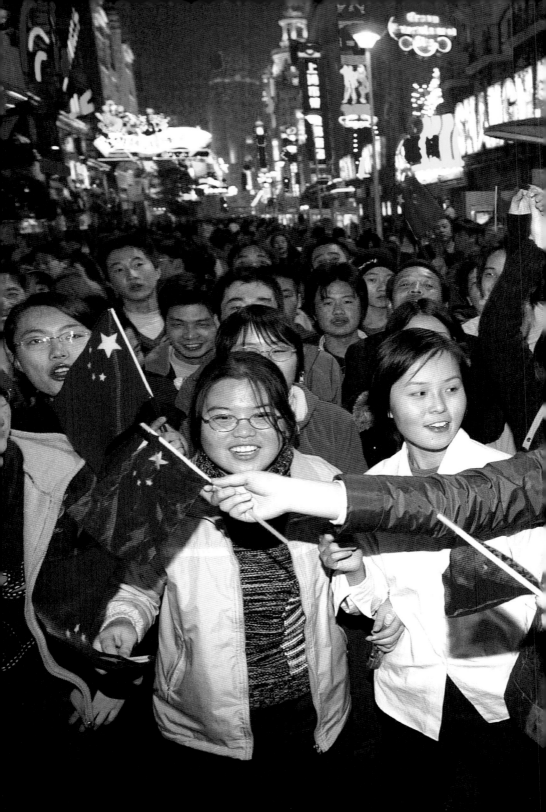

THE SHANGHAINESE

The inhabitants of China's richest city are not particularly loved by other Chinese, but that doesn't seem to faze the consumer-oriented Shanghainese

The Shanghainese are very much like their cutting-edge city: smart, hip and – yes – arrogant about it. They are admired, but only grudgingly so, by Chinese from other parts of the country. This doesn't seem to bother the Shanghainese a jot: after decades of being under Beijing's thumb, Shanghainese confidence and self-respect have bounced back strong and healthy. Its people are once again convinced that Shanghai is *the* future, and that it will stand again with New York and London as one of the great cities of the world. There is an unspoken pact between the Shanghainese from the mayor down to the kids on how to achieve this goal as quickly as possible – the mayor works on highways, the kids on hairstyles.

A migrant town

The bright lights of Shanghai have attracted migrants for centuries. When asked why the Shanghainese are so smart, a former mayor famously replied, "It's not that the Shanghainese are smart. Smart people come to Shanghai."

Greater Shanghai sprawls over 6,340 sq km (2,448 sq miles) with a population of 15 million, including some 3.8 million migrant workers from other parts of China. It is a port and an immigrant town, like New York, with the forefathers of its residents mostly hailing from other cities and districts of East China. Shanghai was already a thriving city in the 18th century, and after the British blasted open the gates of China with the Opium Wars in the early 1840s, they chose Shanghai as one of their settlements to promote trade. The foreign settlements became a powerful magnet for Shanghai's economic development as the surrounding areas of East China were torn apart by periodic wars and famine over the following decades.

One of the dominant influences on the development of Shanghai's language, cuisine and personality is the southern seaport city of Ningbo, perhaps best known for its bankers (well into the 1940s, Ningbo bankers ran Shanghai's financial industry). There was also a prominent Cantonese community in 19th-century Shanghai, who had followed the British in as compradors.

The migration process continues unabated

PRECEDING PAGES: Shanghai youth celebrating the city's winning bid to host the 2010 World Exposition; demonstrating the art of drinking tea at Zhabei.
LEFT AND RIGHT: contrasting scenes of Shanghai life.

today. Shanghai's economic boom of the past decade has attracted a new wave of immigrants – ambitious young turks from the rest of the country, Uighur traders from the northwest of China and small-time business people from the surrounding provinces. The Taiwanese too are becoming a huge force in Shanghai, and it is said there are 300,000 living in the city. As Hong Kong has waned since the late 1990s, increasing numbers of its people have moved north to seek their fortunes, reversing the flow of half-a-century ago when immigrant Shanghainese fuelled Hong Kong's prosperity.

Since the days of the Concession, Shanghai

has always had a strong foreign presence. Today, the number of Europeans, Americans, Koreans and Japanese continues to grow dramatically. Exact figures are hard to come by, but there are around 50,000 foreigners, less than the number of foreign residents in the 1940s when cosmopolitan Shanghai was hailed as the Paris of the East. As Shanghai moves to take its place in the pantheon of world-class cities, the authorities are encouraging the influx of foreigners wanting to participate in the new China boom.

Changing lifestyles

China's one-child policy, implemented in 1979 to slow down an explosive population growth rate, has had a huge impact on the life of the Shanghainese. Virtually every young person in Shanghai today is the product of a one-child family. It is natural for parents and grandparents to spoil their only child silly; in fact, bratty male offspring are *xiao huangdi*, or "little emperors". There has been some official concern about this; children are now encouraged to view cousins as siblings, and the policy is also being quietly relaxed – offspring from one-child familes who marry someone who is also an only child are allowed to have two children.

Up to the 1990s, Shanghai was one of the world's most densely populated cities. Then began what is arguably the biggest construction project China has ever attempted – the reconstruction of central Shanghai and the development of vast housing estates around its perimeter. More than 2 million people have been shifted out of the old housing in the central districts since 1995, a process which continues to this day.

The *longtang* or lane houses which characterised Shanghainese life for so many decades are fast disappearing. Those that haven't been razed are largely populated with older people – their children have moved to newer and better accommodation. Much is lost in the process, but then much is gained as well – the old lane houses were jerry-built, have no inside toilets or running water, and are often dark and cramped. Younger Shanghainese seem to miss the old alleys much less than sentimental foreigners do, although the older residents do lament the loss of neighbourly *longtang* life. The new standard for Shanghai living today is an apartment in a high-rise block at a housing estate with a small pet dog yapping to be taken

SHANGHAINESE DIALECT

The Shanghainese language bears virtually no resemblance to Mandarin and is almost completely incomprehensible to Chinese living in other areas of the country. On Shanghai streets, it's probably the most common language used, yet in local media it's almost completely absent. The Beijing government has for decades tried to encourage the city's residents to accept Mandarin or *putonghua*, the official language of China, and the campaign has had significant impact. Modern Shanghainese spoken today is heavily influenced by Mandarin, and younger Shanghainese often use Mandarin words and phrases, or break into whole sentences of Mandarin, during conversation.

for a run on the small piece of grass outside.

In this new Shanghai, people have something that they have never had before – privacy. In the alleys, everyone knew everything about everyone else; the walls were paper thin and gossip spread quickly when women washed out the chamber pots in the morning. In the new estates, people tend to not know their neighbours. Life has moved from one extreme to the other.

Young people in Shanghai enjoy an independent urban lifestyle but still have the advantage of the traditional Chinese family support system. Increasingly, young people will rent their own apartments, but they will typically

western China than in Shanghai, probably because there is much more opportunity here.

Mobile phones and SMS messaging, Internet chatrooms, and even online virtual families, are now a central part of life for Shanghai's young. They enjoy rising salaries in an overall deflationary consumer environment, allowing them to spend more on clothes, computers, food and travel. The white-collar middle managers from foreign joint-venture companies have led the way in the past decade, and as firms increasingly localise to cut costs, the Shanghainese are moving up into leadership positions, creating an affluent yuppie, or "Shuppie", class.

return to see their parents on the weekends – and not just to get their clothes washed. Attitudes towards sex have changed dramatically as well, and many young Shanghai people now openly live together before marriage.

But there is a generation gap as technology changes and Shanghai integrates itself into the outside world. Linguistically and technologically, it is hard for older Shanghainese to keep up. Teenage angst in the city, however, is not high. Signs of alienation are more likely to be found among young people in northern and

What makes a Shanghainese?

When they get together, Chinese people love to discuss regional differences in character – and Shanghai people are an obvious target. There is a caricature that all agree upon: Shanghainese are arrogant and aloof, smart but somewhat false, self-conscious, guarded. The men are docile, the women domineering. Everyone seems to have an agenda, everyone seems concerned about impressions, substance often seems secondary. It's partly jealousy, of course. Shanghai is, after all, China's richest and most sophisticated city.

Shanghainese men, according to the cliché, have what it takes to be good at business. They lack the natural openness of northern Chinese.

LEFT: a "little emperor" hitches a ride on his dad.
ABOVE: typical scene at an old-style lane house.

They hesitate before answering because they are mulling over what you may think about what they will say. And they are famous for their street arguments that never degenerate into brawls – the Shanghai man, in the famous phrase, "moves his mouth, not his fist". They are supposedly docile at home (ideal husbands for domineering wives, you could say) and they are seldom big drinkers.

Shanghai women are seen as strong-willed and calculating, and they are certainly the country's best-packaged females, a

NO ALCOHOL PLEASE

Shanghainese men are seldom big drinkers – many foreign beer companies in the 1990s foundered on the mistaken belief that Shanghainese would match their Beijing brethren glass for glass.

the coastal edge of East China's pregnant bulge, one of the most sophisticated parts of China. The region's older cities such as Suzhou, Hangzhou and Ningbo were noted for their culture. Their Mandarins ruled China and composed poetry, while the merchants collected jade, porcelain and concubines. They were not warriors but a feudal upper middle class, and, as war and revolution pulled apart the fabric of their world from the 1840s until the Japanese invasion in the 1930s, they fled in waves to

reputation that goes back to the days of the cigarette girl ads in old Shanghai. A Shanghai man bemoaned the fact that his girlfriend refused to have even the one child permitted by the government. "She says it will ruin her figure and interrupt her career, she won't listen to me." Like most clichés, this one overstates reality, yet contains some truth.

What, then, accounts for the perceived strength of the Shanghai female and the more delicate nature of the male? History contains some clues. Shanghai's character as an immigrant town was formed in the late 19th and early 20th centuries when the social fabric of old imperial China was falling apart. The city sits on

the safety of Shanghai, their pockets stuffed with jade. The character of Shanghai men, therefore, could be said to have been founded on old China's intellectual business culture.

The psyche of Shanghainese women can be traced to the time when the city was a refuge for girls escaping the constricting life of old China – bound feet, concubinage and slavery. They had to assert themselves to survive, which made them focused and forceful, convinced that the end always justifies the means.

ABOVE: higher disposable incomes allow young Shanghainese a lifestyle their parents never had.
RIGHT: making fashion statements along Huaihai Road.

Taking the middle road

Someone once said that a Shanghai extremist would be a contradiction in terms, and the rough psychological profiles discussed here would support this. Shanghai people as a whole generally lack the passion of conviction to be extremist. They are too self-involved and calculating, too detached. But that also makes them perfect for administration, politics and management. Shanghainese are also good at business and they understand the art of compromise – qualities which help make this city the commercial capital of China and a magnet for foreign investment.

As in most major world cities, there is a degree of tension between natives of the city and people from the provinces. In Shanghai, the locals are often too ready to make assumptions about others, either seriously or in jest, based on which district they were born in or which school they went to. Some class-conscious Shanghainese are dismissive of those they view as being beneath them – especially people from rural areas. A potent put-down is to call someone a "peasant", a country bumpkin – it means they are not smart enough, too slow on the uptake, too unsophisticated, too... un-Shanghainese. It feels, just a little, like Manhattan.

Such attitudes, born in Shanghai in the 1920s

TRENDY FASHIONISTAS VS PYJAMA POWER

Shanghainese women are China's fashion trendsetters. They have everything necessary to be so: increasingly sophisticated tastes, high disposable incomes, an insatiable thirst for international trends and, most importantly, attitude. Shanghainese women were China's first to start perming their hair after the Cultural Revolution of the 1960s. Today, they are the economic engine driving China's rapidly expanding fashion industry. Women's fashion dominates both the growing numbers of megamalls as well as the posh boutiques and department stores that line Nanjing Road and and Huaihai Road. One of the best places to feel the pulse of Shanghainese women's fashion is at the open-air Xiangyang cloth-

ing market at the junction of Huaihai Road and Xiangyang Road, a crowded labyrinth of tiny stores selling fresh-from-the-factory garments, shoes and accessories.

Not every Shanghainese woman espouses Gucci and Prada, however. Perhaps a reaction to the couture culture is a fashion trend so avant-garde that it has become the subject of government condemnation: pyjamas. At any time day or night, it is not difficult to find a woman on the street wearing her nightclothes. Government-controlled media have decried that public pyjama wearing, particularly during daylight hours, does nothing to help the city's image. Now who's going to tell that to the 25-year-old in pink bunny slippers?

and 1930s, were stifled first by the Japanese invasion in 1937, then by the Communist takeover in 1949. During the Cultural Revolution years, personal ambitions that would have been condemned as bourgeois by the Communists lay dormant inside their ubiquitous Mao jackets. Then, as the political winds changed direction, middle-class dreams re-emerged. Shanghai people now want to buy their own apartments, drive big cars and send their children to the best schools. And as they move up the social scale, a new generation of immigrants arrives from the farm to handle the menial tasks the locals no longer wish to do.

The Shanghainese are typically more open to ideas from the West – or, as Chinese people from other areas might see it, more slavish in their pursuit of foreignness. It began in the old Shanghai with something called Yangjingbang Culture, Yangjing Bang being the name of the creek which separated the French Concession area of Shanghai and the Chinese city. The term refers to the amalgam of Chinese and Western ideas and influences into something that was uniquely Shanghainese, in terms of language, clothes, food, lifestyle and attitudes. The trend is visible again today (although other parts of China are catching up).

Shanghainese are more likely to assume that the way the foreigner does it is better. Naturally, it compares itself more to cities outside China than to those within, just as Japan would prefer to compare itself to Europe and the US rather than to neighbouring Korea and China.

Conspicuous consumerism

Shanghainese are always looking for bargains – they like quality, fashionable products, but are highly price-conscious. The classic mode of shopping is to go to a major department store to identify an item, then head for the local knock-off market to buy a copy of the same thing for a tenth of the price. But increasingly so, with rising affluence, buying the real McCoy carries a certain cachet of having arrived, of being one-up on their designer knockoff-togged neighbours.

A key feature of the consumerist lifestyle is fads, and Shanghai, which has the highest standards of living in China, follows the latest trends in clothing, mobile phones and nightclubs. People from other parts of China see Shanghainese fashion and lifestyles as something to emulate. Huaihai Road, the city's key fashion shopping street, is the epicentre of fashion trends in China. But as quickly as people try to emulate the Shanghai look, it morphs into something else, leaving the "outsiders" (*waidiren*) permanently outside.

Shanghainese girls particularly are moving swiftly from being followers to leaders and before this decade is out, Shanghai fashion trends will probably be leading those in Japan.

Shanghai people are more ambitious, more focused on succeeding than other Chinese. They are less satisfied with comfort, more likely to fight for luxury. But they are not natural politicians or philosophers. While a conversation with a Beijing taxi driver can cover vast territories, it's difficult to get a tight-lipped Shanghai taxi driver even to tell you how business is going.

Sichuan province in the heart of China is more likely to produce the great Chinese novelists of the 21st century than practical-minded Shanghai – people here tend to be focused on their careers, and leave concerns about the meaning of life to others. Thanks to the Shanghainese, the city will undoubtedly be the powerhouse that drives China through this century, becoming once again the dominant East Asian, if not world, metropolis. ❏

LEFT: Shanghainese enjoying the good life.

Shanghainese Trailblazers

The Shanghainese are the over-achievers of China and the city has produced more than its fair share of high profile individuals in both the business and arts world. Here are thumb sketches of some of the city's most prominent children.

Chen Yifei: Acknowledged as contemporary China's most famous and commercially successful artist, Chen Yifei is best known for his oil paintings of old Shanghai, including winsome beauties wearing delicate Chinese *qipao*, that mirror photographs in their exactitude. He was born in Shanghai and studied in New York from 1982 to 1992. His earliest works reflected a view of Chinese Communist revolutionary history, and in the mid-1990s, he moved on to a series of paintings depicting Tibetan people and landscapes. Today, Chen is involved in many other business ventures to which he lends his name, including film-making, a mid-price fashion chain called Leyefe, and home furnishings. In the eyes of many Chinese, however, Chen is more a businessman than a cultural figure.

Wei Hui: Derided by the Chinese Communist Party as "decadent, debauched and a slave of foreign culture", Wei Hui is a novelist and author of the international sensation *Shanghai Baby*. The tale of a young Shanghainese woman's self-discovery and sexual coming-of-age via an affair with a German man living in Shanghai, *Shanghai Baby* sent waves through the literary world for its modern and sexy portrayal of Chinese youth. Conventional wisdom has it that Wei Hui's writing ability is limited at best, but it is her timing and self-assuredness that have catapulted her to the position of darling of the West within the Chinese literary world.

Joan Chen: Shanghai-born Joan Chen became a celebrity in China at the age of 14 with her role in the 1979 Chinese film *Little Flower* as a deaf-mute girl whose first words after being cured through acupuncture were, "Long live Chairman Mao!" Seven years later she made her Hollywood debut and began steadily landing supporting roles in films, culminating with her role as the opium-addicted empress of Bernardo Bertolucci's *The Last Emperor*. Chen also earned significant recognition in her role as Josie Packard in the 1990

American cult classic television series *Twin Peaks*. After a brief foray into action films, Chen later reinvented herself and made her debut as director in 1998 with her film *Xiu Xiu: The Sent Down Girl*. The film was filmed without approval from the Chinese government, for which she was banned from China. Chen now resides in San Francisco.

Jiang Zemin: While not a native of Shanghai (he was born in nearby Yangzhou, Jiangsu Province), Jiang Zemin is inextricably linked to the city. He was educated in Shanghai at the prestigious Jiaotong University, where he graduated in 1947. It was during his days there as an engineering student that Jiang registered as a member of the Communist

Party in 1946. After venturing into the Soviet Union to learn about automobile factories in 1955, Jiang returned to China a year later to manage several automobile factories, including one in Shanghai.

Jiang's association with Shanghai was strengthened by his term as the city's mayor from 1985 to 1988. It is believed that his handling in 1989 of the democracy protests in Shanghai gave him significant momentum in his rise to General Secretary of the Communist Party, State President and head of the powerful Military Commission. He relinquished the first and second posts in 2003 but not the third and apparently plans to play the same role as the late Deng Xiaoping did in his final years – a father figure retaining significant power. ❑

RIGHT: Shanghai-born author Wen Hui signing copies of her controversial novel *Shanghai Baby*.

PERFORMING ARTS

Chinese opera, music, drama, dance and cinema are all staging a comeback, and Shanghai looks set to claim its past glory as a world cultural centre

The Shanghai Grand Theatre *(see page 142)* stands on the northwest side of People's Square, a gleaming glass and steel structure with an aluminium roof that arcs gracefully toward the heavens. With its French design, German construction, Japanese stage and American acoustics, the theatre has set the standard for venues across China and enticed the world's top performing arts companies to Shanghai. That Shanghai should have the country's first world-class theatre is fitting, since it was here that many of the arts that fill Chinese stages today were incubated, refined and born.

Glory days of the arts

Shanghai was the undisputed performing arts capital of China in the 1920s and 30s, a magnet for aspiring and established artists from around the country. The greatest Chinese opera stars dazzled audiences with their interpretations of classic operas in private and public performances. Professional story-tellers mesmerised crowds in teahouses, relating tales so long they took months to finish. Acrobats, jugglers and contortionists cavorted before crowds in the narrow streets around the Yu Garden. In the foreign concessions, the Shanghai Municipal Orchestra filled the Lyceum Theatre with the works of classical and contemporary European composers. Movies were so popular with Chinese and foreigners alike that it was front-page news when a new theatre opened.

But then came war, revolution and an entirely new system for governing the arts. After 1949, private opera troupes were disbanded and reorganised under government auspices. Itinerant performers were obliged to stop their wanderings. The foreigners who comprised the bulk of the Shanghai Municipal Orchestra left or were expelled. Beijing emerged as the cultural centre of China and Shanghai's performing arts were forced to play second fiddle.

PREDEDING PAGES AND LEFT: scenes from *kunju* opera *The Peony Pavilion*, staged by Shanghai Kunju Company.
RIGHT: a cellist leaving the Shanghai Grand Theatre.

Neglect, the passage of time and 10 years of suppression during the Cultural Revolution did great damage to the arts in Shanghai. Yet, somehow, many have withstood the odds and are still being performed today. These art forms divide neatly into those traditional to China and those imported into Shanghai from the West and Japan.

Chinese opera (Peking)

Chief among traditional performing arts is Chinese opera, a broad term for sung drama that includes more than 360 different types. Chinese opera is a highly demanding art that requires its performers to begin studying as children – in old China, child performers were actually bought and sold for their talent. Actors must learn to sing and dance, acquire an extensive repertoire of highly stylised gestures and even do acrobatics. Hard as Chinese opera is to perform, it is also challenging to watch. In a traditional staging, there are few props and the audience must use their imagination to fill in considerable blanks. Characters are role types recognisable by their facial make-up and costumes – the clown always has a white nose, the general wears flags – and interpretative differences are often so nuanced that only connoisseurs can appreciate them. Sadly, modern audiences prefer more passive entertainment, like television, and Chinese opera is losing its fans, especially in the cities.

Shanghai has for the past century been home to four different kinds of Chinese opera: Peking, Kunju, Shaoxing and Huju. Peking opera is the best known of them all, recognisable by its falsetto singing, vivid facial painting, percussion-based music, striking acrobatics and librettos based on the heroic exploits of legendary heroes.

In old Shanghai, Peking opera was king. The country's greatest stars – including Mei Lanfang, renowned male interpreter of women's roles – came here from Beijing, enticed by wealthy patrons like the mobster Du Yuesheng. Though many performances took place during banquets in private gardens, others were held in teahouses, guild halls and pleasure palaces like Great World.

So seductive was the profusion of performing arts available in Shanghai, that Peking opera troupes began to borrow from other art forms and a Shanghai school of Peking opera called *haipai* developed. *Haipai* was – and is – characterised by a willingness to experiment. It was

DYING FOR THEIR ART

The Cultural Revolution (1966–76) was a political campaign and power struggle, disguised as an effort to create a new socialist culture by ridding China of traditional and Western art forms. It was launched from Shanghai by Jiang Qing (Mao Zedong's wife) and her cronies in the Gang of Four.

For 10 years, virtually all performing arts were banned except eight "model operas" which Jiang Qing helped create. These included five modern Peking operas, two ballets and a revolutionary symphony. The Shanghai Peking Opera Company's *Taking Tiger Mountain by Strategy* and the Shanghai Ballet's *White-Haired Girl* were performed countless times because they had Jiang Qing's offficial sanction.

Although the performing arts suffered immensely during this period, the artistes suffered more. Virtually all significant performers of "feudal" or "Western" arts were subjected to public criticism sessions in which they were humiliated, beaten and locked away in make-shift jails. The tools of their art – instruments, opera costumes, sheet music – were confiscated and burnt. Unable to withstand this cruelty and abuse, many artistes simply gave up and killed themselves. At the Shanghai Conservatory alone, 17 students and professors committed suicide in the first years of the Cultural Revolution. At the Shanghai Symphony, the conductor Lu Hongen was executed – because he criticised Mao Zedong.

the first to use mechanical scenery and special effects, and to adapt scripts from outside the traditional repertoire. This willingness to innovate is criticised by purists, but has helped Shanghai's Peking opera company maintain its vitality and remain one of the strongest in the country.

Kunju, Shaoxing and Huju opera

Kunju, named after nearby Kunshan, is sometimes known as the mother of Peking opera. Its music is gentle and melodic, dominated by the bamboo flute, and its librettos are long and lyrical, read to this day as literary classics. Its beauty is perhaps too ethereal for the modern

a punch. In 1998, the Shanghai Kunju Company and New York's Lincoln Centre attempted to stage this opera in New York and Paris. But Shanghai culture officials were so shocked by the erotic and political content of the 20-hour production that they refused the theatre company permission to leave the country. The ban became front-page news in the US and Europe, but Shanghai never relented.

Shaoxing opera, which originates from Zhejiang town, has a repertoire of mainly tragic love stories like *A Dream of Red Mansions*, with music augmented by violins and cellos. Interestingly, it is performed – and watched – almost

era, and there are only five Kunju companies left nationwide. The Shanghai Kunju Company is the best and has twice sparked renewed interest in the dying genre, once with a 1950s production of *Fifteen Strings of Cash* and more recently with *The Peony Pavilion*.

Written by Tang Xianzu in 1598, *The Peony Pavilion* is one of the most popular operas in the Kunju repertoire, best known today as a love story. It has 55 acts, a cast of 100 and although more than 400 years old, it still packs

exclusively by women. It first became popular in the 1920s – when fans would throw gold and jewellery on stage to their favourite actresses – and has a large cult following of housewives to this day. Indeed, so ardent are Shaoxing opera fans that many become groupies of performers – usually those who play male roles – and follow them to performances around the region, often sending them flowers before a show.

Huju is a strictly local opera form sung in Shanghai dialect and rarely performed in theatres but is sometimes still staged outdoors near the Temple of the Town God (Chenghuang Miao), a gathering place for itinerant performers from the Ming Dynasty up to 1949.

LEFT: *pingtan* story-telling is accompanied by traditional instruments like the *pipa* and *san xian*.
ABOVE: modern stage drama in action.

Huajixi and Pingtan

Though the wandering performers of old Shanghai are gone, a few of their arts have survived, including Huajixi, Pingtan and acrobatics. Huajixi is a kind of stand-up comedy performed in Shanghainese that has a narrow audience in Shanghai and none outside it. Pingtan, on the other hand, is a respected art form of storytelling with close links to music. It is usually performed by a man and a woman who use only a fan or a teacup as props but keep audiences spellbound with animated facial expressions and virtuoso musical accompaniment on Chinese string instruments like the *pipa* and *san xian*.

Contemporary drama

Westerners began introducing their own performing arts to Shanghai soon after the Opium War. Plays were staged by the Amateur Dramatic Club as early as the 1860s, but had little reach beyond the foreign community. The first spoken (as opposed to sung) drama performed by Chinese was a 1907 adaptation of Harriet Beecher Stowe's *Uncle Tom's Cabin*, staged by leftist students who had discovered the art form in Japan. Their motivations were as much political as artistic, since they saw drama as a useful tool for promoting left-wing politics and social causes.

In the 1920s, young authors like Tian Han

ACROBATIC ARTS

Acrobatics did not originate in Shanghai but was so popular pre-1949 that the city became a centre for acrobatic troupes from around the country and the first port of call for circuses and magic shows from overseas. After 1949, acrobatics was promoted heavily by the government as a proletarian art form and was one of the few arts permitted in the Cultural Revolution. Though it remains popular in rural areas, urban residents tend to view it as peasant entertainment and the audience in Shanghai is comprised primarily of overseas tourists. This is unfortunate because the Shanghai Acrobatics Troupe *(see page 182)* is one of the best in the world.

began writing plays and, in 1933, The China Travelling Dramatic Troupe was founded to take spoken drama from Shanghai to the rest of the nation. Its greatest moment was the 1936 premiere of Cao Yu's *Thunderstorm*, a tragedy that remains a classic of the Chinese stage. Drama is still associated with politics and is thus carefully controlled in Shanghai. Though the city still supports several drama companies, it has contributed little to the art form in recent decades.

Orchestral music

The Shanghai Symphony dates to 1879, when it began as a Town Band for the International Settlement. Over the years, the band became a symphony, and from the 1920s to 40s it was led by an Italian named Mario Paci under whose baton it became known as "the best orchestra in the Far East". Initially, the musicians were all foreigners – including many White Russian and Jewish refugees – but after 1938, it started recruiting Chinese musicians. The presence of so many foreign musicians in Shanghai attracted aspiring Chinese musicians from around the country and led the great music educator Xiao Youmei to establish the country's first music school – now the Shanghai Conservatory – here in 1927.

Graduates of the Conservatory were instrumental in persuading the Communist Party that classical music could "serve the people" and many went on to be key forces in the post-1949 development of Western music and opera. Western classical music in turn became a major influence in the reform of Chinese music – traditional instruments were modernised, new instruments were created and Western-style orchestral ensembles were formed. Both the Shanghai Symphony and Shanghai Conservatory remain strong institutions. The city also supports a second major orchestra, the Shanghai Broadcast Symphony as well as the Shanghai Opera Orchestra. Although the opera has been plagued by financial problems in recent years, it stages several co-productions a year at the Grand Theatre with companies from overseas.

Ballroom and ballet dancing

Dance was wildly popular in old Shanghai among Chinese and foreigners alike, but more as a participatory activity than as a performing art which people watched in a theatre. It was closely linked with jazz and – together with movies – was the prime means through which jazz was introduced. In the 1920s and 30s, Shanghai had enough dance halls to support 500 jazz bands, mostly comprising Filipino musicians. Ballroom dance remains popular today – often performed on sidewalks in the early morning – and the nightclub band circuit is again dominated by Filipinos. Jazz is even

---

FUSION MUSIC

The Shanghai Traditional Music Orchestra is an ensemble modelled after the Western symphony orchestra, but using traditional Chinese instruments in place of Western ones.

---

making a comeback, and once again many of the musicians are foreign. The close association of dance with popular music in Shanghai is likely one of the reasons the city has never developed a significant rock-and-roll scene.

Ballet and contemporary dance were brought to Shanghai by the White Russians in the 1920s and a ballet school was opened in 1936. After liberation, Soviet Russians came to help develop the art form and the Shanghai Ballet School and Shanghai Ballet were

founded, producing some of China's greatest dancers. Their repertoire was dominated by Russian classics up until the mid-1960s when Jiang Qing (Mao Zedong's wife and key perpetrator of the Cultural Revolution) encouraged the creation of a proletarian ballet with Chinese characteristics. Classic poses from Peking opera were integrated into ballet and the choreography was made more "revolutionary", meaning that ballerinas danced with clenched fists and rifles, their eyes ablaze with the fire of class hatred.

Today's repertoire includes both European and proletarian ballets, but unfortunately many of Shanghai's best dancers left the country in

---

FAR LEFT: performer from Shanghai Acrobatics Troupe.
LEFT: Shanghai Symphony rehearsing at Grand Theatre.
RIGHT: a ballet star in the making.

the 1980s and the Shanghai Ballet is still rebuilding from this talent loss. The Shanghai Dance Ensemble, which combines elements of contemporary, classical and traditional Chinese dance, is a stronger group and has several rising young stars. Shanghai also has a new modern dance company founded by the renowned modern dancer Jin Xing who moved here from Beijing. Jin Xing – who used to be a colonel in the People's Liberation Army and is as famous for her widely-publicised sex change as for her dancing – is a strong and provocative choreographer whose work is shaking up Shanghai's modern dance scene.

Shanghainese cinema

Cinema also got its start in Shanghai, where the first film ever shown in China was presented as the interlude between magic tricks and a fireworks display in an 1896 vaudeville show. The first films made in China were produced by foreigners in Shanghai and the first Chinese-produced films were also made here.

By the 1930s, movies were the biggest form of entertainment, with first-run Hollywood films shown in lavishly decorated auditoriums that could seat nearly 2,000 people. The first Chinese "talkie" was produced in Shanghai in 1931, starring the legendary actress Butterfly Wu, and the industry soon prospered despite the continued popularity of Hollywood movies.

The Communist Party quickly recognised the usefulness of film as a propaganda tool, and gave considerable support to the industry after 1949. Today, however, Shanghai's film industry is moribund, as is the industry nationwide.

In the early 1990s, China had 15,000 cinemas, but by 2000 there were fewer than 4,000. Less than 100 feature films are produced each year, and of these only a handful are made in Shanghai with 80 percent of them losing money. Virtually the only time crowds fill the theatres is during the annual Shanghai International Film Festival. Conservative critics blame Hollywood for the difficulties of China's film industry, but Shanghai's past experience contradicts this.

What the future holds

Unfortunately, Shanghai's film industry and all its performing arts suffer because the government maintains a contradictory, and ultimately unsustainable, arts policy. On the one hand, the government recognises that performing and other arts are essential to Shanghai's drive to be a major global city – and has invested much money and resources into building first-rate performance venues. Yet, it treats professional arts companies as government propaganda vehicles. Although their subsidies have been sharply cut, performing arts groups remain saddled with burdensome quotas for performances at factories and schools. They must be ready to appear at a political event on a moment's notice, even if it means cancelling a long-scheduled public performance. In addition, all scripts for plays and films must be submitted to cultural censors for approval.

Sadly, the degree of artistic interference in Shanghai works to negate the many commendable efforts the city is making to again become a great cultural centre. Lost – or deliberately overlooked – in the rush forward is the simple fact that old Shanghai was the nation's performing arts capital because it was open, cosmopolitan and relatively free. Shanghai is fortunate that so many of its stellar performing arts companies survived a century of war, revolution and chaos. But only when artists are allowed to create and perform with relative freedom will Shanghai have a chance of reclaiming – or exceeding – its past glory. ❏

LEFT: Jin Xing, modern dance luminary.

Modern Literature

So important is Shanghai in the history of modern Chinese literature that nearly every great writer of the first half of the 20th century lived here at some point. Lu Xun, Guo Morou, Ba Jin, Mao Dun, Xu Zhimo, Qian Zhongshu, Cao Yu, Tian Han, Ding Ling – the list goes on. The reasons these authors settled in Shanghai are as varied as their writings. Some were escaping the Japanese or Kuomintang (KMT) forces, some sought a place where they could discuss poetry openly, while others simply wanted to be close to their publishers.

Whatever their motivations, they found themselves in a city primed to support a literary revolution. The Shanghai region had for centuries produced great poets, painters and calligraphers – arts that are intertwined in traditional Chinese thinking. When Westerners settled here after the Opium War, they spread their own literature and ideas through missionary schools and universities. In time, graduates of these schools began to study overseas and returned with new world views. When the "old culture" of the traditional literati met the "new culture" of the Western-influenced students, great literary ferment was inevitable.

Shanghai became a nucleus of literary experimentation, a role made easier by its commercial base as a printing and publishing centre. The pinnacle of the written word in China had always been poetry, but in Shanghai the novel – written in the vernacular, rather than classical Chinese – became vogue. Famous novels penned or set here between the 1920s and 40s include Mao Dun's *Midnight*, Ding Ling's *Miss Sophie's Diary*, Ba Jin's *Family* and Qian Zhongshu's *Fortress Besieged*.

But poetry, too, became a form for experiment. The new-style bards tossed aside the strict technical rules for writing Chinese poetry and immersed themselves in the flowing verse of such poets as Whitman and Tagore. Guo Morou wrote ardent, Whitman-inspired verse like:

Earth, my mother
The skies already brighten with the early dawn
You arouse the child at your bosom
Now I clamber upon your back
Earth, my mother.

Xu Zhimo wrote of love, ideals and freedom; he lived his life as passionately as he wrote his poetry and remains a romantic idol to this day.

RIGHT: monument to the writer Lu Xun.

The essay also held an important place in Shanghai's literary world, its greatest practitioner the legendary Lu Xun. Lu Xun moved to Shanghai in 1927 and died here of tuberculosis in 1936. He is buried in Hongkou Park, near the site of his former home *(see page 210)* and memorialised in an excellent museum of his life and work. Lu Xun wrote with an acid-tipped pen, criticising the entire fabric of Chinese society. During his Shanghai years he was at odds with the KMT and many of his essays revolved around political or revolutionary topics. However, he is best known in the West as the author of such short stories as *The True Story of Ah Q* and *Diary of a Madman* which lampooned Chinese character and culture.

Sadly, there is little to say about literature in Shanghai from 1949 until 1976, an era characterised by political movements in which writers were forced to reflect a vision of socialist "reality" and produced little of literary merit. When the Cultural Revolution ended, some writers picked up where they had left off but most of the old generation were either dead or too disillusioned to write. In the late 1990s, several young writers published passionate accounts of individuals struggling to find love or meaning in the modern city. Wei Hui's sexually-charged *Shanghai Baby* has been translated into several languages (but it is banned in China) and the teenage Han Han's novels that condemn China's education system have become nationwide bestsellers. ❏

VISUAL ARTS

A heady mix of both traditional and cutting-edge contemporary art forms
has made Shanghai an exciting centre of artistic expression

Shanghai's progress in transforming itself into a cultural centre is nowhere more apparent than in the visual arts. Indeed, in less than a decade, the city has become the nation's standard-bearer for museum design and management, and a key centre for contemporary art. Remarkable as this transformation is – especially given that just a few years ago the city was best known in art circles for the speed with which it shut down avant-garde art exhibitions – it nonetheless feels like destiny.

Old Shanghai was an important arena of artistic experimentation, a meeting place for artistic methods and philosophies from China and the West. Its booming commercial life enabled it to support artists, patrons and collectors, and its cosmopolitan atmosphere made them feel at home. In traditional China, the arts had long been looked upon as a gentleman's pursuit rather than a professional's metier, but in brash, business-minded Shanghai it became acceptable to combine culture with commerce – and still be respected. The city's prosperity also made it a centre for the production of many crafts and folk arts that were executed by anonymous, but highly talented, artisans.

Chinese painting

Painting is traditionally considered the greatest of the arts in China. It is intimately related to calligraphy, which holds a similarly exalted status, and to seal-carving. In old China, some facility in painting or calligraphy was a virtual requirement for any self-respecting literati, a cultural belief so deeply embedded that to this day Chinese leaders feel obligated to demonstrate their calligraphic skills in public.

As part of the propserous Jiangsu-Zhejiang region, Shanghai was heir to a tradition of highly accomplished gentlemen painters. In this tradition, painting was a meditative and philosophical art that was considered as much a reflection of the artist's inner moral being as his

artistic skill. Brushwork was of paramount importance, its intent to reflect the essence of whatever was portrayed rather than its true appearance. Tradition reigned supreme; a painter who wished to portray a mountain was as likely to study a past master's representations of mountains as to go and look at one him-

self. Though many Chinese painters were aware of such Western techniques as perspective and shading, they eschewed them, considering their own way of painting to be infinitely superior.

But, as Shanghai became increasingly cosmopolitan in the late 19th and early 20th centuries, a new school of painting called *haishang* began to develop. *Haishang* is essentially a combination of different styles and techniques, its most distinctive feature being openness to new ideas – it is the visual arts equivalent of Chinese opera's *haipai*. This *haishang* broadmindedness grew to encompass Western art when the printing industry blossomed at the turn of the 20th century and painters could see

---

LEFT: Shanghai-born abstract artist Zhou Tiehai.
RIGHT: horses are a recurrent motif for artist Xu Beihong.

reproductions of Western masterpieces. Art students began to paint still lifes and nude models, and to take their easels outdoors and sketch what they saw on-site – methods which were inimical to traditional art. Shanghai became the destination of choice for students interested in Western painting, including such renowned painters Liu Haisu and Xu Beihong.

Liu Haisu, whose work can be seen in Shanghai's eponymous museum, studied in Paris and Japan and founded the Shanghai Art School in 1920. A great admirer of such artists as Van Gogh and Cezanne, Liu sparked a scandal when he organised an exhibition of nude paintings, which was quickly shut down by the police. Liu eventually returned to brush-and-ink painting, but his traditional-style works still reveal the influences of his Western education.

Xu Beihong studied in Paris and Berlin and spent much of his career moving between Western and Chinese-style painting. At its best, his work combines elements of both, as seen in his famous galloping horses which seem ready to run off the scroll with their flowing brush strokes and bulging muscles.

The vivacity that characterised painting in Shanghai largely ended with the Sino-Japanese war. In the years after 1949, Soviet-style realism

MUSEUMS APLENTY

When the Shanghai Museum moved to its urn-shaped building to Renmin Square in 1996, it was seen as proof that Shanghai was serious about improving its cultural standards. The new museum became an important catalyst in Shanghai's artistic revival and a model for museums around the country. Its success fuelled a plan to refurbish and build many more museums in Shanghai, both public and private – the long-term goal is 100. Already open are the new Shanghai Art Museum, the Urban Planning Centre, the Shanghai Public Security Museum and even the private Sex Museum. Museums for science, cars, tobacco and much more will soon open.

became the main influence, and the subject matter of both traditional and Western-style painting tended to be revolutionary. Traditional paintings often included trains and tractors and the practice of drawing people dwarfed by landscape ended – workers, peasants and soldiers had to dominate nature, not be overshadowed by it. In the Cultural Revolution, Western-style portrait painting was widely practised but there was only one subject – Mao Zedong. Poster art was also prominent, most of it "red, bright and shiny".

After the Cultural Revolution ended, artists quickly picked up their brushes and began to paint in both traditional and Western styles – many even began to portray Mao in political pop art paintings that have been eagerly snatched up by Western buyers. Shanghai became a centre of this political pop art with painters like Wang Ziwei becoming rich and famous by contrasting Mao with such American icons as Mickey Mouse and Donald Duck.

A different path to the same destination of fame and fortune was taken by Chen Yifei, who is perhaps best known for his lush old-master style paintings of women from old Shanghai. In typical Shanghai style, Chen has branched out from painting in recent years and now owns a trendy store in Xintiandi that sells his branded art products and acts as a modelling agency.

like a memory that flutters just beneath the consciousness. Shanghai is also known for artists who employ modern techniques such as photography and computers to comment on society.

Zhao Bandi's series of posters of himself with a stuffed panda are ubiquitious in Shanghai, even in government sponsored anti-smoking campaigns. Zhou Tiehai has turned self-promotion into an ironic art by placing himself on the cover of such international magazines as *Time* and *Newsweek*. The works of all these Shanghai-born and based artists can be seen in Shanghai galleries, as can the works of many non-Shanghainese artists.

Abstract art

In recent years, Shanghai has become known as a centre for abstract art, often inspired by traditional painting. Shen Fan's abstract works, some of them using only a single colour, are reminiscent of Chinese calligraphy. Ding Yi's mesmerising paintings of tiny crosses resemble textiles more than canvases, and, indeed, are sometimes painted on tartan cloth. Wu Yiming uses traditional techniques to paint figures from old China who are faceless and cloaked in mist,

LEFT: Liu Haisu's work is reminiscent of French Impressionists. **ABOVE:** Chen Yifei is best known for his lush paintings of women from old Shanghai.

Sculpture, bronze and jade

In old China, sculpture was primarily seen in temples and at royal tombs. Sculpture spread with Buddhism during the Tang dynasty and many of the greatest examples are Buddhist. The Shanghai Museum has an excellent collection of stone Buddha sculptures and the Jade Buddha temple is home to the exquisite Jade Buddha statue. Interestingly, modern Shanghai is a major producer of Buddha statues, since its foundries are capable of casting the huge metal figures that are favoured these days by monasteries.

The city is also heir to a tradition of Western sculpture that grew up alongside Western-style architecture in the Concession era. It is perhaps the only Chinese city that has public sculptures of famous figures from arts and literature – the writer Tian Han, the composer Nie Er, and even the Russian poet Alexander Pushkin. It also has its fair share of Mao statues, mainly on university campuses. Public sculpture is a priority of the government, which recently founded a commission to oversee the creation of sculpture for public areas. Its tastes tend toward whimsical crowd-pleasers, such as the many life-size, bronze sculptures of typical Shanghainese going about the business of daily life – a young woman talking on a cellphone, a couple pushing their child in a stroller, a man on a bicycle.

Cast bronzes, carved jades and porcelain were produced by anonymous artisans and collected by emperors, literati and wealthy merchants. In addition to beauty and age, bronzes were also prized for their inscriptions and supposed ability to drive away ghosts and evil spirits; jades because they were thought to embody every virtue and to contain much qi, the vital life force; and porcelain for its lustre, feel and melodious ring when struck. Shanghai was not a major production centre for any of these crafts, but many wealthy collectors lived here and the Shanghai Museum has excellent galleries devoted to each of these.

SUZHOU EMBROIDERY: A DYING CRAFT

Embroidery is a craft that has been passed from mother to daughter in rural Suzhou for centuries. At the end of the Qing Dynasty, there were 100,000 "embroidery girls" at work in the area, but the number has fallen to 10,000 today and most of the "girls" are now quite elderly.

Embroidery girls work in their homes on pieces assigned to them by Suzhou factories that maintain embroidery stations in the villages. A complex piece – like a dragon robe that might be worn by an emperor – could take one woman stitching alone five years to complete. To speed up the process, the girls often work together, stitching toward each other from opposite sides of the embroidery frame.

They also work together when doing Suzhou's famous two-sided embroidery, in which each side of the cloth is identically embroidered – usually with a kitschy kitten surrounded by flowers and butterflies.

Although there is great demand for hand-embroidered goods, embroidery is slowly dying because peasant families have become prosperous enough that they no longer need the work. The embroidery girls' daughters often have little time for the craft and the extra cash that grandmothers earn is put to such uses as paying for the college tuition of a granddaughter – who is unlikely to become an embroiderer.

Embroidery and folk crafts

The Jiangsu-Zhejiang region was the nation's key producer of silk, with imperial silkworks located at Suzhou, Hangzhou and Nanjing until they were closed in 1894. Sericulture is intimately linked with embroidery, and nearby Suzhou became an important centre of this craft. Of the four nationally recognised styles of embroidery – which include Hunan, Sichuan and Guangdong – Suzhou's was considered the most elegant *(see box on opposite page)*, and was used for the heavily embroidered gowns worn by the Emperor and his family. Suzhou was also the main supplier of the embroidered insignia, or rank badges, worn by the nine different levels of civil and military officials in imperial China. The market for such robes and insignia ended with the demise of the imperial system in 1912, but the embroidery industry stayed alive because of demand for opera costumes, household items and export goods.

Wood-block printing is an ancient craft that fell into steady decline after the introduction of mechanical printing in the 19th century, but was revived in Shanghai in the 1920s and 30s. Its rebirth came about because the renowned writer Lu Xun, an ardent admirer of the craft, hired a Japanese artist-engraver and organised a class for young artists at which he himself acted as interpreter. Lu continued to devote his time, money and reputation to promoting wood-block printing, encouraging students to depict society as they saw it. The results are frequently bleak – starving children, downtrodden refugees, industrial landscapes – but nonetheless beautiful; samples from his collection can be seen at the Lu Xun Memorial Hall. The craft has remained alive in Shanghai, as have silk-screening and other related methods of artistic printing.

As a major cosmopolis, old Shanghai was a destination for itinerant folk artists from around the country – paper-cuts, lanterns, batiks, musical instruments, fans and every other folk art imaginable could be purchased in the city in pre-revolutionary days. Though many of these items can still be bought, they are generally

mass-produced for the tourist trade. The government officially encourages folk arts, but this sometimes results in kitschy products like dolls made from ping pong balls.

SHADOW PLAY

Shadow puppetry is gone as a theatrical art, but its magic lives on in exquisite puppets made from donkey or water buffalo skin. The Shanghai Art Museum has an excellent collection.

Experimental art

But if attempts to revive folk arts have been less than successful, the government's support of painting, calligraphy, sculpture, photography and even video and performance art is of of great significance. This backing is generally indirect, often grudging – untold num-

bers of experimental art shows have been shut down in the past – and largely a corollary of efforts to ensure that showcase projects like the Shanghai Arts Fair and the Shanghai Biennale become respected international events.

Nonetheless, the result is that Shanghai now has dozens of private galleries that sell the work of local and national artists and a burgeoning community of artists. It has frequent shows of experimental art and the Shanghai Biennale has grown into an important international exhibition. Once again, Shanghai's winning combination of culture and commerce, creativity and connoisseurship has enabled it to emerge as a key centre of the visual arts. ❏

LEFT: Suzhou embroidery is a rarity these days as it involves painstaking hours of work.

RIGHT: modern art on display at the Shanghai Biennale.

CUISINE

Shanghainese cuisine is best described as earthy and hearty comfort food
but the city is also home to scores of sophisticated eateries

From crispy fried dough crullers for an early morning breakfast to a late-night snack of plump steamed dumplings, Shanghai is a city that loves to eat – 24 hours a day. At first light, cooks begin crowding the astounding produce markets, starting the cycle of shopping, preparing food, eating and endless conversations about food that is central to the Chinese way of life – a place where people greet each other with 'have you eaten rice yet?' (*Ni chi fan le mei yo?*)

For sheer variety alone, Shanghai is one of the best places to eat in China. Dining choices range from makeshift street vendors where takeout is the only option to swanky eateries like M on the Bund, named one of the 50 best restaurants on the planet. The geographical diversity is just as breathtaking, with culinary offerings from Africa to Brazil, India to the Mediterranean, the Americas, Europe and Southeast Asia, and styles ranging from the simple to the sublime, fast food and fusion, as well as an impressive array of Chinese regional cuisines.

Comfort food

Shanghai's own cuisine has its roots in hearty peasant cooking, with none of the grand flavour statements, enormous variety or subtle complexities of, say, Cantonese and Beijing cuisines. With its long-simmered stews and sauces sweetened for the child in all of us, this is comfort food, not haute cuisine. An insistence on seasonality and freshness lifts it from the ordinary, although Shanghai gourmands say that increased fish farming and hot-housing of fruits and vegetables has irrevocably changed the original flavours of classic Shanghai dishes.

Shanghai cuisine is a subset of Huaiyang cuisine, Huaiyang being the lush region between the Huai River and the Yangzi River that encompasses both Zhejiang and Jiangsu provinces, a place so rich and fertile that it is known

as the land of fish and rice – which is also an apt description of Shanghainese cuisine.

The sea and rivers that feature so prominently in Shanghai's history play an equally important role in shaping its largely seafood-based cuisine. The most famous dish is Shanghai's signature Dazha "hairy crab". More popularly known in

CLASSIC SHANGHAI DISHES

Most local food aficionados will agree that the following dishes constitute classical Shanghainese cooking: *dazha* (hairy crab); *tipang* (pork rump); *hong shao rou* (red-cooked pork); *shizi tou* ("lion's head" meatballs); *shui jing xia ren* (crystal prawns); fish head with *fenpi*, a jelly made of bean starch; *menbao shansi* (eel casserole); *hong shao huang yu* (red-cooked yellow croaker fish); *su ji* (vegetarian chicken) and *su ya* (vegetarian duck); *zuiji* ("drunken" chicken); *shi yu* (hilsa herring); *jiao bai* (wild rice stems); *cao fu* (wheat gluten); *pao fan* (ricepot dregs made into *congee*, or porridge); *xiao long bao* (pork dumplings); and *shengjie mantou* (potstickers).

PRECEDING PAGES: Shanghai hairy crabs.
LEFT: pan-frying *shengjie mantou* snacks.
RIGHT: pork rump, or *tipang*, is another local delicacy.

Asia as "Shanghai hairy crab" *(see page 85)*, the finest versions of this autumn delicacy come from Yangcheng Lake in Jiangsu province. The crustacean gets its name from the black hairs found on its legs. To retain their exquisite taste, the crabs are steamed lightly and served with a soy sauce, black vinegar and raw ginger dip.

The city that grew up on the banks of the Huangpu River is especially fond of its denizens. River fish like yellow croaker (*huang yu*) and carp – crucian carp, variegated carp and black

OFFERING A TOAST

When toasting, hold a glass with one hand with the other placed underneath. Eye contact is made around the table, the contents drunk in one swallow, the glass lifted, and eye contact made again.

stewed to a melting tenderness, is a Shanghai classic, as is *hong shao rou* or "red-cooked" pork, fatty cubes of pork stewed in a soy sauce marinade until it practically melts in the mouth.

Poultry plays only a minor role, featuring in the classic appetiser *zuiji* or "drunken" chicken (chicken marinated in Shaoxing rice wine), *feng ya* or "wind-dried duck", which is dried outdoors and preserved for the winter, and duck and taro soup. There is also Jinhua processed ham, from Zhejiang

carp – are typically "red-cooked", prepared in a sauce of soy and sugar. River eel is cooked in casseroles, clams are stir-fried with ginger and scallions, and mussels are cooked with soy sauce and chilli. The classic Shanghai prawn dish is "crystal prawns", marinated in egg white and brine and stir-fried, while the hilsa herring (*shi yu*), now rarely prepared, is renowned for its succulent scales. Fish head is considered especially sweet, and, when stewed with *fenpi* (a sheet of bean starch jelly), soy sauce and red chilli in a claypot, makes another favourite dish.

Turning inland, pork plays a more prominent role in the cuisine than poultry: the rustic *tipang*, a great hunk of pork rump on the bone

province, often sliced and steamed with rock sugar and added to fish dishes and soups, or stir-fried with vegetables.

Traditionally, the vegetables of Shanghai cuisine – either cooked with meat or as dishes on their own – are fresh from the farm and seasonal, from the fat spring bamboo shoots to their more delicate-tasting winter counterparts, baby lima beans, lily buds, Chinese broccoli, *ji cai* or "shepherd's purse", asparagus lettuce, leafy *mixi*, and the quintessential Shanghai vegetable dish, *jiao bai* (wild rice stems).

With its country roots, the preparation of Shanghai cuisine is far less complex than its Cantonese or Beijing cousins, with only three major methods of preparation: *hong shao* or red-cooked (with sugar and soy sauce), stewed or simply stir-fried with ginger and scallions. Garlic is never used in Shanghainese cooking.

Nonetheless, Shanghai's famous style is revealed in its cold dishes, artistically arranged *hors d'oeuvres* of dazzling variety: plates of julienned vinegary pickles, tiny raw crabs marinated in rice wine called *zuipanxie*, spiced broad beans, "drunken" chicken marinated in wine, and sweet marinated wheat gluten (*kao fu*), all laid out in picturesque arrays at street stalls.

Bakeries and borscht

The cosmopolitan influence on Shanghai's design, architecture and fashion also left culinary footprints. Many of the first generation Communist leaders, notably Deng Xiaoping and Zhou Enlai, spent time in Paris, and it was their passion for croissants, say the Shanghainese, that perpetuated the Euro-style bakeries that were first brought to Shanghai by the French. After falling into disfavour during the Cultural Revolution, Shanghai's neighbourhood bakeries have undergone a renaissance, and today number in the thousands. Their shelves are filled with croissants, brioches, jewel-like teacakes – and Shanghai's fabulous sponge cakes.

Shanghai's pastry tradition has a distinctly French accent. Light, fluffy sponge cakes several layers high are generously iced with a white whipped cream frosting – with elaborate curlicues and pastel roses – and smothered with fruit. Many bakeries install their pastry chef behind a glass window, and crowds watch in fascination as he crafts a sugar-spun fantasy from the most basic of ingredients.

About the same time that the French were baking croissants, Shanghai's White Russian population, which swelled after the 1917 Russian Revolution, was brewing borscht. Those Russian restaurants are long gone (although a new one, catering to a new generation of Russian residents, recently opened), but *luo song tang* (literally "Russian soup") remains a fixture on many local restaurant menus.

Shanghai continues to seamlessly incorporate new influences into its cuisine. Not to be left behind by the likes of MacDonald's and Burger King who are lining the streets of Shanghai, the street vendors who fry up spring rolls in great bubbling woks of oil also now slice up potatoes into french fries, accompanied by a watery ketchup – localisation at its best.

Fruits of the soil

Happily, Shanghai is still a place where menus are defined by the seasons, with specialities supplied by nearby farms. Each seasonal speciality is eagerly anticipated, deftly incorporated into dishes and eaten – until the next delicacy arrives at the markets.

Bamboo shoots are characteristic of Sichuan and Hunan cuisines, home of lush bamboo

WET MARKETS AND PEDDLERS

The wet markets of Shanghai make fabulous theatre as well as a fascinating introduction to Shanghai food: the philosophy of freshness is encapsulated here, where everything is just-picked and fresh-killed, and cooks shop daily, tailoring their menus to the seasons' constantly changing produce. The mind-boggling display of items includes vegetables, fruit, live poultry and seafood, tofu and noodles, and even clothes and household sundries. But it is the itinerant peddlers, wandering Shanghai with shoulder baskets filled with produce from nearby farms, who are the first with the newest offerings, often selling rare delicacies that never make it to the markets.

LEFT: a grand banquet-style meal.
RIGHT: vegetable vendor at Yong An Road market.

forests, but Shanghai's fat spring bamboo shoots, called orchid bamboo shoots because of their fragrance, come from nearby Sheshan in Songjiang County. The bamboo shoot is sliced and often "red-cooked" on its own, as well as used in other dishes; winter brings a more subtly flavoured shoot.

With springtime comes the small, succulent and intensely flavoured strawberries and red cherries, including a brief, glorious season of yellow cherries. The itinerant peddlers in old Shanghai who would crush the juicy summer *yang mei* berry, a cousin of the bayberry, into a thirst-quenching drink are long gone now, but

Street food and snacks

For all its amazing eateries, one can still eat extraordinarily well and never set foot in a proper restaurant in Shanghai: street food abounds throughout the city, from Muslim-style Xinjiang roasted mutton kebabs to streetside bakeries and Shanghai dumplings, at all hours of day and night.

Breakfast is almost always eaten on the run, with *you tiao*, the long fried dough cruller, always a favourite. The classic Shanghai way to eat *you tiao* is to wrap it in a sticky rice cake and eat the two together – experiencing both soft and crunchy sensations in one bite – and washing it

sugar cane juice vendors still ply the streets of Nanshi, the long mottled stalks of succulent green sugarcane balanced precariously on their bicycles their calling cards.

The Barbie-pink peach blossoms of spring, more substantial and pinker than their famous cherry blossom cousins, yield to summer's Nanhui honey peach, a delicate and juicy thin-skinned white peach with a subtle yet distinctive flavour. The peach has both a round and flat variety, the latter sold as "designer fruit" in the US. Along with the autumn hairy crab, November brings fresh figs from Baoshan, while the winter months see deliciously sweet miniature oranges from the offshore islands.

down with freshly brewed soybean milk. That same sensation is found in breakfast rice cakes (*ci ba*), deep fried squares of compressed rice that make a filling morning meal. Another favourite is *pao fan*, the ricepot dregs which are steeped, then made into a *congee*, or porridge. And then there's the more familiar omelette called *jianbing*, cooked on steaming griddles and topped with chilli sauce and rolled up for take-away.

Snacks and street food are available on virtually every corner of Shanghai, but the best

ABOVE: typical Shanghainese breakfast fare: *jian bing* (left), fried rice cakes (middle) and *you tiao* (right).
RIGHT: modern-day moon cakes *á la* Häagen-Dazs.

selection of Shanghai snacks is found at Yu Garden *(see page 151)*. Such is the fame of Shanghai street food and snacks that hordes of Chinese tourists patiently wait in line at Yu Garden's Nanxiang Steamed Bun Restaurant, purportedly the best place for *xiao long bao*, the tiny pork-stuffed dumplings with translucent skins for which Shanghai is famous.

The lines are just as long for the so-called potstickers, *shengjie mantou*, pan-fried in giant crusty black pans and sprinkled with scallions, and for *anchun jiaozi*, soft, sweet "pigeon-egg" dumplings made with glutinous rice flour and filled with the flavours of the osmanthus flower and mint. Originally a summertime treat, they are now eaten year round. *Tang yuan*, glutinous rice dumplings with a sweet filling in a soup of fermented rice, is a traditional New Year delicacy, as is *nian gao*, literally "New Year cake". Other favourite snacks include crisp-crusted *meimao su* or "eyebrow" shortcake, a pastry named for its arched shape and filled with sweet or savoury stuffing, and *chou doufu*, or smelly beancurd, more politely known as fermented beancurd and an acquired taste, from Fenxian county on the outskirts of Shanghai.

Unrivalled dining scene

Dining out in Shanghai has blossomed from glum state-run restaurants into a thriving international culinary scene: new restaurants open every month, and one local publication lists 35 different types of cuisines in its restaurant directory. Add to that the enormous variety of eateries, from hole-in-the-wall digs to sophisticated palaces of haute cuisine, and you have a dining scene that is unrivalled on the mainland.

As a city of immigrants, Shanghai's restaurants represent a veritable microcosm of China. Along with the major cuisines – Cantonese, Beijing, Sichuan – are endless variations in between. Sichuan hotpot (*huoguo*) restaurants where a communal pot of chilli-laced bubbling soup, sitting on a flame, is used for dipping and cooking vegetables and meats, are popular, as are dim sum (*dian xin*) buffets. Sensing opportunity, well-known restaurants have opened branches in Shanghai, including Beijing's famous Quanjude Peking duck, northern-style dumplings at Chang An, Xinjiang cuisine at Afunti and the Cantonese Be There or Be Square chain.

FESTIVAL FARE: FROM RICE DUMPLINGS TO CHOCOLATE MOONCAKES

Discouraged by Sun Yat-sen's Kuomintang government and almost entirely eradicated by the Communists, Shanghai's festivals and the special food associated with them are now undergoing a renaissance. Perhaps because they were so sorely missed, many festival foods are now available year-round in Shanghai.

Chinese New Year, the biggest and most important festival, usually falls in January or February. It's a great excuse for the fish-loving Shanghainese to eat fish dishes – *yu*, or fish, is a homonym for prosperity in Chinese, and considered a particularly auspicious New Year's dish, and *tang yuan*, the soft glutinous rice dumpling always ends the meal.

Qingming or the springtime tomb-sweeping day is mostly observed with ceremonies at the gravesites of Communist martyrs, but the *qing* cake, made of glutinous rice paste and stuffed with a sweet filling, has returned for Qingming. Summer's Dragon Boat Festival is the time to eat *zongzi*, the lotus-leaf wrapped glutinous rice dumplings now available year-round, followed by autumn mooncakes, probably the most popular festival food in Shanghai. Although newspaper polls say that Shanghainese prefer traditional mooncakes, creative options like Häagen-Dazs ice-cream mooncakes and gourmet chocolate mooncakes have made serious inroads, particularly amongst young trendsetters.

Chinese cuisine trends sweep Shanghai every couple of years or so, leaving a host of restaurants in their wake: first, it was the food of the ethnic minority Yunnan people, then came the cuisine of lakeside Hangzhou, and lately, spicy Hunan food from Mao Zedong's home province.

Local Shanghainese restaurants run the gamut from neighbourhood gems like Baoluo, where lines form each evening for good, downhome Shanghainese cooking in a studiously unpretentious setting, to the considerably more

DINING SCHEDULES

Lunch is served from 11.30am to 2pm, and restaurants close from 2 to 6pm. At 6pm, all of Shanghai eats – including taxi drivers, making cabs hard to find at that hour.

here for Li's delectable smoked fish and special Shanghai dishes no longer available elsewhere. (Note: These days even the best Shanghainese restaurants, including Shanghai Uncle, include non-Shanghai dishes on their menus.)

Shanghai has a variety of eateries that span the globe, but the best of these, regardless of the cuisine served, have a strong sense of place. Located in a 1920s Bund building, M on the Bund serves a European-Mediterranean menu in a 1930s-inspired modernist interior, its views of the water-

upmarket confines of Ye Shanghai at Xintiandi, a Hong Kong import serving nouvelle Shanghai cuisine in an old *shikumen* (stone gate) house. The trendiest Shanghainese restaurants, however, like 1221 and Henry, are a combination of the two: homestyle Shanghai cooking in a stylish setting that even Shanghai's nouveau-riche would be pleased to be seen in.

By far Shanghai's best Shanghainese restaurant is Shanghai Uncle, owned by Li Zhongheng, an erudite gourmet who has inherited the tastebuds of his mother Virginia Lee, the co-author, along with American food critic Craig Claiborne, of the classic *The Chinese Cookbook*. Nostalgic Shanghai gourmands come

front unparalleled. Across the river, the Grand Hyatt's On Fifty Six features three restaurants on the 56th floor of the silver Jin Mao Tower – Italian at Cucina, Continental at The Grill and Japanese at Kobachi – all overlooking the sweep of the city from China's tallest building. Face Restaurant's exotic Asian eateries (Hazara and La Na Thai) are located in a garden manor; T8 restaurant serves fusion in a refurbished *shikumen* house at Xintiandi; and French haute cuisine is served in an old Russian church called Ashanti Dome – under a ceiling painted with cherubs. ❑

● *See page 296 of Travel Tips for restaurant listings.*

ABOVE: grand views and food at Grand Hyatt's Cucina.

A Feast of Hairy Crabs

Naturally, the signature dish for the place known as "the city above the sea" comes from its waters. Ancient poets have inscribed verses on the joys of savouring hairy crabs and sipping wine under a ripe harvest moon, and the tradition endures today. Autumn is the season for the Dazha crab, known throughout the world as the Shanghai hairy crab, but actually indigenous to the lower reaches of the Yangzi River.

The crab's journey to the platters of Shanghai's restaurants begins in springtime, in May, when millions of the migratory crustaceans swim eastwards to the mouth of the Yangzi River to spawn. The baby crabs swim into the nearby connecting rivers and lakes, where fishermen snap them up and rear them in crab farms until they mature in the autumn.

The immense popularity of the hairy crab has instigated the development of crab farms throughout the region, from Chongming Island in the east to Dianshan Lake in the west, but connoisseurs still insist that the crabs from Yangcheng Lake are beyond compare. Pollution-free and with water so clear that the sunlight fills its depths, experts say that it is the unique ecology of the lake that helps create such delectable creatures. Genuine Yangcheng Lake crabs all sport distinctive shiny green shells, pearl-white bellies, golden legs covered with long, thick hair – and spit foam continuously.

The fresh and fragrant taste of the crabmeat is its primary lure, but its inaccessibility adds cachet: the deep waters of the lake make retrieving the precious booty a challenge. That, coupled with its short life cycle – the crab is available only during the autumn months – has made it a rare treat.

Conservationists in the US prohibit the capture of roe-bearing female blue crabs, but there are no such restrictions on the Shanghai hairy crab in China – in fact, the roe is one of the most eagerly anticipated delicacies of the crab season. The female crab becomes available first, in October, while the male crab is ready in November. Each female crab bears just a few roe, making it an expensive delicacy, but the rich flavourful taste, say connoisseurs, is habit-forming.

Crab gourmands have strict criteria when it comes to selecting the perfect crab. Crabs are always kept alive until selected, their legs usually

RIGHT: the best and most succulent roe-filled Shanghai hairy crabs come from Yangcheng Lake.

tied with twine and kept in aquariums. They should be flat and, most importantly, alert. The legs should be long, with long hairs, and the crab's apron, the "cover" at the rear, should be as white as possible.

Because the taste of the crabmeat is so prized, preparation is focused on preserving that natural flavour as much as possible. The crabs are steamed to a gorgeous shade of vermilion, sometimes with ginger, and are served with a dipping sauce of raw minced ginger, soy sauce and black vinegar. With much ceremony, the apron and carapace are taken off, at which point the roe is extracted and savoured. Next, the crab legs are

pulled off, and the meat inside extracted with a chopstick, then a cracker is used for the claws. Finally, the great, succulent chunks of meat inside the main body of the crab are tackled. Everything but the lungs are eaten, and particularly adept crab eaters manage to put the entire crab back together after eating it, as if it had never been touched.

Hairy crabs are considered by the Chinese to be "cooling" to the body so the sherry-like Shaoxing wine, from neighbouring Shaoxing province, is usually offered to rebalance the body's *yin* and *yang*. Like some crab gourmands who can put a whole crab back together again after tearing it apart, the human body, too, needs to return to its pre-crab eating state. ❑

SHOPPING

Leaving culture to Beijing, brash Shanghai has sidelined glitzy Hong Kong and reclaimed its former role as China's fashion and design hotbed

Since the mid-1990s, the rise of private enterprise and an increasingly sophisticated local clientele have rejuvenated Shanghai's shopping scene. Even jaded shoppers have trouble restraining themselves when faced with Shanghai's tantalising array of goods, from ubiquitous knock-offs to high-quality items made for the local and export markets – all at bargain basement prices.

Between the two World Wars, Shanghai's shopping culture blossomed as smartly dressed ladies and their taipan husbands plied the foreign concession shops in search of accoutrements for their elegant mansions and European lifestyles. Famous stores sported names like Wing On, Sincere and Sun. The old Sun Store on Nanjing Road, now called the Shanghai No. 1 Department Store *(see page 137)*, is a local landmark whose distinctive façade has been the backdrop for countless Chinese tourist photos in the recent past. When the austere Communists took over in 1949, the big name retailers fled to Hong Kong, taking sophistication, a culture of customer service and glamour with them. The old store buildings, however, stood firm in the ensuing years, filled with low-quality goods and surly clerks who seemed to know only two words: "*mei you*" (Chinese for "don't have").

A shopping renaissance

Today, Shanghai's second shopping renaissance is well underway. Major department stores have returned to their historic Nanjing Road and Huaihai Road stomping grounds while also expanding into new areas like Pudong and the weekend consumer mecca at the junction of Zhaojiabang, Caoxi and Hongqiao roads in the Xujiahui district. Here, in cavernous mall-cum-entertainment centres, is where Shanghai's younger generation escape from their crowded living quarters and tiny office cubicles.

Youthful Shanghai, the city of the future, is a city where almost any money-making idea can become reality. This translates into a lively ferment among entrepreneurs, both local and international. Whether indulging in China's tradition of copying as an art form, finding ways to funnel made-for-export designer goods into local shops or taking inspiration from Shanghai's cosmopolitan atmosphere to design unique

East-meets-West products, the sky's the limit.

Shanghai offers many adventures for the intrepid shopper. For a slice of Shanghai life – with the added bonus of unique goods and great bargains – venture from the main thoroughfares and into local markets, back streets and private showrooms. The warren of shops around Yu Garden *(see page 151)* is where kitsch battery-powered Panda bears, carved walking sticks and fake chirping crickets can be found. Everyone knows that bustling Yu Garden Bazaar is a good-natured tourist trap. But close your eyes and allow yourself to be transported back to the days when this area, home to the Temple of the Town God, was the heart of the old Chinese walled city.

LEFT: bolts of colourful Suzhou silk brocade.
RIGHT: the famous Shanghai No. 1 Department Store.

Knock-offs and copies

Xiangyang Fashion Market, or Xiangyang Shichang *(see page 165)* at Huaihai and Xiangyang roads, is Shanghai's one-stop knock-off fashion centre. Hundreds of stalls along the bustling lanes vie for the shopper's attention with their displays of brand-name purses, watches, clothing and accessories. Rest assured that the merchandise reflects the latest trends among Shanghai's fashionistas. After a hard day of window-shopping on Nanjing Road, most savvy locals repair to Xiangyang market for the final kill. Although they love the prestige of brand names, few ordinary Shanghainese can afford the real thing, leading to a thriving market for knock-offs. Negotiating is *de rigueur.* If you don't see a certain luxury brand displayed, chances are that the company's big brass is in town. Just ask, and the shopkeeper will probably pull it out from under the counter.

In-the-know local customers rarely buy a top-quality knock-off wallet or handbag off the shelf. Instead, they ask to see the shopkeeper's catalogue of "A Grade" products with brands ranging from Louis Vuitton to Chanel. Do the same, even if you don't speak Chinese. Pointing and miming is very effective and most merchants speak some English. Once you've cho-

THE FINE ART OF COPYING

Copying has deep cultural roots in China. Since the 6th century, Chinese painters have been judged by six aesthetic principles developed by scholar Xie He. One principle, *chuanyi muxie*, encouraging replication, says "by copying the ancient models should be perpetuated". Copying ancient masters allowed a painter to preserve revered traditional techniques. Admittedly, it's a far cry from ancient masters to a Prada handbag. But China-made goods of foreign design are often subject to complicated business arrangements where the end producer may not have a clear idea of who owns the original design. Also, some local companies don't understand the concept of design copyrights. While copyrights are protected under Chinese law, many foreign companies choose not to battle in courts due to cost and time commitments. All this, plus the consumers' appetite for knock-off goods, has contributed to the counterfeiting trade.

Thanks to consumer education and increased vigilance by companies, the situation is improving. The value of counterfeit goods seized by the US Customs has fallen over the years. While this may not present a true picture of the exact business turnover, a post-WTO push is underway to educate locals about copyright laws. As incomes in Shanghai rise and the value of original goods gain a certain cache, trendy Shanghainese may follow their Tokyo neighbours in their quest for the real McCoy.

sen the styles you like from the catalogue, the shopkeeper will fetch the goods from his "warehouse". This can take up to 30 minutes. Carefully check the merchandise for scratches and flaws, and overall finishing. Now you're ready to start haggling. One good rule of thumb is to start at one-third and end at one-half to two-thirds of the original asking price. The final sum − which can range from RMB 100 to 500 − will depend on a delicate combination of the seller's disposition and your bargaining skills.

> **BARGAINING PRIMER**
>
> Decide how much you want to spend, buy in bulk for cheaper prices, be prepared to walk away, and remain calm and friendly. And remember: the shopkeeper will always make a profit.

Watches and CDS

Shopping for knock-off watches is a real adventure as top-quality fake Rolexes and Longines are only sold surreptitiously at Xiangyang market. If you're game, respond positively to vendors who approach you with whispers of "want a watch?" as you thread your way through the market. Although perfectly safe, less intrepid shoppers may want to embark on this quest with a companion because your watch vendor will likely lead you to a hidden salesroom tucked in one of the neighbourhood mazes adjoining the market. After dodging hanging laundry and groups of card-playing grandpas, your guide will duck into a dimly lit building entrance, open a nondescript door and usher you into a room chock full of glittering watches. With a diligent quality check, friendly attitude and hard bargaining, you should be able to get a nice watch for about RMB 200–300.

The men will go weak-kneed at Xiangyang's open displays of bootleg DVDs and VCDs, and Game Boy and Nintendo games. But be forewarned that the quality found here can vary. Roughly one out of three copied disks is flawed, and pirated DVDs sometimes don't work on the high-end DVD players sold in the West. Game Boy and Nintendo items are good buys and generally work fine.

Xiangyang is also good for one-of-a kind designer fashion bargains. Seek out its stalls selling unique clothes with a sophisticated East-meets-West edge. If you're tempted by one of the trendy jackets or dresses (RMB 300–800) and can wait 3–4 days, they can make one to fit you.

LEFT: Shanghai tailors can copy any design you wish.
RIGHT: Xiangyang Market's designer watch knock-offs.

Chinese furniture and curios

Most old-style Chinese furniture shops are in the vicinity of Wuzhong Road *(see page 196)* just minutes from the Hongqiao airport. The prices are usually much lower than what you would pay in other countries. All the shops stock restored as well as unfinished pieces. Ask to visit the warehouse area, where you can stroll among dusty piles of rickety trunks, kitchen cabinets, calligraphy tables, austere chairs and wedding chests. Once you have cho-

sen your piece, the store's craftsmen will restore and refinish it to your specifications. Most of the furniture here is newly made of old wood, or has been aged to give them an "antique" look. Shop owners will usually tell you the real provenance of the piece. But, as with all Shanghai shopping, *caveat emptor*. The warehouses will also help ship your purchases.

For smaller curios and typical Shanghai items from the 1920s and 30s, try the Dongtai Road market *(see page 156)* where opium pipes, cigarette girl retro posters, lanterns, porcelain and other trinkets spill from the dusty shops onto the street. Flea market shoppers should also visit the five-storey Cang Bao Building *(see page 154)* near Yu Garden. Local antique and curio collectors shop at dawn on Sundays for the best bargains, as this is when smaller vendors and country folk set up tables here to sell their wares.

Original goods at local prices

If China is the world's factory, Shanghai is its showcase. Labour-intensive products manufactured in central China are sent down the Yangzi River to be exported via Shanghai's port – the largest in mainland China. The significance for shoppers? It all ends up in Shanghai, from original Western designer-brand clothing to silk and freshwater pearls from neighbouring provinces.

Export-bound and China-made original Nike, Reebok and other branded sportswear from local factories sometimes takes a detour on the way to Shanghai's port – usually ending up in one of the hole-in-the-wall shops along Shanxi Road (S). Keep an eye out also for original American fashion labels like Liz Claiborn and Nordstroms as well as European brands on leather jackets, coats and dresses. These made-in-China merchandise often gets siphoned directly from the factory with money exchanged under the table. Shanxi Road (S) is a fun shopping outing; you never know what you'll find, and there's always plenty of local colour here.

Since ancient times, China has cornered the world's silk market. Legend holds that the concubine Lei Zu discovered the silk-making process when she accidentally dropped a silkworm cocoon into her tea over 3,000 years ago. By 200 BC, the precious "woven wind" fabric was being dispatched to Western markets via the fabled Silk Road. China is still the world's largest exporter of silk, with most of the fabric produced around Shanghai. Peasants raise silkworms less than 100 km (60 miles) away in mulberry tree-carpeted Deqing County, near Hangzhou, heart of China's silk producing region. Naturally, Shanghai is home to all varieties of silk, from stiff brocades to slinky materials.

Fabrics and pearls

Plenty of bargains also await fabric hunters at Dongjiadu market *(see page 157)*. Before shopping, be sure to explore the traditional neighbourhood first. After a bowl of noodles at one of the mom-and-pop stands, you will be ready to stake out the sprawling fabric market, Shanghai's best for silks, woollens, cashmeres and linens. Most of the shops have tailors on the premises, but you'll have to work hard at communicating. If you brought a piece of your own clothing to be copied, the tailors usually do a good job. Incidentally, "copy" is an English word understood by most Shanghai tailors.

If you don't have time to poke around at

Dongjiadu market, try visiting one of the Silk King stores around town. These government-run emporiums offer quality silk as well as a variety of excellent (but pricey) fabrics like cashmere. To transform your silk into a traditional Mao jacket or *qipao*, a Chinese-style slim fitting dress, check out the tailors on the premises. As a bonus, they can also custom-make shoes to match your outfit.

Cultured pearls are one of the Shanghai's best bargains. The Yangzi River Delta and the network of canals and ponds surrounding Shanghai is home to China's thriving freshwater cultured pearl industry. In fact, the Chinese were the first to develop the technique for producing cultured pearls in the 5th century. Pearl quality has improved greatly since the modern industry began in the 1960s. Round, lustrous gem-quality pearls as well as multi-coloured baroque, seed and coin-shaped pearls are sold in many specialised stores in Shanghai. And if you have a few days, the shop's craftsmen can produce jewellery to your specifications.

Although jade is inextricably linked to Chinese culture and history, it is surprisingly difficult to find reputable dealers in Shanghai or even Beijing. However, inexpensive "jade" trinkets are available in the jewellery and souvenir shops around Yu Garden.

Shanghai chic

Local and international entrepreneurs, inspired by Chinese tradition and Shanghai's cosmopolitan atmosphere as well as the easy access to raw materials, produce high-quality goods primarily for export at select locations in town. The French were among the first to combine elegant design with local craftsmanship and materials.

French-owned Shanghai Trio (181 Taicang Road) is popular with expats for silk, linen and cashmere home and fashion accessories while locals adore the Zen-like tableware at Chine Concept's store hidden in a leafy street in the former French Concession (74 Wu Yuan Road). The Singaporean-owned Simply Life chain of home décor stores in trendy Xintiandi (No. 5 Xintiandi) and elsewhere offers a lovely selection of minimalist concept items, including bone china by AsianEra, produced by a local

Chinese-American entrepreneur and exported to exclusive boutiques around the world. For more of the same, visit the Taiwanese-owned ShangPin lifestyle store at 227 Shanxi Road (S) for its range of home accessories.

While at Xintiandi, stop by clothing designer Anthony Xavier's boutique at No. 15, darling of expat ladies from Hong Kong to Australia. His "X" store is a treasure trove of whimsical fashion and accessories.

SoHo meets Shanghai (well, sort of) at Taikang Road (at Sinan Road), Shanghai's "official" art street. Stroll into Lane 210 and peek into American potter Jeremy Clayton's

studio. Further down the lane at No. 2, see local photographer Deke Erh's latest showing. Across the lane at No. 3, an old factory has been converted into a design incubator for young talent: here are art, fashion, design and gift products. The second floor Jooi design studio offers contemporary home and fashion accessories incorporating fine Chinese craftsmanship. Continuing down the alleyway, new stores and cafés are emerging weekly. The latest developments include Shanghai's first DJ record store and a hippie clothing shop hidden in a renovated courtyard that bills itself as an alternative to the chic Xintiandi area. ❏

● *See page 308 of Travel Tips for shopping listings.*

LEFT: silk cushion covers and other trinkets.
RIGHT: cultured pearls are another good buy.

SHANGHAI NIGHTS

Bop till you drop takes on new meaning in the city – whether your tastes run from nasty drink dives, elegant be-seen pubs or all-night karaoke

A classic 1930s pop song entitled *Nighttime Shanghai* trilled the tribute, "You really are a city that never sleeps". In the 1950s, the Communists outlawed Shanghai's wild nightlife and the licentiousness that made it famous, but today, some aspects of its exciting past have started to re-emerge. While contemporary Shanghai cannot claim the endless after-hours bustle of its historical heyday, the city does keep busy until the neon gives way to dawn.

The bar scene

Like much of modern Shanghai's revival, the nightlife owes a large debt to foreign investment. Most of Shanghai's successful bars are opened and run either by foreigners or by Chinese "returnees" who have studied abroad. Yet, also like so much else, Shanghai has translated the foreign-invested bars into something uniquely Shanghainese, a seamless blend of the indigenous and the imported.

Appearances count for everything in Shanghai, including its bars. Other Chinese cities are dominated by earthy and unpretentious dives, but in Shanghai, even the casual is carefully crafted. Its most famous bars, like Face in the Ruijin Guesthouse and Goya on Xinhua Road, are posh and pricey, with elaborate decors that recall the upmarket neighbourhoods of Western cities or Hong Kong – with prices to match. These rarified, elegant settings often contain a surprisingly colourful mix of both foreigners and locals. Shanghai is a true melting pot, and alcohol its flame. While social rank matters, the lines between the castes are lightly drawn and highly permeable. Even in expatriate enclaves, the crowds are often half local.

Shanghai's bar denizens are as varied as the city itself. At many nightspots, ubiquitous Western faces are joined by Shanghainese white collar workers. Shanghai's upwardly-mobile and college-educated yuppies, or "Shuppies", enjoying middle-management positions and salaries

their parents never dreamed of, are generally bored and eager for new experiences. Many Shuppies are also eager to assert their sophistication – which in Shanghai translates to being Westernised – and thus prefer foreign bars.

Local students – Shuppies in training, with lower budgets – usually congregate at campus

bars, rock dives and dance clubs. Chinese student dives usually offer cheap drinks, unpretentious environments and a low-key crowd. Places like Time Passage on Huashan Road and the Hard Rock Bar on Zhengtong Road by Fudan University are the top favourites. In addition to students, these places attract an interesting roster of local artists, writers and other creative folk.

Foreign students frequent places like Windows Too on Nanjing Road (W): packed, dingy rooms offering RMB 10 drinks in plastic cups. At the opposite end of the spectrum are the Hong Kong and Taiwanese communities, who like to spend extravagantly at the swanky see-and-be-seen

LEFT: making all the right moves at Shanghai's Pegasus club. **RIGHT:** tending the bar.

clubs like Fuxing Park's California and Guandi clubs, and Pegasus and Maya on Huaihai Road.

Given such conflicting demands, opening a bar in Shanghai is a Darwinian undertaking, and most have the shelf life of an open can of club soda. Trend-obsessed barflies follow the "hot new thing", currently the Xintiandi development *(see page 160)*. With its collection of restaurants, bars and shops in converted *shikumen* (stone gate) housing, Xintiandi is trendy enough to attract the Shuppies, expensive enough to placate the Hong Kong and Taiwanese contingents, and exotically elegant enough for the expatriates. Top hotspots include

Che and Luna, but the entire complex is packed every night of the week.

The hot place before Xintiandi was the far less genteel Maoming Road (S) bar strip *(see page 164)*, which is still hopping but drained of its vitality after the police shut it down at its prime in 2000. It was allowed to reopen after a few months, but the police presence remains ominously obvious. Populated by middle-aged Western men on the Chinese girlfriend prowl (the young women prowling back) and twenty- and thirty-something party crowds, Maoming Road (S) is a place charged with sex. Judy's Too, at No. 176, the seamy soul of the strip, has

STRANGERS IN THE NIGHT

Shanghai is a city with flagrant prostitution but no prostitutes. Instead, there are "fishing girls", KTV misses, hair-washers and gold-diggers. A Western man cannot enter a Maoming Road bar without being accosted by a girl demanding, "Hello! Buy me drink!" She will often secure cash from him and then return from the bar sipping a glass of water, the money stashed in her bra. These *diaomazi*, or "fishing girls" charge for their company, but not necessarily for sex. Similar ambiguity surrounds the KTV *xiaojie*, or KTV miss, whose job is to accompany male karaoke patrons. KTV misses at most establishments are, for the right tip, also available for anything from groping

and kissing up to and including sex. If a wealthier KTV client takes a shine to a particular *xiaojie*, he may upgrade her to his personal "canary" (*jinse niao*). Most wealthy Chinese, Hong Kong and Taiwanese men keep at least one mistress in Shanghai, showering upon her an apartment, designer clothing and cash. Even women who are not full-time canaries expect boyfriends to spend lavishly on them, and a fat wallet (or a foreign passport) can make any man a Don Juan. The only straightforward sexual exchange in Shanghai occurs in barbershops, where RMB 10 buys a shampoo and scalp massage – and RMB 100 buys something a great deal more lascivious.

become synonymous with the older Western-man-with-young-Chinese-girl phenomenon, while Buddha Bar nearby has become the headquarters of the chemically-induced generation.

A step lower on the sleaze barometer is the Julu Road strip, Shanghai's oldest bar street. Its collection of tiny bars feature dim lighting, darts, and again, older Western men with Chinese girlfriends in tow, but these can be cozily intimate in a "Cheers" sort of way when compared to the crowded, pounding anonymity of Maoming Road. Julu Road recently added a few more mainstream spots, attracting a younger clientele.

Less intrepid expatriates and business visitors congregate at Shanghai's "Little America" along Nanjing Road (W) near the Portman Ritz-Carlton. Malone's American Café serves up the best burgers in town and live cover tunes, while business at the Hard Rock Café is reputedly so good that only hookers must pay an entrance fee. The Long Bar upstairs is infamous for its nightly "model shows", where it is the models, and not their clothing (or lack thereof) that are on show.

Nightclubbing – Shanghai style

Shanghai's booming DJ scene dominates dozens of nightclubs, inexplicably labelled "discos" despite bearing no connection to the 1970s American music genre. The offering is uniformly Techno and Hip-Hop mixed by a handful of homegrown DJs, some Chinese but mostly new arrivals who grew up in Japan, Canada and America. Shanghai has also become a requisite tour stop for internationally famous DJs like Paul Oakenfield, and weekend clubs like Rojam on Central Huaihai Road and La Belle on Tongren Road justify their cover charges with DJs visiting from the near-abroad of Beijing, Hong Kong or Tokyo.

DJ-driven nightclubs attract an edgy subsection of Shuppies and younger foreigners. They are also popular with Shanghai's recreational drug users who, high on ecstasy, head-shake or *yaotou* to the trance music. The same crowd attends the periodic raves organised in the suburbs by local DJs.

LEFT: Chinese-girl-and-Western-man pairings are the rage these days in Shanghai.
RIGHT: typical club "headshaker".

NEW HOTSPOT

Taikang Road, off Sinan Road, is the latest upmarket nightspot, with posh restaurants and trendy clubs interspersed with art galleries, shops and a live music house.

Another type of nightclub caters to an entirely different group of Shanghainese youth. Playing perky remixes of Top 40 and Mandopop tunes, discos like Real Love at Hengshan Road provide an oasis of innocence in Shanghai's wild nightlife. The atmosphere recalls that of a junior high school dance, with groups clinging shyly to their same-sex friends while the waiters deliver notes from equally shy young men. After four years, Real Love remains the busiest place in Shanghai, and a whole collec-

tion of mellow little bars have sprung up to accommodate its runoff. The neighbourhood coexists peacefully with the expensive, ostentatious Promenade complex down the block.

The kiddie discos were all the rage in the early and mid-1990s, when they were still a novelty. Until a few years ago, they also had *yaotou* and aggressive pick-up scenes, but the DJ clubs have since siphoned them off. Reduced clientele due to proliferating entertainment options has spelt the death knell for most youth-oriented nightclubs. A few, such as Real Love or SOS at Xujiahui, have survived downtown, while others like Buff Disco and Apocalypse Now thrive in the northern "low-corner" and student districts.

Rock, jazz and pop music

Shanghai has a small but strong and growing rock scene *(see page 99)*. Xintiandi Ark, featuring a couple of local pop-rock bands every week, holds weekend afternoon rock parties and hosts a steady line-up of Japanese rock luminaries and underground American bands. Music Factory on Taikang Road caters to Shanghai's artsy, rebellious punk and metal bands with its industrial grunge décor. It also regularly features cutting-edge Beijing bands. Guaer, located on Huangxing Road near Fudan, is the music scene's great equalizer. Reached by walking through a scrap metal heap, it showcases the city's big names of all styles and allows new bands to cut their teeth.

Shanghai's jazz scene is better integrated with the mainstream, foreign-oriented bar scene than its rock music, but is also less original. There are a few prominent roving jazz musicians, such as the band Five Guys on a Train and the singer Coco, but most regularly operate in-house at Shanghai's jazz clubs. The Cotton Club, located on Huaihai Road, and the House of Blues, at Maoming Road (S), have both been around for years and feature nightly performances by mostly local musicians. M on the Bund's Glamor Room has a regular jazz line-up, and most five-star hotels, like the Ritz-Carleton and the Four Seasons, have jazz bars featuring mostly American singers backed by local or Filipino musicians. Tourists prefer the Peace Hotel Jazz Bar, with nightly performances by an elderly pre-Liberation band.

Shanghai's biggest homegrown pop star is the sophisticated, jazz-influenced singer-songwriter Li Yuan. Mandopop and Cantopop stars from all over China, including Coco Lee, Yu Quan and Zheng Jun, perform regularly in Shanghai, usually at the Shanghai Stadium but sometimes at smaller venues in bars and clubs. Aspiring young singers often vie for the spotlight at M-Box on Huaihai Road, and one regular there, pop duo UTM, seems to have a good shot at stardom.

Local pastimes

While Shuppie hipsters live it up at foreign bars, dance clubs and music dives, their elders and their lower-income peers opt for more time-tested activities. Despite the Starbucks invasion, teahouses remain a favourite first-date spot. These establishments, however, are a far cry from the traditional Chinese teahouse: boys sip beer, the girls pearl tea – a sweet, thick concoction containing glutinous balls, or "pearls", that are slurped up through an extra wide straw. Celine Dion wafts as thick as the cigarette smoke from the nervous youngsters who play cards to avoid awkward first-date conversation.

Although its vogue has been fading since a mid-1990s peak, bowling is popular with a certain segment of low-income youth. Attached to larger recreational facilities offering video games, snooker and go-carting, most bowling alleys are open 24 hours to accommodate young male slackers and hustlers, joined after-hours by their girlfriends, mostly bar and KTV girls.

GAY SHANGHAI

Shanghai's gay bars are the picture of civility compared to the aggressive sexuality flaunted at the city's straight bars. Anonymous gay sex is relegated instead to late nights at parks and People's Square. The small number of "out" gays in Shanghai, led by cross-dresser and bar owner Phil and jazz singer Coco, ensures a collegial atmosphere, and new friends are always welcomed. Although equal parts Western and well-educated Chinese, the scene is predominantly male. Homosexuality was no longer considered a mental illnesss in 2001, essentially decriminalizing it, but the taboo remains, forcing Shanghai's gay bars to relocate regularly.

The ubiquitous Karaoke parlour, or KTV (Karaoke TV), enjoys something of a double life. The dozens of outlets of the immensely popular Cashbox KTV chain draw a steady flow of Shanghainese of all ages and classes, predominantly the same young crowd one might see at Real Love. Singing is taken seriously at Cashbox, which can even record the evening's session for aspiring impresarios – but rarely at other less salubrious places. The real point of the latter form of KTV is the KTV girl, Shanghai's equivalent of the hostess. A customer selects from a line-up of pretty young things to sing with, and pays an hourly rate for her com-

along with sauna, steam room and Jacuzzi, there are special pools containing pearls or rose petals for supposed medicinal benefits. After donning the obligatory house-issued pyjamas, one can head upstairs for a meal, a massage, a movie, Karaoke, billiards, miniature golf, mahjong, a manicure or facial, or even fly fishing. Alternatively, a glimpse of ordinary folk can be had at the old-style bathhouses *(see text box page 98)* in the Old City, particularly along Fangbang Road and the "low-corner" districts.

Ordinary Shanghainese with limited means are resourceful at concocting budget forms of entertainment. Ballroom dancing, banned as

pany, with tips for more physical services. Many of the upmarket bars and discos have KTV rooms (and girls) upstairs for their middle-aged male clientele. The middle-aged Chinese and Taiwanese men who frequent such establishments come in groups, often on expense accounts to entertain clients and government officials.

Nouveau riche business types also congregate at posh new-style bathhouses like Sea Cloud Garden on Panyu Road. In glaring marble and crystal, these luxurious, multi-storey complexes feature elaborate bathing options:

LEFT: Peace Hotel's Jazz Bar musicians.
ABOVE: bathhouse scene where anything goes.

Western and decadent during the Cultural Revolution, was the rage in the early 1980s and remains popular among retirees, although some Shuppies have also started to take to it. Stereototing elderly Shanghainese often invade downtown parks like Xujiahui Park at dusk, playing music that sends crowds of dozens twirling merrily. There are also indoor social dance halls which charge a small entrance fee, stay open all day and offer classes.

Shanghai is famous for the insular communities contained in its traditional *longtang* (lane) housing, where Shanghainese pass their days and nights socialising with neighbours, often outdoors in the lanes. Children play soccer and badminton, teens strum guitars and elderly men compare birds. After dinner, the lanes fill with a clacking sound like an invasion of locusts from mahjong games, both indoors and out. Regardless of season, older men prop up tables and carry out stools to play cards. Even as the lanes disappear, the stubborn Shanghainese hold onto their traditions, shifting the setting of their outdoor games to bustling city pavements.

After-hours entertainment

Most of Shanghai's bars and clubs ebb around 2am on weekends, and even the busiest dives start to close shop by 4am. Yet as the revellers stumble homewards, some are waylaid by the promise of detoxifying nutrition.

Street kitchens start wheeling up their carts, unloading tables and stools, and firing up the coal brickets from 9pm onwards every evening. Shanghai does not have one central area for after-hours street food; instead, stalls are scattered around the downtown area. The traditional staples are wonton soup (*huntun*), Shanghai and Cantonese-style fried noodles (*chao mian, chao hefen*) and fried rice (*danchaofan*). Many noodle and dumpling shops downtown close late on weekends, and larger hotpot restaurants advertise 24-hour service. Franchises like the Soy Milk

OLD-STYLE BATHHOUSES

Until a decade ago, most Shanghainese lived in dense *longtang* (lane) housing without central plumbing. In the summers, underwear-clad men would bathe outside, still a common sight, but most bathing was conducted in public bathhouses (*yushi*). In addition to showers, they contained changing rooms, a sauna, an attendant offering a full-body loofah (*chabei*), and, in a few, a hot tub. Customers would linger over tea, enjoying the heat and the company of their neighbours. Nowadays, with the suburban migration to high-rise housing, the old bathhouses are disappearing, replaced by elegant new complexes that make public bathing a matter of luxury rather than necessity.

King chain serve breakfast dim sum items like soy milk and *you tiao* (fried dough sticks) around the clock. Convenience store chains also carry hot, greasy snacks to satiate late-night customers.

The anti-vice crackdown in 2000 ushered in a law ordering all bars and nightclubs to close by 2am. While this rule is regularly ignored, Mazzo, the only place to flout it, manages to do so by only opening its doors at 3am. Dancing, drinking or dozing, these hardcore "nightizens" usher in Sunday morning, biding their time until church, breakfast or bed takes over. ❑

● *See page 304 of Travel Tips for nightlife listings.*

ABOVE: card-playing octogenarians.

Shanghai Rocks

Shanghai has one of China's best and most diverse rock scenes. Although it has fewer bands than Beijing, and only one independent record label, it makes up for quantity with quality. Most bands in China's other, grungier urban centres are alternative to the point of being more about performance art than music. Shanghai's rockers, like the city itself, take a pragmatic and commercial approach, composing more mainstream, accessible music to appeal to their primary audience of Shuppies looking to vent their urban alienation.

Alternative music in Shanghai developed mostly independent of the rest of China, taking its musical influences from abroad rather than from other Chinese bands. Its earliest roots lie in the street side guitar bands of the early 1980s. With often homemade instruments, groups of neighbourhood youth reinvented tunes by 1970s Taiwanese pop icon Teresa Teng or composed their own ribald ditties, hoping to outshine rival groups down the block. Shanghai also produced China's first nascent rock star, Zhang Xing, who was so ahead of the times he was arrested in 1985 on charges of hooliganism.

For 15 years, Shanghai rock stewed underground, with only a handful of bands around at any given time, and playing only at the obscure dive, The Tribesman, and at annual underground rock parties. By the late 1990s, however, a couple of young, ambitious bands had secured gigs at more mainstream bars, and their names and songs started to infiltrate public awareness. At the same time, rock parties were being held more often and more publicly, wooing coverage from the reluctant Shanghai media by featuring more-established Beijing bands as well as local groups. Now that the city has a number of regular venues and its own independent record label, Fanyin, Shanghai has the infrastructure needed to nourish its growing rock scene.

Shanghai really has two separate rock scenes. One, which prefers to be called "alternative" or "independent", derives its influences from Brit-rock like U2, the Cure, Radiohead, and even the Beatles. Its music is pleasantly melodic but still intense and hard, and has a crossover appeal for those with little interest in the sort of rock that Shanghainese would label "too loud". This scene is figureheaded by the Honeys (Tianmi de Haizi) and Crystal Butterfly (Shuijingdie), the only extant Shanghai bands

with albums out and who regularly perform with visiting foreign, Mandopop and Cantopop stars.

The other Shanghai rock scene is more underground in nature – and punk, grunge and metal in its inclinations. Headed by radio DJ, poet, singer, music critic and concert organiser Sun Mengjing, known as the "Godfather of Shanghai Rock", these bands take Kurt Cobain and Che Guevara as their idols, romanticising authenticity, suicide and the rejection of commercial compromise. As such, they shun the mainstream, and instead of albums, they produce an annual compilation demo CD for private circulation. Shanghai's main underground bands include punk groups Godot (Geduo), Amplifier

(Kuoyinqi) and Top-floor Circus (Dinglou Maxituan) and the heavy metal Capital Crimes (Sizui).

Alternative bands perform most often at Xintiandi Ark, a Japanese-owned venue that draws upon the expertise of the Tokyo rock scene and attracts a more starched crowd with its modern décor and steep drink prices. Underground bands are more at home in the industrial grunge of the Music Factory on Taikang Road, but both sorts of bands play at both places. They also mingle at Guaer, a concert space located at the SUS2 Music School near Fudan University. Guaer has shows most weekends, and Xintiandi and Music Factory feature original groups a few times a week, plus nightly gigs by the house cover bands. ❑

RIGHT: Crystal Butterfly's lead guitarist Wei Wei.

EVENTS AND FESTIVALS

In contemporary Shanghai, Western-influenced celebrations take precedence over traditional and ritual-heavy Chinese festivals

On any given day, Shanghai has countless exhibitions, plays, concerts, cocktail and theme parties, and raves going on. Given the city's chaotic, anything-goes, Wild West atmosphere, it is little wonder that most events are organised at the last minute, with little forewarning. The annual recurring holidays and festivals make less splash than the daily ongoing events, so visitors are better off planning around the weather than any particular celebration.

Traditions eclipsed

China is not the place for traditional Chinese holidays: in fact, it's fair to say that China is really not all that Chinese. Such spectacles as lion dances and dragon boat races are more commonly found in Hong Kong, Taiwan or in the Chinatowns of Southeast Asia and the West, where emigrants have made a concerted effort to preserve their heritage. In mainland China, these traditional displays are, ironically, staged only for the benefit of tourists, if at all.

After 1949, China's Communists "liberated" the country's rural population from its "feudal superstitions". Most traditional practices which centred on placating spirits, ancestors and deities were banished to the underworld by Socialist secularism. Antipathy towards the old ways heightened during the 10 years of the Cultural Revolution, when even the slightest expression of tradition could destroy an entire family by attracting the "counter-revolutionary" label.

In post-Cultural Revolution times, some traditions have slowly returned but deprived of their original spirit. The significance of the ritualised traditions are lost on the younger generations, and at best are empty gestures practised with a sense of detached irony.

Two fundamental traditions have persisted, however, even through the darkest days of the Cultural Revolution: food and family. The mainstay of every Chinese holiday – and even the

Western ones observed these days – is a huge family meal of auspicious and expensive foods.

If Chinese tradition has fared badly in China, it has done even worse in Shanghai, a place whose only tradition is being as non-Chinese as possible. In the Concession era, Chinese traditions coexisted with Western-influenced

habits, but even then the more urbane Shanghainese scoffed at such devotion to old beliefs. Obsessed with the future and being modern, the Shanghainese now celebrate the Chinese holidays more as habit and entertainment.

Spring Festival

China's most enduring traditional event and most important holiday remains Spring Festival (Chunjie), or Chinese New Year, marking the beginning of the lunar calendar.

Spring Festival has always witnessed an annual pilgrimage to family hearths, but in the late 1990s, the government gradually extended the days off from work for the Spring Festival

---

LEFT: Chinese New Year, or Spring Festival, decorations.
RIGHT: Yu Garden all lit up with lanterns during the annual Spring Festival.

to its current full week. Accordingly, migratory patterns have increased; China's entire migrant labour population returns to its hometown to deliver money and tales from the big cities, clogging the country's massive railway grid for weeks surrounding the holiday.

Attempts to travel during New Year, or the other two week-long holidays, May Day and National Day, provide the most visceral experience of China's huge population. Flights and trains are booked months in advance, and homebound peasants think nothing of enduring standing-room-only space on a 72-hour train ride home for Chinese New Year.

guests to an elaborate and expensive banquet, has encouraged eating out on New Year's Eve. Reservations at posh Shanghainese restaurants are frequently booked solid months in advance.

Wherever it is eaten, the New Year's Eve dinner is always held near a television set. Since the introduction of television to China in the early 1980s, the Chinese Central Television (CCTV) Spring Festival Variety Show has been as central a tradition as dinner. Reaching some 90 percent of the Chinese, it is also the single most widely watched television show in the world. Running from 8pm until 2am, it features performances of skits, dance, Revolutionary Bal-

Spring Festival resembles Easter in that it consists of several small celebrations over the course of two weeks. The most important, however, are Chinese New Year's Eve and New Year's Day. New Year's Eve is celebrated by food, family, fireworks and, yes, television. In most places in China, the women spend all day labouring in the kitchen preparing the repast. In Shanghai, however, it is the domesticated Shanghainese husbands who cook the all important meals, while the comely women press fruits, candies, cigarettes and alcohol upon visitors.

The accelerating pace of life in Shanghai, combined with the "face" gained from treating

let, pop songs, a two-person comedic dialogue called *Xiangsheng*, and the famously irritating (to foreigners) yet amusing (to Chinese) Mandarin-speaking Canadian performer Da Shan.

After-dinner hours are spent visiting assorted friends, neighbours and extended family. At each new home, visitors will be sat in front of the television and plied with candy, nuts, oranges and – if male – cigarettes. Refusal, no matter how stuffed one feels, is considered rude. After staying for a polite spell, it is on to the next house for more CCTV and snacks.

One purpose of the visits is the distribution of little red envelopes, or *hongbao (see box on page 103)* containing cash. *Hongbao* is usually distributed by the wage-earning adults to the elderly and children – the latter defined as all family members not yet married, regardless of age.

The city government throws huge annual fireworks shows on the Bund and around town to discourage their private firing of crackers but to no avail. The racket of rockets and crackers, traditionally to drive away the spirit of the old year, but now more for entertainment and the flaunting of wealth, begins before dark, turning all of Shanghai a dusty and smoky grey. The crescendo continues on sidewalks and in the streets – traffic be damned – peaking at midnight.

New Year's day is devoted to resting, more TV and more food. The following days all hold varying significance, such as welcoming the God of Wealth (Haisheng) on the fifth day. On the 15th day and night of the first full moon, the Lantern Festival (Yuanxiaojie) is observed. Yu Garden *(see page 151)* holds a dazzling display of traditional lanterns, while the average folk buy paper lanterns for their children and consume *tang yuan*, a sweet glutinous rice ball soup.

January – February

Locals and expatriates alike celebrate the Western New Year with aplomb at bars, restaurants, hotels and private parties. Shanghai's office workers are given the first three days of the year off, presumably for hangover recovery.

Spring Festival (Chunjie) falls in either January or February and is observed with food and fireworks. The festival concludes after the 15th day with the Lantern Festival (Yuanxiaojie). Longhua Temple, which also holds a bell-ringing ceremony for the Western New Year, holds a traditional temple fair.

Valentine's Day is one of Shanghai's favourite Western holidays. Office girls compete over the size of their bouquets, and couples exchange gifts and have a romantic meal out.

March – April

On International Women's Day on March 8, Chinese women, who "hold up half the sky", are honoured for all the underpaid work that they do for the year. Some offices give women a day or half-day off.

LEFT: both food and family take prime focus at most Chinese festivals.
RIGHT: *hong bao* packet embossed with the Chinese symbol for good luck.

The first week of April brings the Clear and Bright Festival (Qingming), known in the West as "Tomb-Sweeping Day", in which Chinese visit the graves of their ancestors, bearing gifts of food or funerary paper cars, houses and money to burn in provision for the afterlife. Although not widely observed in Shanghai, a few filial urbanites flock to Suzhou, which has burial grounds for the recently deceased.

Late in April, the International Tea Festival is held in Zhabei, in the public square outside the Shanghai Train Station. Tea aficionados congregate here to attend tea ceremonies and workshops, and sample different tea brews.

HOLIDAY BRIBERY

One surviving custom has taken on a new meaning in the atmosphere of corruption and greed that has emerged in the post-reform era. The giving of *hongbao* – red envelopes of cash to children and the elderly at Spring Festival – and boxes of mooncakes during the Mid-Autumn Festival have become a common front for bribery.

Successful businesses order mooncakes by the truckload to cultivate good relations with clients. It is not uncommon for government officials and business moguls to receive gold- and jewel-encrusted boxes of mooncakes, and their children red envelopes bulging with many thousands of dollars.

May – June

May Day is one of the two most important holidays in Shanghai after Spring Festival – not for any deep empathy which Shanghainese may have for the workers of the world but rather for the week off from work. Given its lack of traditional associations or family pressures, May Day sees the most pleasure tripping. A common joke asserts that, for the first week of May, the entire population of Shanghai relocates to Thailand, while masses of peasants take their places on the crowded streets. Fireworks shows are held at the Bund and elsewhere on this day.

Recent additions to the calendar include the

Shanghai International Fashion Festival. Held for 10 days at the end of April till the beginning of May, the event attracts designers from all over Asia and spotlights the city's growing fashion industry. Chic Xintiandi and trendy Westgate mall are some of the best places to catch some of the action.

International Children's Day on 1 June sees Shanghai's "little emperors" getting their way and running wild in public even more than usually.

The Shanghai International Film Festival, held in the second week of June, is generally dominated by second-rate Hollywood fare, but international films are also screened, and Chinese independent films sometimes sneak in.

July – August

The birthday of Guanyin, the Goddess of Mercy and the Buddhist patron saint of the Chinese, is on the 19th day of the seventh lunar month (July or August). Most Shanghainese pay no notice, but small ranks of the devout will head to temples or Guanyin's birthplace on the nearby island of Putuoshan.

The Chinese Communist Party (CCP) was founded on 23 July 1921 in Shanghai, an event celebrated on 1 July. War dramas, CCP documentaries and elderly cadres singing old revolutionary songs dominate television for a month.

The reintroduction of the old Seven Sisters Festival (Qiqiaojie) on the seventh day of the seventh lunar month (July or August) livens up the otherwise quiet months. The various legends it derives from tells of immortal lovers separated by the heavens and only allowed to meet this one day. Its newfound appeal lies in its status as Chinese Valentine's Day, and (unfortunately) it's observed with the same commercial impulses as its Western equivalent.

September – October

The Mid-Autumn or Moon Festival (Zhongqiujie) arrives on the 15th day of the eighth lunar month and is the most important Chinese holiday after Spring Festival as well as the only other one widely observed in Shanghai. Mid-Autumn festival centres around the buying, giving and eating of mooncakes, round pastries filled with sweet red bean or lotus nut paste. Mooncakes are always given by businesses to clients and by individuals to family, and can get passed around much like Christmas fruitcake. They have become a big business: advertising begins weeks in advance and the likes of Häagen-Dazs offer trendy nouveau mooncakes filled with ice cream.

Also in September, the Shanghai government throws the annual Tourism Festival, a giant street party on Nanjing Road. Huge outdoor stages are set up for music and dance performances, while the Huangpu District government showcases Shanghai bands with a two-week Rock Festival in People's Park.

National Day, commemorating the founding of the PRC on 1 October 1949, brings the annual televised parade of military might in Beijing's Tiananmen Square plus pompous pronouncements of "10,000 years to the Motherland!" on signs dotting every Shanghai street. Most Shanghainese use the week off to go shopping.

Sports buffs' high-point of the year is the Heineken Open at the Xianxia Tennis Centre in October, which attracts tennis luminaries like Andre Agassi and Michael Chang.

Halloween is also popular with younger Shanghainese – one suspects because of the Chinese fascination with the supernatural – who wear costumes to restaurants and bars on the Saturday closest to the 31st.

November – December

November is arts month in Shanghai. The month-long Shanghai International Arts Festival features an impressive line-up of international and Chinese theatre, music and dance

includes a full and a half marathon, plus a 4 km (3 mile) fun-run.

On the Chinese calendar's first day of winter, either 21 or 22 December, the Shanghainese eat *zhongzi*, meat packed into rice dumplings, wrapped in lotus leaves and steamed.

Christmas is widely celebrated by the Shanghainese, usually with a big Western meal with friends or family on Christmas Eve. Bars hold Christmas parties to allow the city's expatriate population to honour the birth of Christ by doing what they do best – drinking themselves silly. Churches around town offer traditional church services. ❑

productions at the Shanghai Grand Theatre and other performance venues. In the same month, the Shanghai Arts Fair brings art galleries of all genres from all over China together for two weeks. The Shanghai Biennale is staged at the Shanghai Art Museum on even years from November to January. It attracts some of the leading names in modern art from around the world as well as showcasing Shanghai's avant-garde works for mainstream audiences.

Also in November is the Toray Cup, which

LEFT: model at the Shanghai International Fashion Festival. **ABOVE:** celebrating Christmas with gusto.

GOING WEST

Given Shanghai's traditional role as the translator between China and the West, it is scarce surprise that Western holidays are widely celebrated by locals, albeit often with a uniquely Shanghainese bent even beyond the "Marry (sic) Christmases" and the Santas with arms raised in a Chairman Mao-like benediction. With typical cultural flexibility, the Shanghainese observe Western traditions with a huge banquet, but usually of Western rather than Chinese food, and fireworks are sometimes set off. As with the Chinese and Western New Year, they celebrate Christmas on Christmas Eve, complete with a "10-9-8...hooray!" countdown at midnight.

ARCHITECTURE

Art deco, post-modernist, Chinese Song Dynasty, Tudor or just plain kitsch,
Shanghai is a stimulating arthouse of architectural treasures

Even world-weary visitors from the globe's most sophisticated urban centres catch their breath the first time they see Shanghai's skyline. The city is in the middle of the biggest urban building boom the world has ever known, and the sheer size, scale and speed of its reconstruction is astounding. Shanghai's juxtaposition of avant-garde glass and steel structures and its old world brick and mortar historic buildings is visually arresting. The result is an almost visceral tension between the ultra-modern and the traditional – a tension that is exciting to some, but unsettling to others.

Nowhere is this tension as palpable as on the Bund promenade along the Huangpu River where the distinguished neo-classical stone monuments to the west and the soaring mirrored towers of Lujiazui, the financial district of Pudong to the east, will fight for your attention.

Some say the space-age Oriental Pearl Tower *(see page 218)*, opposite the Bund, with its needle-point spire and garish pink baubles was commissioned with symbolism in mind, to divert attention from the city's "humiliating" colonial past and toward its shining future. If true, its design is a smashing success, as the tower is now the most recognised structure in the city. Before it was built, the dramatic sweep of the Bund, where the Western powers left their architectural stamp, was the indisputable symbol of the city – a powerful image, to be sure, but also an unwelcome reminder that it was not the Chinese but foreigners who first put Shanghai on the world map.

Look East, or West?

For 40 years after the establishment of the People's Republic of China in 1949, construction virtually halted in Shanghai because the Communist leadership feared that the city's capitalist culture could undermine its efforts to create a New China. When restrictions on Shanghai's development were lifted in the early 1990s by the Communist Party leadership, the city was a veritable time capsule of pre-1949 architecture.

Today, in an effort to catch up with the times, old sections of the city are being razed over and replaced with modern highrises and green open

XINTIANDI: CHANGING ATTITUDES

Just south of the brightly lit office towers of Central Huaihai Road lies Xintiandi, the first major adaptive re-use project involving Shanghainese *shikumen* (stone gate) lane housing. With the help of Boston-based architects Wood & Zapata, the old neighbourhood was gutted and rebuilt as a modern shopping/entertainment venue, with some entirely new structures mixed in with preserved grey brick facades. It's not historic preservation, really, but defenders of Shanghai's architectural patrimony generally approve of the project for its success in raising awareness of the value of the city's historic buildings: Xintiandi almost single-handedly made *shikumen* houses cool again.

spaces. The resulting mix of old and new, and East and West is quintessentially Shanghainese style (*haipai*). Shanghainese are well known for their ability to adopt ideas from elsewhere and weave them into their local culture. Creativity is another hallmark of Shanghai's energetic people, and this is readily evident in the leeway given to the city's architects and planners in their designs for the new city.

While it is sad to see so many bricks and beams fall to make way for chrome and glass, it is vital to remember that Shanghai has always been about being modern. This in the 1920s was symbolised by art deco buildings like the Peace

Hotel; in the 1990s, by the futuristic Oriental Pearl Tower. In the 21st century, it is likely that Shanghai architecture will look for solutions that resolve the contradictions between the two.

As China becomes less rigid ideologically and more open economically, the Shanghainese are slowly coming to terms with their architectural identity. They still want modernity, the latest that the world has to offer, but they are also confident enough to celebrate, however subtly, the unique history of their city. Apartment buildings, for example, are now often built with architectural references to the lane dwellings of old Shanghai. The rejection of "bourgeois" art, which reached its extreme during the Cultural Revolution of 1966–76, has given way to a rich architectural environment in which themes from the world over – including its own turf – all contribute to the dramatic skyline of today's Shanghai.

Shanghai modern

Shanghai's most successful modern buildings include references to Chinese or Shanghainese architecture, or push the high-rise design envelope in some way. The 1998 Grand Theatre on People's Square does both. Designed by Frenchman Jean-Marie Charpentier, it resembles a hyper-modern transparent temple to the arts – until you realise that the convex curvature of the thick white roof is a clear homage to the heavy roofs and upturned eaves of traditional Chinese palace architecture.

At the time of its completion in 1989, the Shanghai Centre complex on Nanjing Road (W) was the only tall building for miles. Its obvious reference to traditional motifs can be seen in the simple, strong red columns that sup-

REACHING FOR THE SKY – JIN MAO TOWER

In the international quest to build the world's tallest buildings – symbolic or silly as the competition may be – Shanghai's Jin Mao Tower stands out: unlike many of its rivals, it is a truly beautiful building. Like much great art, it appeals in different ways to different eyes. For many Westerners, the Jin Mao's design is a successful reference to art deco masterpieces in New York and Chicago – the latter city being home to Jin Mao's chief designer, Adrian Smith of Skidmore, Owings, Merrill.

Smith says that the design is grounded in the tradition of Chinese pagodas and Chinese numerology: "There are 88 storeys. The lowest segment of the building is 16 storeys,

and each succeeding segment is 1/8th smaller. In the top section, the vertical segments shrink from 8 down to one storey." Whatever the inspiration, this building "works" from any perspective.

For those who believe size matters: Jin Mao Tower at 420 metres (1,378 ft) is taller than all save Kuala Lumpur's Petronas Towers at 452 metres (1,483 ft) and Chicago's Sears Tower at 442 metres (1,450 ft). When the Shanghai World Financial Centre is completed in 2008, adjacent to the Jin Mao, it will pip them all at 460 metres (1,509 ft). But for some, aesthetically, the Jin Mao Tower will still stand taller than the rest – always.

port the entrance portico. Less obvious is the monumental reference that architect/developers John Portman & Co. designed into the building – it is in the shape of the Chinese character for mountain, *shan*. The same company has gone on to further successes in Shanghai. It designed both the Tomorrow Square and Bund Centre buildings – the latter's lotus-topped tower changed the Bund skyline forever when it was completed in 2002.

Next to the Shanghai Centre is Plaza 66, a building that "works" without reference to traditional architecture. Its clean, simple lines state "modern" in the long Shanghai tradition of striving for the cutting edge. Plaza 66 architects Kohn Pederson Fox Associates of New York also designed the Wheelock Square project on Yan'an Road (W), which at 290 metres (951 ft) will overtake the 288-metre (945-ft) Plaza 66 as the tallest building west of the Huangpu River when completed in 2007. The Shanghai World Financial Centre, another Kohn Pederson effort, is set to be the tallest on earth when it is completed in 2008.

Post-modern European architects have been equally popular in Shanghai. The seagull-inspired Pudong International Airport – a 2000 landmark in glass and brushed aluminum – was designed by Paris-based Paul Andreu. The airport is far less controversial than another of Andreu's Chinese commissions, the National Theatre in Beijing. So pleased were the city fathers with this effort that they hired Andreu to design Pudong's new Oriental Arts Centre, scheduled for completion in 2004.

Other areas of the city studded with impressive examples of contemporary architecture include Central Huaihai Road (near Huangpi Road), the Xujiahui area, Lujiazui in Pudong and Century Boulevard (Shiji Da Dao) near Dong Fang Road in Pudong. All of these areas are easily accessible by subway.

Shanghai Chinese

The best Shanghai-style buildings have successfully combined elements of both traditional Chinese architecture and Western design to great effect. The city's older buildings fall into a number of distinct styles – it's best to learn how to discern the different types and then keep your

eyes open wherever you find yourself in the city.

A few examples of Ming Dynasty Yangzi River Delta style (Jiangnan) architecture can still be found within the old Chinese city, south of the Yu Garden Bazaar area. These are distinguished by their whitewashed walls, distinctive rooflines, undulating "dragon" walls, latticework and keyhole windows.

The structures inside Yu Garden are also of the Jiangnan style – if your itinerary doesn't bring you to Suzhou, this is an excellent place to indulge in an afternoon of the region's traditional architecture. "Shanghai Old Street", a newly built tourist area west of Yu Garden,

mimics the Jiangnan style of buildings which would have been found inside the walled Chinese city a century ago and earlier.

Longhua Pagoda was built (and re-built many times) in the Southern Song style in 922. This Shanghai landmark has borne witness to much of local history, including a front-row seat during the Japanese Occupation of Shanghai from 1941 to 1945 – when it was used as an anti-aircraft gun emplacement. The Jade Buddha Temple (Yufo Si), though constructed in 1918, is also built in the Southern Song manner.

Jing An Temple (formerly called the Bubbling Well Temple), which has stood at its Nanjing Road (W) location since 1216, has not

---

LEFT: Jin Mao Tower rises 88 storeys to the sky.
RIGHT: Chinese roof lines at Yu Garden Bazaar.

been so fortunate in terms of preservation: it underwent a complete transformation in 2002 when the last of its older bits were razed in favour of today's tourist-oriented temple with an adjoining mall of shops.

There are very few late 19th-century Chinese-style urban houses left in Shanghai today, but until the early 1900s, most of the city consisted of such dwellings. Characterised by their Chinese-style wood-frame construction, they featured commercial space at street level and living space on the floor above, with cantilevered porches jutting out from the main structure. Visitors with sharp eyes will discern some exam-

ples surviving in greatly altered form, with their porches enclosed or amputated – but these are fast falling to the demands of urban renovation.

Lane houses

The most representative Shanghainese architectural form is the attached lane dwelling, rows of which are arranged within a block in a matrix of alleys called *longtang* or *lilong*. The perimeter of a *longtang*'s exterior walls is pierced by several openings that can be closed off by iron gates. Individual homes within the earliest *longtang* blocks were entered through *shikumen* (stone gates) that were arranged in rows along

RELIGIOUS ARCHITECTURE

Old Shanghai's international character is reflected in its places of worship, many of which are intriguing architecturally as well as historically. Catholic, Protestant, Islamic, Jewish, Russian Orthodox and even Shinto monuments dot the city. The 1853 Dongjiadu Cathedral was built by French Jesuits in a pleasing Mediterranean style, whereas the famous 1906 red-brick Xujiahui Cathedral soars in Gothic splendour. The 1931 Mu'en Church is a neo-Gothic study by Ladislaus Hudec, one of old Shanghai's most talented and versatile architects. Here, Hudec set bricks at different depths, creating an undulating effect evoking movement. His copper-roofed church in

Hongqiao is a more daring, modernist neo-Byzantine study; unfortunately, it is currently not open to the public.

A real delight for those who enjoy combinations of architectural traditions is the Peach Orchard Mosque in the old Chinese City, which combines Chinese, Islamic and art deco elements. The Ohel Rachel Synagogue, unusual in that its architectural inspiration is the Greco-Roman tradition, is now occupied by the Shanghai Education Commission and not open to the public; ditto for the former Shanghai Jewish School on the same grounds. Happily, the former Russian Orthodox St Nicholas Church on Gao'lan Road is now a fine French restaurant that welcomes (hungry) visitors.

the alleys, creating a pleasing visual repetition.

Shikumen blocks were built in Shanghai from the 1860s to the 1930s, mutating slowly during that period in response to fashion and economic development. Over time, land prices and reinforced concrete impelled developers to build higher dwellings, which eventually lost their vestigial courtyards and came to resemble modern urban apartment buildings. Early ornamentation incorporated neo-classical themes, which were superseded later by the Mediterranean, Tudor and art deco styles favoured in Shanghai during the 1920s and 30s.

Shikumen housing once provided the vast majority of urban housing in Shanghai, but since the 1990s, many have been demolished by a municipal government intent on razing these now-dilapidated neighbourhoods in order to modernise the city's appearance, upgrade utilities and decrease city-centre population density. Redeveloped *shikumen* projects like Xintiandi are rare *(see text box page 109)* and architectural preservationists seem to have little influence in the process. Sadly, it may not be long before the best place to learn about *shikumen* lane dwellings will be in a museum.

Early Western structures

Although the earliest Western buildings in Shanghai are mostly gone, there are a few significant examples still left standing today. The venerable 1870s edifices found within the former British Consulate compound at the top of the Bund are built in the grand two-storey, arched portico style typical of British colonial times. An even earlier structure, dating to the 1850s, can be seen at Fuzhou Road just to the rear of No. 9, on the Bund. The sturdy dark stone building with simple Gothic arches is the former warehouse of one of the earliest trading companies to set up operations in Shanghai, Russell & Co. of the US.

The late 19th-century commercial buildings on Jinling Road are also of note, as they still sport their tall-columned "five-foot ways" which facilitated the movement of goods and people during inclement weather. Also worth a look are the three-storey brick buildings with lovely arched

---

LEFT: Russian Orthodox St Nicholas Church.
RIGHT: the Bund buildings are best seen after dark.

doors and windows on many streets behind the Bund – typical of Western residential blocks built before reinforced concrete technology arrived in Shanghai in the second decade of the 20th century.

The magnificent Bund

No visit to Shanghai is complete without a stroll along the Bund, with its striking panorama of European-style buildings. About half of the 24 structures on the Bund were built during the 1920s, and nine during the first two decades before that.

SHIKUMEN STYLE

A *shikumen* doorway is formed by three pieces of solid stone with rounded upper joints, and an inward-opening set of wooden doors leading to a small courtyard.

Most incorporate the neo-classical themes that predominated the design of public buildings then. The queen of them all is the 1923 Hong Kong & Shanghai Bank building at No. 12 (now the Shanghai Pudong Development Bank) – regal from the top of her magnificent domed crown to the base of the amber marble columns of her breathtaking interior.

The most famous of the Bund beauties – the 1929 Cathay Hotel (now the Peace Hotel) and the delightful Bank of China building next door – are art deco gems. The prolific firm of Palmer & Turner (responsible for seven Bund buildings, almost a third of the total) made sure that these two edifices complemented each other.

The former Bank of Communications at No. 14 is the youngest building on the Bund (completed in 1948), and has a later, stripped-down art deco style. The 1906 Palace Hotel (now the Peace Palace Hotel) is the only edifice along the road that still proudly sports its original brick exterior. The owners of the former Commercial Bank of China (1906) at No. 6 and the quaint China Merchants Steam Navigation Co. (1901) at No. 9 must have felt their brick facades looked old-fashioned next to the stone-faced behemoths that went up near them in later decades: at some point they plastered over their facades to update their appearances.

by Shanghai's high-ranking Party officials, who favour this area like the taipans before them.

Certain old houses have been converted to commercial use, however, and welcome visitors. The grand former residence of the Secretary General of the French Municipal Council (and later, of the first Communist mayor of Shanghai, Chen Yi) on Fenyang Road is now the Shanghai Arts and Crafts Museum. Close by, on Taiyuan Road, is Taiyuan Villa, a French mansion built for the Comte du Pac de Marsoulies, and, later, a favourite haunt of Mao's wife Jiang Qing. An art deco masterpiece on Lane 18, Gao'an Road is now the Xuhui Dis-

French Concession homes

The International Settlement was considered *the* place to do business in old Shanghai, but from the 1920s onwards, the *nouveau riche* of all nationalities preferred the tree-lined streets of the western part of the French Concession for their homes. Stroll down Fuxing Road, Wukang Road or Xinhua Road, and you'll still see the lovely Mediterranean, Tudor and art deco homes that set the architectural fashion some 70 to 80 years ago. Be content to view most of these homes from the street: some have been multiple-family dwellings since the 1950s or 60s; some are now rented out to foreigners at exorbitantly high rents; and others are occupied

trict Children's Palace. The former fanciful residence on Shaanxi Road (S) of a Swedish businessman named Moller is now the (Hengshan) Moller Villa, a boutique hotel.

And then there are the delightful French Concession apartment buildings. Apartment living was the height of modernity in the 1920s and 30s, and architects were given free reign to use the latest ideas in their designs. art deco styles, with their emphasis on linearity, verticality and man's relationship to the world, were perfectly suited to these structures. Almost any walk in Frenchtown will take an observant visitor past these old beauties, with evocative names like the Astrid, the Picardie and the Gascogne.

The Shanghai of tomorrow

The pace of change in Shanghai over the past 15 years has been exhausting, but it is only likely to accelerate. The development focus in the 1990s was Pudong – a project so large in scope that many observers openly scoffed when it was announced. The initiatives on the drawing boards for the next decade are of equal or greater sweep.

The largest will be the redevelopment of some 74 sq km (29 sq miles) along the banks of the Huangpu River. Much of the area will be devoted to green public space, with wide setbacks from the river's edge and building height limited to 30 metres (98 ft) to protect precious

Within this huge redevelopment zone, only a handful of historic structures – their facades, really – will survive. The news is not good for the remaining old sections in the city proper, either. The authorities anounced in mid-2002 that some 28 million sq metres – almost half of Shanghai's historic residential areas – had already been demolished, and 640,000 residents relocated.

Recent Shanghai urban planning and development has reflected an almost stereotyped Modernist vision of vertical skyscrapers and landscaped greenbelts criss-crossed by wide avenues and superhighways – with city plan-

views of the water. The area south of the Nanpu Bridge will be turned into a huge complex for the World Expo in 2010, and the Shiliupu wharf area will be transformed from an unsettling no man's land of dingy warehouses into a lively waterfront marketplace inspired by The Rocks area in Sydney.

North of the Waibaidu Bridge, an international passenger terminal and related shopping and entertainment projects are slated to replace the run-down shipyards and warehouses in the Hongkou and Yangpu districts.

ners following the trends set by architectural gurus like Rem Koolhaas.

However, others – like Shanghai's own Pu Miao, now teaching at the University of Hawaii – advocate new concepts like "designing for density" that confront the urban realities of cities like Shanghai. This is a more sensitive approach as it attempts to preserve the human scale and public interaction that has traditionally characterised many Asian cities.

Given the scale of development that Shanghai has set its sights on for the future, it may be in in this city that these two schools of thought vie for dominance in bricks and mortar and glass and steel. ❑

ABOVE: the steel and glass towers making up the Lujiazui financial zone in Pudong.

PLACES

A detailed guide to the city, with the principal sites clearly cross-referenced by number to the maps

Shanghai is a city poised on the cutting edge of the past – and of the future. Relics of the days when it was Asia's most modern city are woven between 21st-century Shanghai's glittering towers of power. Layers of old and new, East and West converge and mingle: chamber pots are washed out next to internet cafés; Starbucks lattés are sipped in the shadow of the city's oldest teahouse.

The limits of this maritime city are defined by its waterways. The Huangpu River separates Shanghai's newest district, Pudong, literally "east of the Huangpu", from the rest of Shanghai, or Puxi, "west of the Huangpu". The Suzhou Creek divides the thriving midsection of Puxi from its quieter northern suburbs. New lines have been drawn, but the shape and feel of the old foreign Concessions and Nanshi, the Old Chinese City are still discernible.

In 2003, all street signs with romanised Chinese *pinyin* were replaced with English ones, part of Shanghai's bold new plan to be an international city. The Chinese characters still remain, but Nanjing Dong Lu, for instance, is now called Nanjing Road (East). In time to come, these English names will trip off the tongues of Shanghainese with ease, but for the moment a rudimentary understanding of the basic street translations will hold the traveller in good stead *(page 287)*. Also useful is the list of main city sights written in Chinese script *(pages 317–9)*.

Shanghai Municipality comprises 16 city districts and three outlying counties. Streets run north to south and east to west in gridlike fashion, except for oval-shaped Nanshi and People's Square, the latter defined by the old racetracks. The major streets run the length of the city and have directional tags: Huaihai (West), Huaihai (Central) or Huaihai (East). Buildings are usually numbered sequentially, odd numbers on one side of the street and even numbers on the other; the numbering on the residential lanes *(longtang)* that run off the main streets has no relationship to main street numbering. To find an address, you should know its cross-street, such as, Huaihai Road near *(kaojing)* Gao'an Road.

The 98-km (61-mile) outer ring road, A20, takes a lap outside the city limits, while the inner ring Zhongshan Road loops around the inside perimeter of Shanghai city and Pudong, changing its name in Pudong and east Hongkou before turning back into Zhongshan Road. The city is bisected from east to west by the Yan'an Road Elevated Highway and from north to south by the Chongqing Road Elevated Highway.

Buses cover most of the city but are packed during peak hours and have Chinese-only information. The sleek subway system, however, is an easy way to get around; the lines are still being extended and are linked to a new elevated light railway system called the Pearl Line. Taxis are an inexpensive and usually plentiful option. ❏

PRECEDING PAGES: Pudong viewed from Puxi, with the Huangpu River in between; Yu Garden Bazaar ablaze with lights; Chinese soldiers walking past the Grand Theatre.
LEFT: the pressing crowds at Nanjing Road (E), Shanghai's foremost shopping street.

Shanghai Huochezhan
(Railway Station)

Jiatong Road

Central

JIAOTONG
GONGYUAN

Shanghai
Railway
Station

Hengfeng Road

Hengfeng Road

Minli Rd

Meiyuan Road

Datong Rd

Tianmu Road (W.)

Gonghe Xin Road

Central Tianmu Road

Xinjiang Road

Tibet (Xizang) Road (N.)

Tianmu Road (W.)

Hanzhong Road

Meiyuan

Gonghe Road

Datong Road

Xinjiang Road

Wuzhen Road

Qufu

Hanzhong Road

Haifang Road

Wusong (Suzhou Creek)

Hanzhong Road

Road

Meiyuan Road

Hanzhong Road

Datong Road

Chengdu Road (N.)

Xinzha Road

Central Tibet (Xizang) Rd

Changping Road

Xinchang Road

Xinzha Road

Xiar

Kangding Road (E.)

Datian Road

Xinzha Road

Huanghe Rd

Xinzha Road

Shaanxi Road (N.)

Kangding Road

Xinzha Road

Shanghaiguan

NI CHENG QIAO (W.)

Xinchang Rd

Beijing Road

Huaihe Rd

Fengyang Rd

Shar No.1 Dept S

Wuding Road

Datian Road

Beijing Road (W.)

Fengyang Road

Huaihe Rd

Guoji Fandian
(Park Hotel)

Jinmen Dajiud
(Pacific Hotel)

JINGAN

Xinzha Road

Taixing Road

Shimen No.2 Road

Beijing Road (W.)

Fengyang Road

Xinchang Rd

People's Park

RENMIN GONGYUA
(PEOPLE'S PARK)

Jiangning Rd

You Tai
Jiaotong
(Ohel Rachel
Synagogue)

Nanhui Road

Nanjing Road (W.)

Huangpi Road (N.)

Shanghai Meishuguan
(Art Museum)

Peo
Sc

Chengshi Gu
Zhenshi

Shaanxi Road (N.)

Westgate
Mall

Maoming Rd (N.)

Shimen No.1 Road

Shanghai Dianshitai
(TV Station)

Chengdu Road (S.)

Shanghai Renmin
Zhengfu (City Hall)

Boteman
(Shangai
Centre)

Plaza 66

CITC Square

Ming Tien
Guangchang
(Tomorrow Square)

Central
Plaza

Shanghai Dajuyuan
(Grand Theatre)

People's Squar
(Renmin Guangcha

Nanjing Road (W.)

Shaanxi Rd (N.)

Weihai Road

Weihai Road

Shangh
Bowugua
(Shanghai Museum

Tongren Road

JC Mandarin

Wusheng Rd

Huangpi Road (N.)

Shanghai
Zhanlan Zhongxin
(Exhibition
Centre)

Weihai Road

Wenxin Dasha
(United Press)

Yan'an Road

Central Yan'an Road

YANZHONG
GONGYUAN (W.)

Hong Kong

Central Yan'an Road

Ma Lei Bie Shu
Fandian
(Moller Villa)

Julu Road

Julu Road

Maoming Rd (S.)

Chengdu Rd (S.)

Jinling Rd

Huangpi Rd (S.)

Central
Plaza

Shui On
Plaza

Julu Road

Changle Road

Rujin No.1 Road

Changle Road

Changle Rd

Central
Plaza

Shaanxi Road (S.)

Lanxin Dajuyuan
(Lyceum Theatre)

Taicang Rd

Xintiandi

Huayuan
Fandian
(Okura Garden
Hotel)

Lao Jinjiang
Fandian
(Old Jinjiang)

Central Huaihai Road

Isetan

Zhonggong Yidahuizhi
(Site of the First National
Congress of the Communist
Party of China)

Madang Rd

TAIPING
GONGY
Xintiandi

Xinle Road

New Hualian Commercial
Building

Nanchang Road

Yandang Rd

Zizhong Rd

XIANGYANG
GONGYUAN

Baisheng Gouwu Zhongxin
(Parkson Department Store)

Shaanxi
Road (S.)

Ashanti Dome
(former St Nicholas
Church)

Sinan Rd

LUWAN

Donghu Road

Central Huaihai Road

Maoming Rd (S.)

Sun Zhongshan Guju
(former residence of
Sun Yat-sen)

FUXING
GONGYUAN

Chongqing Road (S.)

Central Fuxing Road

Aigenisi Shimotejia Jinju
(Agnes Smedley's former residence)

Madang Road

Yinyue
Xueyuan
(Conservatory
of Music)

Xiangyang
Shichang
(Fashion Market)

Xiangyang Road (S.)

Shaanxi Rd (S.)

Nanchang Road

Central Fuxing Road

Zhou Enlai Gongguan
(former residence of
Zhou Enlai)

Hefei Road

Road

Fenyang Road

Central Fuxing Rd (S.)

Central Fuxing Road (S.)

Wenhua Guangchang
(Cultural Square)

Rujin No.2 Rd

Rujin Bin'guan

Maoming Rd

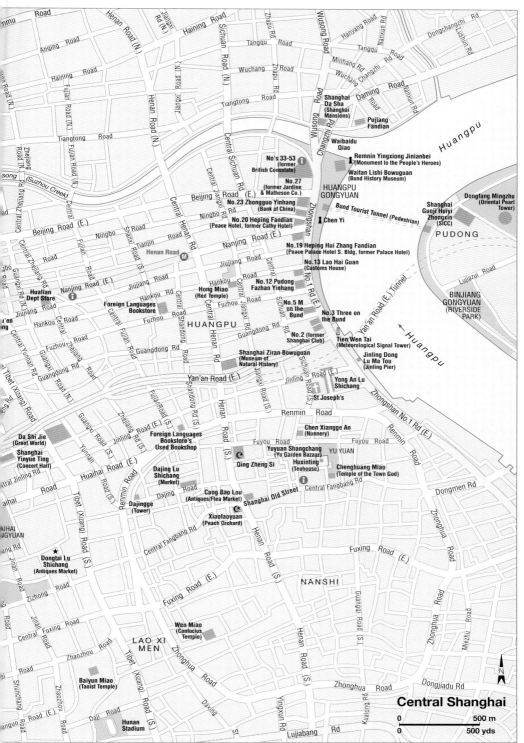

Central Shanghai

0   500 m

0   500 yds

THE BUND AND BEYOND

For the visitor, the Bund is the perfect introduction to Shanghai's past. Its glorious examples of European architecture tell stories of pride and subjugation, commerce and culture

Map on page 128

"On this small oblong plot of land, about the size of Manhattan Island from the Battery to 58th Street, are jammed all but a handful of the foreign banks and all of the important native ones, all the office buildings, the hotels, the important shops and big department stores, most of the clubs... The industry, the finance, the amusements of the fifth biggest city in the world". So wrote *Fortune* magazine in 1934. Shanghai in the 21st century may be a city defined by a breathtaking, warp-speed journey into the future, but its signature sight remains the **Bund** (Waitan). The 2-km (1.2-mile) sweep of historic waterfront buildings is a Concession-era time capsule, a sepia portrait in a Kodachrome world.

The sight of so many magnificent buildings all at once – each more beautiful, more stately, more glamorous than the last – is nothing short of breathtaking, particularly when the Bund is lit up at night and glows, as if from within. Yet Shanghai has a love-hate relationship with the Bund. The stretch of European buildings (despite the Chinese flag flying above each one) is both a politically incorrect symbol of foreign domination and the city's most well-known sight, a conflict that seems to have slowed down development plans for the area and helped to maintain its original character.

Along Shanghai's famous stretch, more than anywhere else in the booming city, the ghosts of the past are palpable. As the rest of Shanghai implodes and regenerates around it, the Bund stands as an unchanging, silent witness to Shanghai's turbulent 20th-century experience. Many of the Bund buildings are empty, some are being renovated while others are occupied by dowdy state-owned enterprises.

An architectural 'museum'

The banks and financial institutions of old Shanghai's Wall Street were anchored along the Bund and behind it in the International Settlement area, where the visitor today will find an uninterrupted treasure trove of architectural imprints made by long-forgotten giants. The grid of narrow streets – not yet widened or greened like so much of Shanghai – immediately creates a retro aura, enhanced by the monumental buildings crowding in. The work of the International Settlement surveyors is still evident in the logical grid behind the Bund; streets running north to south bear the names of Chinese provinces while those going east to west are named after China's cities.

Like the buildings that line it, the word "bund" is itself a legacy of the colonial era. The British signatories to the 1842 Treaty of Nanjing, which ended the First Opium War and opened Shanghai to foreign trade (separate treaties were signed by the US and France in

LEFT: street entertainer showing off his skills in front of the Peace Hotel. **BELOW:** Peace Hotel, circa 1932, known then as the Cathay.

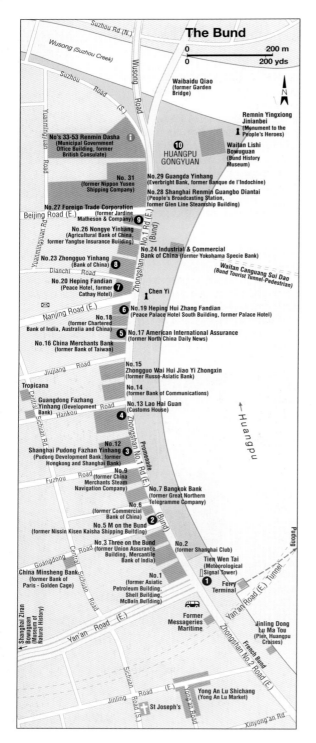

The Bund

0   200 m
0   200 yds

Waibaidu Qiao
(former Garden Bridge)

Suzhou Rd (N.)

Wusong (Suzhou Creek)

Suzhou Road

Wusong Road (S.)

Yuanmingyuan Road

Remnin Yingxiong Jinianbei
(Monument to the People's Heroes)

No's 33-53 Renmin Dasha
(Municipal Government
Office Building, former
British Consulate)

⑩
HUANGPU GONGYUAN

Waitan Lishi Bowuguan
(Bund History Museum)

No. 31
(former Nippon Yusen
Shipping Company)

No.29 Guangda Yinhang
(Everbright Bank, former Banque de l'Indochine)

No.28 Shanghai Renmin Guangbo Diantai
(People's Broadcasting Station,
former Glen Line Steamship Building)

No.27 Foreign Trade Corporation
(former Jardine
Beijing Road (E.)   Matheson & Company) **⑨**

No.26 Nongye Yinhang
(Agricultural Bank of China,
former Yangtse Insurance Building)

No.24 Industrial & Commercial
Bank of China (former Yokohama Specie Bank)

No.23 Zhongguo Yinhang
(Bank of China) **⑧**

Dianchi Road

Zhongshan No.1 Rd (Bund)

Waitan Canguang Sui Dao
(Bund Tourist Tunnel-Pedestrian)

No.20 Heping Fandian
(Peace Hotel, former
Cathay Hotel) **⑦**

Chen Yi

✉

Nanjing Road (E.) **⑥**

No.18
(former Chartered
Bank of India, Australia and China)

No.19 Heping Hui Zhang Fandian
(Peace Palace Hotel South Building, former Palace Hotel)

⑤   No.17 American International Assurance
(former North China Daily News)

No.16 China Merchants Bank
(former Bank of Taiwan)

Jiujiang Road

No.15
Zhongguo Wai Hui Jiao Yi Zhongxin
(former Russo-Asiatic Bank)

Tropicana

No.14
(former Bank of Communications)

Guangdong Fazhang
Yinhang (Development   Road
Bank)   Hankou

No.13 Lao Hai Guan
(Customs House)

Central Sichuan Rd.

Zhongshan No.1 Road (E.)

Promenade No.1 Rd (E.)

H u a n g p u

No.12
Shanghai Pudong Fazhan Yinhang **③**
(Pudong Development Bank, former
Hongkong and Shanghai Bank)

No.9
(former China
Merchants Steam
Navigation Company)

Fuzhou   Road

No.7 Bangkok Bank
(former Great Northern
Telegramme Company)

No.6
(former Commercial
Bank of China) **②**

No.5 M on the Bund
(former Nissin Kisen Kaisha Shipping Building)

No.3 Three on the Bund
(former Union Assurance
Building, Mercantile
Bank of India)

Guangdong   Central   Sichuan   Road

China Minsheng Bank
(former Bank of
Paris - Golden Cage)

No.2
(former Shanghai Club)

Tien Wen Tai
(Meteorological
Signal Tower)

No.1
(former Asiatic
Petroleum Building,
Shell Building,
McBain Building)

①
Ferry Terminal

Pudong

Shanghai Ziran Bowuguan
(Museum of Natural History)

Former
Messageries
Maritime

Yan'an Road (E.) Tunnel

Jinling Dong
Lu Ma Tou
(Pier, Huangpu
Cruises)

Yan'an   Road   (E.)

Zhongshan No.2 Road (E.)

French Bund

Jinling   Road   (E.)

Sichuan   Road

Yong An Road

Yong An Lu Shichang
(Yong An Lu Market)

St Joseph's

Xinyong'an Rd

1844), brought with them a new vocabulary, some of it borrowed. Bund comes from the Hindi word *band* for artificial embankment, a word that the British applied to the embanked quay along the shores of the settlements in their Chinese treaty ports and in British colonies from Ceylon to Malacca.

Old Shanghai's maritime soul determined the strategic location of the Bund – on the shore of the Huangpu River where great trading ships sailed in from the Yangzi. Originally a muddy mess with sewerage and refuse strewn on its banks, it was only when the strip was filled and "bunded" in the late 1880s that the classic Bund, lined by jetties, with trading houses and financial institutions just behind them, began to take shape. Waitan, the Chinese name for the area, means "outside beach".

A four-lane highway now runs where once the great mass of coolies hauled crates into the trading houses and rickshaw pullers ran. A raised promenade, lined with umbrella-topped photography booths, has replaced the old jetties, and it is a sign of the times that most of the tourists who pack the promenade want to be photographed against the Pudong skyline *(see page 215)* – not the Bund.

River cruises

In the pre-aeroplane age, the Bund was the first sight that greeted vessels approaching Shanghai on the Huangpu River. Visitors today can replicate that vision on cruises from the **Jinling Pier** at 219–239 Zhongshan No. 2 Road (E), with riverside views of the Yangpu and Nanpu bridges (several cruises ranging from 1–3½ hours are available). The cruise boats slide past an eye-popping array of freighters, ships and barges, a sign of the vibrant activity in China's largest port. Across the street from the pier is the former French **Messageries Maritime**, an art deco high-rise and one of the few original buildings left on the French side.

The boats that ply the river once received typhoon warnings from the 31-metre-tall (102-ft) **Meteorological**

Map
on page
128

Signal Tower ❶ (Tien Wen Tai: daily 10am–12pm; entrance fee), north of the Ferry Terminal. Jesuit priests at Xujiahui Observatory would telephone in weather information to the Meteorological Signal Tower, which was then known as the Gutzlaff Signal Tower. The tower, which is Shanghai's only surviving art nouveau building, was built in 1908 on the Quai de France (the French Concession part of the Bund), and has since been moved inland 80 metres (263 ft) to accommodate the widening Bund. It now houses a ground-floor museum and an outdoor terrace café with excellent perspectives of the length of the Bund.

Cross the pedestrian bridge that spans the junction of Zhongshan No. 1 Road and Yan'an Road (E), the old border between the Quai de France and the International Settlement's Bund, to the beginning of the Bund proper at **Zhongshan No. 1 Road (E)**. Highlights along this road – which faces the Bund promenade along the Huangpu River – are described in the following pages (*for a complete list of all the Bund buildings, see page 139*). At No. 1 is the former **Asiatic Petroleum Company** – dating back to 1915 – and now used as offices.

Famous Long Bar – a power barometer

The old boys' club which controlled Shanghai ran it from the leather-and-whiskey soaked confines of the former **Shanghai Club** at No. 2, where membership was restricted to white men of a certain class. Even the famous 34-metre (112-ft) Long Bar on the second floor was subject to a strict hierarchy: the prime Bund-facing end of the L-shaped mahogany bar was the territory of bank managers and taipans, with the social scale falling as one moved down the length of the bar. The club had all the requisites of a proper gentlemen's club: a smoking room and a library – reported to hold more volumes than the Shanghai Public Library – a

Meteorological Signal Tower has a café with excellent views.

BELOW: dance practice at the Bund promenade.

TIP

The cognoscenti sip
classic martinis at
M on the Bund's
Glamour Bar *(see this
page)*, from where
there are amazing
views of the landscape
behind the Bund. If the
wallet doesn't allow
this, head for the
rooftop bar of the
Peace Hotel, where
drinks are slightly
cheaper.

BELOW: Queen of
the Bund –
Shanghai Pudong
Development Bank.

billiards room, the massive Italianate Grand Hall dining room for long, boozy lunches, and guest rooms on the top two floors. The Long Bar has long since been dismantled, but the lofty grandeur of the colonnaded Grand Hall on the first floor remains intact, as do the caged lifts tucked into the curve of the Sicilian marble staircase. After ignominious years as a seaman's club, backpacker hotel and Kentucky Fried Chicken outlet, the building now stands empty.

At No. 3, the 1922 former **Union Assurance Building** now goes by the swanky name of **Three on the Bund** – housing **Nobu** and **Jean-Georges**, branches of acclaimed restaurants owned by their namesake celebrity chefs. Both are due to open in December 2003. The 1925 **Nissin Kisen Kaisha Shipping Building** (No. 5) now houses the Huaxia Bank, but its most famous contemporary tenant is the seventh-floor **M on the Bund ❷** restaurant (entrance at 20 Guangdong Road; tel: 6350 9988), considered by many to be Shanghai's best Western restaurant. Restaurateur Michelle Garnaut has revived the old glamour in 21st-century fashion, which is enhanced by the city's best view of the Bund.

Shanghai's constant rebuilding missed out the rare Victorian Gothic building of the former **Commercial Bank of China** (No. 6). Now empty, it once served as the original Municipal Council Hall, housing the governing body of the International Settlement; this was also where the Shanghai Volunteer Corps billeted its mercenary Russian troops until 1937.

Duck into Fuzhou Road, where adjacent to No. 9 is the oldest Bund building, the squat 1850s red-brick Gothic former **Russell & Company** warehouse at 17 Fuzhou Road, now a seedy apartment block. The impressive Tudor-style building on the northern side of the street, a few paces west at No. 44, were the former offices of wine importers **Calbeck and MacGregor**, now occupied by Chinese companies.

The Beauty of the Bund

Head back up to the Bund, passing the segregated entrance to the Chinese section of the former **Hongkong and Shanghai Bank**. "Dominate the Bund" was the instruction given by the Hongkong and Shanghai Bank to architects Palmer & Turner. Today, the domed neo-classical building at No. 12, "the grandest building East of Suez", is still the beauty of the Bund. Renamed the **Shanghai Pudong Development Bank ❸** (Shanghai Pudong Fazhan Yinhang), it remains guarded by the bronze lions Protection and Security. These are replicas of the originals, but passersby still carry on the old tradition of rubbing them for luck. Opened in 1923 and restored in 1999, the bank's magnificent 2,000-sq metre (21,500-sq ft) banking hall and adjacent office building are open to the public.

Map on page 128

An arched neo-classical entrance at the Shanghai Pudong Development Bank.

No expense was spared on the building of this edifice, with almost every piece crafted overseas. The four marble columns that support the hall, each weighing more than 7 tonnes and hewn from a single piece of marble, are among only six solid marble pillars of this size in the world – the other two are found in the Louvre Museum in Paris.

Above the octagonal entrance lobby is the spectacular domed mosaic ceiling: eight panels depicting the eight cities in which the bank had its branches in 1923, along with the eight words of the bank's motto, *"Within the Four Seas all men are brothers"*. The 12 signs of the zodiac ring the dome, and panels on the walls illustrate, in Latin, 16 lofty qualities, including temperance, truth and prudence. When the Communists seized Shanghai in 1949, the bank, worried that the mosaic would fall victim to the proletarian cause, had it hidden under layers of thick white paint, where it remained during the half-century the building served as the seat of the Shanghai Municipal Government. Only when the

BELOW:
rubbing the bronze lion for good luck.

BANKING ON BRONZE LIONS

Mythical dragon-lion creatures flanking Chinese doorways are traditional, but the Western-looking lions that guard the main entrance of the Shanghai Pudong Development Bank, formerly the Hongkong and Shanghai Bank, are an unusual sight, and their origins even more unusual.

Named Protection and Security, one rests peaceably while the other roars aggressively. Sculptor Henry Poole cast four bronze lions: two for the branch in Hong Kong and two for the Shanghai branch, and then broke the mould. Contemporary accounts tell of Shanghainese passersby who rubbed the lions for good luck until the beasts acquired a golden sheen on their teeth, nose and ears. A rumour began to spread among the local Chinese that the lions were, in fact, made of gold.

When the lions disappeared during the Japanese Occupation, it was assumed they had been melted down for use as cannon fodder. There were sporadic sightings of the lions languishing in the bank after the war but one day they inexplicably turned up in the basement of the old Shanghai History Museum in the 1980s, where they were later displayed. Today, one of them can be seen at the new Shanghai History Museum *(see page 218)*. The replica lions guarding the bank continue to be rubbed and patted till this day for good luck.

Mosaic detail from the ceiling dome of the Customs House.

BELOW: ceiling frescoes of the Shanghai Pudong Development Bank. **RIGHT:** the Customs House is another classic Bund structure.

Shanghai Pudong Development Bank began restoration work was it revealed.

In the southwest corner, where foreign exchange transactions are now handled, stood a separate bank for Chinese customers that was decorated in the bright reds and shiny golds favoured by its clientele. All that remains today are Chinese designs in the ceiling mouldings, cornices and ventilation covers, and in the Chinese characters for fortune in the trim and on the walls. The bank manager's offices, now VIP meeting rooms, still have their original parquet floors and Bund views.

The fourth floor, under the domed rooftop, once housed the Royal Air Force Club of Shanghai. Restoration work found no signs of the seal of the RAF and the images of World War I aircraft that the Fly Boys were said to have laid in mosaic on the floor. A separate entrance, just north of the bank's main entrance, leads to the office buildings and the lovely second-floor **Bonomi Café** (Room 226, No. 12; tel: 6329 7506) that looks over the courtyard.

One of the few commercial buildings in Shanghai to have the same role for over a century till today, the **Customs House** ❹ (Lao Hai Guan) at No. 13 next door was first located in a Chinese temple that was destroyed in an 1853 Taiping uprising. A castle-like Gothic brick building took its place before this neo-classical Palmer & Turner building and its distinctive clock tower was built in 1925. Fondly referred to as the "Big Ching", the clock tower sounded every 15 minutes until the Cultural Revolution when its chimes were replaced with loudspeakers which broadcasted revolutionary slogans. The clock chimes were restored in 1986 and repaired recently again in 2003 to ensure that its chimes can be heard above the street's din. The Communist People's Peace Preservation Corps once holed up in the Customs House to fight for the liberation of Shanghai, and a detailed carving in the entrance lobby commemorates its contribution.

Inside, strips of jarring neon outline the low ceiling, while an interior dome mimics the grander one in the Pudong Development Bank next door. The mosaic here depicts the different types of Yangzi clippers.

There is more colonial history at the **China Merchants Bank** (No. 16) – Japanese colonial history. Built as the **Bank of Taiwan** in 1924 during the Japanese occupation of Taiwan, the bank's main gallery features blossoms on the columns, original alabaster lamps and a second-floor gallery from which bank managers still carry out their supervisory duties.

The fabulous Peace Hotel

The **American International Assurance (AIA) Building** ❺ (No. 17) was the tallest on the Bund when it was completed in 1923 as the North China Daily News Building – the "Old Lady of the Bund". The oldest and most important newspaper in the city, the *North China Daily News* ran from 1864 to 1951, and at some point during the 1930s, rented space to the American Asiatic Underwriters, founded in Shanghai in 1919. The firm went on to become the insurance giant AIA, and leased its old premises back after extensive renovations. Much of the old building was gutted but the vaulted mosaic ceilings of the entrance hallways remain intact, as does the (repaired) motto of the old newspaper chiselled on the exterior: "Journalism, Art, Science, Litterature (*sic*), Commerce, Truth, Printing".

At No. 19 is the south wing of the Peace Hotel *(see page 134)*. Known as the **Peace Palace Hotel** ❻ (Heping Hui Zhang Fandian) – entrance at 23 Nanjing Road (E) – this stately Edwardian red-brick structure was built in 1906 as the **Palace Hotel**. Its ornate wood-panelled and gilt Edwardian lobby with its brightly painted ornamental plaster ceiling certainly reflects the palatial theme.

Map on page 128

TIP

Beware of scams in the Bund area. Locals sometimes approach tourists and suggest going for coffee to practise their English. The "coffee" ends up as an expensive meal when the new-found friend leaves "to go to the bathroom" and never returns.

BELOW: enterprising salesperson at the Bund promenade.

Just outside the original art nouveau revolving doors, a panel commemorates the 1909 meeting of the International Opium Commission. Ironically, it was in this city – whose foundations rested on the right to trade in opium – that the world's first steps towards narcotics controls were taken.

The star of the Bund is the fabulous art deco **Peace Hotel** ❼ (Heping Fandian) at No. 20 – entrance at No. 20 Nanjing Road (E). Built in 1929 as the luxurious **Cathay Hotel**, and originally located on the fourth to seventh floors of Sassoon House, the hotel was considered Shanghai's finest – and tycoon Victor Sassoon's showpiece. Scion of the great opium trading firm E.D. Sassoon, Victor Sassoon's domination of Shanghai's property market defined the skyline. In addition to his taste for the high life and fast women, Sassoon was apparently also enamoured of greyhound racing – very popular in Shanghai at the time. Two greyhounds dominate the carvings below the hotel's roof and on the exterior.

'Spiritual' water from silver taps

The first of three Palmer & Turner buildings standing together on this stretch of the Bund, the Cathay Hotel was a legend in a city of legends: pure spring water from the Bubbling Well *(see page 182)* flowed from silver taps into its imported marble tubs, and every luminary who came to town stayed here: Charlie Chaplin, George Bernard Shaw, and Noel Coward, who wrote *Private Lives* in his Cathay suite.

Although the standard rooms have been halved and modernised into anonymity by current owners Jinjiang Group (whose delivery of food and service is mediocre at best), many of the interior details of the public areas have remained, especially on the eighth floor: the stunning Chinese art deco ceilings of the Dragon and Phoenix Restaurant, the classic Deco detailing of the Grill

The wide stretch between the Bund buildings and the Huangpu River is a legacy of its use as a tow path where trackers would pull in the boats. The 1845 Chinese Land Regulations stipulated a space of 9 metres (30 ft) between the buildings and the shore.

BELOW: the Peace Hotel lobby.
RIGHT: welcoming Peace Hotel bell boy.

Map on page 128

Room and the magnificent ballroom, where Sassoon held his fabled fancy dress parties. The tycoon's penthouse suite, now a function room, still has the Lalique crystal fish on the doors. The roof garden, where Shanghai famously danced as the Communists knocked, is now a café with spectacular views of the Bund, the river and Nanjing Road. Renamed the Peace Hotel in 1956, its ground-floor bar is packed with tourists who come to see the "Old Man Jazz Band", a group of elderly, and not particularly good, musicians playing vintage tunes.

Bank of China design: A favourable fusion

Directly across from the Peace Hotel stands the **statue of Marshal Chen Yi**, on the spot where a statue of British diplomat Sir Harry Parkes had stood before it was melted down by the Japanese. One of China's legendary "10 marshals", Chen Yi liberated Shanghai on 25 May 1949 and later became the city's first mayor.

Next door to the Peace Hotel is another Palmer & Turner building. Its harmonious blend of Chinese, classical and art deco themes conspire to make the **Bank of China** ❽ (Zhongguo Yinhang) at No. 23 a fusion jewel. Reminiscent of an ancient drum tower and built in 1935, the building was commissioned by H.H. Kung two years before the Japanese occupied Shanghai. Kung was the Kuomintang Finance Chief, Bank of China director and the husband of Ai Ling, one of the famous Soong sisters. Originally occupied by the fanciful Teutonic Club, built in 1906, which became Kuomintang government property after World War II, the building is remembered as the institution responsible for the ruinous hyperinflation of post-war China.

The building features traditional Chinese elements like a blue-tiled Chinese roof, ancient dragon designs on the bronze entrance gates, cloud motifs on the columns and "latticework" panels on the façade. The steps to the main building are in three groups of nine, like Beijing's Temple of Heaven. The Chinese theme continues in the beamed ceilings of the marble lobby and the square pillars. The Bank of China asked Palmer & Turner to make its building taller than Sassoon House next door, and so it was – until Victor Sassoon countered with a tiny cupola on his roof.

The final building in the Palmer & Turner trilogy along this stretch is the classical Greek-themed **Industrial and Commercial Bank of China** (No. 24), built in 1924 as the **Yokohama Specie Bank**.

At No. 27, the offices of the **Shanghai Foreign Trade Corporation** ❾ are located in what was one of the main hives of commerce in old Shanghai, the **Jardine Matheson & Co.** building. Completed in 1922, it was known as Joyful and Harmonious Trading House, or *"yihe yanghang"* in Chinese. One of the great old *hong* or trading houses on the China coast, the granite-clad seven-storey building with its marble and terrazzo floors, mosaics and high-ceiling parquet offices, was located across from Jardine's own jetty.

During the Japanese Occupation, Jardine rented out its top-floor offices to the British Embassy. They looked directly into the top-floor offices of the German Embassy in the **Glen Line Steamship Building** next door, now the **Shanghai People's Broadcasting Station** (No. 28). The Japanese had confiscated the

TIP
Yuanmingyuan Road, northwest of the Bund, is a surprisingly untouched corner where old Shanghai's social institutions slumber: the YWCA, Royal Asiatic Society, the *Wenhuibao* newspaper offices, a HK bank branch and the Rotary Club.

BELOW: statue of Chen Yi presiding over ballroom dancers.

Huangpu Park's towering Monument to the People's Heroes is a favourite picture backdrop.

BELOW: mural at the base of the Monument to the People's Heroes.

Glen Line building and given it to the Germans but after the war, it became the home of the US Consulate and the US Information Agency until 1949.

The oldest buildings on the Bund proper are the very last ones: the former **British Consulate**, now the **Municipal Government Office Building** (Nos. 33–53). The British Consulate oversaw the development of Shanghai from its perch at the end of the Bund, and the buildings included the consul's residence (No. 34), the British Court of Justice (No. 33) – now the Antiques and Curios shop – the British Naval Office (No. 35), the residence of the vice-consul (demolished) and the Office of Works (No. 51). Built in 1873 on a site acquired by Shanghai's first British Consul, Sir Rutherford Alcock, the buildings have a simple dignity and a commanding location that befitted the British Empire.

Across the street is **Huangpu Park** ❿ (Huangpu Gongyuan: daily 6am–6pm; free), the former Public Gardens. Laid out in 1868 by a Scottish gardener brought to Shanghai specifically for the job, the park was the site of the famous (some say fictitious) "No Dogs and Chinese Allowed" sign. Actually, the sign listed a number of prohibitions, including restrictions against dogs and unaccompanied Chinese. This was particularly humiliating as the park was financed by municipal taxes which were paid by both Chinese and foreigners. Today, a socialist-realist statue stands at the site of the old British bandstand, and in the mornings, many Chinese gather in front of it to practise *tai chi*. Along the waterfront facing the park stands the **Monument to the People's Heroes** (Renmin Yingxiong Jinianbei), its three pillars commemorating those who died fighting the Opium Wars, the May 4th movement and Liberation. The **Bund History Museum** (Waitan Bowuguan: daily 9am–4pm; admission fee) located underground beneath the monument features period photos of the buildings of the Bund.

Maps on pages 128 & 137

A favourite shopping street for all Chinese

Two blocks south is "China's No. 1 Shopping Street", **Nanjing Road (E)** Ⓐ, which has attracted tourists from the rest of China for over 80 years. Now overshadowed by glitzy Huaihai Road *(see page 165)*, the street – particularly the pedestrian strip from Tibet Road (Xizang Lu) to as far as Central Henan Road – is still packed with Chinese tourists, giving it an almost carnival feel. A giant screen broadcasts propaganda, couples snuggle and a tourist tram plies the walking street. Most of the shops have now acquired a glossy look, including Shanghai's famous "Big Four Department Stores", staples of old Shanghai which have all been refurbished and updated for a new generation: **No. 1 Department Store** (formerly Sun) at 800 Nanjing Road (E); **Shanghai No. 1 Provisions Store** (Sun Sun) at 729 Nanjing Road (E); **Hualian Department Store** (Wing On) at 635 Nanjing Road (E); and the **Shanghai Fashion Store** (Sincere) at 479 Nanjing Road (E).

A block south is the old banker's street of Jiujiang, lined with stately banks in styles ranging from Victorian to art deco. At the intersection with Jiangxi Road stands the 1866 **Red Temple** Ⓑ (Hong Miao), a classic 19th-century Gothic church now used as government offices. Along the old street of publishers, Hankou Road, a block south, stands the former **Joint Savings Society Building** (now the **Guangdong Development Bank**) at the corner of Sichuan and Hankou roads, created by master architect Ladislau Hudec, while at the same intersection is a slice of the past at the **Tropicana** nightclub (261 Sichuan Road). Russian dancing girls and salsa are the attractions of the Cuba-in-the-1930s club, set in a beautiful old bank building with a rooftop garden.

The middle section of **Fuzhou Road**, a block south is lined with bookshops

Every neighbourhood in Shanghai still has a glassed-in box displaying the day's paper, a way of making sure that the party's message reaches the people.

LEFT:
shoppers along
Nanjing Road (E).

Beyond the Bund

0   200 m
0   200 yds

Map on page 137

Crowning glory atop the Bund Centre – the striking building houses the Westin hotel, apartments and offices

BELOW: a wooly mammoth exhibit at the Shanghai Museum of Natural History.

like the **Foreign Languages Bookstore** (390 Fuzhou Road), the slick **City of Books** (456 Fuzhou Road) and stationery shops selling calligraphy tools and paper, paints, ink and school supplies. Fuzhou Road in old Shanghai was a red-light district, the haunt of Shanghai's famous "sing-song girls".

From the bookshops, head east for a block to a quartet of buildings – three art deco skyscrapers and a low-rise building – at the intersection of Fuzhou Road and Central Jiangxi Road. On the northeast corner is the **Metropole Hotel** and on the southeast corner, its almost identical twin, **Hamilton House**. Both have 14 floors, were built by Victor Sassoon in the 1930s and designed by Palmer & Turner. Hamilton House now houses the **Magic Restaurant** (tel: 6328 2782) and various offices. The refurbished Metropole is still a hotel and has kept the old logo of a pair of greyhounds over its revolving door. Across from the plainer apartment house on the square is the former **Shanghai Municipal Council Building**, now government offices; a manhole cover outside reads "SMC PWD" (Shanghai Municipal Council Public Works Department). West on Fuzhou Road at No. 209 is the lovely red-brick Georgian-style **People's Court**, built in 1924 as the American Club.

Continue east to Sichuan Road, then southeast under the Yan'an Road (E) overpass to Jinling Road and turn left into the **Yong An Road Market** (Yong An Lu Shichang), a lively street market that blankets two blocks of Yong An Road in the mornings. Vendors sell an array of vegetables, fruits, chickens, fish, turtles and frogs, along with tofu, noodles, dumplings and clothes. The street specialises in sewing supplies, and each shop, in a different product: ribbons in one, buttons in another, thread in a third. A few minutes' walk southwest, at 36 Sichuan Road (S), are the charcoal Gothic spires of the Catholic **St Joseph's Church** (Sichuan Nan Lu Ruose Tang), rising like a fairytale castle next to the school it adjoins. A big stained glass window dominates the 1950s French-built church, which has statues in four niches on its façade. On Sunday mornings a church service is held.

Shanghai's own Xinjiang

A 20-minute walk west to 260 Yan'an Road (E) is the **Shanghai Museum of Natural History** (Shanghai Ziran Bowuguan: Tues–Sun 9am–4.30pm; entrance fee), which houses some of the Royal Asiatic Society's collection in a stately neo-classical building. The exhibitions trace everything from amoebas and a ceiling-scraping Sichuan dinosaur on the first floor to mammals on the third. This is a rare old-style museum in modern Shanghai, with plenty of badly stuffed, formaldehyde-soaked specimens.

Across the street is the red-brick art deco tower of the former **Chung Wai Bank**, owned by Shanghai's chief mobster Du Yuesheng, now an office building. Next door is the **Bund Centre**, the area's new jewel. Designed by John Portman Associates, the complex includes the **Westin** hotel, apartments and offices.

Immigrants from the predominantly Muslim area of Xinjiang in southwestern China have settled in **Little Xinjiang** , a 20-minute walk west in the area around Guangdong Road and Central Zhejiang Road. It is a colourful area: restaurants serving spicy barbecued food, noodles and *nang* bread, lively Xinjiang music, and the distinctly sharp-featured faces of Arab children. ❏

Bund A–Z

Everyone knows of the Peace Hotel, but what about the other Bund treasures? This walking tour covers every single building along the Bund. It begins with the first building on the southern end of the Bund at Zhongshan No. 1 Road (E), and ends with the former British Consulate at Nos. 33–53. (There is the occasional gap where a building was demolished, or, in the case of No. 4, an unlucky number in China, simply glossed over.)

No. 1 Former Asiatic Petroleum Company. Dates back to 1915, now used as offices.

No. 2 Former Shanghai Club. Dates from 1910, now unoccupied.

No. 3 Former Union Assurance Building (later Mercantile Bank of India), now a restaurant complex called Three on the Bund. Built by Palmer & Turner in 1922.

No. 5 Former Nissin Kisen Kaisha Shipping Building, now the Huaxia Bank (Huaxia Yinhang) and M on the Bund restaurant.

No. 6 Former Commercial Bank of China, now unoccupied. Former headquarters of the original Municipal Council, which ran Shanghai.

No. 7 Former Great Northern Telegramme Company, now Bangkok Bank Building.

No. 9 Former China Merchants Steam Navigation Company, now unoccupied.

No. 12 Shanghai Pudong Development Bank, formerly Hongkong and Shanghai Bank). Built in 1923 by Palmer & Turner.

No. 13 Customs House. A neo-classical Palmer & Turner building with a clock tower, built in 1925. Still retains its original function.

No. 14 Former Bank of Communications, now used by Shanghai Trade Union.

No. 15 Former Russo-Asiatic Bank, now China Foreign Exchange Trade Centre and Shanghai Gold Exchange.

No. 16 Former Bank of Taiwan, now China Merchants Bank. Built in 1924.

No. 17 Former North China Daily News Building, now the American International Assurance Building. The tallest on the Bund when it was completed in 1923.

No. 18 Chun Jiang Building, formerly the Chartered Bank of India, Australia and China. Now called Bund 18 housing offices and shops.

No. 19 Peace Palace Hotel, former Palace Hotel. Entrance at 23 Nanjing Road (E).

No. 20 Peace Hotel, former Cathay Hotel. Entrance at 20 Nanjing Road (E).

No. 23 Bank of China. The only Chinese-style building on the Bund. Still retains its original function.

No. 24 Former Yokohama Specie Bank, now the Industrial and Commercial Bank of China.

No. 26 Former Yangtse Insurance Building, now the Agricultural Bank of China. The building once housed the Italian Chamber of Commerce and the Danish Consulate.

No. 27 Former Jardine Matheson & Co. Building, now Shanghai Foreign Trade Corporation.

No. 28 Former Glen Line Building, now Shanghai People's Broadcasting Station.

No. 29 Former Banque de l'Indochine, now Everbright Bank.

No. 31 Former Nippon Yusen Shipping Company, now used as offices.

No. 33–53 Former British Consulate, now Municipal Government Office Building and the Antiques and Curio shop (No. 33). ❑

RIGHT: art deco chandelier at the historic Peace Hotel, located at No. 20 along the Bund.

PEOPLE'S SQUARE

The town square area contains the best of Shanghai, including a world-class museum of Chinese art and craft, and a magnificent theatre that showcases the city's orchestra and ballet

Map on page 142

The People's Square area is Shanghai's centre, its exact geographical mid-point, according to the city's mapping and surveying department. Shanghai's subway lines all converge here at this new town square, bringing people throughout Shanghai to the city's cultural and political hub. The core of People's Square is Showcase Shanghai, the best of the city's world-class museums, a state-of-the-art theatre and the imposing Shanghai City Hall in the middle of it all. The buildings, all raised during the late 1990s and each one a significant architectural statement, seem to have been lifted from a futuristic urban planner's utopia. With these buildings, new Shanghai has arrived: no longer does the city government have to take pride in a symbol of the foreign oppressors, the Hongkong and Shanghai Bank building *(see page 131)*, because it couldn't afford any better; no longer do foreign artistes shy away from Shanghai because the facilities here are inadequate.

But the area's magnet as the city centre appealed to a Shanghai of yore as well, and one of its great attractions is that all around the sparkling core, like an antique frame, is a historical ring of the legends that defined old Shanghai: the tallest hotel, the best theatre, the wildest entertainment stand in the shadows of their modern counterparts, creating a rich and contrasting texture.

LEFT: Shanghai Grand Theatre with the equally striking Tomorrow Square rising behind it. **BELOW:** Shanghai Art Museum.

Horses once raced here

Although there is little to remind you of the past in **People's Square ❶** (Renmin Guangchang) itself, the place was once so deliciously bourgeois that it had to be razed and paved over before it was fit for proletarian Shanghai. The perimeter of People's Square, Nanjing Road (W), Huangpi Road (N), Central Tibet Road (Xizang Zhong Lu) and Wusheng Road once defined pre-Liberation Shanghai's race course, where millionaires would ride their steeds and their wives would wager fans and sun-bonnets because betting money was too, too vulgar.

The wartime Japanese command used the racetrack as a holding camp and the postwar Kuomintang turned it into a sports arena. By 1952, the new Communist government had paved over part of it into a parade ground and turned the rest into a verdant park. **People's Park** (Renmin Gongyuan: daily 6am–6pm), just behind People's Square and separated by the massive buildings on People's Avenue, is much smaller than what it was previously. Although the park has almost as much concrete as green, it remains popular with both the elderly and the young.

Virtually the only remnant of the race track's glory days is the 1933 Shanghai Racing Club, which houses today the **Shanghai Art Museum ❷** (Shanghai Meishuguan: daily 9am–5pm, last ticket 4pm;

The anniversary of the Grand Theatre's opening in August heralds a world-class line-up of musicians, ballet companies and local arts troupes. Highlights include the Chinese-language revolutionary plays and musicals now rarely performed but still remembered almost word-for-word by a keen (older) audience.

entrance fee) at 325 Nanjing Road (W). The letters SRC are still engraved over the granite building entrance and "Big Bertie", the clock tower, still ticks, but the RMB 70 million renovation in 1999 – which left behind the horseheads on the ironwork banisters – removed the Turkish baths, bowling lanes and its old atmosphere, including the ghost of the inebriated socialite who slipped into a gigantic punchbowl one Christmas on a dare.

Temporary exhibits of varying quality occupy the first floor, while the second floor houses China's first permanent modern art collection, with pieces from the 1940s to the present. The third floor shows prints and exhibitions from the Shanghai School of Painting as well as Chinese shadow puppets. On the rooftop, palettes have yielded to palates at the fine-dining restaurant **Kathleen's Fifth** (tel: 6327 0004) with its spectacular views of the surroundings.

The tallest building in Puxi, the 280-metre (920-ft), 60-storey **Tomorrow Square** (Ming Tien Guangchang) skyscraper with its needle-sharp pyramid top, lies just west of the museum at 399 Nanjing Road (W). The Marriott-managed office-residential-hotel complex, designed by John Portman Associates (Shanghai Centre, Bund Centre), offers excellent views of downtown Shanghai.

Less than a block to the east is the **Old Shanghai Art Museum** (Lao Shanghai Meishuguan; daily 9am–5pm; entrance fee) at 456 Nanjing Road (W) – confusingly housed in a new building – has mainly exhibitions of traditional Chinese art.

A magnificent "crystal" theatre

BELOW: light-filled interior, Shanghai Grand Theatre.

To the south, **San Jiao Park** (San Jiao Gongyuan), unobtrusively tucked into the corner of Huangpi Road (N) and Wusheng Road, is haunted by elderly men who hang their caged songbirds from the trees. It may well be haunted, too, by

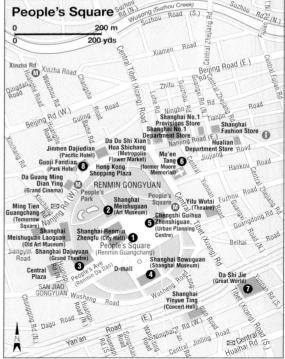

the spirits of those who were buried here when it served as the cemetery for Jewish stable hands from the race course.

Across the street are some of the most important institutions in the city, all built in the late 1990s to symbolise the new, energetic Shanghai. Foremost is the **Shanghai Grand Theatre** ❸ (Shanghai Dajuyuan) at 300 People's Avenue (Renmin Da Dao). Here, French architect Jean-Marie Charpentier has created a futuristic glass confection with flamboyantly upturned eaves – mimicking a traditional Chinese roof – that glows magically at night. Completed in 1998 and dubbed the "Crystal Palace" by locals, the 1,800-seat, 10-storey theatre is the home of the Shanghai Broadcast Symphony Orchestra and the Shanghai Ballet. The city's epicentre of highbrow culture has a packed season of ballet, classical music and opera, as well as the occasional musical and revolutionary opera. Self-guided tours of the theatre (daily 9am–4.30pm; entrance fee) take visitors behind the scenes to rehearsal rooms, performance spaces and the high-tech stage.

A collection of Chinese art

A landscaped plaza fronts the **Shanghai Museum** ❹ (Shanghai Bowuguan: daily 9am–4pm; entrance fee) across the street at 201 People's Avenue. The neatly manicured gardens and flowerbeds are dominated by a soaring musical fountain, whose jets cool Shanghai children during the steamy summer months. Allow a full morning or, better yet, a day, to tour the museum. Designed by Chinese architect Xing Tonghe of the Shanghai Architectural Institute, the massive five-storey granite structure was officially opened in 1996.

Shaped like a *ding*, an ancient round bronze tripod cooking vessel, the museum focuses on the arts and crafts of China in its 11 permanent galleries, arranged the-

Ancient bronze "ding" vessel which inspired the shape of the Shanghai Museum.

BELOW:
Shanghai Museum all aglow at night.

TIP

To save money on
individual entrance
fees to two of People's
Square's big sights –
Shanghai Grand
Theatre and Shanghai
Museum – buy a
combination ticket
from the ticket booth
(daily 8.30–11am
and 2–4pm) near the
main (south) entrance
of the Grand Theatre.

BELOW:
Qing dynasty
calligraphy at the
Shanghai Museum.

matically across four floors. Cleverly laid out and lit, with excellent Accous-tiguide taped commentaries and informative introductory panels in each gallery, the museum houses one of the largest collections of Chinese art in the world – rivalling Taipei's National Palace Museum – and is easily the best in the country.

The first floor's **Ancient Chinese Bronze Gallery** has one of the world's fin-est and most comprehensive collections of bronzes, including very rare pieces going back to China's first dynasty, the Xia (21st to 16th century BC). Compris-ing a variety of food and wine vessels, weapons and other implements, the col-lection is laid out chronologically. Highlights include a Shang dynasty square *lei*, or wine vessel, with finely crafted dragon decorations; a Western Zhou dynasty bell embellished with tigers; and an enormous *jian* wine vessel, with four myth-ical creatures grasping the rim and peeking into it, from the tomb of King Fu Chai of the Wu Kingdom. On the same floor is the **Ancient Chinese Sculpture Gallery**, with its excellent displays of pottery, and stone and bronze sculptures.

Most of the second floor is devoted to the **Ancient Chinese Ceramic Gallery**, which traces this born-in-China craft from the Neolithic Yellow River cultures to the Qing dynasty. Especially beautiful are delicate Tang dynasty *Sancai* ceramics with their three-colour glazes, and blue-and-white Ming and Qing pieces. There is also a potter's workshop, model kilns and pottery-making demonstrations.

A rotating exhibit of the nation's largest and most extensive collection of Chinese paintings, including Tang and Song album leaves and hand scrolls, and masterpieces such as *Eight Noble Monks* by Liang Kai, *Misty River and Mountains* by Wang Shen, as well as works by masters of the Yuan, Ming and Qing dynasties, are showcased on the third-floor **Chinese Painting Gallery**.

Also on this floor is the **Chinese Seal Gallery**, which displays intricately

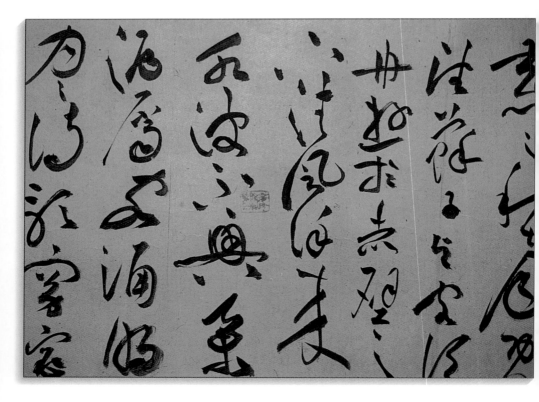

carved seals of ivory, jade, amber and crystal, which served as signatures in ancient letters and contracts. The **Chinese Calligraphy Gallery** on the same floor traces the development of this ancient form of brushstroke writing, from early inscriptions on tiny oracle bones to flowing Qing dynasty scripts.

The **Ancient Chinese Jade Gallery**, on the fourth floor, explores the mystical beliefs associated with the stone while the **Coin Gallery** displays Chinese currencies through the ages. Also on the fourth floor is the **Chinese Minorities Nationalities' Art Gallery** – a firm favourite – with a vibrant collection of colourful costumes and masks from China's 56 ethnic minorities, while the **Furniture Gallery** has antique rosewood and sandalwood furniture from the different Chinese periods. Reproductions and souvenirs are available at the first-floor gift shop.

Subterranean mall and an urban museum

Subterranean **D-mall** (Dimei Gouwu Zhongxin), north of the People's Square fountain, is a maze of hip-hop fashion boutiques, and tattoo and piercing parlours in an underground rabbit warren. Fearful that the 1960 Sino-Soviet split would precipitate a nuclear war, Mao exhorted the people to "dig deep, store grain and resist hegemony". The result was underground bomb shelters like this which snake under Shanghai.

Across People's Avenue, the exhibitions at the **Shanghai Urban Planning Centre ❺** (Chengshi Guihua Zhenshiguan: Wed–Sun 9am–4pm; entrance fee) at 100 People's Avenue help make sense of the Shanghai building frenzy. Nearly a twin of the Grand Theatre, with which it flanks **City Hall** (Shanghai Renmin Zhengfu: closed to the public), the square building has the same clean lines though its startling flat roof is an almost kitschy departure. Designed by Xing

Map on page 142

Shanghaied, the verb, entered the English language in the 1870s to describe the act of drugging and kidnapping sailors for compulsory service aboard ships bound for China... presumably the treaty port of Shanghai.

BELOW: Shanghai Urban Planning Centre showcases the city's development.

Great World was the hub of Shanghai nighlife in the 1930s (see page 147).

BELOW: Beijing Opera staged at Yifu Theatre.

Tonghe (of Shanghai Museum fame), urban Shanghai's past, present and future are encapsulated in the brick, tile, cement, pebble and asphalt path to the entrance – a visual metaphor of Shanghai's progress from pebble paths to superhighways.

A recreation of the Sino-Western architecture and *longtang* (lane) houses that dominated the pre-Liberation era is found in the basement. Look out for a wall relief in the lobby area depicting a commonplace urban Shanghai moment: the relocation of residents from old lane houses. Second-floor exhibits tell the story of Shanghai's development from fishing village to Concession, while the third floor focuses on the government's efforts at providing modern housing, with visitors putting on 3-D glasses for a peek at the buildings of Pudong. The 500-sq metre (5,380-sq ft) scale model of downtown Shanghai depicts every building over six storeys high, including future ones. The fourth floor has a blueprint of the city's plans for the 21st century while the top floor has perhaps the best exhibit of all – a circular window from which to view the city itself, as seen from its heart.

The innovative mark of Ladislau Hudec

The museum's basement leads directly to more underground shopping at **Hong Kong Shopping Plaza** (Xiang Gang Zhongxin: connects to D-mall and is accessible through People's Park subway station), with plenty of accessories and brand-name fashions. Come up at the corner of Tibet and Fuzhou roads and head north to the red **Mu'en Church ❻** (Mu'en Tang) at 316 Central Tibet Road.

Originally named the Arthur J. Moore Memorial Church after the Texan who donated funds for its construction in the late 1920s, the church was rebuilt by the prominent Czech architect Ladislau Hudec in 1931, and features characteristically innovative design elements such as the concave-and-convex brickwork

that encases the structure. Used as a middle school during the Cultural Revolution, it was the first church in Shanghai to reopen in 1979.

Two blocks away at 701 Fuzhou Road is the **Yifu Theatre** (Yifu Wutai), which hosts regular weekend performances of Beijing Opera (Sat–Sun 1.30pm and every evening 7.15pm; tel: 6351 4668) as well as other forms of Chinese opera. The wedding cake structure of the infamous **Great World** ❼ (Da Shi Jie: daily 9am–9.30pm; entrance fee) is located several blocks south at 1 Tibet Road (S). Its first owner was a Chinese pharmacist named Huang Chujiu, who made a fortune with "Yellow", a brain-boosting tonic popular at the time. By the 1930s, the building was controlled by the head of the French Concession's Chinese detective squad, Huang Jinrong, or "Pockmarked" Huang. Stories linger of smoky gambling dens, where scions of Shanghai's first families lost their fortunes, of dance hostesses, and of the staircase to nowhere – where those who had lost it all could take the desperate and quick way out.

These days, however, the amusement centre has acrobats performing amazing feats in the open-air courtyard, while a smorgasbord of activities go on in the four floors above: Beijing Opera performances, video game arcades, bumper cars, and a genuinely scary Ghost Train ride. Give the rather lame Shanghai Guinness Book of World Records exhibition, however, a miss.

The major renovation that levelled much of Yan'an Road, west of the Great World, in 2003 to bring it in line with the modernity of People's Square also moved the 1930 Greek classical **Shanghai Concert Hall** (Shanghai Yinyue Ting) – home of the Shanghai Symphony Orchestra – to the south in a new park setting.

How Park Hotel inspired I.M. Pei

Nanjing Road (W), at the intersection of Tibet Road, just behind the Grand Theatre, is a nice antidote to the newness of People's Square, but there was a time when the gracious old buildings here defined progress. When the eight-storey **Pacific Hotel** (Jinmen Dajiudian) was built in 1924 at 104 Nanjing Road (W) as the Union Insurance Building, it was the tallest building in the city and its bell tower used by ships for navigation. It was soon outdone by Ladislau Hudec's 24-storey **Park Hotel** ❽ (Guoji Fandian) at 170 Nanjing Road (W), which Shanghai-born architect I.M. Pei cites as his career inspiration. In his memoirs, Pei recalls coming out of the **Grand Cinema** (Daguangming Dian Ying) at 216 Nanjing Road (W) – another Hudec jewel – when he saw the just-completed Park Hotel. Immediately he took out his pencil and began drawing its outline. Its interior has been renovated and its status as Asia's tallest building long since surpassed, but the Park's brown-tiled tower still dominates this section of Nanjing Road (W).

Built for the Joint Savings Society, whose art deco headquarters was on the premises, the Park Hotel also served as the first hotel school for Chinese students. Old cutlery, monogrammed china and photographs are displayed on the second floor. During the Cultural Revolution years, the hotel was draped with ugly banners ("Do not forget the class struggle" and "Politics is in command") because it symbolised decadence. ❑

Map on page 142

The Shanghai Athletics Association (Shanghai Tiyu Hui), next to the Park Hotel, was where enemies of the state were held for questioning during the Cultural Revolution. It was here that the daughter of author Nien Chieng ("Life and Death in Shanghai") perished.

BELOW: the glazed brick Park Hotel.

NANSHI

Map on page 150

Visit the famous Yu Garden and its adjoining bazaar by all means. But, to see the real China, wander around the Old City's narrow winding alleys for the sights and sounds of a vanishing way of life

A 1934 guidebook to the city, published by Shanghai's University Press, warned that "Shanghai is not China". For a peek at the real China, the book suggested a visit to its Chinese city – advice that still applies today. While parts of Shanghai's original city, **Nanshi** ("Southern City") may be self-consciously Chinese, as in a theme-park vision of Ming China, the spirit of the Old City remains very much alive in the tightly-packed lanes and crowded old markets along the back streets, defined by the constant din of *ri nao* ("hot noise").

Although the back lanes are still buzzing, every day great swaths of Nanshi fall to the wrecking ball, and old 19th-century wood-and-brick Chinese housing is replaced by new tourist-friendly sites and green space, as residents continue to move out to the suburbs. It's definitely worth seeking out this endangered way of life while it's still here. A walk along an old lane or alleyway may be rewarded by scenes of children playing in the streets, chamber pots being washed out, and women shelling peas outside century-old doorstops.

Some 2,000 years before foreigners arrived and carved out the Concessions, a small fishing town called Hu was already established on the site of today's Nanshi. Renamed Shanghai in 1280, the original settlement here grew and became prosperous, although it never gained any historical importance.

LEFT: a cultural performance at Yu Garden bazaar.
BELOW: pan-frying *shengjie mantou*, a local snack.

A refuge for the lawless

Strictly speaking, Shanghai's Chinese population was to live in the Chinese city during the Concession era, but that stricture quickly broke down. Developers found that building housing for Chinese who were seeking the safety of the policed Concessions during the Taiping Rebellion was too lucrative to miss out on.

Chinese soon lived throughout the Concessions – they paid taxes, but had no voice in the municipal government – leaving the Old City as a squalid ghetto that remained purely, utterly Chinese, with its mysterious maze of lanes, exotic sights and strange smells. It was a lawless place that foreigners did not dare visit – save the missionaries who came to convert the heathen. For some – rebels plotting to overthrow the government or gangsters and criminals – it was a place in which to hide.

Japanese pirate incursions instigated the building of a 4.8-km (3-mile) long, 8-metre (27-ft) high wall and a moat enclosing the city in the 1550s. The structure had two watchtowers and six gates that were firmly locked at midnight. The Kuomintang demolished the wall, but its contours still define the 4-sq km (1.5-sq mile) area of Nanshi. The walls today are the high-speed highways of Renmin Road to the north and Zhonghua Road to the south.

The former northern gate is still an ideal entry point to the Old City. But now, instead of the forbidding

wall, the two-block stretch of northern Renmin Road at Henan Road (S) offers the surreal sight of rows of Cinderella-at-the-ball wedding dresses and glittering evening gowns; some hung up on lines along the pavements. Brides on a budget rent their gowns from the shops here. They may be fussier and more frou-frou than those at the upmarket wedding boutiques on Huaihai Road (*see page 169*) but – at RMB 150 a night – are only a fraction of the cost.

The **Foreign Languages Bookstore's Used Book Division** at 89 Sheng Ze Road (daily 9am–5pm), Shanghai's only second-hand English bookshop, is tucked in a small lane off the wedding dress street. One famous customer was Soong Ching Ling, who might well have enjoyed its well organised selection of books on a wide range of topics, including rare books on Shanghai, and magazines.

Continue south along Henan Road (S), stopping at the **Fuyou Road Mosque** (Qingzheng Si), the city's first, built in 1853 by Muslim traders. Move on to **Yu Garden Bazaar ❶** (Yuyuan Shangchang) – bordered by Anren Street, Fuyou Road, Jiujiaochang Road and Central Fangbang Road – a bold and brash,

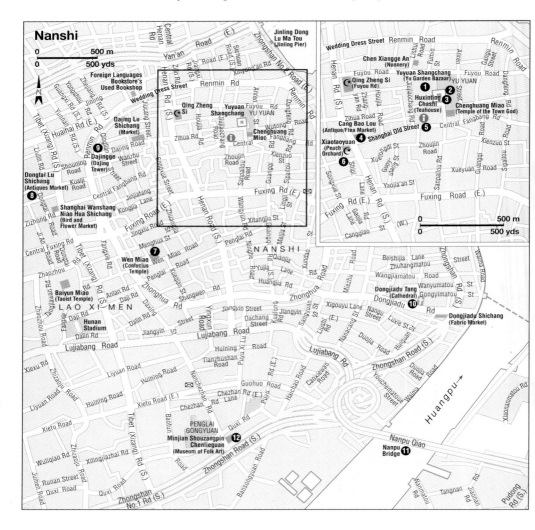

vehicle-free, reinvented Ming-era Chinese experience centred on speciality shops and delicious local snacks *(more details on page 153)*.

Located at the southern entrance to Yu Garden Bazaar, at 1 Yicheng Road, is the **Temple of the Town God** (Chenghuang Miao: daily 7am–4pm; entrance fee), dedicated to the gods that protect Shanghai. Each city in old China had a town god temple that served as its hub, a place where traders gathered and festivals were celebrated; this tradition continues at the adjoining bazaar. Built in 1726, the Temple of the Town God succeeded the 15th-century Jinshan Miao (Golden Hills Temple) and, like the latter, is dedicated to legendary general Huo Guang. After being used as a factory during the Cultural Revolution, images of the general and his Taoist deities have been restored. Incense is again burnt under the splendid carved roof and, on Sundays, a market trades in the courtyard.

Suzhou-style garden

At the centre of the bazaar is Shanghai's most famous garden, the 16th-century **Yu Garden ❷** (Yu Yuan: daily 8.30am–5pm; entrance fee), at 218 Anren Street. Referred to in local maps and literature as Yuyuan Garden, it occupies the northern portion of the Old City. The garden was built in 1577 by Ming dynasty official Pan Yunduan to please his elderly father – "Yu" means peace and comfort – and after years of neglect, was restored in the mid-18th century.

Yu Garden, its walls encircled by an undulating dragon, is a petite 2-hectare (5-acre) classical Suzhou-style garden that has all the ingredients that create a microcosm of the universe – the defining hallmark of the classical Chinese garden. It has 30 pavilions connected by bridges and walkways, interspersed with fishpools, rockeries and ingenious views. Unfortunately, like the Suzhou gar-

Temple bells like this one are rung on special festival days.

LEFT: deities from the Temple of the Town God.
BELOW: pavilion at Yu Garden.

The best Chinese tea, according to tea connoisseurs, is brewed in tiny Yixing teapots like these (see text box below).

BELOW:
Mid-Lake Pavilion Teahouse can only be reached by a twisting bridge.

dens, Yu Garden is often invaded by tourist groups with loudspeaker-blasting guides, crowding what is meant to be a space for quiet contemplation.

The **Grand Rockery** (Dajiashan), a 2,000-tonne mountainous sculpture of yellow rocks from Zhejiang Province, stands 14 metres (46 ft) tall as the centrepiece of the garden, with the best views from the aptly named **Hall for Viewing Grand Rockery** (Dajiashan Tang) that stands just opposite the rocks. On the garden's east side is the enormous **Exquisite Jade Rock** (Yu Ling Long), acquired by the Pan family when the boat carrying the rock to the emperor in Beijing sank off the coast of Shanghai. Also on this side is the **Hall of Heralding Spring** (Dianchun Tang), which in the early 1850s served as the headquarters of the Small Swords Society, the local branch of the Taiping rebels. A small museum in the hall recounts the Taiping Rebellion, now embraced by the Communist government as China's first large-scale peasant uprising.

Sip tea to a view of willows by the lake

Leave Yu Garden by the main entrance, closest to the **Three-Ears-of-Corn Hall** (San Sui Tang) – with grains and fruit carved on window frames and beams to suggest a bumper harvest – and find yourself face-to-face with the Old City's best-known sight: **Mid-Lake Pavilion Teahouse ❸** (Huxinting Chashi: daily 8.30am–9pm; tel: 6373 6950), set in the centre of a man-made lake. Leading to the five-sided teahouse with its classical pointed roof is the zigzagging **Bridge of Nine Turnings** (Huxinting Qiao), built on the supposition that spirits cannot turn corners. In reality, the bridge seems to have acquired a few more turns over the years.

Perhaps because Huxinting has hosted the likes of Queen Elizabeth and former US President Bill Clinton, a cup of tea here can be expensive. However, sip-

YIXING'S TINY TEAPOTS

At the Mid-Lake Pavilion Teahouse, waitresses pour tea from the tiny maroon-brown spout of a Yixing teapot, the vessel that tea connoisseurs say brews the finest tea anywhere. Made from the purple clay found only in Jiangsu Province's Yixing County, the teapots remain unglazed, both inside and out, and this porous quality allows it to become seasoned over time from both the colour and flavour of the tea. Usually, only one type of tea is used in a pot to maintain its purity, and it is said that one needs to only add hot water to a seasoned Yixing teapot in order to enjoy a flavourful cup of tea.

The Yixing teapot has an impressive legacy. First created during the 10th century, the teapots flourished during the Ming dynasty, when tea-leaf infusions replaced tea powder. The tiny teapots were originally created for personal use. During the Ming dynasty, the pocket-sized teapots were carried around by their owners, and tea would be drunk directly from the spout.

Yixing teapots are sold throughout Yu Garden Bazaar, in a range of prices and quality. Take a tip from the experts, who say a quality teapot should be rough, both on the outside and on the inside, make a clear sound when struck, and the tea should pour out from the spout in an arc.

ping delicate Chinese tea from a Yixing teacup on the second floor, to views of willows and the tops of the trees in Yu Garden, is a rare experience.

Among the Yu Garden Bazaar's newly built Ming-style buildings housing restaurants, food stalls and hundreds of small speciality shops are a labyrinth of lanes, made all the more confusing by the crowds of visitors. The central plaza, in which sits a giant sculpture of an ancient Chinese gold piece, is an endless source of entertainment: toy vendors demonstrate their products and tourists bounce along in sedan chair rides. There are larger department stores selling overpriced jewellery and antiques, but the individual speciality shops make for more interesting shopping. A sight to behold is the incredible range of products in shops specialising in chopsticks, canes, buttons, fans, kites, scissors and wigs; one of the latter shops was a supplier to Madam Mao.

Famous Shanghai snacks

As well as shopping, Yu Garden Bazaar is known for its snacks. Domestic tourists line up at the food stalls for a taste of Shanghai's famous delicacies: the bite-sized, translucent *xiao long bao* (pork dumplings) from Nanxiang, sweet glutinous rice pigeon-egg dumplings (served opposite the Bridge of Nine Turnings), and the eyebrow-shaped shortcake. The queues for the snacks are almost always worthwhile, but the same can't be said for the area's best-known restaurants. Places such as **Old Shanghai Restaurant** (Shanghai Lao Fandian), which has been in business since 1875, and **Green Wave Pavilion** (Lubolang) all serve the famous snacks along with a menu of Shanghainese dishes, but the atmosphere is too much that of a tour-bus stop, and the prices are ridiculously high.

The bustling commerce spills out onto the streets that ring the bazaar and

Map on page 150

The Mid-Lake Pavilion Teahouse is supposed to be the subject of the "Blue Willow" pattern plates, first created in 1790 during the heyday of the China trade by Josiah Spode. He based it on an original pattern called the Mandarin.

BELOW: freshly fried noodles at Yu Garden Bazaar.

Buyer beware: if every stall carries the same item, it is unlikely to be a genuine antique.

BELOW: traditional-style architecture predominates in the shops around the Yu Garden area.

these are lined with shops selling everything from Chinese decorations to kitchen equipment, temple supplies and stuffed animals. Antiques join the list at the **Cang Bao Building** ❹ (Cang Bao Lou: daily 5am–5pm) at 459 Fangbang Road, west of the bazaar's southern exit. The modern five-storey building with the Chinese roof, the tallest structure in the area, is fairly quiet on weekdays, but turns into a lively antiques market on weekends. Then, as early as 5am, traders begin laying out their wares on the top floor, and shop owners from all over the city begin jamming the aisles. Go early, as the real finds are gone by 8am.

The Cang Bao Building is a successor to the former Fuyou Road Sunday "ghost" market and still has that street market feel to it; most of the antiques are obviously scrounged from homes and have more sentimental than antique value. Even if you don't buy anything, you would have gained an unusual insight into old Shanghai. This is especially true on the fourth floor, where vendors sell relics from the Concession era, such as monogrammed cutlery from the old clubs, factory cards, photographs from the old studios, rare books – some from old Shanghai libraries – and Cultural Revolution memorabilia. The third floor's furniture corner has a good supply of Shanghai art deco pieces from the 1920s and 1930s, including fixtures such as doorknobs, while the first and second floors have a melange of smaller collectibles which include vintage clocks, watches and genuine Shanghai advertising posters from the 1930s.

Shopping is more focused on **Shanghai Old Street** ❺ (Shanghai Laojie), which runs for 825 metres (2,706 ft) along Central Fangbang Road, east of Henan Road, and is lined with two-storey buildings that progress architecturally from the Ming to the Qing and to the Kuomintang era. The shops sell tradi-tional Chinese-themed souvenirs: the famous "purple clay" Yixing teapots,

Map
on page
150

Chinese lanterns and crafts, tea blends, temple paraphernalia and antiques. Also on this street are old-style teahouses – like the venerable **Old Shanghai Teahouse** (Lao Shanghai Chaguan) at 385 Fangbang Road (tel: 5382 1202) – which capture the soul of old Shanghai with leisurely cups of tea that are sipped amidst surroundings filled with historical maps, pictures and collectibles.

For the real Shanghai old street, continue east for about five minutes, passing the Temple of the Town God *(see page 151)*, until Central Fangbang Road becomes a narrow lane lined with old apothecaries, pickle stores with gigantic jars and Shaoxing wine merchants, transporting you into a mediaeval time warp. Cotton candy sellers pump vintage machines to spin sugar, corn is roasted on outdoor grills and sugared fruit is speared onto sticks. Turn left into Anren Street which leads to Fuyou Road and its fabulous **Fumin Street Smallware Market** (Fumin Shang Sha; daily 8am–5pm), an enormous dime store stocked with seemingly everything under the sun. China is the world's factory and this market seems to sell it all – and at heavily discounted prices. The range of goods is truly mind-boggling and combing the market, plus the shops outside the building, will take a dedicated shopper hours.

People wear their pyjamas on the street throughout Shanghai, but especially in the back lanes of the Old City. The practice dates from a time when only the better-off could afford to wear pyjamas.

A figurine for each of Buddha's 348 disciples

West of the Fumin Street market, the legacy of Yu Garden's founding Pan family lives on outside the bazaar area at the **Chen Xiangge Nunnery** (Chen Xiangge An: daily 6am–4pm; entrance fee), the city's largest, at 29 Chenxiangge Road. Restored in 1994 after an interlude as a factory during the Cultural Revolution, the temple is renowned for its 348 Buddha figurines that represent the 348 disciples of the Buddha.

Shanghai's Chinese Muslim community, the Hui people, worship at the **Peach Orchard Mosque** ❻ (Xiaotaoyuan: daily 8am–7pm; free), south of the nunnery at 52 Xiaotaoyuan Road, near Central Fangbang Road. The mosque, with its distinctive green spheres on the roof, was built in 1917 and renovated in 1925, but is surprisingly modernist with a restrained fusion of Arabic, Western and Chinese architecture that includes round art deco windows more frequently seen in the French Concession.

Students – and their anxious parents – still pray at the sunny yellow-walled **Confucius Temple** ❼ (Wen Miao: daily 9am–5.15pm; entrance fee), just south of the Peach Orchard Mosque at 215 Wen Miao Road, particularly during "black July", the time of college entrance exams. As Confucius is the patron of scholars, the literary theme is strong here. There are the **God of Literature Pavilion** (Kui Xing), with its Chinese roof, and **Respecting Classics Tower** (Zunjing), a library for Chinese classics that also served as the state library during the Kuomintang period, and a lecture hall. The last served a less-than-literary purpose during the Taiping Rebellion as the headquarters of the rebels' Shanghai branch, the Small Swords Society.

The literary theme continues in the temple courtyard, the site of a regular book market that includes vintage English books, and the lanes around the temple, which are crowded with book vendors. Originally

BELOW:
statue of Confucius
at the temple
named after him.

*Everything a tailor
needs can be found
at the Dongjiadu
Fabric Market (see
page 157).*

(see page 157).

a temple for the Zitang clan (the temple was reconstructed in 1855), its new sheen comes from more recent renovations after its destruction by the Red Guards during the Cultural Revolution.

The quietness of the **Baiyun Taoist Temple** (Baiyun Miao) at Xilinhou Road, just off Wen Miao Road, dating back to 1873, belies its historical importance for Shanghai's Taoists. Taoist monk Xi Zhicheng extended the former temple on this site, Leizu (Ancestor of Thunder), in 1882. In 1888, when he brought over 8,000 scriptures from Beijing's Baiyun Temple, Leizu was renamed Baiyun. The temple's three halls were built in 1892, but sustained major damage during the Cultural Revolution, including the destruction of its magnificent collection of paintings and scriptures. The restored Baiyun now proudly displays its seven bronze Taoist gods that survived the Cultural Revolution and is once again a functioning temple. Baiyun also serves as the headquarters for Shanghai's Taoist Association, as well as a research centre for Taoist culture.

Shanghai's biggest antiques market

Take a brief detour out of the Old City – yet stay within its spirit – to the **Dongtai Road Antiques Market ❽** (Dongtai Lu Shichang: daily 10am–4pm) on Dongtai Road and Liuhekou Road. This biggest market in Shanghai has 100 booths, as well as two-storey shophouses, with a mix of serious antiques and kitsch, including fresh-from-the-factory reproductions of bestsellers, such as china figurines depicting Cultural Revolution-era heroes. A delightful stop is Stall No. 88, which specialises in vintage lighting fixtures, many from grand houses and restaurants that have since been torn down. The "showroom", on the second storey of the shophouse behind this stall, is a tiny bedroom turned into

BELOW: vendor at
Dongtai Road
Antiques Market.

a fairyland of chandeliers, lamps and sconces in all shapes and sizes. The garrulous proprietor, who speaks only Chinese, has a story for every one.

Shanghai's increasing wealth has meant a proportionate increase in luxury
items – such as pets, which are sold on the eastern side of Dongtai Road at the
Shanghai Wanshang Bird and Flower Market (Shanghai Wanshang Niao Hua
Shichang: daily 7am–7pm). The covered pet section is stocked with several breeds
of puppies, kittens, rabbits, hamsters and pot-bellied pigs, and a good selection of
birds and impressive handmade cages. During the summer cricket season, an
entire segment is devoted to the chirping insects. The corner of Zhonghua and Fuxing Road (E), south of the bird market, is the site of an active junk market, where
buyers and sellers haggle over used appliances, furniture and electronic goods.

Head back into the Old City's northwestern quarter, just off People's Road to
Dajing Road, for the theatrical **Dajing Road Market** (Dajing Lu Shichang). The
market is at its best in the morning, when housewives do their shopping for the
day. The vibrant colours of the mounds of fruit and artistically arranged vegetables are often outdone by the shouts of the vendors advertising their goods.

Continue on Dajing Road to **Dajing Tower** ❾ (Dajingge: daily 8.30am–4pm;
entrance fee) at 269 Renmin Road, a simple structure with a Chinese roof, and
all that has remained of the Old City wall. The museum inside has an interesting collection of photographs of life in the old days – its festivals, markets and
history – along with a miniature model of the Old City's original layout.

Moorish baroque church

The southeast quadrant of the Old City is a wasteland of ugly government-built
apartments. Thus, coming upon the beautiful **Dongjiadu Cathedral** ❿
(Dongjiadu Tang) at 185 Dongjiadu Road is all the
more surprising. The Moorish baroque church, built
by the Spanish Jesuits in 1853, was Shanghai's first
Catholic church. Restored in 2000, it is still an active
church, holding Sunday Mass at 7.30am.

A few minutes' walk east along Dongjiadu Road
leads to the covered **Dongjiadu Fabric Market**
(Dongjiadu Shichang), which has a rainbow of fabrics
in Chinese silk and cotton, along with fabrics for curtains, bed linen and napkins, accessories such as buttons – and tailors who can put the whole thing
together. A 10-minute walk from Dongjiadu Road to
Zhongshan Road (S) leads to the **Nanpu Bridge** ⓫
(Nanpu Qiao: daily 8.30am–4pm; entrance fee), the
beautiful suspension bridge from which to take in
sweeping views of Pudong and the Old City.

Shanghai has an estimated 100,000 collectors and
many of these exhibit their often arcane collections
at the **Museum of Folk Art** ⓬ (Minjian Shouzangpin
Chenlieguan: daily 9am–4pm; entrance fee), east of
Nanpu Bridge at 1551 Zhongshan Road (S). Past exhibitions have included butterflies, tiny shoes for bound
feet, cigarette labels from the 1930s, school badges
and ship models. The museum building is worth a
visit on its own. Built in 1909 as the Sanshan Guild
Hall with funds raised by a Shanghai-based Fujian
fruit dealer, the hall is the only remaining one of several that used to line this area. ❑

Map on page 150

TIP

Chinese markets
are not for the
faint-hearted. Not very
different from a small
zoo, there are live
chickens, pigeons,
snakes, frogs, turtles,
prawns and fish:
any of which are killed
and cleaned in front of
the customer to
ensure freshness.

BELOW: Shanghai
Wanshang Bird and
Flower Market.

FUXING PARK AND ENVIRONS

Map on page 163

Ideological idols Sun Yat-sen, Soong Ching Ling and Zhou Enlai once lived in the area, and the French Concession's streets are still elegant, with many notable restaurants and nightspots

In old Shanghai, it was said that the British in the International Settlement would teach you how to do business, but in the French Concession, you would be taught how to live. That remains true in the surprisingly well-preserved area surrounding Fuxing Park, the old heart of the French Concession that is today the soul of the city's good life. Lucien Bodard's description in *Les Français de Shanghai* still rings true: "A charming residential area dotted with imposing villas and large avenues with their venerated names… sidewalk cafés, boutiques with the latest styles, nightclubs… French savoir faire, elegance and gentility reigned supreme in the Concession."

Élan may have attracted high-living sybarites of all nationalities, but it was the protection of the French police that attracted wealthy Chinese fleeing the Taiping Rebellion (although later, the rabid disorganisation under the Concession's chief of Chinese detectives and triad leader, "Pockmarked" Huang, permitted revolution to brew). When the British and Americans unified their Concessions into the International Settlement in 1863, the French decided to go it alone in the area south of the Settlement. Thus, the French Concession was established, bounded by a creek that later became Avenue Edouard VII (now Yan'an Road), expanding westward over the years. A bizarre situation arose: the north side of the street was policed by His Majesty's turbaned British Sikh police officers while the south side was patrolled by helmeted Annamite guards from French Indochina. The electrical, plumbing and telephone systems on each side were completely different.

LEFT: striking a pose in front of the Site of the First National Congress of the Communist Party of China.
BELOW: *tai chi* practice at Fuxing Park.

First secret Communist congress

Shanghai's contradictions come to a head at the **Site of the First National Congress of the Communist Party of China** ❶ (Zhonggong Yidahuizhi: daily 9am–5pm, last ticket 4pm; entrance fee) at 76 Xingye Road. Here, in 1921, the Communist Party of China was formed in an attractive but bourgeois 19th-century charcoal-and-red brick *shikumen* (stone gate) house that was the home of delegate Li Hanjun. The table around which the 13 delegates, including a young Mao Zedong, held their first secret Congress, is set with 13 stools and 13 teacups, as if waiting for the return of the delegates. Although that first Congress wasn't completed here – the delegates fled on the eighth day when news of the illegal gathering reached the Concession's gendarmes – this remains one of Communism's sacred sites. The escapees went on to complete the meeting on a pleasure boat on Nanhu Lake in Zhejiang Province.

An adjacent exhibition hall recounts the history of the Chinese Communist Party, with grainy pictures of the original delegates – in a chilling foreshadowing of Mao's later campaigns of terror, 11 of the 13 were

Marx and Engels honoured at Fuxing Park.

killed, quit or left to join the Kuomintang – the horrors of the capitalist treatment of workers, a wax-figure tableau of the first congress, and special exhibitions that include relics of Communist history such as Mao's swimming trunks. The gift shop has a selection of Mao buttons and other Communist paraphernalia.

Xintiandi: Shanghai's most happening nightspot

More contradictions appear after a five-minute walk from Xingye Road south to Madang Road. Here, in identical *shikumen* houses, you can order a Starbucks' latté, shop for designer duds or nibble French pastries. The **Xintiandi** ❷ complex (at Taicang and Madang roads) is a two-block area of refurbished *shikumen* housing that is currently Shanghai's most happening restaurant-bar-entertainment scene. Developed by Ben Wood (his resumé includes Boston's Faneuil Hall and Singapore's Boat Quay), it has gourmet restaurants at every turn, haute couture boutiques, a rock music venue and a state-of-the-art theatre showing vintage Shanghai movies. Brand names fill the old houses: the Aman luxury hotel group's sophisticated fusion restaurant, **T8** (tel: 6355 8999); Hong Kong superstar Jacky Chan's **Star East** (tel: 6311 4991); and even a Vidal Sassoon salon. An old *shikumen* museum recreates the interior of an authentic lane house, a memorial to the hundreds of homes surrounding Xintiandi that were felled to create the 4-hectare (10-acre) lake and new high-rise offices and residences on the 50-hectare (124-acre) development.

Yandang Road, a walking street lined with modern Chinese restaurants and herbal medicine shops in refurbished old buildings, is a short stroll west and a pleasant way to reach **Fuxing Park** ❸ (Fuxing Gongyuan: daily 6am–6pm; entrance fee) on Chongqing Road (S). A plaque on the red-brick apartment build-

BELOW: Xintiandi is Shanghai's latest entertainment hub.

ing on the southeast corner of the Chongqing Road-Central Fuxing Road inter-section identifies it as the former **residence of Agnes Smedley**. Smedley is the American journalist who chronicled the Chinese Communist revolution in books such as *Battle Hymn of China* and *Chinese Red Army Marches*. Accused of espionage (though never charged), she is considered a heroine of the revolution.

Enter Fuxing Park at the Chongqing Road entrance, where the odd sight of an old piece of machinery, used in a factory that was located in the park, sits under glass. Laid out by the French in 1909 and known as the French Park, Fuxing Park – which served briefly as a Japanese parade ground – honours its heritage in European landscaping interspersed with Communist symbols. Statues of Karl Marx and Friedrich Engels smile benevolently upon the carnival of Chinese martial arts, aerobics, sword play, ballroom dance and *tai chi* exercises that awaken the park at dawn each day. In front of the children's playground and ferris wheel is **Park 97** (inside the park, entrance at 2 Gaolan Road), a collection of mediocre restaurants and the hot nightspot **California Club**.

Dine in a historic Russian church

Exit the park on Gaolan Road and cross Sinan Road to the **Ashanti Dome ❹** (16 Gaolan Road; tel: 5306 1230), a chic restaurant housed in the former Russian Orthodox **St Nicholas Church**. The elaborate church was frequently used for weddings, including local ones, and served the White Russians who flooded Shanghai after the 1917 Russian Revolution. The figure of Christ, surrounded by 12 apostles, no longer graces its onion-shaped domes, nor are the four patron saints of Moscow on its four walls, but it has acquired a portrait of Chairman Mao on the entrance façade, painted during the Cultural Revolution to protect

Art lovers visiting Fuxing Park will want to drop by ShanghART (2A Gaolan Road; daily 10am–7pm). One of Shanghai's first independent art galleries, it showcases brand-name Shanghai contemporary artists.

BELOW: old world interior at Ashanti Dome restaurant, formerly the St Nicholas Church.

BELOW:
Sun Yat-sen
lived here from
1918–24.

the church from desecration. The best table in the house is upstairs, underneath the interior dome, where original paintings of pink-cheeked cherubs against puffy white clouds smile down on diners. Four exquisite depictions of Michelangelo's *Virgin* grace the room, painted by the People's Liberation Army when they occupied the premises after 1949.

Modern China's founding fathers

Leave the restaurant heading east on Gaolan Road and walk a block south to **Sun Yat-sen's Former Residence ➎** (Sun Zhongshan Guju: daily 9am–4.30pm; entrance fee) at 7 Xiangshan Road. The Kuomintang party that he established in 1905 sought to replace the ailing Qing dynasty with democratic leadership, and finally succeeded in 1911. Considered the father of modern China, Sun – who has the distinction of being the only political figure revered by both Taiwan and the mainland – lived here with his wife Soong Ching Ling from 1918–24. Listen to the taped introduction of the tour emanating from a gramophone, and you will realise that the Edwardian-era house reflects a China on the brink of modernity. Among the plush Chinese carpets, artwork and gleaming blackwood furniture – all supposedly originals despite the house having been looted by the Japanese – is a 1924 picture of Sun and Soong in front of the first aeroplane in China.

Tree-shaded Sinan Road, lined with a dozen different architectural styles, is also the site of **Zhou Enlai's Former Residence ➏** (Zhou Enlai Gongguan: daily 9.30am–5pm, closed 11.30am–1pm; entrance fee), at No. 73, where he lived in 1946 when he was head of the Shanghai branch of the Communist Party. Elaborately-carved ceiling medallions and mouldings contrast with the bare wooden floors and simple furnishings in this 1922 Spanish-style villa.

Aside from a small bedroom on the first floor, where Zhou's battered suitcase sits poignantly next to his desk, the rest of the house was devoted to the underground revolution: Communist newspapers were produced on the second floor and the third floor housed a dormitory for comrades who needed a safe house. From the porch, the Kuomintang surveillance house that kept a constant watch on Zhou is visible. In a separate building, an exhibition hall documents his life, and a statue of the young Zhou with fresh flower offerings at his feet is a testament to his status as one of China's best-loved leaders.

Past **Ruijin Hospital** (Ruijin Yi Yuan) at 197 Ruijin No. 2 Road, one of the city's major hospitals set in the tranquil grounds of the former French Aurora University, a short walk along Shaoxing Road leads to the antique-filled and atmospheric salon of photographer Deke Erh (Erh Dongqiang), the **Old China Hand Reading Room** (Hanyuan Shuwu) at 27 Shaoxing Road. This is a good place to browse through architecture books; particularly apt is *Frenchtown*, part of a series on old Shanghai architecture photographed by Erh and written by Shanghai architectural historian Tess Johnston.

Map below

Statue of Sun Yat-sen at his former residence. Sun is considered by historians to be the father of modern China.

From racing dogs to restaurants

The busy traffic choking Ruijin No. 2 Road yields to the sprawling lawns and grand manor houses of the **Ruijin Guesthouse** ❼ (Ruijin Bin'guan), at 118 Ruijin No. 2 Road, the former Morriss estate. H.E. Morriss, Jr, son of the founder-owner of the *North China Daily News*, built the estate with its four villas in 1928. Morriss, an avid horse and greyhound breeder and racer, would walk his greyhounds through a back door in the estate and out directly to the greyhound race track, the Canidrome, which is today the Jingwen Flower Market

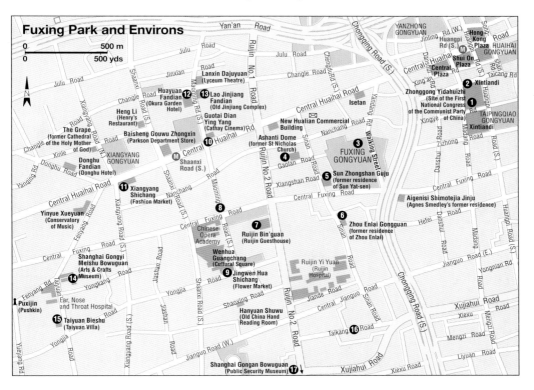

Fuxing Park and Environs

(see below). Building 3, which houses the **Art Deco Garden Bar and Café** (Maoming Road (S) entrance; tel: 6472 5222 ext. 3006), also harbours a magnificent piece of stained glass, depicting a tiger in a jungle. It is Shanghai's only surviving piece of stained glass from the Siccawei (Xujiahui) Orphanage stained glass workshop – the rest were smashed during the Cultural Revolution.

The Morrisses lived well until the very end; the date on the stained glass is 1949 and the last Morriss lived out his years in the estate's gatehouse. Guests at the Ruijin Guesthouse today live well too, socialising at the chic restaurants and bars that now fill the old estate's villas. In addition to Art Deco Café, there is **Face Bar and Restaurant** (Building 4; tel: 6466 4328), a Southeast Asian fantasy of deep colours, candlelight and carved wood. It has a tented Indian restaurant (Hazara) downstairs and a Thai restaurant (La Na Thai) upstairs.

Where nightbirds and flowers converge

Leaving Ruijin by the Maoming Road gate takes one directly to the nightlife centre on **Maoming Road (S)** ❽, a rowdy strip filled with dancers, ravers and the Shanghai "head shakers", who toss their heads to the screaming techno beat. Hot clubs change like chameleons, but **Judy's Too** (176 Maoming Road (S); tel: 6473 1417) is a stalwart, always packing in crowds every night of the week, and the nearby **Buddha Bar** (172 Maoming Road (S); tel: 6415 2688), where Buddhist icons gaze down on frenzied night moves, has a big following as well. For the most sophisticated French meal (and the best profiteroles) in the city, head for **C'est la Vie** (207 Maoming Road (S); tel: 6415 9567) in the next block.

The **Jingwen Flower Market** ❾ (Jingwen Hua Shichang, also known as Shanghai Wenhua Guangchang: daily 7am–7pm) is to the west, at the end of

Maoming Road, located in a portion of the old Canidrome. On weekends, the entrance to the flower market is crowded with wedding cars being decorated. Inside, masses of tulips, roses, lilies, gerberas, tuberoses and other exotica ring the perimeter of the fan-shaped building, while suppliers race through the narrow corridors, weighed down with blooms and elaborate floral arrangements. In the northwest corner, the terraced steps where the Canidrome boys used to race up and down collecting betting slips are now given over to the making of silk flowers.

Head back north on Shaanxi Road (S) to **Central Huaihai Road** ❿. One of Shanghai's major streets, Huaihai Road cuts an east–west swath through the city *(see map on page 163)* but this middle section is the city's most fashionable stretch for shopping. The outdoor plaza of the **Parkson Department Store**, corner of Central Huaihai Road and Shaanxi Road, is the venue for lively weekend entertainment such as modelling shows and interactive art, while a block north into Shaanxi Road (S), between the designer knock-off shoe boutiques, is the popular Shanghainese restaurant **Henry** (Heng Li) at 8 Xinle Road (tel: 5403 3448), serving up home cooking in a simple yet chic setting.

A centre for fakes and cheap originals

Heading west from Parkson, Huaihai is packed with shops, boutiques and restaurants. Pause at the gargantuan **Xiangyang Fashion Market** ⓫ (Xiangyang Shichang), a big, brash bazaar. Stalls burgeon in every direction, spilling their wares in seeming disarray (each one actually bears a number and a licence), and the variety is astounding. Xiangyang is known for its fakes – brand-name bags, clothes, shoes, watches – but there are illegally gotten genuine products as well. There are down jackets, linen tablecloths, beaded bags, DVD holders, silk table runners, Chinese *qipao* dresses, Hawaiian shirts, candles and Red Army hats. Strange characters out of a Dickens novel pop up at every turn, hoarsely whispering, "CD? DVD?" It's a constantly shifting scene; overwhelming to some, but perhaps paradise to others.

To recover from a shopping spree – or to plan one – while enjoying an overview of the market, ask for a table on the second-floor balcony of **Café Montmartre** (55–57 Xiangyang Road (S); tel: 5404 7658), just by the market's Xiangyang Road (S) exit.

Xiangyang Park (Xiangyang Gongyuan: daily 6am–6pm; free), across the street from the market on Huaihai, with its ancient trees and park benches, is another soothing alternative. At this point, Huaihai yields to upscale furniture showrooms, ending at designer department store **Maison Mode** (Mei Mei). Across the street, the building that looks like a Marseilles villa originally housed the families of the French Concession police officers. Today, the families of Chinese police officers live here.

Retrace your steps eastwards on Huaihai, past the art deco **Cathay Cinema** (Guotai Dian Ying Yuan), at 870 Central Huaihai Road, that screens the latest movies in Chinese, and take a short detour south into Maoming Road for its cluster of fashion boutiques and expert tailors, as well as the restaurant **1931** (112 Maoming Road (S); tel: 6472 5264), serving home-style Shanghainese food amidst evocative old Shang-

Bootleg DVDs are aplenty at Xiangyang market. However, the pirated stuff may not work on your expensive DVD player back home.

BELOW: Jingwen Flower Market.

hai décor. Back on Huaihai, continuing east, the street is jammed with department
stores: **Hualian Commercial Building**; **New Hualian Commercial Building**,
a major children's department store; Japanese giant **Isetan**; IT mall **Hong Kong
Plaza**, which also has the wild **Rojam** disco (tel: 6390 7181) on its top floor; and
Shui On Plaza, linked to **Central Plaza** by a walkway interspersed with wedding boutiques displaying flamboyant ballgowns *(see page 169)*.

The **Okura Garden Hotel** ⓬ (Huayuan Fandian) at 58 Maoming Road (S),
north of Central Huaihai Road, with its spreading lawns and fountains, is a welcome
oasis after the buzz of Huaihai. The original entrance lobby (on Maoming Road)
of the former Cercle Sportif Francais, or French Club, still features the grandeur of
glittering gold mosaic, polished marble columns and a dramatic stairway, all
designed in 1926 by the French Concession's master architect, Paul Veysseyre.

The club – which once had 20 lawn tennis courts, an indoor pool, a rooftop
terrace for dancing al fresco and a ballroom with a stained glass ceiling that is
still intact – became a private guesthouse for Mao on his Shanghai journeys
before its conversion into a hotel. This could be the reason why the Grecian
nudes holding up the ballroom lobby's columns were not destroyed during the
Cultural Revolution but were merely covered up; although Mao is definitely the
reason for the eight-room reinforced concrete bunker built in case of a nuclear
attack. The bunker – the entrance of which is found in the inconspicuous garden shed by the fountain and is usually locked – connects to the **Old Jinjiang
Complex** ⓭ (Lao Jinjiang Fandian) across the street.

The complex comprises several buildings, chief of which is the historical
Jinjiang Hotel. The brainchild of tycoon Victor Sassoon, the hotel was a risky
investment when it was built as the Cathay Mansions in 1928. It was the first high-

rise to be built on swampy ground, and there was no guarantee that downtown sophisticates would want to live in what was then the countryside. As it turned out, Cathay Mansions was so successful that the company built two more housing complexes on the premises, the Grosvenor House (now an all-suite hotel) and the low-rise Grosvenor Gardens, now used as offices. The Jinjiang secured its place in contemporary Shanghai history as the venue where US President Richard Nixon and Chinese Foreign Minister Zhou Enlai signed the Shanghai Communique in 1972, the first step towards normalising US-China relations. Jinjiang's international food street, an alley to the right of the Maoming Road entrance, includes the upscale **Tandoor Indian Restaurant** (tel: 6472 5494) and **Mazisaka** (tel: 6415 7979), which serves Japanese cuisine. Also found here is a **Shanghai Tang** store, which sells funky Chinese-inspired clothing and accessories.

Margot Fonteyn danced at the Lyceum

Continuing north on Maoming Road, on the Changle Road corner, is **Lyceum Theatre** (Lanxin Dajuyuan) at 57 Maoming Road (S), built in 1930 as the home of the British Shanghai Amateur Dramatic Society – and where the great ballerina Margot Fonteyn performed as a girl. Today, the theatre hosts acrobatics and Chinese opera. Across the street is the stylish **JJ Dickson** shopping mall (400 Changle Road), offering Versace and Lalique, and across from JJ Dickson is "*qipao* row", a string of boutiques specialising in the traditional high-necked and form-fitting Chinese silk dresses.

The sapphire-hued onion domes of the former **Cathedral of the Holy Mother of God**, a 1931 Russian Orthodox Church, are located two blocks southwest along Xinle Road. Stripped of its former glory, it is now home to the popular Shanghainese restaurant **The Grape** (tel: 6472 0486) and a stylish Continental eatery called **Dome** (tel: 5404 4388). Inspired by the Cathedral of the Saviour in Moscow, it used to hold 2,500 worshippers. Locals say its paintings of six cherubim and seraphim, now gone, resembled the faces of the local artist's lovers.

Continue west on Xinle Road and take a detour left towards the old wing of the **Donghu Hotel** (Donghu Fandian) at 70 Donghu Road. This was a generous gift to the Green Gang Triad boss, Du Yuesheng, though he never actually lived here. The adjacent restaurant, **The 7** at what else – 7 Donghu Road (tel: 6415 7777), serves Shanghai cuisine in a grand brick villa overlooking a manicured lawn.

Students at the prestigious **Conservatory of Music** (Yinyue Xueyuan), a short walk south to 20 Fenyang Road, give classical music concerts on Sunday evenings (7pm, during the school year only). Continuing south on Fenyang Road, head for the **Shanghai Arts and Crafts Museum** ⓮ (Shanghai Gongyi Meishu Bowuguan: daily 9am–4.30pm; entrance fee). Its collection of dying crafts includes the indigenous *hai-pai*, or East–West fusion art characteristic of early 20th-century Shanghai. Set on lush grounds, the grand whitewashed mansion, its curved façade reminiscent of the American White House, was designed by Ladislau Hudec in 1905 for the director of the French Compagnie des Tramways, and was also the home of

Map on page 163

TIP

Past the Pushkin statue at 150 Fenyang Road is Paulaner Brauhaus (tel: 6474 5700), a microbrewery and one of the city's most popular bars. The renovated old villa is packed to the rafters on weekends.

BELOW: Margot Fonteyn once performed at the Lyceum Theatre.

Map
on page
163

*Blue-and-white
Chinese pottery for
sale at a Taikang
Road warehouse.*

BELOW:
Shanghai Arts and
Crafts Museum

Shanghai's first mayor, Chen Yi. Just south of the museum, where Fenyang and Yueyang roads intersect, stands a **bust of Alexander Pushkin** (Puxijin). Dedicated in 1937 on the centennial of his death, the statue was damaged in the Cultural Revolution but has since been restored.

A five-minute walk south, past the Shanghai Ear, Nose and Throat Hospital, is **Taiyuan Villa** ⓯ (Taiyuan Bieshu) at 160 Taiyuan Road, a mansard-roofed mansion straight from France. Built for the Comte du Pac de Marsoulies in the 1920s, it was General George Marshall's residence while he was trying to broker a last-minute deal between the Communists and the Kuomintang, and was later commandeered by Madam Mao. It's now a guesthouse, and her Shanghai-deco furnished suite is available to guests. The interior is remarkably intact, with a spiralling wrought-iron staircase and the Comte's coat of arms in the fireplace.

The **Taikang Road** ⓰ art quarter, to the east, is an industrial-chic series of old warehouses and factories in an anonymous side street that has been turned into an arts space. It is anchored by a 3,200-sq metre (34,445-sq ft) former candy factory that now serves as the offices of advertising and design firms. Photographer Deke Erh has a studio here, the **Shanghai Deke Erh Centre** (Erh Dongqiang Zhongxin) at No. 2 Lane 210 (daily 9am–5pm), as does artist Chen Yifei next door, while the **Hands in Clay** pottery studio is at No. 1.

Further south, the **Shanghai Public Security Museum** ⓱ (Shanghai Gongan Bowuguan: Mon–Sat 9am–4.30pm; entrance fee) at 518 Ruijin Road (S) caters to crime connoisseurs. See the wax figure of a red-turbanned Sikh guard and a pistol with a gold folding handle that crime boss "Pockmarked" Huang once carried, as well as a selection of artefacts that offers glimpses of Shanghai's evil underbelly – pornographic porcelain vases and hand-painted courtesan's cards. ❏

Playing Dress Up: Shanghai Brides

As the sepia wedding photographs in the antiques markets show, Shanghai's brides have been dressing up in clouds of tulle and lacy white gowns for at least a century now. After a brief post-Cultural Revolution respite, when wedding photographs consisted of black-and-white portraits of couples dressed in their best Mao suits (cheeks and lips hand-tinted), the wedding belle dream has burst into full flower.

More specifically, the white wedding gown photograph. The gowns displayed in the windows of the ritzy salons found along **Central Huaihai Road** are not for walking down aisles or kneeling at altars, they are there for the all-important bridal portrait. Bigger than the wedding banquet and certainly much bigger than the civil ceremony, the bridal photograph session is *the* most important day in a Shanghai girl's life. A wedding day may last 24 hours, but pictures are forever.

Lured by the fairytale-like dresses in the shop windows, potential customers are thrust a thick photo album showing portraits of satisfied customers in their wedding finery and the different packages to choose from, in different combinations of dresses, photographic backgrounds, makeup and hairstyles.

Downstairs, porcelain-skinned women, often seated before giant mirrors in front of the shops' glassed streetside frontages, have make-up patted on, transforming them from ordinary mortals into flawless visages of ruby-lipped, wide-eyed beauties. Upstairs, they search through the racks for the gowns of their dreams: Cinderella white? Scarlett O'Hara red, with ringlets to match? Bright blue, festooned with roses, or off-the-shoulder taxicab yellow? Or, perhaps, a Chinese *qipao*? Or probably all of the above. Unfettered by notions of Western tradition, they select fabulously flamboyant hoop gowns, with built-in bust enhancers and big seams, which nimble tailors adjust to the customers' size within moments.

For most brides, the wedding outfits are a once-in-a-lifetime dress-up indulgence, and the whole get-up can cost anywhere from RMB 2,000–10,000 – a year's salary for some. Photographs can take place several months before the wedding banquet, and the photo is often used in the wedding invitation.

Brides-to-be and their adoring husbands pose for the camera against backdrops of Paris or ancient China, with the women (and some men) changing outfits and hairdos each time. Some choose to be photographed outdoors against the backdrop of Shanghai's most famous sights and gardens, and may be seen tramping down the street with their entourage, or leaning atop the decorated Mercedes that is the modern-day sedan chair.

It is enough to make someone who was married during the Communist heyday envious, but China's entrepreneurs have thought of that, too. Shanghai's Twilight Red studio caters to those who missed out the first time, offering gowns sized for women over 40 and photographers who are patient with costume changes by 60-year-olds. ❑

RIGHT: a white Western-style wedding gown is what every Chinese bride dreams of.

HUAIHAI AND HENGSHAN

By day, view quiet, stately mansions – once the homes of taipans, consuls and concubines – for a feel of old Shanghai. By night, hole up in the best live jazz bars the city has to offer

Map
on page
172

The upscale Huaihai and Hengshan area has a split personality, drawing both sedate, highbrow residents and a swinging crowd. Diplomats, high-ranking party officials (and even the infamous Gang of Four in the past) like the prestigious address for its wide boulevards, tree-lined streets, generously sized villas – and the rare quality of quiet – in a downtown location. Even the "common people", the Chinese parlance for the average man, in this area aren't so common after all. Former missionary school graduates populate the parks and markets, and several still live in the shabby grandeur of apartments and houses built by their families half a century ago, waiting for someone to pay the million-dollar price tag that these properties now command.

The road, too, reflects the character of its residents: Huaihai Road is a brash consumer paradise to the east (*see page 165*) but here it is toned down. Yet it's not all well-behaved matrons in this stylish part of the city: Nightfall sees Shanghai's party animals heading for the throbbing, neon-lit strip of bars, restaurants and discos – and the best jazz in town.

The country manors of the French Concession were located here when this was the Avenue Joffre – and their size and grandeur have made them a prime diplomatic enclave. The corner of Huaihai and Urumqi roads (Wulumuqi Lu) is rich with consulates, the flags of five nations flying over vintage mansions. Prime among these, at 1431 Central Huaihai Road, is the Mediterranean-style **French Consul-General's Residence ❶** (Faguo Lingshiju; closed to the public), built for the French Basset family in 1921, and later home to colourful characters such as American taipan Frank Raven, whose years of high living put him in jail for defrauding his company's investors.

The residence changed hands several more times over the years, becoming the French Consul's residence in the 1980s. The house, with its original tiled floors, circular sun-room and lush garden, is opened to the public for charitable events such as the Historic House and Garden Tours (send an e-mail to *SHHA-subscribe@topica.com*). Otherwise, curious visitors can glimpse the roof and cheerful sunflower tiles that line the top of the house over the high walls.

A taipan's mansion

Across the street, at 1469 Central Huaihai Road, straight-backed guards protect the rambling mansion which has served as the **US Consulate-General ❷** (Meiguo Lingshiguan: closed to the public) since 1980. Despite its decidedly neo-classical Western appearance, the house was built in the early part of the 20th century for a prominent Chinese entrepreneur and Qing government minister, Shang Shu. After stints as the resi-

LEFT:
traffic policemen
along the tree-lined
residential section
of Huaihai Road.
BELOW:
French Consul-
General's residence.

RIGHT: the 1924
Normandie building
is reminiscent of
New York's Flatiron.

dence of the Jardine Matheson taipan and the Swiss Consulate, it was bought by
Rong Hongyuan of the powerful Rong family, one of Shanghai's wealthiest industrial dynasties. The house, apparently still owned by him, stands today because it
was placed under lock and key during the Cultural Revolution. Briefly a state
guesthouse before the American government rented it, its 1½ hectares (3½ acres)
includes a vast lawn, a traditional Chinese rock garden and a lovely orange grove.

Next door, at 1517 Central Huaihai Road, stands the massive neo-classical
Japanese Consul-General's Residence (Riben Lingshiju: closed to the public), built in 1900 and once the home of northern warlord Duan Qi Rui. It is said
that the same construction firm built all three houses, and reports of an underground tunnel linking the three buildings remain unconfirmed. Across the street
on Urumqi Road is the former **Singapore Consulate** (now unoccupied) at 400
Urumqi Road (S) and its Spanish-style neighbour on 17 Fuxing Road (W), the
Consulate of the Islamic Republic of Iran, whose bulletin board on the outside
wall shows the best marketing effort of all in its alluring travel posters of Iran.

Asia's largest library

The stately air of the consulates is enhanced by the white-tiled **Shanghai
Library ❸** (Shanghai Tushuguan: daily 8.30am–8.30pm), standing at 1555
Central Huaihai Road, next to the Japanese Consul's residence. The Greek-
style amphitheatre that fronts the building attracts early morning sword dancers
and library employees who do their morning exercises here, both in winter and
summer. The light-filled spacious facility, opened in 1996, is Asia's largest
library. It has collections of old and rare Chinese books, the Chinese Cultural
Celebrities Manuscript Library, Concession-era photographs and archives, and

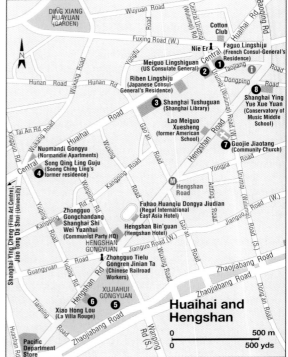

**Huaihai and
Hengshan**

0   500 m
0   500 yds

Map
on page
172

a genealogy section for Chinese throughout the diaspora. Of particular note is a rare 8,000-volume Ming dynasty edition of the *Taoist Scripture*.

From the intellectual to the material: lifestyle shops such as **Simply Flowers** (1554 Central Huaihai Road) and **Lee's Décor** (1586 Central Huaihai Road) are crammed into the tiny shop spaces across the street, offering candles, designer homeware, lamps and frames. Further west along Huaihai Road is the red-brick **Normandie** (Nuomandi Gongyu), a local landmark that dominates the north side of the street. Almost identical to Manhattan's Flatiron building, the structure is known locally as the Titanic because of its remarkable resemblance to the great cruise liner. Built in 1924, the Normandie – also known as the Intersavin Society (I.S.S.) apartments – was built with 76 apartments on six floors and 30 servants' quarters. Today, 700 people fit into that space.

The Soong House

Charlie Soong locked his daughter Ching Ling in her room to prevent her from marrying the much older and still married Dr Sun Yat-sen, but she made history by climbing out of the second-storey window of **Soong Ching Ling's Former Residence ❹** (Song Qing Ling Guju: daily 9am–4.30pm; entrance fee) to elope with Sun. Located at 1843 Central Huaihai Road, directly across from the Normandie, the lovely house is where she returned after Sun's death, having donated their Sinan Road house as a museum. Today, Soong's house – where she lived from 1948 to 1963 – stands as a monument to her, and as a triumph for the Communist Party, to which she remained loyal despite her family's leadership roles in the opposing Kuomintang government. Her house is incongruously furnished with 1960s furniture but of interest are the photographs of Soong with a host of legends

A young Soong Ching Ling at her residence.

BELOW:
porch and gardens at Soong Ching Ling's house.

from Mao to Nehru. A modern building in the compound documents the extraordinary Soong clan in letters and artefacts, and in the garage sit two ebony limousines: a 1952 Jim presented by Stalin and Soong's own Chinese Red Flag. The lanes behind the house make up a nice walk well imbued with local atmosphere.

The **Shanghai Film Art Centre** (Shanghai Ying Cheng), southwest on 160 Xinhua Road, is the site of the annual Shanghai Film Festival that screens both local and international movies. Next door is the **Crowne Plaza Shanghai** at 400 Panyu Road, a popular business hotel in a slightly out-of-the-way location. Continuing west, restaurants and embassies are housed in impressive mansions along this tree-shaded street renowned for its architectural variety. **Goya** (357 Xinhua Road; tel: 6280 1256), a candlelit, trendy little vodka bar with an impressive selection of house-infused vodkas and martinis, is a favourite hangout of the artsy crowd.

China's second-oldest university

Shanghai's prestigious **Jiao Tong University** (Jiao Tong Da Shui), southeast from here on 1954 Huashan Road, is China's second-oldest university and counts China's leadership among its graduates. The extensive campus is dotted with stately early 20th-century buildings, now home to the university's renowned science and engineering faculties. The **C.Y. Tung Maritime Museum** (Dong Zhi Yun Chuan Yun Bowuguan: open daily 1–5.30pm; free), dedicated to the late Shanghai-born shipping tycoon and housed in a refurbished 19th-century dormitory, has exhibits on the history of Chinese shipping and the legacy of the Tung's family shipping business. C.Y.'s son, Tung Chee Hwa, is presently the chief executive of Hongkong, and although often criticised soundly for his ineffective leadership in the city, is well-regarded by the Communist powers that be.

Newly woven reed wattle fences are an old sight making a comeback in this neighbourhood. Look for the fences around Soong Ching Ling's house, the Shanghai Communist Party Headquarters and the red-brick mansion on the corner of Kangping and Wukang roads.

BELOW: main entrance to Jiao Tong University.

Map on page 172

Exit the university on leafy Kangping Road, where the French Concession aura is enhanced by broad pavements and quiet streets. Part of the quiet stems from the fact that many of the high-powered residents who live here work at the ominous grey building that stretches around the corner at Wanping Road. This is the unmarked **Headquarters of the Shanghai Communist Party** (Zhongguo Gongchandang Shanghai Shi Wei Yuanhui) and is closely guarded by sharp-looking soldiers with equally sharp eyes – watch for a moment too long the shiny black cars with darkened windows that drive in, and you'll be sent on your way.

Head south on Wanping to Hengshan Road and the pristine, manicured grounds of **Xujiahui Park ❺** (Xujiahui Gongyuan: daily 6am–6pm), which is part of the city's ongoing greening project. There are neat beds of flowering plants, a shimmering lake and a controversial raised glass bridge (concern that peeping Toms might gather underneath resulted in its glass floor being boarded over).

La Villa Rouge ❻ (Xiao Hong Lou; tel: 6431 6639), a restaurant and bar housed in a red-brick villa at 811 Hengshan Road along the park, is the former EMI studio that has recorded some of Shanghai's most famous voices, including Zhou Xuan, the legendary "golden throat" of the 1930s, and Nie Er, the composer of the Chinese national anthem. The building remained a recording studio throughout Shanghai's turbulent history: under the Japanese, the Kuomintang, and finally as the Shanghai branch of China Records. The present occupants have assembled a small museum housing the vintage recording equipment that was used here. A smokestack from a British factory stands incongruously in the park's southern corner, dominating the landscape like an industrial-age pagoda.

Tai chi exponent at Hengshan Park.

When in Shanghai, bar-hop as the locals do

Cross the street to the small island at the intersection of Hengshan and Guangyuan roads, where stands the **Chinese Railroad Workers Memorial**, a twisted helix sculpture made from railroad tracks that was a gift from the American state of Illinois. Far less tranquil is the pocket-handkerchief sized **Hengshan Park** (Hengshan Gongyuan: 6am–6pm; free), across the road on the corner of Wanping and Hengshan. Formerly Petain Park, it was laid out by the French in 1935 and re-landscaped in 1987. Half a century's worth of lush greenery gives the park an almost tropical feel. Beginning at dawn, the park buzzes with *tai chi* practitioners in one corner, fan dancers in another, and crowding the entrance, elderly ballroom dancers waltzing to the tunes of yesteryear.

Many of these elderly dancers would remember the refurbished **Hengshan Hotel** (Hengshan Bin'guan) at 534 Hengshan Road across the street when it was the Picardie Apartments, built in 1934. Next door, the **Regal International East Asia Hotel** at 516 Hengshan Road is making history of its own as the home of the city's most exclusive health club and tennis centre, favoured by diplomat spouses and party officials.

Going northeast, warm up at Hengshan Road's shops and boutiques before the bar strip begins. Bar-hopping is an integral part of Shanghai's nightlife culture, and come nightfall, party animals begin working their way down Hengshan Road with options from the English pub-like **Sasha's** (9 Dongping Road,

BELOW: another mansion-turned-restaurant, La Villa Rouge.

House 11) to raucous **Bourbon Street** (191 Hengshan Road), the downright seedy **Hello**, and the throbbing disco-beat **Real Love** (10 Hengshan Road).

The stately red-brick building next to Real Love club is the former **Shanghai American School**, the first signpost of the American community that once flourished here. The school was set up in 1912 to educate the children of American missionaries and moved to this location in 1923. By 1934, a booming Shanghai saw enrolment at the school pass the 600 mark. Designed by American architect Henry Murphy to resemble Independence Hall in Philadelphia, the building today houses a naval research facility and is closed to the public.

Every Sunday, a small community of Christians gather to worship at the ivy-covered **Community Church** ❼ (Guojie Jiaotang) at 53 Hengshan Road, founded by a group of Americans around 1925. The beautiful red-brick Protestant church, with its rosewood pews and high ceilings, is worth a visit at any time of the day, but particularly during services. Chinese-language services are especially popular, with the congregation spilling onto the lawn. To curb proselytising, Chinese nationals must worship separately from foreign passport holders. The latter may attend the Chinese services, as celebrities from Jimmy Carter to Bishop Tutu have, listening to the translated service through headphones.

Elegant restaurant quarter

Past **41 Hengshan Road**, one of the city's most elegant apartment houses, is a mini-restaurant quarter. Down what looks like an unpromising lane, **Yang's Kitchen** (No. 3 Lane 9 Hengshan Road; tel: 6445 8418) serves good, old-fashioned Shanghainese cuisine. Further down the block are **Sasha's** (9 Dongping Road, House 11; tel: 6474 6166), where French cuisine is served on the second floor in an old world setting and **Simply Thai** (5-C Dongping Road; tel: 6445 9551), whose piquant cuisine is served amidst elegant minimalist decor. **The Blarney Stone** (5-A Dongping Road; tel: 6415 7496), the city's most authentic Irish pub – complete with Irish lads and lassies – serves stick-to-your-ribs pub grub. All three restaurants, located round the corner on Dongping Road, are fortunate enough to occupy the grounds of the **Shanghai Conservatory of Music Middle School** ❽ (Shanghai Ying Yue Xue Yuan), which has an idyllic pond and resident geese and goats.

The Western brick villas in the compound were the former Shanghai home of the powerful Soong family, who lived here like dynastic royalty. Sasha's restaurant was the home of T.V., the most prominent of the three Soong sons, who served as Kuomintang finance minister and was once said to be the richest man in the world. The villa to the right of Sasha's was the home of Kuomintang leader Chiang Kai-shek and Soong May Ling, the sister of Ching Ling and a power-broker in her own right. To the right of the Chiangs was the home of H.H. Kung, financial wizard, Bank of China head, briefly Kuomintang finance minister, and husband of Soong Ai Ling, the oldest sister. Only Ching Ling lived apart from the rest of the Soong clan, and only Ching Ling remained in China. In fact the Chinese say of the three Soong sisters: "May Ling loved power, Ai Ling loved money, but Ching Ling loved China".

TIP

English-language Sunday services are held 4pm at the Community Church on Hengshan Road, along with Sunday school. The largest Protestant church in Shanghai also conducts Christmas and Easter services in English.

BELOW: Sunday service at the Community Church.

Where jazz is king

Jazz was old Shanghai's signature tune – 1,200 jazz bands, it is said, performed here in the 1930s – and new Shanghai seems to have embraced it as well. From Dongping Road, its a 10-minute walk northwest to the darkened, smoky **Cotton Club** (8 Fuxing Road), a local legend in Shanghai jazz circles. There are jazz clubs elsewhere in the city, but this is the one by which all others are measured by. Cotton Club's house band plays jazz standards with such verve that even Wynton Marsalis stopped by to jam some years ago when he was in town. Tuesday is open mike night, when the atmosphere at the club is imbued with an almost underground feeling.

A five-minute walk west, past two of French Concession architect Paul Veysseyre's classic art deco apartment buildings on the northeast and northwest corners of Fuxing and Urumqi roads, are a Tibetan accessories shop, a small antique shop and further down (closer to Wukang Road) **Madam Mao's Dowry** at 70 Fuxing Road (W) (daily 10am–6pm), a gallery that features innovative exhibitions such as the art of the Cultural Revolution.

The lovely oasis called **Ding Xiang Garden** (Ding Xiang Huayuan) at 849 Huashan Road is a 10-minute walk to the northwest. The stucco-and-wood English-style house, with its porches and gingerbread trim, was built in 1900 by an American architect. The Qing dynasty reformer Li Hongzhang acquired the house for his favourite concubine Clove (Ding Xiang), and stored his vast collection of books here. The building is currently used by high-ranking party officials, but the **Xian Yue Hien Restaurant** (tel: 6251 1166) in the compound allows both access and delicious views of the garden and its pavilion, surrounded by walls topped with writhing dragons. ❑

Map on page 172

The wide, beautiful expanses of green in Shanghai's parks are strictly off-limits; visitors are confined to the concrete walkways and plazas built expressly for the purpose of walking. Kite flying, too, was recently forbidden.

BELOW: jazz reigns supreme at the Cotton Club.

JING AN

This posh area takes in the larger-than-life, architecturally confused Shanghai Exhibition Centre, the swanky one-stop Shanghai Centre's restaurants and shops, and the long-suffering Jing An Temple

Map on page 180

Top-of-the-line office buildings, showy shopping malls and a constellation of five-star hotels define the prestigious business and commercial area of **Jing An**, home to some of the most expensive real estate in Shanghai. Outside the foreign Concessions until the boundaries expanded in 1899, Jing An's wide open spaces attracted the Hardoons and the Kadoories, two of the richest Jewish families in old Shanghai. Each built concrete symbols of their wealth in the form of magnificent mansions just minutes away from each other. Here, too, were the rambling Bubbling Well cemetery and the Bubbling Well temple, whose Chinese name – Jing An, or "Tranquil Repose" – gives the area its name, as well as the legendary Paramount nightclub.

The cemetery has yielded to a park, the actual "bubbling well" has long been smothered by a busy highway, and the lavish Hardoon mansion has become the site of a Sino-Soviet symbol of friendship. But not everything is radically different. Following an almost continuous period of renovation, prayers are offered again at Jing An Temple. They're dancing again at the Paramount, and the moneyed class is flocking to the area's prestigious office buildings and shops. The road's western flank, Nanjing Road (W), dominating the area, can still lay claim to being "one of the seven most interesting streets in the world", as a 1930s guidebook avowed when the stretch was known as Bubbling Well Road.

A hotel out of a fairytale

The fairy-tale steeples and spires of **Moller Villa** ❶ (Ma Lei Bie Shu Fandian) rise like a fairytale Gothic fantasy at 30 Shaanxi Road (S). After spending the post-Liberation years as the Communist Youth League, the house that Swedish shipping magnate Eric Moller built in 1936 has been restored to something of its former splendour as a boutique hotel owned by the Hengshan group. Moller was a passionate racer of horses, and a statue of his favourite steed stands in the garden; its body is rumoured to be buried on the grounds.

Across the road, at the intersection of Shaanxi and Weihai, a banner proclaims the beginning of the rather more pedestrian "car parts" street. Streets specialising in particular trades are a Shanghai tradition, and these two blocks running north along Weihai Road boast every imaginable car part, all stuffed into narrow shops. In-between stands the **United Press Building** (Wenxin Dasha) home of Shanghai's largest-circulation daily newspaper, the *Xinmin Rebao*, and the **Four Seasons Hotel** (Si Ji Jiudian) at 500 Weihai Road, which adds a little panache to the neighbourhood.

The ivy-covered Greek Revival **Ohel Rachel Synagogue** ❷ (You Tai Jiaotong) at 500 Shaanxi Road (N), a short walk northwest, was built in 1920

LEFT: historic Moller Villa is now a boutique hotel. **BELOW:** interior, Moller Villa.

*Meilongzhen
restaurant at Nanjing
Road (W) is well
known for its
delicious
Shanghainese fare
(see this page).*

by Jacob Sassoon in memory of his wife Rachel. The synagogue, facing Jerusalem, served as the spiritual home for the city's wealthy Sephardic Jewish community until 1952. It was used as a stable by the Japanese during World War II and later as a warehouse and lecture hall, complete with a portrait of Mao over the ark, during the post-Liberation years.

It was only in 1998 that the synagogue was renovated and sanctified for the visit of former US First Lady Hillary Clinton and Secretary of State Madeleine Albright. After granting the Jewish community the use of the synagogue for a Rosh Hashanah service in 1999, the government – which does not recognise Judaism as an official religion – has been tight-fisted about permitting its use for regular worship services. The building is now on the World Monuments watch list. Next door is the former **Shanghai Jewish School**, established by Horace Kadoorie in 1932. Both the synagogue and school officially belong to the Shanghai Education Bureau and are not open to the public.

Designer malls where Shanghai's yuppies shop

Head south to Nanjing Road, where grimy 1930s buildings begin to give way to Starbuck's cafés, one in every other block. The Fifth Avenue vibe gathers momentum on the north side of Nanjing Road (W), which is wall-to-wall with designer malls: CITC **Square**, **Westgate Mall** and **Plaza 66**, where Shanghai's yuppies flock to sip lattés, savour Häagen-Dazs sundaes and shop at Burberry's. In stark contrast, sunburnt fruit pedlars from the countryside stand outside the gleaming white malls, balancing shoulder poles carrying baskets full of the season's offerings.

Directly across the street from Westgate Mall is **Meilongzhen** ❸ (No. 22 Lane 1081 Nanjing Road (W); tel: 6253 5353), one of the city's most famous

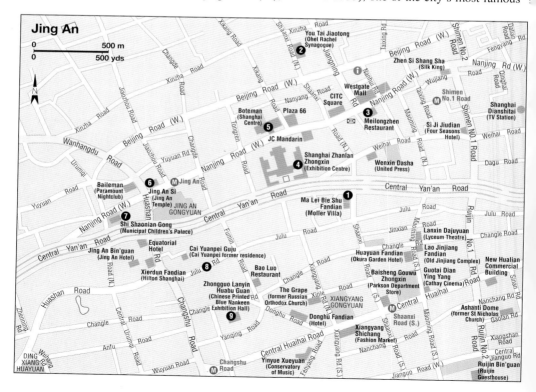

Map on page 180

Chinese restaurants, located in a pink-brick French-style mansion on an unpretentious lane. Briefly Communist Party headquarters, the restaurant serves Shanghainese delicacies in a Victorian dining room where vintage Chinese lanterns and red-lacquered columns coexist agreeably with English rose wallpaper.

The south side of the street has older shops, including the venerable **Silk King** (Zhen Si Shang Sha) at 817 Nanjing Road (W) in the Shanghai Silk Commercial Building. Silk King is a purveyor of Chinese silks to diplomats, aristocrats and tourists (Shanghainese prefer the local fabric markets). The porcelain and souvenir shops here also tend to be overpriced, due in part to two nearby five-star hotels.

A Sino-Soviet symbol of solidarity

One of the two hotels is the **J.C. Mandarin** at 1225 Nanjing Road (W), which, along with the **Shanghai Exhibition Centre** ❹ (Shanghai Zhanlan Zhongxin; entrance at 1000 Yan'an Road) next door, sits on the grounds of *Aili*, one of the Concession-era's most sumptuous estates. *Aili* ("Beloved Li") belonged to Silas Hardoon, a Sephardic Jewish man who arrived penniless in Shanghai and worked his way up from watchman to Shanghai's richest man. His estate, named after his half-French, half-Chinese wife, Luo Jialing *(see margin text right)* was once dotted with pavilions, arched bridges, lakes and bamboo groves.

The Shanghai Exhibition Centre was one of the many buildings constructed in major Chinese cities during the 1950s as an expression of the common cause of the Soviet Union and the People's Republic of China. Designed by a Russian architect, the 9.3-hectare (23-acre) centre is created on a scale for a giant and in a cacophony of styles, including Communist stars, Christmas wreaths, a Roman central dome and a socialist-realist Atlas sculpture – all topped by the

The wife of Silas Hardoon, a Jewish millionaire, was herself a much-whispered about Shanghai legend. Orphaned as a child, Luo Jialing sold flowers and her favours in the old Chinese city, but later became a born-again Buddhist.

LEFT: futuristic Plaza 66 Mall. **BELOW:** Socialist-inspired Shanghai Exhibition Centre.

106-metre (348-ft) gold-plated steeple, inspired by Russian Orthodox church architecture. Once *the* place in China to host exhibitions – Mao Zedong, Deng Xiaoping and Georges Pompidou all passed through these portals – it was eclipsed in the 1990s by newer, more technologically adept exhibition halls. An extensive renovation in 2002 has put it back in the running.

Across the street, the John Portman-designed **Shanghai Centre ❺** is at 1376 Nanjing Road (W). The city's first international residential, business and hotel complex is ground zero for the expatriate population, who need never leave its comforts. There is an upscale grocery shop, bank, post office, clinic, tennis courts, a pool, a Hard Rock Café, the **Portman Ritz-Carlton Hotel** (Boteman Lisi Kaerun Jiuan) and its clutch of restaurants. The **Shanghai Centre Theatre** (Shanghai Shangcheng Juyuan) within the complex is the home of the Shanghai Acrobatics Troupe *(see margin tip)*, or Shanghai Zaji Tuan, which carries on a 2,000-year-old tradition that would dazzle even the most jaded soul.

Heading west, the elaborately festooned neo-classical twin white houses, next to the Shanghai Centre, once belonged to the wealthy Kwok family, owners of the former Wing On Department Store along Nanjing Road. It is now occupied by the **Foreign Affairs Bureau of the Shanghai Municipal Government**.

Don't miss the Shanghai Acrobatics Troupe at Shanghai Centre. Tickets for the nightly 7.30pm show are often sold out, so book ahead (tel: 6279 8663).

BELOW:
lush Jing An Park.

The "Bubbling Well" located

At **Jing An Park** (Jing An Gongyuan), two blocks west on Nanjing Road (W), elderly men sit on benches shaded by an arcade of plane trees that once lined the entrance to Bubbling Well (Yong Quan) cemetery, the park's previous incarnation. The bubbling well itself, a 3rd-century carbonic gas spring that stood at the intersection of Nanjing and Wanhangdu roads, was considered supernatural by the locals. The well has been paved over, but the park has built a reproduction in an area devoted to the eight famous scenes of ancient Jing An Temple. The idyllic **Bali Laguna** restaurant (189 Huashan Road; tel: 6248 697) in the park serving Southeast Asian cuisine has an outdoor terrace that overlooks a lily pond.

The lively **Jing An Temple ❻** (Jing An Si: daily 7.30am–3.30pm; entrance fee) has stood at 1686 Nanjing Road (W) since 1216, when the lapping waves of the Suzhou Creek eroded the foundations of the original temple, built on its banks in 247. Originally called Hudu Chongyuan Temple, it was renamed Jing An in 1008, but became more popularly known in pre-1949 Shanghai as the Bubbling Well temple. Dedicated to Sakyamuni Buddha, whose statue is worshipped in the Grand Hall, the temple has suffered much over the years. It lost many of its statues and scriptures during the Cultural Revolution, when it served as a factory. It also lost its old architecture in 1998, and again in 2002 when a major renovation project was started to reflect its status as one of Shanghai's major tourist attractions – with all-new construction and a shopping mall. You can visit parts of the temple but the reconstruction is only expected to be completed in 2005.

The temple is noted for its rare Mi shrines from a sect that is all the more unusual because its modern development dates to the Communist era. The Mi sect is a branch of Buddhism with its own gods and prac-

Map on page 180

tices, which originated in India and flourished briefly in China during the Tang dynasty. The Japanese took the religion, along with other arts and culture from the Tang era, back to Japan. By the 10th century, the Mi sect had disappeared in China, but not in Japan, where the monk Zhisong found it. He brought it back to China in 1953, when Jing An's Mi shrines were first built, but the vicissitudes of the Cultural Revolution and his own death have meant that the religion is no longer practised.

Playgrounds for adults and children

The **Paramount** (Baileman) at 218 Yuyuan Road, west of Jing An Temple, was one of old Shanghai's great nightclubs, but languished as a movie theatre after 1949. A renovation in 2001 has removed all trace of the original and created a nightclub for new Shanghai, with bright blue neon flashing on the clean lines of the tower and silk roses under the glass dance floor.

To the south is the **Municipal Children's Palace ❼** (Shi Shaonian Gong) at 64 Central Yan'an Road, where gifted children are trained in art, music, drama, dance and, more recently, computers. There are several Children's Palaces in the city but this is the largest and most visited. Built as the Marble Hall – marble was used throughout the house, particularly in the gorgeous fireplaces and hallways – for the fabulously wealthy Jewish Kadoorie family, the mansion was completed in 1924 after six years of construction. Run by a coterie of 43 servants, this was the first house in the city to have air-conditioning. Visitors can come here and watch apple-cheeked children perform under the 5½-metre (18-ft) tall chandeliers in the magnificent ballroom.

The sunny Atrium Café at the **Hilton Shanghai** (Xierdun Fandian) at 250

Jing An Temple, Shanghai's wealthiest, was once famous for its equally wealthy and flamboyant abbot, the towering Khi Vedhu, who kept seven concubines and had White Russian bodyguards.

BELOW: Jing An Temple.

Map on page 180

TIP

For great city views, take a night ride in the glass elevator to the 39th floor of the Hilton Hotel (Xierdun Fandian) at 250 Huashan Road. Note: the elevator is closed in winter.

BELOW: no-holds barred Julu Road nightlife.

Huashan Road, a block south, is a favourite weekend spot for brunch. Across the street at No. 16 Lane 303 Huashan Road is **Cai Yuanpei's Former Residence** (Cai Yuanpei Guju: daily 8.30am–4.30pm, closed Mondays; entrance fee)**,** a German-style villa where education reformer Cai Yuanpei lived in 1937. An exhibition tells the life of the man who was the first Kuomintang minister of education and past president of Jiao Tong University.

One of Shanghai's raunchier strips

On Sundays at 8pm, chamber music concerts by the Shanghai Symphony are performed within the ornate wood-carved interior of the San Diego Room in the 1920s-era **Jing An Hotel** (Jing An Bin'guan) at 370 Huashan Road. The musicians alternate between Western and Chinese classics.

Things are rather less highbrow on **Julu Road ❽**, across the street, one of Shanghai's most notorious bar streets. When the lights dim, the working girls come out. One of Shanghai's raunchier night spots, the strip is packed with no-frills darkened bars and drunken revellers weaving down the street in the wee hours. Tucked among the bars, an old air force compound with its mock Tudor buildings is the colonial setting for the Vietnamese restaurant **Cochin China** (Block 11, 889 Julu Road; tel: 6445 6797). A right turn on Fumin Road leads to **Baoluo** restaurant (271 Fumin Road; tel: 5403 7239), where a seemingly permanent queue attests to its heartwarming Shanghainese cuisine.

Take a right on Changle Road for a vista of "Tudor-bethan" houses, then head to No. 24 Lane 637 Changle Road, where the **Chinese Printed Blue Nankeen Exhibition Hall ❾** (Zhongguo Lanyin Huabu Guan: daily 9am–4.30pm; free) displays Shanghai's famous indigo batik *(see information panel on right)*. ❏

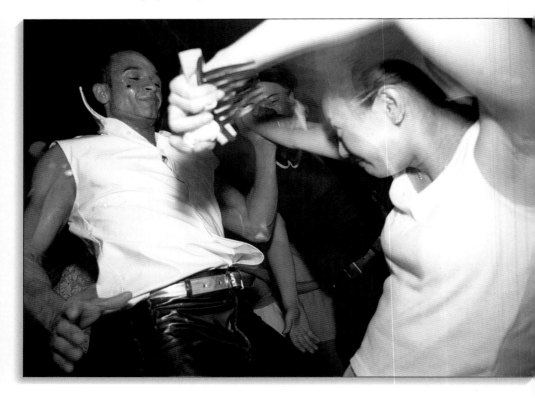

Blue and White Nankeen

Inky indigo dyes from the Silk Road explode into stunning patterns on coarse cloth at the **Chinese Printed Blue Nankeen Exhibition Hall** (No. 24 Lane 637 Changle Road) Once the preserve of farmers and peasants, *nankeen* (as the indigo batik is called in China) is enjoying a renaissance among the fashion-conscious both in the city and on the international runways.

Local lore credits Huang Dapo, a Jiangsu Province weaver, with bringing the craft to the Jiangnan region. The wax-resistant dying technique (much like batik) proved enormously popular, and locals began applying the technique on their own *nankeen* cloth, a brownish-yellow fabric woven from the *gossipium religiousum* cotton indigenous to the region. Named after the capital of pre-Liberation Jiangnan, Nanking (Nanjing), *nankeen* was such a hit in England that the English soon began dying cotton to approximate the colour of *nankeen* – and exporting it to China.

Today, *nankeen* is found all over the country, with coarse cotton handloom and silk substituting for the increasingly rare *nankeen* material. In fact, today, *nankeen* is a generic term referring to indigo batik rather than the cotton material of yesteryear.

Nankeen designs are made by cutting stencils by hand – each pattern has a name, linked to folk tales or traditional symbols of Chinese culture. The stencils are pinned to the fabric, and molten wax is then dripped into the stencil holes. The wax is left to dry, then dunked into a steaming dye bath of indigo leaves – indigo that first came to China from India via the Silk Road – and finally, the wax is painstakingly scraped off to reveal the intricate designs.

Shanghai's *nankeen* headquarters is housed in a pre-1949 mansion, where boss Zhu Ru Qing holds court. Surrounded by bolts of indigo fabric, he tells the story of the revival of this ancient Silk Road folk art. Back in the 1980s Zhu worked for a Shanghai trading company which, among other things, did business with Japan. He met Japanese folk art patron Madam Ku Bo Ma Sa, who had been collecting *nankeen* from the country-side for years. Determined to revive the moribund state of the craft, Ku and Zhu opened the *nankeen* shop in 1982, with a small museum adjacent to the shop displaying some of Madam Ku's collection.

The small, dusty museum displays faded photographs of the process of making *nankeen*, as well as stencils and samples of antique fabric. The shop is lined with bolts of fabric in an endless array of patterns, ready to be turned into clothing and accessories (including sneakers, mobile phone covers and stuffed animals). The coarse cloth was once considered farmer's gear, but its appearance on international runways has won over Shanghai's famously fashionable young women.

Zhu takes pride in the fact that his *nankeen* products are all-natural, and touts its anti-mosquito and anti-inflammatory properties as well. He's not the first: Pliny noted that "in physicke there is use of this Indigo, for it doth assuage swellings that doe stretch the skin". ❑

RIGHT: Chinese blue and white *nankeen* is currently enjoying a new found popularity.

CHANGNING

Middle-class Changning offers a less lofty but no less enjoyable itinerary: you can swim among sharks, visit China's only sex museum, or learn about the ceramic pottery craft of Jingdezhen

Map
on page
188

Sparkling high-rises fade and the construction slows in the western Changning area where, despite a sprinkling of baroque mansions, an altogether shabbier ambience reigns. Officially outside the Concessions in pre-Liberation days, this area attracted Shanghai's "B" list, a heady brew of revolutionaries, missionaries and spies who sought land and a life removed from the law. A second-class citizen's aura still clings to this down-to-earth community of working-class people, many of whom live packed five families to a floor in vintage apartments or squeeze several families into houses originally built for single ones. The modernising tide that has swept Shanghai is encroaching, though. New apartment buildings are beginning to emerge next to old-style lane houses, and a new boutique, pastry shop or art gallery intermittently punctuates the worn streets.

An English country estate

At the edge of the renegade neighbourhood is a touch of old-world gentility at the **Xingguo Guesthouse** ❶ (Xingguo Bin'guan), commissioned in 1934 by the Butterfield and Swire company. British architect Clough Williams-Ellis created an English country estate complete with playing fields on the serpentine curve of Avenue Haig, now Huashan Road. Today, the vast lawns and spreading camphor trees meander around an architectural mélange of French, Italian and neo-classical whitewashed mansions, still evoking a gracious weekend-in-the-country air. Butterfield and Swire quit China in 1950, but the mansion remained in favour with another powerful figure. Whenever he was in Shanghai, Chairman Mao Zedong enjoyed staying at **Building Number One**, with its dramatic, sweeping staircase, stately Ionic columns and broad outdoor terrace.

Today, the guesthouse remains a preferred government official accommodation. Now under the management of the **Radisson Plaza Xingguo Hotel**, Number One is still a luxury guesthouse (but only open to guests when it is not occupied by state visitors), while the other houses on the estate serve as offices and restaurants. More recent 1990s pre-fab Canadian-built houses occupied by expatriates sit on the old playing fields, while the Radisson Plaza Xingguo's modern high-rise hotel is on the cusp of the estate, its café overlooking the traffic snarls on Huashan Road as it joins Jiangsu Road.

Jiangsu Road north of the hotel is a bustling thoroughfare lined with shabby office buildings, shops and the occasional ostentatious former residence of a Kuomintang official. There are signs of upward mobility at luxury spa **Lotes** (326 Jiangsu Road), with its expensive French potions and soothing massage rooms, and the **Yuan Chu** pastry shop at No. 328, where like a carnival side show, a baker ices fluffy

LEFT: manicured gardens of the Radisson Plaza Xiingguo Hotel.
BELOW: interior of Building Number One, formerly a British taipan's residence.

white cakes in the window. On a lively, residential lane, vibrant with ringing bicycle bells, is the **Interdit Boutique and Art Gallery** (Lane 162 Jiangsu Road, Building No. 3), whose entrance stands just outside the lane's communal sink. The red-walled boutique owned by French expatriates features chic clothing and accessories that fuse traditional Chinese design elements with French style. The adjoining gallery displays custom-made furniture and jewellery, and hosts regular exhibitions of modern art and sculpture by Shanghainese and expatriate artists.

The alma mater of the Soong sisters

The Chinese say of the three Soong sisters: "May Ling loved power, Ai Ling loved money, but Ching Ling loved China".

A vestige of the street's old incarnation as Edinburgh Road surfaces across the street, on the corner of Jiangsu Road and Wuding Road (W). The Gothic turrets and stained-glass windows of the **No. 3 Middle School for Girls ❷** (Di San Nu Zhong) indicate its origins as the McTyeire School for Girls, founded in 1890 by the Southern Methodist Mission and named after Bishop Holland McTyeire, the Mission's head in China and chancellor of Tennessee's Vanderbilt University.

McTyeire was once the city's most fashionable and exclusive school for the daughters of Shanghai's power elite. When the precocious Soong Ai Ling entered its gates at the age of five, her enchanted older classmates made her the school mascot, dubbing her "Soong tai-tai" (Madam Soong). Three decades later, the world would come to know the Soong sisters – Ai Ling, Ching Ling and May Ling, McTyeire girls all – as the wives of wealthy banker H.H. Kung, Kuomintang leader Sun Yat-sen and Generalissimo Chiang Kai-shek, respectively.

After a brief respite as a co-educational school during the Cultural Revolution, the city's privileged daughters are back at the renamed top-ranked girls' school. In egalitarian blue track suits, they line up in the shadow of the dove-grey

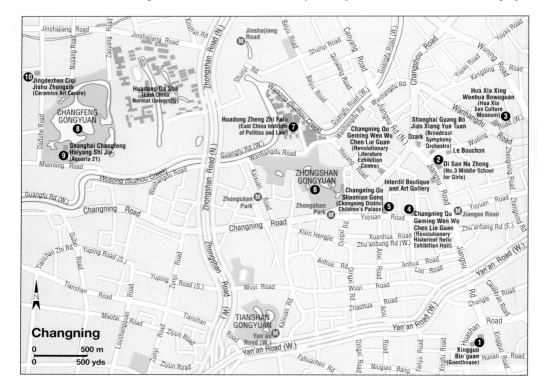

Gothic buildings. Every spring, the girls still play baseball, a McTyeire American tradition that has somehow survived Communist China.

Two blocks north and round the corner on Wuding Road (W) at No. 1498 is the newly refurbished building of the **Shanghai Broadcast Symphony Orchestra** (Shanghai Guang Bo Jiao Xiang Yue Tuan), its black ironwork gates embellished with treble clefs and the SBSO logo. The orchestra inherited the mansion from the Shanghai Opera School, which had claimed it after the Communist victory – Western opera apparently not being bourgeois enough to be outlawed. A stone fountain, its edges carved with grotesque grimacing masks, runs in the overgrown garden, while inside, the mansion has regained something of its former glory, boasting a first-floor bar and a cigar lounge.

China's 6,000 years of erotica

Continue east to 1133 Wuding Road, where a sign announces, "Ancient Chinese Sex Culture", heralding the **Hua Xia Sex Culture Museum** ❸ (Hua Xia Xing Wenhua Bowuguan: daily 10am–6pm; entrance fee). Shanghai University sociologist and sex expert Professor Liu Dalian has gathered his collection of 1,200 sex-related exhibits, covering 6,000 years of sexual history. Liu, a co-author of the first major modern study of Chinese sexuality, opened China's only sex museum with the aim of educating people about the vast erotic history of a country that has treated sex as obscene and unmentionable in more recent times.

It does manage this feat tastefully. Divided into 10 sections, the comprehensive collection includes fertility idols, antique sex toys, chastity belts, tools for foot-binding, sculptures of sex organs in ivory and jade, and the somewhat shocking "sensual Buddhas" – sculptures of goddesses mounting meditating

All the prime buildings in Shanghai have guards, many of whom will deny entrance at first. Smile, be polite, conceal cameras, and tell them you'd like to "*kan yi kan*", or look around, and they'll usually let you in.

BELOW: artefacts at the Hua Xia Sex Culture Museum invite raised eyebrows.

Buddhas. A gift shop stocks sex tonics and various sex-related paraphernalia.

Heading back southwest, in an early 20th-century *shikumen* (stone gate) house on Lane 1376 Yuyuan Road, is the **Changning District Revolutionary Historical Relic Exhibition Hall and Editorial Offices of the Bolshevik** ❹ (Changning Qu Geming Wen Wu Chen Lie Guan: Mon–Fri, 9am–5pm; free). The Communist revolutionaries who produced underground publications, such as the *Bolshevik*, preferred the less-policed area outside the Concessions, where their activities were less likely to be detected. This house, tucked into a warren of lanes, must have been ideal. Displayed are books, maps, faded army jackets and copies of revolutionary literature, labelled in Chinese. Upstairs, bare bedrooms with iron cots and worn blankets recreate the spartan living conditions.

A palace beside a middle-class estate

A few houses west at No. 31 Lane 1136 Yuyuan Road, the florid Teutonic castle exterior of the **Changning District Children's Palace** ❺ (Changning Qu Shaonian Gong: call 6252 4154 to arrange for a visit, or just look around the grounds) hints at its colourful history. The dream house of the Kuomintang Communications Minister created a stir when it was built in 1930, next to a middle-class estate. The 5,000-sq metre (53,820-sq ft) flower garden once had small bridges with flowing water and pavilions nestled among the flowers and trees. The main building's marble columns, Gothic arches and 32 rooms are still intact.

During the War of Resistance against Japan (World War II), this was the home of the head of the Japanese-recognised Kuomintang puppet government, the traitor Wang Jing-wei. After the war, Kuomintang spies took over the house and it became a prison and execution ground for Communist revolutionaries. Pressed into use as government offices after 1949, the building has served peaceably as the local Children's Palace since 1960, an after-school activities programme offering gifted children training in art, music, dance and drama.

A futuristic glass pyramid on Changning Road, two blocks west, encases the subway stop at **Zhongshan Park** ❻ (Zhongshan Gongyuan: daily 6am–6pm; free) and is a design accessory to the slick, landscaped plaza that fronts the glass and chrome ticket booth. Inside the park, the contours of the old Jessfield Park remain. Jessfield was said to be named after a little girl called Jessie, who was rescued from the circus in Hongkou by a wealthy Portuguese gentleman. He sent her to university in America with a missionary chaperone, and later married her – naming his country estate after her. Anchored by a lake, the grounds are a favourite weekend destination for children who love the carnival atmosphere with its games, rides and proximity to McDonald's, just outside the park gate.

The back entrance of the park on Wanhangdu Road leads to the leafy green campus and syncretic Sino-Anglo buildings of the **East China Institute of Politics and Law** ❼ (Huadong Zheng Zhi Falu) at 1575 Wanhangdu Road. It was founded in 1878 by the American Episcopal Mission as St John's University, the Harvard of China, which accounts for the campus' distinctly Ivy League-on-the-Huangpu feel. St John's

The bizarre game of paintball, where camouflage-clad teams fight each other using pump guns (and the occasional grenade) filled with washable paint pellets, is a Zhongshan Park fixture.

BELOW: children at the Changning District Children's Palace practising the *pipa*, a string instrument.

alumni occupied the highest echelons of Shanghai and overseas Chinese society; chances are the elderly gentleman who just greeted you "Good day" in perfect English is a St John's graduate. Originally part of the Jessfield estate, the campus, with its century-old trees, makes for a nice stroll. The headmaster's house fuses 19th-century gingerbread design with classical Chinese eaves and roof.

Northwest and across Suzhou Creek, sprawling **Changfeng Park** ❽ (Changfeng Gongyuan: daily 6am–6pm; entrance fee) is a breathe of fresh air in a gritty neighbourhood, particularly during the spring flower festival when vibrant tulips, daffodils and peonies bloom, and sculptures are fashioned from flowers.

Map on page 188

Sharks and ceramics

At Changfeng Park is **Aquaria 21** ❾ (Shanghai Changfeng Haiyang Shi Jie: daily 9am–5pm; entrance fee), Shanghai's first modern aquarium, with a South American jungle theme. Lush greenery enhances the aquatic exhibits, which include recreations of rivers, rainforests and oceans. At its ever-popular shark's tunnel, toothy sharks and giant rays swim overhead and certified divers can arrange for a swim with the sharks. Children especially love the "touch pool" which allows hands-on experiences with starfish, shrimps and crabs.

Northwest of Changfeng is the **Jingdezhen Ceramics Art Centre** ❿ (Jingdezhen Ciqi Yishu Zhongxin: daily 9.30am–4pm; free) at 1253 Daduhe Road, where 60,000 ceramic works by masters from the great pottery centres of Jingdezhen and Yixing are on display. Jingdezhen's kilns produced ceramics for imperial China, and, like the pottery villages of old, there is an apprenticeship centre, where young potters and interested visitors may train under a master, as well as an auction centre, where regular auctions of fine pieces are held. ❑

Close-up view of a Jingdezhen ceramic urn.

BELOW: Jingdezhen artists painting designs on pottery.

HONGQIAO AND GUBEI

This expatriate enclave has all the expected shops and services, but in welcome contrast to the modernity are the Soong Ching Ling Mausoleum, rows of antique shops and the zoo

Map on page 195

T he expatriates who live in Hongqiao and Gubei's high-walled compounds, each bigger and fancier than the last, are merely the latest to seek the lifestyle of the gentry in Shanghai's suburbs. A century ago, this was all rolling land, perfect for large country estates, horseback riding – and the unique Shanghai Paper Hunt. Brought to Shanghai in the late 19th century by military officers who had "hunted" in other parts of the world, paper hunting involved a 16-km (10-mile) cross-country ride on horseback, following a twisting, turning trail of paper to the finish line. Today, the area is known as Shanghai's new foreign concession, with its expensive, albeit characterless villas, expatriate-oriented shops, and the occasional tidbit from the past.

The rapid development of Hongqiao and Gubei into a foreign enclave took place before the lifting of decades-old policies that sought to restrict the areas in which foreigners were permitted to live. But even without those restrictions, many foreigners prefer living in an environment that is closer to home, surrounded by other foreigners who speak the same language, and protected by a staff of *ayi* (maids), drivers and secretaries. The Scandinavians have an enclave, as do the Americans and the Taiwanese. Not so different, after all, from their predecessors a century ago...

LEFT: Hongqiao area with the Yanan elevated highway.
BELOW: Soong Ching Ling Mausoleum.

Resting place for heroes and patriots

There is perhaps no more concrete evidence of foreign presence in Shanghai than the "Foreigners Tomb Area" in the **Soong Ching Ling Mausoleum ❶** (Song Qing Ling Lingyuan: 8.30am–5pm; entrance fee) at 21 Songyuan Road. Built in 1909 as the International Cemetery, the entrance to the Foreigners' Tomb Area is marked by two faded poppy wreaths, but the tombstones are hidden in patches of grass. Identical stone markers and strange spelling ("Feliks, Nanooer, Eoolc, Marly Jone") suggest that the original graves were moved and new markers recreated. Joseph Sassoon Gubbay and Aaron Sassoon Gubbay, a branch of the family who built the Peace Hotel, are here, having died within three days of each other in August 1946. There is a tombstone for Sir Elly Kadoorie, whose magnificent Marble Hall still stands as the Municipal Children's Palace *(see page 183)*, and Lady Laura Kadoorie, who died trying to rescue her children's nanny when their home went up in flames.

Also on the grounds is a "celebrity cemetery", with tombstones carved in the likeness of the dead. Here rest patriots, war heroes and martyrs, as well as Zhang Leping, creator of the lovable San Mao cartoon, holding his bug-eyed creation. The centrepiece of the graveyard is Soong Ching Ling's gravesite. One of the three Soong sisters and wife of Sun Yat-sen, Ching

Ling is the only one of the influential Soongs who remained in China. A white marble statue of Soong sits in front of the gravesite.

A huge square spreads out from the statue and is marked out in smaller squares. Children come here to pay homage to the childless Soong, who was instrumental in setting up the Shanghai Children's Palaces – an after-school programme offering gifted children training in art, music, dance and drama. The grave itself, marked by a simple stone slab and surrounded by pine trees, is dominated by the graves of her parents. The grave to the left of her parents' is of her faithful maid Yan'e. An exhibition hall recounts Soong's life as an exemplary Communist and on the grounds is the **Children's Museum** (Shanghai Ertong Bowuguan: daily 8.30am–5pm; entrance fee). Scientific education through entertainment is its purported philosophy, though its non-interactive toy hall, navigation hall and aviation hall are not very child-friendly.

Antique lovers' haven

The sparkling international department-store feel of the massive **Friendship Shopping Centre** (Hongqiao Youyi Shangcheng) north of the mausoleum at 6 Zunyi Road, is a far cry from the dowdy Friendship Stores that once were the only shopping available to foreigners in Communist China. Traditional Friendship Store souvenirs such as *qipao* (Chinese-style dresses), carpets and porcelain vases are just a fraction of what is available for shoppers today.

Head west along Hongqiao Road to **Antiques Row ❷**. Cavernous shops such as **Shanghai Sugu Furniture Shop** (No. 1438), **Alex's Antiques Shop** (No. 1970) and **Chine Antiques** (No. 1660) are an antique lover's dream, offering a window into a China where bridal dowries arrived in wedding baskets, gin-

Soong Ching Ling's tombstone at her mausoleum lies in the only cemetery left in Shanghai today. Modern Shanghai cremates its dead.

BELOW: Chinese silk is a good buy.
RIGHT: Friendship Shopping Centre.

Map
on page
195

ger was preserved in porcelain jars, and washbasins and chamber pots were commonplace. Some of the cabinets, chairs, altar tables and beds have been refinished, but the shops also offer custom refinishing and shipping. Watching the craftsmen at work is a real treat. Take a break from antiques at the **Big Fan** (1440 Hongqiao Road, behind Shanghai Sugu Furniture Shop; tel: 6219 7514). This Old Shanghai theme restaurant is set on manicured grounds among the Mediterranean-style buildings of the former Granada Estates.

The **Sheraton Grand Tai Ping Yang Hotel** (Tai Ping Yang Fandian) at 5 Zunyi Road (S) to the north is a favourite gathering place for suburban expatriates, who especially like the deli and **Giovanni's**, one of the city's best Italian restaurants. Children simply love the **Traffic Park** (Jiao Cong Gongyuan: daily 6am–5.30 pm; admission fee, *see margin tip*), located north along Zunyi Road at the corner with Xianxia Road. Here, electric vehicles such as cars, bikes and carts cruise along the streets of a mini-Shanghai, complete with scale landmarks of the Oriental Pearl Tower and Park Hotel.

TIP

Admission to the Traffic Park is free for those under 1.2 metres (3.9 ft). Everyone else has to pay a fee.

Where the expats shop

Gubei's expat central is concentrated on **Shui Cheng Road (S)**, where supermarket giant **Carrefour** ❸ (Jialefu: daily 8.30am–10pm) still manages to create the circus atmosphere of a Chinese outdoor market, as vendors compete to shout out their wares and local delicacies such as pig's feet are displayed a few steps away from Shanghai's best cheese selection. Walk south along the road to soak up the atmosphere: the neighbourhood Starbucks café is across the Shanghai International School and surrounded by over-the-top neo-classical apartments and villas, popular with overseas Chinese as well as Western expatriates.

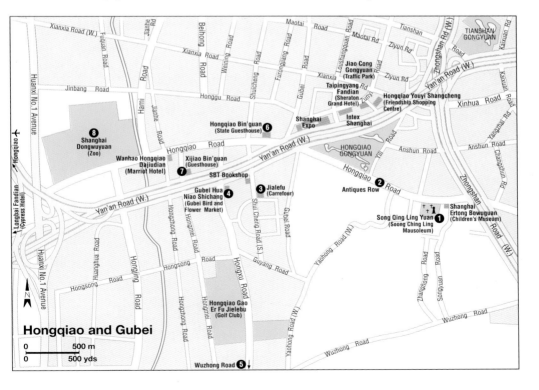

If you notice a rather larger than usual number of young Chinese women here, it's no coincidence. Gubei is known as a "concubine village", where Taiwanese businessmen keep their Shanghai *er nai* (mistresses). The preponderance of women has been the catalyst for a concentration of females-only bathhouses and beauty parlours, such as the upscale **Eliza Lady Spa & Beauty Organisation** (1665 Hongqiao Road, in Luo Cheng Plaza), where communal, single-sex baths and plenty of gossip are followed by traditional Chinese massage, facials and nail care.

All about birds, blooms and beasts

Birds on sale at the Gubei Flower and Bird Market.

The **Gubei Flower and Bird Market** ❹ (Gubei Hua Niao Shichang) at 1778 Hongqiao Road, west of Shui Cheng Road, is stocked with seasonal blooms and a motley selection of songbirds and parakeets, lizards, chameleons and fish. The expat-oriented shops in the market sell crockery and tableware, vases, peasant paintings, placemats and napkins, and will usually custom-make an order.

The 18-hole **Hongqiao Golf Club** (Hongqiao Gao Er Fu Jielebu) is a few minutes' drive south at 567 Hongxu Road. Further south on **Hongxu Road** and **Wuzhong Road** ❺ is another strip of antiques shops and warehouses. On Hongxu Road are the enormous **Zhong Zhong Antiques Warehouse** (No. 28) and **Shanxi Antique Furniture** (No. 731). Wuzhong Road warehouses include **Kang-Da Antique Furniture Factory** (No. 1245), which, as its name implies, turns out reproductions, and **Annly's Antiques** (No. 1255). For an impressive pick of antiques, go to **Hu & Hu** (1685 Wuzhong Road), whose co-owner was raised in the US and trained at Sotheby's.

BELOW: Chinese antiques shop along Hongxu Road.

Back north along Hongqiao Road is some exceptional accommodation, starting with the **Hongqiao Guesthouse** ❻ (Hongqiao Bin'guan). Set within some

40 hectares (100 acres) of lush gardens are a collection of vintage villas in architectural styles ranging from art deco to Spanish colonial, with the privacy of the long-term residents and VIP visitors ensured by trees.

The well-guarded **Xijiao Guesthouse ❼** (Xijiao Bin'guan), farther west, is where notables such as the Queen of England and the Emperor of Japan have stayed. The complex includes a stunning Frank Lloyd-Wright inspired house, now Building No. 4, built for a Chinese entrepreneur in 1949. Set on a sloping hill, its sliding roof, use of glass walls and indoor garden with a Japanese bridge create a link between the interior and exterior. A stream runs through the peaceful compound, whose vast lawns include a lake and pavilions. Across the street from Xijiao is the low-rise **Shanghai Marriott** (Wanhao Hongqiao Dajiudian) at 2270 Hongqiao Road, whose café is a popular expatriate brunch spot.

It's a short walk west to the rolling grounds of the former Hungjao Golf Club which became the **Shanghai Zoo ❽** (Shanghai Dongwuyuan: daily 7.30am–5pm; entrance fee) in 1954. The grounds are dotted with pavilions and streams stocked with swans, pelicans and mandarin ducks, but the zoo, like most zoos in China, is not idyllic. The lethargic Giant Pandas, a symbol of China, are on most tourist agendas, but far nicer are the Yunnan golden monkeys and the rare Southern Chinese tigers, or feeding the ducks and stroking the goats at the petting zoo.

Continuing west, the **Cypress Hotel** (Longbai Fandian), at 2419 Hongqiao Road, is set in the verdant country estate of Jewish millionaire Victor Sassoon, who built the Peace Hotel. His half-timber faux-Tudor mansion formerly called **Sassoon Villa** and scene of many a wild party given by the horse-racer and man about town in the 1930s, still stands next door. The mansion is owned privately today and is not opened to visitors but the beautiful grounds are. ❑

Map on page 195

East of the zoo entrance is an architectural jewel, an abandoned country church with a striking Byzantine copper roof. It was the handiwork of master architect Ladislau Hudec (Lane 1115 Hami Road, House No. 1).

BELOW: Panda bear seeking solace on a block of ice at the Shanghai Zoo.

XUJIAHUI AND LONGHUA

*Scattered within this area of shopping complexes are historic
sights such as Xujiahui Cathedral, Longhua Temple and Longhua
Cemetery of Martyrs, commemorating the White Terror slaughter*

Map
on page
200

An improbable combination of mass market shopping and two of the city's
most ancient, revered holy sites, Xujiahui fairly bristles with a chaotic
cacophony, heightened by the confused flow of traffic at the confluence
of eight roads. Crossing over from the tranquillity of Xujiahui Park and the
elite Huaihai/Hengshan neighbourhood, it is almost as if an invisible line has
been crossed – and in a way, it has. Xujiahui, known as Siccawei or Ziccawei
in the Concession after its Shanghainese pronunciation, lies on the western border of the former French Concession. The modern city has grown out here, but
Xujiahui still offers the real estate bargains that attracted the churches, temples, airports and prisons of yesteryear. Today, it houses cathedrals of commerce and condominiums for yuppies who can't afford downtown prices.

Meaning "Xu family village", Xujiahui is named after China's first Catholic
family. Ming dynasty court official Xu Guangqi (Paul Xu), who was born here
in 1562, was Jesuit missionary Matteo Ricci's first convert as well as his personal assistant. Xu's legacy lived on for centuries afterwards, sometimes in
unexpected ways: illustrious Xu descendants include another Shanghai first
family, the Soongs (on their mother's side).

A French-Gothic Catholic cathedral

The soaring twin towers and flying buttresses of the
French-Gothic **Xujiahui Cathedral** ❶ (Tian Zhu
Jiao Tang), at 158 Puxi Road, stands on land that Xu
donated for the founding of a Jesuit community – who
built the first St Ignatius Cathedral here in 1846. Originally named after the founder of the Society of Jesus
order, the cathedral has remained essentially
unchanged since a 1910 expansion – with the notable
exception of the dramatic amputation of the 50-metre
(165-ft) twin towers during the Cultural Revolution,
when the church was closed. Now restored with the
towers back in place, the church grounds feature a
charming grotto with a statue of the Virgin Mary with
floral offerings at her feet. Services in Shanghainese
are still held daily to a packed congregation, and
masses at Christmas and Easter are especially popular.

The meteorological observatory that Xu established
on the grounds of Xujiahui Cathedral is gone now, but
its legacy lives on at the Shanghai Meteorological
Bureau, a five-minute walk south of the cathedral. Just
next to the Bureau on a grassy plot of land is a **Statue
of Paul Xu** ❷, the scholar who made all this possible.

Directly north of Xujiahui Cathedral at 1 Hongqiao
Road stands another shrine, this one to shopping. Sunlight floods the glass dome of the **Grand Gateway**
(Ganghui Guangchang) mall, the city's largest, glint-
ing on the escalators that glide up six floors – four

LEFT: the French-
Gothic inspired
Xujiahui Cathedral.
BELOW: the
cathedral's interior.

levels of shopping and two of restaurants and entertainment centres, plus a street-level food alley. The mall, which opened in 2000, has eclipsed its mega-mall predecessor to the south, the mid-market **Orient Department Store** (Dongfang Shangchang) at 8 Caoxi Road (N).

Grand Gateway also caused the demolition of some of the church buildings that once dominated this area, but others remain. After a tasteful restoration, the old convent, south of the cathedral, is now the **Old Station Restaurant** (Lao Huo Che Fandian: tel: 6427 2233) at 201 Caoxi Road (N). The restaurant serves Shanghainese cuisine in an interior embellished with beautiful floor tiles, carved wood and coloured glass; diners can also elect to be seated in the vintage train car at the rear of the restaurant.

The **Shanghai Film Studios** (Shanghai Dianying Zhipianchang), a short walk south, is the site of the very popular Shanghai genre of movies (the studios are usually closed to the public, but the sound stages in the western suburbs are open to visitors: *see page 225*).

Tucked into an unremarkable row of shops and restaurants one street east is the city's best Shanghainese restaurant, **Shanghai Uncle** (Hai Shang Ah Shu: tel: 6464 6430) at 211 Tianyaoqiao Road. "Uncle" Li Zhongheng, whose beaming countenance appears on all the restaurant promotional material, is the octogenarian founder and son of Virginia Lee, the noted Chinese chef who collaborated with former *New York Times* food critic Craig Claiborne on the classic tome *The Chinese Cookbook*. Li, a physicist who speaks fluent English, is a microcosm of Shanghai history. An array of dishes, made with Li's own family recipes and updated for the 21st century, is sometimes delivered with a liberal dose of old Shanghai stories from "Uncle" himself.

The spitting habit that you frequently witness comes from the Chinese belief that excess phlegm must be cleared, at the risk of ill health. The more refined may spit into handkerchiefs or trash cans, but if you hear a throat being cleared – move!

RIGHT:
bronze saxophonist
at Xujiahui's Grand
Gateway mall.

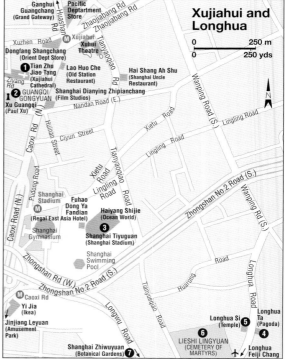

Continuing south on Tianyaoqiao Road leads to the east gate of the huge **Shanghai Stadium** ❸ (Shanghai Tiyuguan) at 111 Caoxi Road (N) – built in 1997 to host the China National Games. Once the pride of the city and home of the popular Shanghai Shenhua football club and one of the projects "built to enhance people's lives", the stadium has been a victim of Shanghai's addiction to progress, and is now surpassed by the Hongkou stadium *(see page 211)* in the northeast, the Shenhua club's new home.

Nearby **Ocean World** (Haiyang Shijie: daily 10am–9pm; entrance fee), at 1111 Longwu Road, is a none-too-clean indoor beach and water play area. For something wilder, you can bungee jump into the stadium or better yet, watch jumpers take their white-knuckled leaps from the comfort of **Top of the World** sports bar at **Regal East Asia Hotel** (Fuhao Dong Ya Fandian), 666 Tianyaoqiao Road, which overlooks the stadium.

Swedish furniture and the season's first fresh fruit

Down the road from the Shanghai Stadium, Shanghai yuppies crowd the Swedish home store **Ikea** (Yi Jia) at 126 Caoxi Road (N), next to the Caoxi Road subway station. The light colours and clean lines of Swedish furniture – the antithesis of classical Chinese dark mahogany and rosewood furniture – have become a hit with the locals, who also stop to nibble on Swedish meatballs in the 500-seat restaurant at Asia Pacific's largest Ikea store. Chefs at Shanghai's finest restaurants are often found on Ikea's front steps – the fruit sellers who station themselves here have a reputation for being the first with seasonal produce – the first yellow cherries of spring, the first peaches of summer.

Head southeast to Longhua Road which leads to Shanghai's only pagoda.

Map on page 200

Shanghai Stadium is also the venue for bungee jumpers. Contact Extreme Sports Centre at tel: 6426 6888 for details, if you are so inclined.

BELOW: football-crazy Shanghainese at Shanghai Stadium.

The striking 44-metre (140-ft) **Longhua Pagoda ④** (Longhua Ta), a major tourist destination in the 1930s, looks as if it popped straight out of ancient China. The yellow wood-and-brick octagonal tower (no entry), whose tinkling bells on upturned eaves could once be heard all the way to the Huangpu River, was first built in 242 by a nobleman from the Wu Kingdom, although its current shape dates from a 922 reconstruction. Rebuilt several times over the centuries, the pagoda served as a flak tower equipped with anti-aircraft guns during World War II, and was papered over with propaganda during the Cultural Revolution. Today, a modern shopping plaza, featuring Chinese-style buildings around the pagoda, has unfortunately robbed it of some of its languid charm.

Shanghai's largest temple

Across the street stands the rambling **Longhua Temple ⑤** complex (Longhua Si; daily 7am–4pm; entrance fee). With its incense-filled courtyards, giant joss burners and imposing Buddha images, this atmospheric temple is Shanghai's largest and most active. Originally built in 345, the Chan (Zen) Buddhist temple has been rebuilt in essentially the same style over the years, and is considered a particularly fine example of Southern Song architecture. The current structure dates from the Guanxu period of the Qing dynasty, although the temple was devastated by Japanese bombs in 1937 and was subsequently restored.

Longhua Pagoda, which dates to 242, has been rebuilt several times over the centuries.

BELOW: the multi-armed Guanyin, also known as the Goddess of Mercy, at Longhua Temple.

Longhua contains some significant Buddha images: Sakyamuni Buddha's Bodhisattva form, in the **Hall of Heavenly Kings**, and in the **Maitreya Hall**, the Maitreya Buddha incarnation, known as the "cloth bag monk". In a departure from tradition, the statues lining the temple halls at Longhua include both *arhat* (Buddhist saints) and the guardians of Buddhist law, which are usually separate.

The **Grand Hall** features a gilded meditating Sakyamuni Buddha, under a spiralling dome, with a statue of Guanyin in the rear, while the **Three Saints Hall** showcases the three incarnations of the Buddha. Striking Longhua's bronze bell 108 times (to erase the 108 worries of Buddhist thought) has become a Shanghai New Year's Eve tradition, as has the reinstituted Chinese New Year temple fair, China's largest, full of folk traditions and dances.

Next door, **Longhua Cemetery of Martyrs ⑥** (Lieshi Lingyuan; daily 9am–4pm; entrance fee) commemorates a tragic moment in Shanghai's history. Hundreds of idealistic young Communists were killed during what has become known as the White Terror, the ruling Kuomintang's reign of terror against the Communists, carried out in Shanghai by the notorious Green Gang. On 12 April 1927, revolutionaries were pulled from their homes, rounded up and taken to the execution grounds at what was then the Longhua Garrison. Each April, Longhua's orchard of peach trees blossoms in remembrance, looking remarkably like the tissue-paper flowers made for funerals.

The cemetery today is all landscaped gardens and high-tech fountains, with a blue-glass Louvre-esque pyramid and a memorial hall to the Communist martyrs. Outside, an eternal flame burns in front of a Herculean sculpture being swallowed up by the earth, and the marble graves of the martyrs lie in a semi-circle.

Lush gardens and fun parks

A corner of the park features the tiny prison cells of the **Longhua Camp Civilian Assembly Centre**, the infamous Longhua prison camp – the setting for much of J.G. Ballard's 1984 autobiographical account of the Japanese Occupation of Shanghai, *Empire of the Sun*. A short walk further south on Longhua Road leads to the vintage **Longhua Airport** (Longhua Fei Ji Chang), waiting for a developer to give it a new lease of life. Used by the Japanese and the Kuomintang during wartime, the terrazzo floor features airplanes, and floor-to-ceiling circular windows offer a view of vintage aeroplanes from the days of the Flying Tigers.

The **Shanghai Botanical Gardens** ❼ (Shanghai Zhiwuyuan: daily, summer 7am–6pm, winter 8am–5pm; entrance fee), at 1100 Longwu Road, further south on Longwu, is a rambling green vista of lakes, pine trees and over 9,000 plants. It is known for its bonsai collection in the Penjing Garden, the Orchid Garden and a pair of 18th-century pomegranate trees, as well as its spring and autumn flower festivals. Fans of Shanghai's blue-and-white *nankeen* fabric should pay their respects at the Huang Dapo Memorial temple in the grounds: Huang is the legendary figure who brought the technique of *nankeen*-dyeing to the Jiangsu region.

Further west, **Jinjiang Amusement Park** (Jinjiang Leyuan: daily 8.30am–5pm; entrance fee) at 201 Hongmei Road is sparsely attended, despite its claim to fame as home of the world's second largest ferris wheel. The ferris wheel is new, but the rest of the amusement park has seen better days – nonetheless, kids universally seem to enjoy the swinging pirate ship and the horror house. Also in Minhang, **Dino Beach** (Redai Fengbao) at 78 Xinzhen Road (open daily 9am–9pm late June to early September; entrance fee) boasts the world's biggest wave pool, along with white water rafting, high-speed slides, tubes and a huge man-made beach. ❏

Map
on page
200

TIP

Guilin Park (Guilin Gongyuan: 7am–5pm; free) to the west of the Shanghai Botanical Gardens is particularly beautiful during the Mid-Autumn festival when it is decorated with lanterns and when its rows of fragrant osmanthus trees burst into bloom.

BELOW: Shanghai Botanical Gardens.

HONGKOU AND ZHABEI

*This unassuming area took major roles on the historical stage:
the base for Japanese occupying forces, the home of writer Lu Xun,
and the largest Far East refuge for Jews fleeing Nazism*

Map
on page
206

Drab blocks of government housing and grimy warehouses define the character of the **Hongkou** and **Zhabei** districts, the area north of the Suzhou Creek. With the memorial hall to Chinese writer Lu Xun as its major tourist attraction, this is paradoxically a very local neighbourhood without the mass market appeal of Shanghai's other big name draws, yet with a rich history of its own that, for the most part, has been left untouched.

Hongkou was little more than a scattering of vegetable farms and swampy ground when the Bishop William Boone – the first Anglican Bishop in China – established the American Episcopal Church Mission here in 1848. It wasn't until six years later, in 1854, that the American Consul raised the Stars and Stripes in Hongkou to commemorate the official establishment of the American Settlement, which merged with the British to form the International Settlement in 1863. By 1900, the Japanese had established their presence here, followed by their wartime occupation of the area. Hongkou's combination of space and proximity to the financial district made it a convenient location for the International Settlement's support systems, such as post offices, prisons, warehouses and waterworks.

LEFT: giving historic Waibadu Bridge a new lick of paint. **BELOW:** the Russian Consulate along the riverfront.

Home of Japanese forces

Kuomintang leader Chiang Kai-shek had big plans for the Hongkou area: a new city, anchored by the Kuomintang's Shanghai government buildings, was already in place in northeast Hongkou by World War II, but the Japanese Occupation of Hongkou and Zhabei materialised before Chiang's plans could. Hongkou played a major role during the war as the home of both the Japanese occupying forces and stateless Jewish refugees *(see page 213)* who were fleeing Hitler's Germany to one of the few places in the world that would accept them.

Zhabei was, and still is, much quieter than Hongkou. A great stretch of government-built housing and factories, Zhabei's claim to fame is its devastation during the Japanese bombing of the city. It was here that the famous photograph of the screaming baby by the bombed out railway lines was taken.

There are signs that a renaissance is beginning slowly in the area. The old warehouses that drove Shanghai's industry are being transformed into art galleries; a Cultural Street commemorates the great literary uprisings of the early 20th century; and Shanghai's old dock area is being redeveloped into an entertainment zone with the world's largest ferris wheel.

Cross into Hongkou the old-fashioned way, across the lovely **Waibaidu Bridge ❶** (Waibaidu Qiao) which spans the Suzhou Creek – and much of the history of Hongkou. Until 1856, the only way to cross Suzhou

Creek into Hongkou was by ferry, but when the International Settlement found that inconvenient, a British entrepreneur built a wooden bridge, naming it the Wills Bridge after himself. His system of requiring the payment of one copper coin from the Chinese who crossed the bridge while foreigners could cross on credit didn't go down well, and the bridge and its toll system were eventually dismantled, succeeded by a floating bridge operated by the Shanghai Municipal Council, and, in 1906, the steel Waibaidu Bridge (known in English then as Garden Bridge).

During the Japanese Occupation, when it served as the demarcation line between occupied Hongkou and Zhabei and the International Settlement, the bridge was guarded by turbanned Sikh policemen from the British forces on the Bund side and fierce Japanese soldiers on the occupied side. Today, the bridge is an excellent vantage point for views of Pudong to the east and the Suzhou Creek to the west.

Buildings with a rich history

Across the bridge, on the western side of 20 Suzhou Road (N) is the imposing 18-storey façade of **Shanghai Mansions** (Shanghai Da Sha), one of Asia's first high-rises, and built in 1935. Known then as the Broadway Mansions, the building was used by the Japanese and later by the American military, but is best remembered as the wartime Foreign Correspondents Club, which occupied the top six floors during the 1930s. From this perspective, some members recorded Shanghai's most memorable events: the 1937 Japanese bombing, and in 1949 (as member Noel Barber recounted in *The Fall of Shanghai*), watching Marshal Chen Yi march in to liberate Shanghai. Now a hotel refurbished beyond recognition, the 18th-floor balcony still has sweeping views of the Bund.

Across the street, along the waterfront, is the **Russian Consulate** (Eluosi

In Mandarin, the characters for Waibaidu Qiao mean "Outer Ferry Bridge", as the bridge stood on the outermost point of the ferry crossing. In spoken Mandarin, a change in the tone of one of the three characters turns Waibaidu Qiao into "Free Outer Crossing Bridge" – which is what it became once the Chinese no longer had to pay a toll.

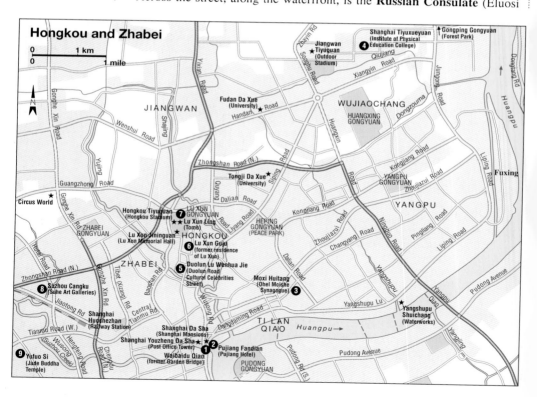

Ling Shi Guan), which has the distinction of being the only Consulate occupying its original location. The Victorian building across the street, the **Pujiang Hotel ❷** (Pujiang Fandian) at 15 Huangpu Road has fallen on hard times. Once known as Astor House, one of Shanghai's most elegant hotels, it is today a backpacker hotel. Built in 1910, the Astor attracted luminaries such as Charlie Chaplin and Albert Einstein, and is said to have effected a slew of Shanghai firsts: electric light, telephone, talkies, dancing ball – even the taxi. Local lore has it that an Astor House bellboy, rewarded for recovering a Russian guest's wallet with its contents, spent a third of it on a car. That car became Shanghai's first taxi and spawned the Johnson fleet, now known as the Qiang Sheng taxi. The interior architecture remains, its sweeping staircases and grand galleries recalling its past grandeur, even under layers of dust.

The **Shanghai Post Office** (Shanghai Yo Zheng Ju) tower, a short walk west, still dominates the area, much as it did when it was built in 1924 to serve both foreigners and Chinese. The post office, which consolidated the work of seven postal units, is still Shanghai's main post office – marble chutes still swoosh the mail from floor to floor and ornamental plaster vines still twine over the ceiling. Just west of the post office, along Suzhou Creek, is the startlingly modern **Embankment House**, now local housing. Built by the Sassoons in 1932, Embankment House was Shanghai's largest apartment house at the time, with 194 rooms.

The banks of the Suzhou Creek, heading east, were Shanghai's dock area, the cradle of Shanghai industry, and were once lined with the factories that fuelled Shanghai's growth. The factories fell into disuse as Shanghai went high-tech, and the government has decided to redevelop the zone into a 3.7-sq km (1.4-sq mile) entertainment extravaganza that will include a 200-metre (656-ft) ferris

Map on page 206

Pujiang Hotel was formerly known as Astor House.

LEFT: the Shanghai Post Office.
RIGHT: a Shanghai yuppie on wheels.

wheel, the world's highest. The project, slated for completion in 2005, will retain some of the area's historic warehouses, including the castle-like **Yangshupu Waterworks** (Yangshupu Shuichang) on the waterfront at Yangshupu Road, built by a British firm in 1881. The waterworks has buildings for each step of the filtration process and Victorian equipment that is still used today. From the Waterworks building, take in the sight of the **Yangpu Bridge** (Yangpu Qiao), the longest suspension bridge in the world.

A refuge for war-time Jews

The redevelopment zone, bordered by Zhoujiazui Road in the north, Wusong in the west and Dalian in the east, may also demolish what is left of Hongkou's old Jewish neighbourhood, which provided a safe haven for 20,000 refugees during World War II. North of the waterworks, a plaque in **Huoshan Park** (Huoshan Gongyuan: daily 6am–6pm; free), on Huoshan Road, commemorates the area as the "designated area for stateless refugees" between 1937 and 1941.

At the heart of the old Jewish area is the **Ohel Moishe Synagogue 3** (Moxi Huitang: daily 9am–4.30pm; entrance fee), a red-brick-and-blue building at 62 Changyang Road that was founded by the Russian Ashkenazi Jews in 1927. Two of the rooms are a photographic museum to the Shanghai Jewish experience, but more powerful is a tour of the neighbourhood with the octogenarian museum tour guide Wang Fa Liang, who grew up here and whose vivid recollections of the days of the Jewish ghetto bring the old neighbourhood to life. The neighbourhood then, as it is now, is a poor, down-at-the-heels area, and has reverted to being entirely Chinese, though with surreal signs of Jewish shops and cafés.

If you have children with you, stop at **Peace Park** (Heping Gongyuan: daily 6am–6pm; entrance fee) at Tianbao Road, with its hundreds of animatronic dinosaurs (some genuinely scary) and an aviary, before proceeding northeast along Siping Road to one of the best-kept secrets in Shanghai.

Chiang Kai-shek built his "new city" centre here, in northeast Hongkou, the core of a grand planned city that would showcase his new government. The Communists changed his plans, but the buildings remain, classic examples of the fusion of art deco and Ming Chinese that defined Nanjing Decade architecture.

The first "new city" building on the wide boulevard is the grandiose **Jiangwan Outdoor Stadium** (Jiangwan Tiyuguan) with a plain white, almost Grecian exterior decorated with Chinese designs in ornamental plaster. A five-minute drive north are the squat clean contours of Shanghai's first indoor swimming pool, still in use. The jewel in the crown, though, is the **Institute of Physical Education College 4** (Shanghai Tiyuxueyuan), housed in the former City Hall at 650 Qiu Yuan Huan Road. A stunning two-storey building with more than a touch of the Forbidden City architecture, the interior is empty, save for a couple of employees who live there, and can be easily explored. From the steps of the old City Hall, two other Chinese-style buildings are visible – at least one was intended to be a library – but are not open to the public.

A 15-minute drive from the stadium leads to the very pleasant **Gongping Forest Park** (Gongping

Famous Jews who lived in Shanghai during the World War II years include pop artist Peter Max, former US Treasury Secretary Michael Blumenthal and "Far Eastern Economic Review" founder Eric Halpern.

BELOW: furniture like the ones used by the Jews of yesteryear are on display at the Ohel Moishe Synagogue.

Gongyuan: daily 6am–7pm; free) at Jungong Road, where visitors can ride on horseback, boat on the lake, fish in the stocked pond, barbecue, or just enjoy the sturdy trees and landscaped flower beds.

Hongkou's literati lane

Head back southwest and straight into Lu Xun territory, which begins at **Duolun Road Cultural Celebrities Street ❺** (Duolun Lu Wenhua Jie) at the corner of Duolun and Sichuan roads. Considered the father of modern Chinese literature, Lu Xun's literary railing against social injustice earned him a place in the pantheon of modern China's most celebrated personalities. Hongkou takes great pride in the fact that he chose to live here from 1927 until his death in 1936, and commemorates his presence at every opportunity.

Lu Xun was part of a circle of literati who lived around Duolun Road and who were instrumental in founding the League of Left Wing Writers. Several of the writers' houses, in styles ranging from Shanghainese *shikumen* (stone gate) houses to Swiss villa, have been restored as museums, as has the **League of Left Wing Writers Museum** (Zhongguo Zuolian Bowuguan) at No. 2 Lane 201 Duolun Road (daily 9.30am–4.30pm; entrance fee). The former Chinese Arts University, where the league was founded in 1930 to "struggle for proletarian liberation" through writing, has preserved its interior. Collections of the league's works are showcased, along with an exhibition on the life of five martyred writers executed by a Kuomintang firing squad at the Longhua garrison during the Communist witch hunts in 1927 *(see page 202).*

The 550-metre (1,804-ft) L-shaped stretch of Duolun Road is dotted with life-sized bronze figures of the celebrities who lived here, posing here and there along

Map on page 206

TIP

The Shanghai Circus troupe performs at the shiny new Shanghai Circus World (Shanghai Maxicheng). Call 6652 7750 for ticket information. Look out for the giant golf ball at its entrance at 2266 Gong He Xing Road.

BELOW:
Duolun Cultural Celebrities Street.

Monument to Lu Xun at his tomb. Widely regarded as one of modern China's greatest writers, Lu Xun died in 1936.

BELOW:
a tribute to Lu Xun (left) in bronze at Duolun Cultural Celebrities Street.

the street. The first floor of the **Hongde Church** (Hongde Tang), with its distinctive Chinese tiled roof, has become a souvenir hall, but on the second floor is an active church. There is also a recreation of a bookshop of Lu Xun's friend, Kanza Uchiyama, originally on nearby Sichuan Road, a cinema and several minimuseums, including one of the world's largest collections of Mao buttons, chopsticks and clocks. The lavish Moorish house at the end of Duolun Road was the home of financier H.H. Kung, husband of Ai Ling, one of the Soong sisters.

Other monuments to Lu Xun

A short walk northeast leads to **Lu Xun's Former Residence** ❻ (Lu Xun Guju: daily 9am–4pm; entrance fee), the plain red-brick Japanese Concession house at No. 9 Lane 132 Shanying Road. Lu lived here from 1933 until he succumbed to tuberculosis in 1936. Smaller than the homes in the European Concessions, the simply furnished house, meant to convey the soul of an unpretentious man of the people, is just as it was when he lived here.

The centrepiece of Lu Xun territory is **Lu Xun Park** ❼ (Lu Xun Gongyuan: daily 6am–6pm; entrance fee) at 146 Dongjiang Wan Road. The lovely park, also known as Hongkou Park, contains both the writer's tomb and a memorial hall. The park's peanut-shaped pond area, which attracts early morning ballroom dancers and *tai chi* practitioners, is a refreshing spot of greenery after Hongkou's gritty streets, and is very popular with the locals.

A bronze seated figure of Lu Xun welcomes visitors to the **Tomb of Lu Xun** (Lu Xun Ling) within the park. The inscription on the tomb is by Mao, and the trees on either side of the grave planted by Zhou Enlai and Lu Xun's widow. The **Lu Xun Memorial Hall** (Lu Xun Jininguan: daily 9am–5pm; entrance fee) to

THE LEGACY OF LU XUN

Modern China's most revered literary figure was a product of the May 4th Movement in 1919. Protests in China broke out when it was revealed at the Versailles Peace Conference that Germany's extraterritorial rights in Shandong Province had been transferred to Japan. The movement ultimately affected politics, economics, language and literature, and is regarded as a cultural watershed. For young Chinese idealists such as Lu Xun, it was about social justice for the downtrodden. He questioned everything; nothing was sacred.

Lu Xun's legacy was a radical new style of writing, *bai hua*, or plain language, that turned its back on the flowery classical style understood only by scholars. The very first *bai hua* short story, *Diary of a Madman*, modelled on the works of Gogol, was a brutal satire of the Confucian society that he desperately wanted to eradicate. His most famous work, however, is *The True Story of Ah Q*, another jab at Confucianism through the persona of a simple man.

Lu Xun's politically correct ideology appealed to the Communists, who made him their poster boy. Yet he never joined the Communist Party and his iconoclastic personality might not have survived Mao's China. By dying young (of tuberculosis), Lu Xun ensured the survival of his legacy.

the right of the park's entrance has recreations of his study, newspaper articles and photographs from the period and translations of works by and about him.

Northwest of the park at 715 Dong Ti Yu Hui Road is **Hongkou Stadium** (Hongkou Tiyuguan), the new 50,000-sq metre (538,200-sq ft) stadium that is home to Shanghai's popular Shenhua "Blue Devils" football team.

Head to the Suzhou creek area and the **Suhe Art Galleries ❽** at Moganshan Road. The warehouses in this seedy neighbourhood that once formed the backbone of Shanghai's industry are now experiencing an artistic renaissance. In the tradition of artists reinventing industrial space, the artists call this area Suhe, an abbreviation of Suzhou Creek in Chinese. The old rice and cotton warehouses are left essentially untouched, with peeling paint on the giant doors adding texture to gallery exhibits.

The Buddhas that were left behind

One of Shanghai's major religious attractions, the **Jade Buddha Temple ❾** (Yufuo Si: daily 8am–5pm, closed 12–1pm; entrance fee) is to the south at 170 Anyuan Road. Almost hidden among the sprawling factories and government housing, the temple's Song-style architecture belies the fact that it is relatively new, dating only from 1918. This is Shanghai's best-known and most-visited temple, thanks to a pair of exquisite jade Buddhas from Burma.

In 1882, the monk Hui Gen of nearby Putuoshan island *(see page 239)* returned from his pilgrimage to Burma with five Sakyamuni Buddha images, each one carved from a single piece of jade. Transporting all the heavy statues back to the island by ferry – particularly the largest, which weighed 1,000 kg (2,200 lbs) – proved impossible, so two were left behind in Shanghai, and a temple was built that same year to house them. The original temple burnt down in

TIP

Shanghai's summer plum rain season is a constant downpour that lasts for two or three weeks in mid-June. The rains are named after the plum fruit that are harvested during this period.

BELOW: artist Pu Jie with his work – typical of the cutting-edge art found at the Suhe Art Galleries.

Map
on page
206

1918, and was replaced with the Jade Buddha Temple on the same site. Hui Gen took the other three jade statues back with him to his monastery on Putuoshan island, but these jade Buddhas have since disappeared.

The saffron-walled temple is entered through the *san men* ("three gate") temple gate, referring to the "three extrications" that every Buddhist must make in this material world in order to enter into the appropriate spiritual state of emptiness, no phenomenon and no action. The temple's five halls include the **Hall of Heavenly Kings**, with an enormous gilded image of the laughing Maitreya Buddha with a quartet of gods representing the elements in harmony, and the **Grand Hall**, with the Sakyamuni Buddha meditating on a lotus, flanked by the 20 warrior-like heavenly kings.

Exquisite faces of peace

The temple is known for its Buddhist paintings and a woodblock-printed set of the complete Buddhist scriptures, but the centrepieces are the two jade Buddhas, housed in separate halls. The seated Sakyamuni Buddha, which weighs 1,000 kg (2,200 lbs) and is 1.92 metres (6.3 ft) tall, rests in a glass case on the second floor of the **Jade Buddha Hall**. The creamy white, almost luminous statue of the beatifically smiling Buddha, draped in a gem-encrusted robe and seated in the lotus position, shows Buddha at the moment of enlightenment. On the ground floor of the **Hall of the Reclining Buddha** is the other smaller but much more exquisite reclining jade Buddha at 96 cm (37 inches), depicting a tranquil Sakyamuni, with the same beatific smile, at the moment of death. Don't confuse this with a larger polished stone version of the reclining jade Buddha, housed in a separate hall on the same floor. ❑

BELOW: Jade Buddha Temple's Reclining Buddha.

Jewish Sanctuary

Shanghai has always had a Jewish presence, beginning with the Sephardic Jewish families such as the Sassoons, Hardoons and Kadoories who built their vast fortunes in the city. They were followed by the Russian Jews, who fled the anti-Jewish pogroms and upheavals of early 19th-century Russia. During the 1930s, the new wave of Jews arriving in Shanghai were those fleeing the Holocaust in Europe.

For many European Jews, the smashing of the synagogues by rampaging anti-Jewish mobs in 1938 was the final push they needed to be convinced to leave their homeland, but doors throughout the world were closed: Shanghai was the only place that did not require a visa or family connections. As a result, between 1938 and 1940, some 20,000 European Jews arrived in Shanghai.

In Austria, Jewish persecution reached a frenzy after it was annexed by Nazi Germany in March 1938. Although Shanghai did not require visas for entry, Austrian Jews who wanted to flee Austria were not allowed to leave unless they had visas to prove to the Nazis that another country had accepted them.

In order to help them, the Chinese Consul-General to Austria from 1938–40, a dapper young man named Ho Fengshan, quietly granted several thousand visas to Austrian Jews – with Shanghai as the end destination. Ho knew that the visas were only a means of escape for Austrian Jews; in reality many of the visa recipients went to other parts of the world. Under his watch the Chinese Consulate in Vienna issued an average of 500 visas a month over the two-year period of his term. Ho is regarded today as China's Schindler and has been honoured for his work by Israel.

The Japanese, who occupied Hongkou and Zhabei, herded the Jewish refugees into a "designated area for stateless persons" in a section of Hongkou. The impetus for this was apparently a visit by the butcher of Warsaw, Joseph Meisinger, who arrived with a canister of poison gas (which was found after the war in Pudong) in Shanghai and suggested that concentration camps be set up on Chongming Island for the Jewish community.

The Japanese declined, instead insisting that all "stateless persons" move into the Hongkou ghetto. Times were difficult and things were scarce, but the refugees made the best of what they had, creating a "Little Europe" with cafés, delicatessens, schools and even a theatre – with financial help from the longer-established Jewish families.

Leaving the ghetto, for those who went to school or work outside, required a pass, which had to be issued by the diminutive, raging Japanese officer called Kwano Goya – virtually every Shanghai Jew who lived in the ghetto has his or her own Goya tale. Hats had to be doffed when crossing Waibadu Bridge, and low bows made to the Japanese sentries. Failure to do so invited abuse.

As hard as life was under the Japanese in Shanghai, many wartime refugees look back fondly on their time in the city. It was a tightly-knit community, they say, a time when people pulled together. It was also a time that saved many from almost certain deaths.   ❑

RIGHT: Ho Fengshan helped Jews flee from Nazi-occupied Austria by issuing them visas.

PUDONG

*Once marshland, Pudong's futuristic façade will encompass
several global superlatives, such as the world's longest
cable bridge, tallest building and highest hotel*

Map
on page
217

P udong is Future Shanghai. Anchored by the rocketship-like Oriental Pearl
TV Tower, this zone east of the Huangpu River with its forest of glittering
skyscrapers – not one built before 1990 – looks like the set of a space-age
film. Much of Shanghai's fast-forward progress since 1990, when plans to
develop Pudong as a special economic area were first announced, has been
telescoped into this 350-sq km (135-sq mile) area. Economic incentives have
lured 45 of the world's financial giants to the Lujiazui financial zone ("Shanghai's Wall Street") as well as the Shanghai Stock Exchange, the Futures
Exchange and the Diamond Exchange. It's no coincidence that skyscrapers are
positioned to face off with the Bund, showing up the colonial masters. Large
areas have been carved out for development: the Waigaoqiao container port,
the Jinqiao export processing zone and the Zhangjiang High-Tech Park.

As the face of 21st-century Shanghai, Pudong is the showcase for the best, the
brightest and the most advanced: the site of China's tallest building, Asia's
largest stock exchange, the world's longest cable bridge, a US$2 billion show-
case airport, technologically sophisticated exhibition centres, and state-of-the-
art museums and theatres. This is an urban planner's Utopia: high rises
interspersed with large sweeps of greenery and straight boulevards – man and
nature coexisting with industry and commerce.

LEFT: Pudong's
fantasy architecture.
BELOW: getting the
Oriental Pearl Tower
in the background
is a must.

Out of the squalor and poverty

Pudong today could be accused of being sterile, a contrast to its pre-1990 self: a country village on the
wrong side of the tracks. During the pre-Communist
era, it was a place of grinding poverty – destitute citizens like the 1940s cartoon character San Mao often
ended up as beggars on the streets. Pre-1949 Pudong
was a place of unhappy ghosts, the place where ruined
gamblers came to *"tiao Huangpu"* – jump into the
river – and where the bodies of sailors who perished
in American ships were buried.

Pudong, meaning "east of the Huangpu", was so
insignificant to Shanghai that the namesake river was
not spanned until the 1990s. Until then, the only way
to get across to Pudong was a five-minute ride on a
ferry from the Bund at **Jinling Pier** at 219–39 Zhongshan No. 2 Road (E). The ferry (daily 6am–6pm) still
makes for an atmospheric ride, with boats and barges
sliding past. On landing, it is but a short walk to the
Lujiazui sights. In contrast, the **Bund Tourist Tunnel** (Waitan Canguang Sui Dao) at Zhongshan Road
(by the Chen Yi statue) is the 21st-century way to
travel: train cars, accompanied by flashing lights and
scenes projected onto the tunnel walls, whisk visitors
to Pudong. It takes a little longer to cross by road via
either the **Yangpu Bridge** (Yangpu Qiao) or **Nanpu**

TIP

If you drive, check the latest Yan'an Road (E) Tunnel policy before you cross. The rules seem to change every few months, and have included: alternate days for odd- and even-numbered taxi licence plates; restricted hours when taxis are not permitted; and a toll.

BELOW:
Jin Mao Tower, the tallest building in China – for now.
RIGHT: Grand Hyatt's Cloud 9 bar.

Bridge (Nanpu Qiao), the world's longest and fourth-longest cable bridges, respectively, but the dramatic spiderwebbed bridges and the travel on space-age elevated highways make the experience worthwhile. The most popular crossing is the **Yan'an Road (E) Tunnel**, which as a result suffers from horrible jams. These should be tempered when three more tunnels are completed: Dalian Road and the Outer Ring Road tunnel at the end of 2003 and, by 2005, the Fuxing Road (E) tunnel, the world's first double-decker tunnel.

The Pudong skyline is dominated by the glittering glass and steel skyscrapers of the **Lujiazui** financial district, home of the Shanghai Stock Exchange and housing a who's who of international banking and finance. The broad swath of green that curves around Pudong's banks is called **Riverside Avenue** (Binjiang Dajie), offering the city's best views of the Bund. There is more greenery at **Lujiazui Park** (Lujiazui Gongyuan: daily 6am–8pm; entrance fee) at Lujiazui Road and Century Boulevard. One of several green lungs in Pudong, the park's open spaces make it a popular spot for lunchtime picnics surrounded by looming skyscrapers.

Have a tipple at the world's highest bar

Despite this stellar company, the **Jin Mao Tower** ❶ (Jin Mao Ta) at 88 Century Boulevard still stands out, and not just because it is the world's third-tallest building at 421 metres (1,381 ft). "I wanted to evoke the subtle memory of a pagoda, the ancient Chinese high-rise and marker for the landscape," explained the building's chief architect, Adrian Smith. Designed around the factor of eight, like the pagoda, the 88-storey building is China's tallest and, with its art deco design elements, makes an architectural summation of the city. The 88th-floor observatory (daily 9am–4pm; entrance fee) offers city views from an almost

identical perspective to the Oriental Pearl Tower (*see page 218*), but at half the price. The world's highest hotel, **Grand Hyatt Shanghai** (Jinmao Kaiyue Daji-udian) occupies the pinnacle of the Jinmao Tower from the 54th floor upwards and is itself a worthy sight. The 56th-floor atrium affords a breathtaking view of the building core, rising in a dizzying concentric spin to the 88th floor. A drink at **Cloud 9**, the highest bar in the world on the 87th floor, is de rigueur. And only at the Grand Hyatt can guests enjoy bubble baths with bird's eye city views.

World's tallest in the making

The much beleaguered **Shanghai World Financial Centre** (Shanghai Guoji Jinrong Zhongxin), which will be the world's tallest building at 492 metres (1,614 ft) when completed in 2007, has resumed construction next door. At first, design plans for an open circle on the roof to cut wind resistance were scuttled after it was pointed out that this would look too much like the Japanese flag; then construction came to a complete halt during the 1997 Asian financial crisis. There are plans now for a glass ferris wheel on top of the 101-storey building.

Cross the street to the only building here that looks as if it might be more than a decade old, the **Lujiazui Development Showroom ❷** (Lujiazui Yingchuan Xiaozhu: daily 10am–5pm; entrance fee). The 1917 home of wealthy shipping merchant Chen Guichen, the wood-and-brick traditional courtyard house, one of Pudong's largest, was once part of a 3,000-sq metre (32,290-sq ft) estate that housed several families and served as the headquarters of the Japanese army. The house-turned-museum offers a glimpse of a Pudong, and a Shanghai, that are long gone. The central courtyard, with its working well, frames a portrait of skyscrapers above, and rooms to the west have been furnished as in pre-

Map below

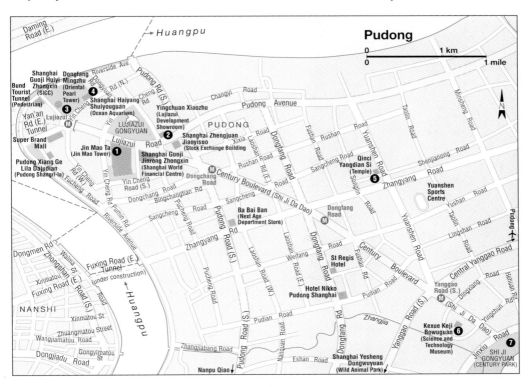

The seemingly endless atrium of the Grand Hyatt. Go up to the 56th floor and peer upwards – it spins all the way up to the 88th floor.

BELOW: Oriental Pearl Tower – an exercise in kitsch.

Liberation times, complete with chamber pots and art deco rosewood furniture. Carved screens, with some of the faces damaged during the Cultural Revolution excesses, hint at its past. An exhibition documents the rise and rise of Pudong year by year over the last decade.

Shanghai's Pearl of the Orient

The **Oriental Pearl Tower** ❸ (Dongfang Mingzhu Guangbo Dianshi Ta: daily 8am–10pm; entrance fee) at 2 Lujiazui Road, a symbol of modern Shanghai that looks like a Jetsons-era rocketship ready for take-off, elicits great passion in locals and mock horror in overseas tourists. The 468-metre (1,535-ft) TV tower, the world's third-largest, has 11 silver-and-cranberry coloured "pearls" in honour of Shanghai as Pearl of the Orient. Only three baubles are open, however.

More than a million visitors have taken the high-speed lift, travelling at 7 metres (23 ft) per second to the second pearl, perched at 259 metres (850 ft). Here, compass points and landmarks are displayed on the windows. The 360-degree view of the city is one of the best ways to orientate oneself – provided it's a clear day. A revolving Chinese restaurant is at 267 metres (876 ft), and above that, the third pearl, at the tower's pinnacle, is the highest point in Shanghai. Souvenir stands on each floor sell Pearl Tower miniatures.

The **Shanghai History Museum** (Shanghai Lishi Bowuguan: daily 8am–10pm) at the Oriental Pearl Tower basement takes one through Shanghai's history, with a Chinese spin on the imperialist invaders. The museum's audio-visual exhibits include re-creations of an early stock exchange, 19th-century cobblestone streets and an arrogant taipan's office (complete with recording), an original bronze lion from the Hongkong and Shanghai Bank *(see page 131)*, a gun from the Opium War's Wusong battles, and finishes up with models of old Shanghai architecture.

The eastern leg of the Oriental Pearl Tower sits on the edge of **Pudong Park** (Pudong Gongyuan: daily 6am–6pm; entrance fee), an idyllic stretch of green with wooden bridges over willow-fringed streams.

Across the street at 158 Yin Cheng Road (N), the **Shanghai Ocean Aquarium** ❹ (Shanghai Haiyang Shuiyouguan: daily 9am–9pm; entrance fee), opened in 2002, is an impressive state-of-the-art facility with a focus on Chinese sea creatures, including the endangered Yangzi alligator. With a high percentage of exotic creatures such as the alien-looking Japanese spider crab and dramatic displays, it has a high "ooh" factor. The shark tunnel, in which sharp-toothed sharks and giant rays swim lazily overhead, is the world's longest at 155 metres (509 ft).

On the other side of the Oriental Pearl Tower, the **Shanghai Natural Wild Insect Kingdom** (Shanghai Yesheng Da Ziran Kunchong Guan: daily 9am–9pm; entrance fee) is a sure hit with kids. The indoor jungle setting exhibits scorpions and spiders, the interactive insect shows (weekends only) allow the audience to touch and feel the creatures, and at an indoor lake, kids can catch (and keep) the fish with nets supplied.

The Lobby Lounge at the gracious **Pudong Shangri-la** (Pudong Xiang Ge Lila Dajudian) at 33 Fucheng Road offers a fabulous, eye-level view of the

Bund, while around the corner, the designer stores of the Thai-owned **Super Brand Mall** at 168 Lujiazui Road are housed in marble splendour. The **Shanghai International Convention Centre** (Shanghai Guoji Huiyi Zhongxin) is one of the very few low-rise buildings in Lujiazui. Flanked by bizarre double globes, it is the official government venue for meetings, including APEC.

Map on page 217

Asia's largest department store

To the east, **Next Age** (Ba Bai Ben) at 5101 Zhangyang Road, Asia's largest department store, has a new sophisticated veneer after a facelift, no doubt to compete with **Time Square**'s collection of designer boutiques across the street, though it needn't have worried: no mall in Shanghai can compare with Next Age in its incredible range of products offered on its 10 floors.

The ochre-walled **Qinci Yangdian Temple ❺** (Qinci Yangdian Si) about 1.5 km (1 mile) east at 476 Yuanshen Road (daily 8am–4pm; entrance fee) with its curved, tiled roof looks a little out of place so close to Pudong's shopping district. First built during the Three Kingdoms period (220–280), the existing temple buildings, housing colourful Taoist god images, date from the Qing dynasty.

Cruise Shanghai's Champs Èlysèe, the magnificent 5-km (3-mile) long **Century Boulevard** (Shi Ji Da Dao), designed by Jean-Marie Charpentier, the architect responsible for the Grand Theatre. The 100-metre (320-ft) wide avenue, with 10 hectares (25 acres) of green belts on either side, allows one of the city's most pleasant drives. At the top end of Century Boulevard, keep an eye out for the distinctive **Shanghai Stock Exchange Building** (Shanghai Zhengjuan Jiaoyisuo), built to resemble an ancient Chinese coin with a square space in its centre. Visitors are not allowed on the trading floor. At 3,600 sq metres (38,750 sq ft), the

Signboard at the Shanghai Natural Wild Insect Kingdom. Children will enjoy the creepie-crawlies on display at this attraction.

BELOW: working the phone at the Shanghai Stock Exchange.

exchange is the largest in Asia and operates an advanced electronic trading system. Take a detour right to a mini-hotel enclave in a gritty neighbourhood, home to the **Hotel Nikko Pudong Shanghai** and the sublime five-star **The St Regis Hotel** at 889 Dongfang Road. The latter's top-floor Italian restaurant, **Danieli's** (tel: 5050 4567), has fabulous food to die for and stunning views of Pudong by night.

A grand show of science

Back on Century Boulevard, veer right at the "Oriental Light" silver sculpture, a giant disk pierced by a spear, to the **Science and Technology Museum ❻** (Kexue Keji Bowuguan: Tues–Sun 9am–5pm; entrance fee). It was in front of the alloyed aluminium sphere that APEC leaders posed in Mandarin jackets during their 2001 meeting. The theme of the US$183-million museum, taking up 68,000 sq metres (731,950 sq ft) of space, is "man, nature, science and technology". The setting is impressive, but the content seems a notch below. The popular IMAX theatre screens daily shows (separate fee), and science halls hold an exploding volcano, a recreated rainforest, technology exhibits and an interactive children's area.

Continue down Century Boulevard to **Century Park ❼** (Shi Ji Gongyuan: daily 6am–6pm; free) at 1001 Jin Xiou Road. Charpentier also designed this beautifully landscaped eco-park, its forest and park area anchored by a huge lake. The park is the site of sporting events such as the annual Terry Fox run and the Shanghai Duathlon, and other large celebrations.

The foreign investments that Pudong attracts have in their turn also attracted legions of foreign employees, many of whom are housed in gargantuan mansions in the Pudong expatriate enclaves, all of which have swimming pools, clubhouses and gyms on their grounds. They have been called the new Ameri-

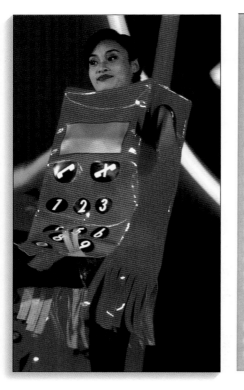

TECHNO-CHIC

Pudong manifests Shanghai's obsession with cutting-edge technology. Young people hunger for innovation, queuing up to try the newest models, and discarding last year's without a thought. Mobile phones (*shoji*) are indispensable and fashionable young women colour-coordinate phone covers with their outfits. Text messaging has become an integral part of life and is a tool for mass marketing. Readers' polls are sent via text, as are holiday greetings.

When Shanghai's young are not chatting into their earpieces, they are chatting online. Helped along by born-in-Shanghai sites *e-tang* and *sina.com*, they *shang wang* (surf the net), though always under the watchful eye of the government. After search engine Google was suspended for weeks in 2002 and users redirected to Chinese sites, surfers on the reinstituted Google found that researching controversial subjects such as the Falungong got them quickly disconnected. On balance, though, things are improving: formerly blocked sites such as the *New York Times* and the *Washington Post* are now accessible.

The cashless economy is becoming a reality. At the largest-circulation *Xin Min Evening News*, a single smart card opens the office door, and pays for lunch and groceries. Prepaid cards pay for taxi and subway rides.

Map on page 217

can Concession because of the concentration of executives from General Motors. The country-club lifestyle doesn't get much better than at the **Tomson Golf Villas**, where the houses edge the golf course.

The butterfly-shaped **Oriental Art Centre** (Dongfang Yishu Zhongxin), designed by Pudong airport designer Paul Andreu, is Pudong's answer to the Grand Theatre. Located near Century Park, the 23,000-sq metre (247,572-sq ft) centre for the performing arts, encircled by a lush garden, has a symphony hall, theatre and cinema, and is due to open in 2004.

Rural Nanhui District, south of the Pudong New Area, is a change in character from Pudong's business-like sterility. **Xinchang Ancient Town** (Xinchang Gucheng), which dates from the Song Dynasty (AD 960–1279) is Pudong's last water village, sensitively restored by one of Shanghai's leading preservationists.

Directly east is **Shanghai Wild Animal Park** (Shanghai Yesheng Dongwuyuan: daily 8am–5pm; entrance fee). The 205-hectare (506-acre) safari park is divided into bus and walking zones by animal type: wilder animals such as hunting leopards and South China tigers are visited from buses, while the walking zones have gentler species such as kangaroos, deer and lemurs. The park has brought back the days of greyhound racing with the modern city's first animal race track, 410 metres (1,345 ft) long, that races dogs, horses and ostriches. Unfortunately, keepers ignore the fact that visitors feed the animals, some of which are unnecessarily tethered, sometimes harshly, during the photo sessions and performances.

Just east of the park is the **Peach Garden Culture Village** (Taoyuan Wenhua Cun), only open during the peach blossom season (March-April) when nature-lovers gather here to admire peach blossoms in bloom.

Travel by magnetic levitation

The route to the new Pudong airport was significantly reduced when the Shanghai Maglev Train (SMT), the world's first commercial train of its kind, started operations in September 2003. The Maglev (short for magnetic levitation) uses electromagnetic levitation to whisk the train at a dizzy 430 km (267 miles) an hour, making the 30-km (19-mile) long trip from Pudong's Long Yang station to Pudong airport in just eight minutes – instead of the 45 minutes by road.

The Maglev, the fastest train in the world, surpassing both the French TGV and Japanese Shinkansen, has gone a long way towards muffling complaints that the slick **Pudong International Airport** (Pudong Guoji Jichang) is in an inconvenient location. City officials argue that it is a matter of time before the city will grow out to Pudong airport as it did with the older Hongqiao.

There is certainly plenty to grow out to: Shanghai's international airport currently handles about 16-million passengers a year (although it is designed for 60 million) in its four terminals, has 28 runways, and its location could make it North Asia's aviation hub. Built on reclaimed tideland that was once fish farms, the building was designed by French architect Paul Andreu to resemble a seagull in flight, a metaphor for soaring Shanghai. He incorporated fish pools and emerald rice fields into the landscaping as reminders of its heritage and as a foil for the light, transparent building. ❑

Instead of conventional steel wheels on rails, the Maglev uses electromagnetic technology to hover and glide above the guide rails. It took 30 years to develop it for commercial use and the Shanghai line cost a whopping US$1.2 billion. German consortium Transrapid built Shanghai's Maglev.

BELOW: Shanghai's Maglev, the fastest train in the world.

WESTERN SUBURBS

Urbanites escape here for the slower pace and a taste of country living. Popular visits are the water villages of Zhouzhuang and Zhujiajiao, but other less well-known stops have their own appeal

Map on page 225

Shanghai

Amusement parks, Ming dynasty canal towns, ancient pagodas and nature spots run riot through the countryside that borders the city's western flank, rejuvenating city-weary souls and simultaneously lining the coffers of their country cousins. It is a symbiotic relationship between city and country that goes back to the creation of the greater Shanghai Municipality, when eight districts, fanning out like petals around the metropolitan core, were carved out of neighbouring provinces to provide the burgeoning city with food and room for expansion, enriching the farmers in return.

A curious mixture of tradition, kitsch and industrialisation, the western suburbs offer a taste of the China of old, with scenes of lonely pagodas brooding on silent hillsides and crumbling Ming houses in forgotten lanes. The rural quiet belies what was a thriving area during the Song and the Tang dynasties, and, in the case of Songjiang County's Songze village, a history that goes as far back as Neolithic times – before the land mass of Shanghai even existed.

Today, Shanghai's long shadow defines the character of the area. Elements of antiquity, so lacking in the city, are tarted up, lit with neon and gift-wrapped for Shanghai tourists. Acres of ripening fields are yielding to the city's relentless progress, as they give way to acres of sparkling factories.

LEFT: the water canal town of Zhouzhuang. **BELOW:** Nanxiang's famous dumplings, *xiao long bao.*

Jiading District

Most people know **Nanxiang ❶**, some 17 km (10½ miles) northwest of Shanghai in Jiading District, as the home of the classic Shanghainese delicacy called *xiao long bao*. The bite-sized pleated dumplings, stuffed with pork and enough boiling liquid inside to do serious damage if popped into the mouth whole, are flogged on every street corner of this small town. Work off a dumpling lunch with a stroll in the bamboo-themed **Garden of Ancient Splendour** (Guyi Gongyuan: daily 8am–4.30pm; entrance fee). Originally called "the beauty of green bamboo" by its designer, bamboo sculptor Zhun Shansong, the Suzhou-style garden retains its Ming contours despite a 1746 reconstruction and 1949 expansion to its present 2.5 hectares (6½ acres). A Song stone pagoda and a Tang stele with Buddhist scriptures stand in the garden. A pavilion built during the Japanese Occupation has a corner left incomplete to signify a broken China under the Occupation.

Just northeast of Nanxiang is **Jiading ❷**, a quiet canal-fringed little town – the largest in the Jiading District. The town's Ming-era **Dragon Meeting Pond Park** (Huilong Tang Gongyuan: daily 8am–4.30pm; entrance fee), named after the five streams that converge here, may be contemplated in relative solitude. At one time, Jiading town was important enough to be the seat of the imperial examinations, held at its

Southern Song-style **Confucius Temple** (Wen Miao: daily 8am–4.30pm, closed 11.30am–1.30pm; entrance fee), at 183 Nan Avenue, west of the park. The temple is also home to the **Jiading Museum** (Jiading Bowuguan: daily 9am–4.30pm; entrance fee). Examination candidates offered prayers to the patron saint of scholars at this temple, first built in 1281, and in return, the Yuan dynasty fish and dragon sculpture over the temple's main gate blessed the scholars with luck. The sculpture is a visual representation of the saying "a carp leaping over the dragon gate", a metaphor for achieving success. There is more symbolism along the dramatic triple archway that fronts the temple, with its 72 stone lions representing the 72 disciples of Confucius.

The graceful Southern Song-era **Fahua Pagoda** (Fahua Ta), rebuilt in 1919, is a five-minute walk north of the temple, while a stroll up north along Lianqiu River leads to the **Garden of Autumn Clouds** (Qiu Xia Pu: daily 8am–4.30pm; entrance fee), Shanghai's oldest garden and laid out in 1502. Across the canal is a large and bustling produce market.

Songjiang County and Sheshan

Songjiang County, 30 km (19 miles) southwest of Shanghai and the site of neolithic remains at Songze village, is known as the cradle of Shanghai civilisation. Its most famous site, however, is much younger. The **Sheshan Cathedral** (Sheshan Tang) and **Sheshan Observatory** (Sheshan Tien Wen Tai: daily 9am–4.30pm; entrance fee), a collection of ageing buildings on the only hill visible for miles is part of Songjiang County's National Tourist Resort of **Sheshan ❸**.

Once one of the most important in Asia, the 1898 observatory, with its century-old 40-cm (15½-inch) aperture telescope still intact, is now a small museum

BELOW:
Jiading's Garden
of Autumn Clouds.

dedicated to the history of Chinese star-gazing. A new telescope was installed just below the crest of the hill, but as recently as 1986, the old machine was used to track and take photos of Halley's Comet for scientific use – just as the Jesuits who built the observatory did when the comet visited in 1910.

The Jesuits also built the sturdy church next door, first as the Holy Mother Cathedral in 1866 and, in 1935, the **Basilica of Notre Dame**. A subtle "M" (for Mary) and "SJ" (Society of Jesus, i.e. the Jesuits) are inscribed in the old iron gate in the southwestern corner of the churchyard. The lovely bronze Madonna and Child on the steeple is a recent replacement for the one that was pulled down during the Cultural Revolution. Pilgrims walk up the south gate, lined with grottoes and shrines, and oddly, play ring-toss games with plastic animals and statues of Mary and Jesus. Local Catholics make a pilgrimage here each May.

The 1898 Sheshan Observatory is now a museum dedicated to astronomy.

The eastern slopes of the hill feature an odd mix of the **Forest Park** (Senlin Gongyuan: daily 7am–4.30pm; entrance fee), the seven-storey **Xiudaozhe Pagoda** (Xiudaozhe Ta: open daily; free) and Shanghai's own leaning tower, the 11th-century **Huzhu Pagoda** (Huzhu Ta: open daily; free) on Tianma Hill. The tilt was created by villagers in 1788, who began pulling out the pagoda's bricks hoping for more of the treasure that was found when a fire that destroyed its wooden portion revealed a booty of ancient Chinese coins. Locals proudly point out that Huzhu leans more steeply than the Leaning Tower of Pisa – and is 100 years older.

A different sort of entertainment awaits at the outdoor sets of the **Shanghai Film and TV Studio Amusement Park** (Shanghai Ying Shi Le Yuan: daily 8.30am–4.30pm; entrance fee), at 495 Beisong Gong Road, a detour south off Highway 320. Created as a backdrop for old Shanghai movies, one of China's most popular film genres, visitors can take original Concession-era trams, rick-

BELOW:
Sheshan Cathedral.

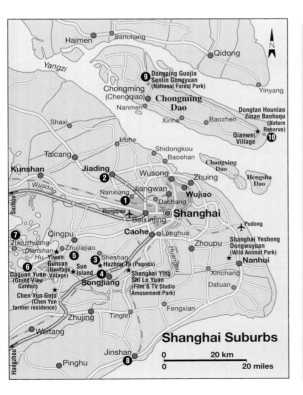

Shanghai Suburbs

shaws and hansom cabs through the streets of old Shanghai: cobblestoned Nanjing Road with the Sincere Department store, the Bund, the Old City, Moller Villa, a row of Tudor mansions or a life-sized cathedral.

Continue on to **Songjiang ❹** town and its pride, the **Square Pagoda** (Fang Ta: daily 8.30am–4.30pm; entrance fee). Built in 1077, the 50-metre (160-ft) structure will reward climbers with views over the countryside. The 14th-century brick screen wall that fronts the pagoda depicts the legendary monster *tan*, with deer antlers, a lion's tail and ox's hooves, who tried to devour the sun but ended up drowning instead – the moral being that greed is not good. The **Garden of Drunken Poet Bai** (Zubai Chi: daily 9am–4.30pm; entrance fee), a five-minute walk west, was built by a Qing official who was a fan of the Tang poet who fell into a pond while drunkenly trying to capture the moon's reflection in the water.

Songjiang's 300-strong Muslims, descended from the soldiers who were part of the Yuan-era Mongol army, flock to the lovely **Songjiang Mosque** (Songjiang Qingzhen Si; open daily 8am–7pm; free) every Friday for prayers. The 1367 Chinese-style mosque is one of the oldest in China.

Qingpu County and Zhujiajiao

Rural **Qingpu County**'s proximity to Shanghai means that it is a favourite playground for city dwellers, who are regular visitors to its parks, water villages and other sights. Retrace your steps to Highway 318, where the **Oriental Green Ship Campsite** (Dong Fang Luzhou Shiyi Yuan: 8.30am–5pm; entrance fee) is found. Created to give city kids fresh air and green space, the complex includes a botanical park, a sculpture garden, water sports facilities and a golf course, and – most strangely – an actual aircraft carrier that can be visited.

China's four official religions are Buddhism, Islam, Taoism and Christianity – both Protestant and Catholic – but Catholics answer to the government, not to the Roman Pope.

BELOW:
typical water canal boat at Zhujiajiao.

The romance of Ming and Qing water villages such as **Zhujiajiao ❺** – just after the park – is rapidly eroding with the onset of tourism. Residents have moved out and are replaced by souvenir shops; shopping plazas ring the historical area and the narrow lanes are elbow-to-jowl with tourists on weekends. Remember that this is a staged recreation rather than an authentic experience, and Zhujiajiao – once you get past the giant parking space and shopping plaza – can be a charming place.

The five arches of the weathered **Fangseng Bridge**, flip-flopping 70 metres (236 ft) across the Caogang River, greets visitors to Zhujiajiao. Market women selling turtles, frogs and fish squat in front of the bridge, first built in 1571 and reconstructed in 1814. Ming and Qing dynasty-style wooden houses open out onto a canal spanned by arched bridges, with second-storey restaurants overlooking the boats floating past. Old shops have been restored, giving an uncharacteristic sheen to the **Handalong Sauce and Pickle Shop** and the **Tong Tian Hu Drugstore**. In-between, small country stores sell regional specialities such as *tipang* (stewed pork rump) and pickles, and country crafts and freshwater pearls while an old barbershop serves the handful of elderly residents who live here. Less well known and less crowded than Zhouzhuang *(see page 228)*, a boat ride on the canal is nevertheless a nice way to get away from the crowds.

Other Qingpu attractions

Also focused on cultural preservation is the **Heritage Village for Arts and Culture** (Yiwen Guncun: tel: 6279 0502, by appointment only; free) at 6622 Huqingping Highway just west of Zhujiajiao. Owner Jeffrey Wong has saved entire buildings *(see page 229)* from destruction – old Ming and Qing houses and the main gate of Shanghai's Jing An Temple for example – and created a unique architectural museum.

A short detour south on the Zhufeng Highway leads to **Sun Island** (Taiyang Dao), a summer resort with an 18-hole golf course and boat rides. Continuing further south, the **Former Residence of Chen Yun** (Chen Yun Guju) and the **Revolutionary Museum of Qingpu** (Qingpu Geming Lishi Jinian Guan: both daily 9am–4.30pm; entrance fee) is at 3516 Zhufeng Gong Road. A statement in marble of the power of the Communist Party, the spacious exhibition hall tells the story of economic theorist, revolutionary and local boy Chen Yun. What makes the visit worthwhile is Chen's narrow, two-storey wooden childhood home, in the rear of the museum, which backs out onto a quiet canal.

Backtrack to Huqingping Highway and ancient China at the **Grand View Garden ❻** (Daguan Yuan: daily 8am–4:30pm; entrance fee), north off the highway on the edge of **Dianshan Lake** (Dianshan Hu). A theme park based on the classic Chinese novel *Dream of the Red Mansion*, the garden's re-creations of the novel's buildings, set in a Suzhou-style garden, are enhanced by Chinese musicians and re-enactments of scenes from the book by actors in period garb. The **Minorities Cultural Village** (Minzu Wenhua Cun: daily 8am–4.30pm; entrance fee), on the edge of Dianshan Lake, recreates China's ethnic minority culture architecture, with regular performances of minority customs.

Map on page 225

Tipang, or stewed pork rump is a Shanghainese delicacy – and you will see it displayed at food shops everywhere in villages like Zhujiajiao and Zhouzhuang.

BELOW:
Grand View Garden tour guide.

Map on page 225

Avoid the tourist
hordes by heading to
either Wuzheng, Xitang
or Tongli – all relatively
untouched water
villages. The best
approach is to hire a
taxi. Your hotel can
arrange this at roughly
RMB 600 for the day.

BELOW: picturesque
boat ride along one
of Zhouzhuang's
canals.

Zhouzhuang

Shanghai's most famous water village, 900-year-old **Zhouzhuang** ❼ (daily 8am–5pm; entrance fee covers most of the village attractions below), 20 km (12 miles) north of Grand View Garden, has become a kitschy Chinese Disneyland of sorts. Listed as a World Heritage site "under preparation", Zhouzhuang was made famous by renowned Shanghai artist Chen Yifei, whose paintings of a pre-tourist Zhouzhuang were snapped up by the likes of the late Armand Hammer, the noted art collector. Now fronted by a shopping plaza and an endless supply of tour buses that ensure crowds at all times, Zhouzhuang's narrow, winding streets are lined with souvenir shops, restaurants, freshwater pearl shops, art galleries, Chen Yifei wannabes earnestly painting the sights, and tourists striking poses on the bridges, the most famous of which is the Ming dynasty **Double Bridge** (Shuangqiao). The bridge – which is somewhat of a disappointment when you actually see it – is made up of two bridges, Shide Bridge, with its curved arch and Yong'an Bridge, with its square arch resembling a key.

Most of the houses that line the canals date from the Qing, Ming and Yuan dynasties, such as the sprawling **Zhang Residence** (Zhang Ting). Built in 1449 alongside the Ruojing River, with six courtyards and 70 rooms, the house has a pond next to its main hall, where riverboats dropping off visitors could turn around. The **Chen Residence** (Chen Ting) to the south, is even more luxurious. A series of wooden two-storey halls, each with a courtyard in between, runs along both sides of the lane, with the river running through the middle, and a second-storey walkway connecting the buildings. The seven courtyards and 100 rooms include separate men's and women's quarters as well as furnished bedrooms, a kitchen and a shrine. Another highlight of the village is **Zhouzhuang Museum** (Zhouzhuang Bowugan), which has a collection of Ming and Qing pottery excavated from the village, and exhibitions on the village's age-old fishing traditions and folk art.

North of the old town, the **Quanfu Temple** (Quanfu Si: daily 9am–4.30pm; entrance fee includes Nanhu Garden below) is renowned for its 5-metre (16-ft) bronze Buddha, surrounded by 21 small gold Buddha statues. The temple gardens, with their pagodas and pavilions, lead into the Suzhou-style **Nanhu Garden** (Nanhu Gongyuan), originally laid out by the Jin dynasty scholar Zhang Jiying.

Jinshan

In rural **Jinshan** ❽, Shanghai's southernmost suburb on Hangzhou Bay, peasant painters have turned ploughshares into art. After the Cultural Revolution, a time starved of art and culture, the village began to develop a local form of folk art. Embroidery, paper-cutting and weaving were transferred to rice paper, recording country life and customs in crayon-bright hues of tempera and chalk. Today, Jinshan's idyllic rural farm scenes have yielded to factories, however, and the farmers now paint at the **Jinshan Exhibition Institute for the Study of Folk Art** (Jinshan Qu Zhu Jing Zhen: daily 8am–5pm; free) at 318 Jiankang Road. There is little in the area aside from the studios, demonstration rooms and galleries at this facility. ❑

Shanghai Heritage House Museum

The price of new Shanghai has been the destruction of old Shanghai, but it's one Jeffrey Wong is not willing to pay. The inveterate collector has started buying up entire historic houses slated for destruction, dismantling them and transporting them to the Heritage Village for Arts and Culture *(see also page 227)* in Qingpu County, near the Zhujiajiao water village. His mission is to save what he can of Shanghai's fragile architectural and cultural heritage before the relentless modernising tide in China completely eradicates the past.

A dirt driveway leads to the village, where a cobbled courtyard fronts the whitewashed Qing dynasty Suzhou-style building with its typical black tile roof that now serves as the Heritage Village office. Wong bought it in its entirety in 2000.

Strewn around the garden are "well stones", the ancient stones that covered wells, and bits and pieces waiting for restoration. When Shanghai's Jing An Temple was dismantled in 2001 and built anew, Wong acquired the main temple building and the entire temple gate with its exquisite temple statuary and elaborately carved wooden girders. When the nearby town of Haining could only afford to maintain one of the poet Xu Zhimo's residences, Wong bought all nine buildings belonging to the 480-year-old *shikumen* family home.

Wong buys the houses through his extensive network of contacts in Shanghai, who are eager to sell off a complete set rather than salvageable parts. Yet despite his efforts at reclaiming the past, Wong does not plan on completely restoring the interiors to their original state.

He would like these houses to be lived in again – perhaps by the artists that he also nurtures in the village – but points out that while period bedrooms and dining rooms may mesh with modern life, Ming bathrooms and kitchens cannot.

At the moment, the Suzhou house, Xu's residence and a rare late 18th-century two-storey house stand on the property. In his warehouse, other projects await: the home of Shanghai's Green Gang triad chief, Du Yuesheng, with the custom-made tiles in the bathroom still intact; an entire Suzhou-style garden; the main Jing An Temple building; and a street of 68 houses along Haining's Xinanhe Street.

Restoration, says Wong, is a slow, expensive and painstaking process. Reconstruction of the old houses has to be done based on the most basic of blueprints, and replacements have to be done with materials of the same vintage, colour and size – which sometimes means waiting for months for another similar house to be dismantled.

Recognising that the dwellings need to be curated with historical accuracy, the Heritage Village for Arts and Culture only focuses on Ming and Qing dynasty-style buildings. A second property due to open soon will display late Qing and 1920s–30s architecture.

Visitors are welcomed but only by appointment, so call beforehand to arrange a visit (tel: 6279 0502). ❏

RIGHT: ceiling detail from a typical late 18th-century Qing-style building.

CHONGMING ISLAND

Not only do the farming villages work hard to provide fresh, live food to assuage Shanghai's voracious appetite, they also provide a wholesome back-to-nature holiday experience

Shanghai

Chongming Island (Chongming Dao) slumbers in silt-muddied waters at the mouth of the Yangzi, a slash of green underscoring the great statement of mainland Shanghai just south. China's second-largest island (after Hainan), Chongming is the *yin* to Shanghai's *yang*. At 1,200 sq km (463 sq miles), Chongming is one-fifth Shanghai's size, with 750,000 residents to Shanghai's 15 million. Chongming's business is its farms – fish, crabs, vegetable patches – that feed Shanghai. The world's largest alluvial island, Chongming has doubled its size over the last half-century through a combination of land reclamation and the constant silting of the Yangzi. And it continues to grow: 140 metres (460 ft) eastwards and 80 metres (262 ft) north each year. With 30,000 hectares (74,130 acres) of beaches and a migratory bird conservation zone, the island may count more wild creatures than people at certain times of the year.

For most of its 1,300-year history, Chongming has battled the sea. The town has been relocated five times – and rebuilt six times – due to the flooding that destroyed the sea wall. The island's attempt to master the sea resulted in a Chongming invention – the Shanghai junk – the classic Chinese boat with a flat bottom that is perfect for the area's shallow coastal waters.

Chongming's rural lifestyle delighted the Cultural Revolutionaries, who sent countless bourgeoisie from Shanghai to farm its lands. Ecologists say the Three Gorges Dam may have environmental repercussions as far up the Yangzi as Chongming in future, but the latter is already affected: 5,000 residents displaced by the Three Gorges Dam were recently relocated to Chongming.

East China's largest man-made forest

The construction of a 25-km (15½-mile) river crossing from Pudong's Waigaoqiao to Chongming Island is in Shanghai's 10th Five-Year Plan (2001–05). For now, the only way to get to Chongming is to board a ferry from one of Shanghai's three northeastern ports of **Wusong**, **Baoyang** and **Shidongkou**. Depending on which of Chongming's three gritty port towns you arrive at – **Nanmen**, **Xinhe** or **Baozhen** – head westward for the **Dongping National Forest Park ❾** (Dongping Guojia Senlin Gongyuan: daily 6am–6pm, 7pm in summer; entrance fee), which covers 360 hectares (890 acres) of the island. Under blue skies, a boulevard of soaring, perfectly cone-shaped deep green metasequoias fringe a canal leading to the entrance of eastern China's largest man-made forest.

The park, 2 km (1¼ miles) by 1.5 km (1 mile), began life as a tree farm in 1959 and has a fishing pond and lake. Its myriad paths – with judiciously placed benches – that crisscross the interior, clean air, birdsong and butterflies are reasons enough to visit.

BELOW:
Chongming Island
is a favourite stop
with Shanghainese
from the mainland.

Map on page 225

However, Chongming's park administration is taking no chances: the lake is stocked with paddle boats; there is a Go Kart track; a slightly grungy swimming pool (and a man-made beach); and even paintball, the bizarre "war" game that involves shooting paint pellets at the enemy. On the forest's edge is a shockingly modern, sparkling silver hotel: the **Bao Dao Resort**.

Most of Chongming's population is concentrated in the port towns, with the remainder in scattered villages, where granite farmhouses painted in pastels loom over neat vegetable fields. **Qianwei Village**, on the island's eastern edge, is a traditional village that practises ecologically sensitive cultivation. In fact, it has been selected by the International Environmental Protection Organisation as one of 500 eco-type villages around the world. Farmers grow organic vegetables, and some have turned their farmhouses into bed-and-breakfast inns, offering TV and air-conditioning (Farm Tour programme: tel: 5964 9261). Qianwei offers demonstrations of folk games and encourages visitors to try out farm living and working in the fields. **Yingzhou Ancient Village Museum** (Yingzhou Lao Shi Bowuguan: daily 9am–5pm; admission fee) occupies a series of thatched-roof earthen houses in Qianwei Village; each one shows a designated task: weaving, cooking or milling grain. A trio of low-rise, simple earthen huts with worn red lanterns hanging outside is a reproduction of the ancient village temple, where women prayed for their husbands at sea.

Trekking into the remote marshes and mudflats at the **Dongtan Nature Reserve** ❿ (Dongtan Houniao Zinan Baohuqu: daily 6am–6pm; entrance fee), on the island's eastern edge, is a highlight *(see below)*. Thousands of birds – which represent one-tenth of the total species in China – flit among the shore grasses, shrieking and cooing, including migratory birds en route from Australia to Siberia. ❑

TIP

The fastest way to get from Shanghai to Chongming is to take the fast ferry (30–40 minutes) from Baoyang Port to Chongming's Nanmen Port.

BELOW:
Chong Ming's nature reserve attracts rare bird species.

DONGTAN NATURE RESERVE

Located midway along the East Asia–Australia flyway for migratory birds, Chongming's nature reserve is an ornithologist's dream. Sandpipers, terns, plovers, gulls, egrets and herons – 116 different species – have been sighted on the island, also a breeding ground for waterfowl. Chongming is committed to protecting its own birds as well as the migratory species, and has signed agreements to this effect with Australia and New Zealand.

RMB15 million has been invested in a conservation zone for the endangered sturgeon, a Mesozoic-era fish that survived 150 million years, only to face the threat of modernity. Chongming's birds are under threat, too. The 3,000 tundra swans, once regular winter visitors, have not appeared in three years; the hardening mud flats a hindrance to getting their food. Pollution kills the shellfish that the birds feed on and grazing animals deplete the shore grasses. The endangered hooded cranes are scared away by the noise of motorised fishing boats. Worse, 15 percent of the protected wildlife on Chongming ends up on Shanghai dinner tables, by courtesy of poachers.

As the delicate balance between ecology and development may be tipping away from the birds some favour, experts say the nature reserve has a difficult mission ahead.

EXCURSIONS FROM SHANGHAI

Nearby trips include ancient capitals steeped in history and enduring beauty, or contemplative, relaxing nature spots

Once, people from other parts of China came to Shanghai to see what the West looked like. Even today, urban Shanghai's go-go energy and cosmopolitan style is not, one is often reminded, the *real* China. Fortunately, some of the country's most famous classically Chinese sights, straight from a Chinese landscape painting, are within a couple of hours of Shanghai. But even in the more sedate, decidedly more Chinese environs of these places, you can't really leave Shanghai behind. There are historical links to the big city, dating from the pre-1949 days, as well as more contemporary connections today, with throngs of Shanghai tourists and spillovers from the Shanghai economic boom affecting life in these neighbouring outposts.

The combination of an efficient train system, high-speed highway and, in the case of Putuoshan, a fast ferry, makes getting out of the city easy. Only on China's three big holidays (Chinese New Year, 1 May and 1 October), when all transport routes are hopelessly jammed, does travelling become a major challenge.

Just an hour away from Shanghai, the pretty mediaeval town of Suzhou captures the essence of Chinese civilisation in her Ming-era classical Chinese gardens, a UNESCO World Heritage site. Two hours further west, what was once the longest city wall in the world contains the historical city of Nanjing, twice the nation's capital in the past and the focal point for some of the most turbulent moments of the last 400 years of Chinese history. Here, too, is one of the region's great scenic spots, the tree-covered and poetically named Purple Gold Mountain.

One of Shanghai's top tourist destinations, Hangzhou, to the southwest of Shanghai, was the capital of China during the Song dynasty. Capturing the 10 best views of mirror-like West Lake, with softly blurred mountains behind it, is the city's main draw, along with ancient temples and pagodas. Just 65 km (40 miles) north of Hangzhou lies a slice of old Shanghai. Almost hidden among groves of thick bamboo are the old vacation villas and churches on Moganshan, the summer hill station resort of missionaries, the Concession elite, and later, Shanghai gangsters and Kuomintang honchos.

It's a different kind of old China on the island of Putuoshan, south of Shanghai across Hangzhou Bay. Dubbed the "fairyland of the immortals", the old cloister is home to one of Buddhism's four sacred mountains. Dotted with monasteries and temples as well as Shanghai's closest beaches, the island – just like all the excursions covered in this section – makes a refreshing escape from urban life. ❑

PRECEDING PAGES: Hangzhou's West Lake bathed in dawn's amber light; stone elephants and other beasts guard the path leading to Nanjing's Ming Tombs.
LEFT: the Twin Pagodas (Shuang Ta) of Suzhou.

PUTUOSHAN

Once the abode only of monks, this serene island is a draw for the religious and the introspective. The 1,000-year-old Puji Temple is one of many that dot a vista of craggy outcrops, forest and beaches

Wide, long beaches, hill-top temples, clean air and an absence of cars and shopping malls makes the island of **Putuoshan ❶** an ideal antidote to Shanghai's buzz. Situated 250 km (155 miles) across Hangzhou Bay, south of Shanghai, the island sees mostly day trippers. One day may be sufficient to cover the major temples but an overnight stay allows the precious solitude of the island to soak in. Ringed by craggy rocks and a crashing sea, Putuoshan is a natural cloister. For centuries, only monks were allowed to live here.

"The little island is literally covered with temples, arbors and monuments… the summit commands a panorama of great beauty, consisting of the blue sea studded with green islands", says a 1924 guidebook. Aside from a change in the sea colour – it's taken on a milky tea-coloured hue today – the description remains an accurate one. Accessible only by ferry, Putuoshan manages to retain its mystical quality even as religious tourism – China's hot new commodity – brings in Chinese tourists by the busloads. "Temple tourism", to a generation raised to believe that religion was the opiate of the masses, results in bizarre scenes, such as tour guides teaching Chinese tourists the proper way to pray. The island's excellent minibus system shuttles visitors between the ferry station and the island's main tourist sites, but along the way, there are plenty of solitary paths and forested copses.

Putuoshan, like all religious entities, was ravaged during the Cultural Revolution. Some temples survived, but both the statuary and population of monks were decimated, with only 29 monks left on the ruined island in the late 1960s, down from the 2,000 at its peak. Today, the tourist dollar goes to the renovation and rebuilding of many of the temples.

It all began with a dream

The "fairyland of the immortals" has been a holy site since the Qing dynasty, when Japanese monk Hui'e, on his way home with a Guanyin statue, miraculously found shelter on Putuoshan during a violent storm. Guanyin, the Goddess of Mercy, told him in a dream that he would be able to return home safely only if he left her behind on the island. Hui'e erected a shrine on the spot that is now **Guanyin Leap** (Guanyin Tiao: daily 8am–5pm; entrance fee), the storm abated, Hui'e went home, and the island has been sacred to Guanyin ever since. Putuoshan is particularly crowded on three dates determined by the lunar calendar: Guanyin's birthday, the day on which she began studying Buddhism, and the day she became a nun.

Today, the 33-metre (108-ft) tall bronze-plated statue of the goddess, gazing over the harbour like a Buddhist Statue of Liberty, is the first sight that greets visitors to the island. The steering wheel she holds in

LEFT: the giant statue of Guanyin welcomes all to Putuoshan island. **BELOW:** Thousand Step Beach, on the east coast of Putuoshan.

her left hand symbolises her protection of the island's fishermen as she steers them away from danger. The platform on which she stands houses 400 statues, representing different Guanyin incarnations, while a pavilion at the base features a series of carved wooden murals depicting scenes of Guanyin coming to the rescue of local villagers and fishermen, for whom she is a patron saint.

Gilded Guanyin image at the Puji Temple, or Puji Si.

Suicide point

The gateway at **Purple Bamboo Temple** (Zhi Zhu Lin Si: daily 6am–5pm; admission fee), directly north on the coast, leads one directly to **Chaoyin Cave** (Chaoyin Dong), near the coast where Hui'e had to leave Guanyin behind. The sound of the waves crashing on this rocky outcrop resemble so closely the call of the Buddha that suicidal monks would gratefully leave the world behind here. A walkway leads to the older temples, tucked into the cliffside, and the chanting of black-robed monks floats over the water to the pine-covered forest.

One of the summer delights on Putuoshan are the wide sandy beaches, **Thousand Step Beach** (Qian Bu Sha: 7am–5pm; entrance fee, free after 5pm) and **Ten Thousand Step Beach** (Wan Bu Sha: 7am–5pm; entrance fee, free after 5pm), north of Chaoyin Cave. Crowded on summer weekends, the beaches are virtually empty on weekdays and during the off season.

Nuns with shaven heads are part of the scene at the **Dasheng Nunnery** (Dasheng An: daily 8am–5.30pm; entrance fee), across from Ten Thousand Step Beach. The place is dominated by a tranquil reclining Buddha in the main hall, while upstairs are hundreds of tiny Buddha statues in meditative poses.

West of the beaches is one of the island's three main temples, **Puji Temple** (Puji Si: daily 6am–9pm; entrance fee), fronted by three lotus ponds with pavil-

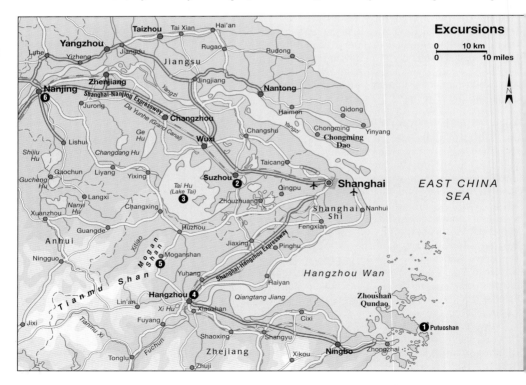

ions, arched bridges and the branches of enormous, ancient camphor trees hanging over the water. The ochre-hued temple buildings were first built in 1080, but the complex has been expanded and rebuilt considerably since then, and the current buildings date from the Qing era. One of the few unreconstructed temples on Putuoshan, Puji Si has a main hall dominated by a gilded seated Buddha that is flanked by colourful Taoist gods, while the secondary hall features the fat, laughing Maitreya incarnation of the Buddha. A Guanyin statue stands at the rear of the temple.

Next to the temple is a cobbled street lined with colourful shops selling religious paraphernalia, from giant origami paper lotuses to an array of joss sticks, and rows and rows of porcelain and gilt statues of various deities. Saffron-coloured bags, similar to those carried by monks, may be purchased and stamped at each temple (for a fee) as a sort of religious passport.

The five-storey Yuan dynasty **Duobao Pagoda** (Duobao Ta: open during daylight hours, free), dating from 1334, stands just east of Puji Temple. Despite its prime location, it has sprouted weeds and the gated grounds are unkempt. It almost seems abandoned, certainly by the tour groups, giving it a certain mystique. Constructed with craggy limestone from Lake Tai, near Suzhou, the pagoda has faded Buddhist holy inscriptions.

Exquisite temple hall from Nanjing

The Ming-era **Fayu Temple** (Fayu Si: daily 6.30am–5.30pm; entrance fee) to the north is a spectacular sight with its 200-odd religious halls, standing among ancient trees along the slope of the mountain in layers. The temple is set against the backdrop of **Foding Hill** (Foding Shan), which rises just behind the complex. Fayu Temple is noted for its exquisite beamless, domed **Dayuan Hall**, in which nine dragons, carved from wood, curl auspiciously around the interior dome of the hall. Originally a Nanjing temple hall, its move to Putuoshan in 1689 is said to have been carried out by order of the Qing Emperor Kangxi. The temple has been the centrepiece of Guanyin's birthday celebrations ever since. Life imitates art when monks, nuns and worshippers come to pray before the statue of Guanyin, herself depicted among monks and nuns.

For hundreds of years, pilgrims have been climbing Foding Hill to the northern **Huiji Temple** (Huiji Si: daily 6.30am–7pm; entrance fee), stopping every three steps to prostrate themselves. Now they can take the cable car (daily 6.30am–5pm; entrance fee), and enjoy remarkable vistas of farmers tilling the land below and the foliage-covered hills, accompanied by the loud quacking of ducks. A tree-lined path leads to the temple, mossy walls adding to its ancient aura (although several temple halls were reconstructed in 2002).

On a clear day, the lookout point on Foding Hill's summit, **Heaven's Lamp** (Tien Ding), a five-minute walk north of the temple, offers spectacular views of the sea and the surrounding islands. Better views are to be had from the state guesthouse that shares the summit; unfortunately the Chinese-roofed mansion is heavily guarded and is not open to visitors. ❑

Map on page 240

TIP

Because Putuoshan caters to tour groups who complete their sights in time to catch the 5pm ferry, the island comes to a halt by 5pm, the time when the mini-buses and the cable cars stop running.

BELOW: Duobao Pagoda silhouetted against the dawn light.

SUZHOU AND LAKE TAI

While its surreal vista of canals and lakes belie a spin-off pearl farming industry, the real Suzhou lies in its serene gardens: to enjoy them is to experience the zenith of Chinese civilisation

Map on page 240

T he ancient moated city of **Suzhou ❷**, whose intricate mosaic of canals and gardens led Marco Polo to describe it as "Venice of the East", is renowned for its classical Chinese gardens, silk-weaving and beautiful women. One of the oldest cities in the Yangzi Basin, Suzhou was founded in 600 BC by He Lu, the Emperor of the Wu Kingdom, but it was not until the completion of the Grand Canal a millennium later that the city began to flourish.

Its prosperity soared, particularly in silk production, when neighbouring Hangzhou, and later, Nanjing, became the imperial capital. It was the imperial officials who first began laying out Suzhou's famous gardens. Unscathed by the Taiping Rebellion and the Japanese Occupation, Suzhou's protected historical district, with its cobblestone streets and ancient stone dwellings, still retains its mediaeval character. The city walls are gone, demolished by the Communists, but the moat that followed the wall's contours remains. Nearly 200 humpback bridges are left, arching like lithe gymnasts over the intricate grid of canals, and one ancient city gate still stands. The historic city is ringed by tomorrow: the Suzhou-Singapore industrial park surrounds old Suzhou, drawing it into a 21st-century world of fast food, superhighways and five-star hotels.

LEFT: the Humble Administrator's Garden, one of Suzhou's most visited attractions. **BELOW:** a lotus in full bloom.

Make time for the tranquil gardens

Just 80 km (50 miles) northwest of Shanghai, Suzhou is a tempting day trip, but the gardens are best explored leisurely, over a couple of days. Suzhou is the region's pearl centre, its picturesque canals and lakes now given over to the increasingly profitable business of pearl farming. A short detour off the main Huqingping highway, just before reaching Suzhou proper, leads to the pearl farm at **Golden Rooster Lake** or Jin Ji Hu (tel: 512-761 4384, by appointment only). Here, farmers take visitors out in small fishing boats to the spot where the pearls are farmed, and pull up a bag of oysters. Back at the jetty, you can dig out your own pearl to take home.

The soul of the city is its tranquil gardens, a UNESCO World Heritage Site, where the zenith of Chinese civilisation comes alive. In the rockeries, gnarled trees and delicate blossoms are expressions of Chinese poetry, philosophy and art. Just 25 of Suzhou's 200 gardens remain; while each has its own distinct personality, all share the basic elements of Chinese classical garden design. Trees, shrubs, fishpools, rocks and pavilions create a microcosm of the world, perfectly balanced in terms of harmony, proportion and variety.

Suzhou's gardens in particular are known for their white pines and weathered stones from Lake Tai. Views through "moon" gates and lattices and cunning reflections in mirrored lakes are all part of the contrived

effect. Everything is imbued with symbolism, from the pine trees (long life) to the fat goldfish (money). There is no off-season for the gardens; they showcase the beauty of each season with judiciously planted autumnal foliage, spring blooms, summer lotuses and sculptured branches, ready for winter's snowy dusting.

Dating from the Qing dynasty, the **Garden of Harmony** Ⓐ (Yiyuan: daily 7.30am–5.30pm; entrance fee), in the centre of town, off Renmin Lu, is one of the newer Suzhou gardens. Zhejiang governor Gu Wenbin studied his predecessors' gardens and incorporated their key elements into his own retreat, adding his own Western-style flower beds – unusual for a Chinese garden.

Don't dine where Emperor Qianlong did

Songhelou Restaurant (Songhelou Caiguan) at 141 Guanqian Jie (tel: 512-727 7006), gets a lot of press as the oldest restaurant in town – Emperor Qianlong is said to have dined here, but standards must have dropped since his day. Much better is **Attaining the Moon Restaurant** (Deyuelou), on the south side of the street at 27 Guanqian Jie (tel: 512-523 8940). Dining rooms are decked out with Chinese lanterns, geometric doorways and Ming-style wooden furniture. Specialities are Mandarin fish, prawns with bean curd, and pork leg stewed in a rich sauce for hours. **Guanqian Avenue** (Guanqian Jie), where the restaurant is found, is lined with fabric shops, boutiques and souvenir shops with tourist prices.

More shopping can be done at the 3rd-century Taoist **Temple of Mystery** Ⓑ (Xuanmiao Guan: daily 9am–6pm; entrance fee), just north of Guanqian Jie – part of its legacy as the grounds of one of the area's greatest temple fairs. This temple was once the heart of the renaissance-style Suzhou bazaar, with performances, acrobats and noisy vendors. It is still a shopping magnet, surrounded by a street

The legendary porcelain skin of classic Suzhou beauties is believed to be the result of washing with Suzhou's pure water and crushed pearl powder, available at pearl shops (and ground on the spot).

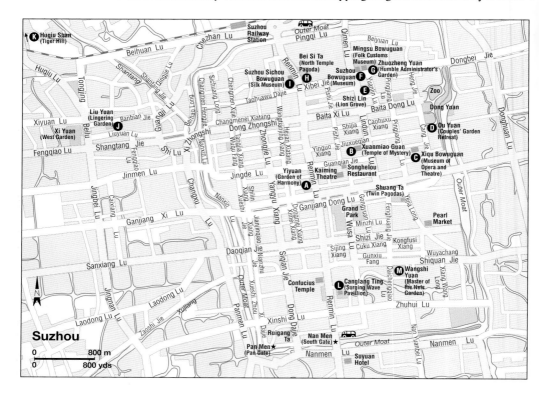

market selling a variety of goods. The temple has an old-China aura and an impressive scale: a great courtyard leads to the massive **San Qing Hall** (San Qing Tang), with its 60 magnificent red-lacquered columns, classic two-tiered roof with upturned eaves and vibrant Taoist gods. The temple was badly damaged during the 19th century – probably by the Taipings – but escaped further Cultural Revolution damage when the Red Guards commandeered it for their own use. Somewhat newer is the mid-1990s landscaped park that now rings the temple compound.

Map on page 244

5,000-year-old Kun opera

A 10-minute walk east, following the canal to narrow Zhong Zha Jia Xiang, leads to the **Museum of Opera and Theatre** ● (Xiqu Bowuguan: daily 8.30am–4.30pm; entrance fee), guarded by a pair of stone lions. The museum chronicles Suzhou's own 5,000-year-old Kunju opera tradition, which pre-dates Beijing opera by 2,000 years. Kunju opera *(see page 65)* is still performed in this Ming dynasty building under a stunning seashell-whorl wooden dome. Across the courtyard, another building houses a display of costumes, opera masks, musical instruments – even a model orchestra – as well as documents the opera's history.

Wall detail from the Museum of Opera and Theatre.

A five-minute walk northeast, at Xiao Xin Qiao Long, just inside Suzhou's outer moat, is **Couples' Garden Retreat** ● (Ou Yuan: daily 8am–4pm; entrance fee), surrounded by water on three sides. Covered walkways lead to a cosy courtyard ringed by a rock sculpture that includes a miniature of Anhui's Yellow Mountain – a tribute from the garden's creator, a former governor of Anhui.

Head north, bypassing Eastern Garden (Dong Yuan) and the rather sad zoo, for **Lion Grove** ● (Shizi Lin: daily 7.30am–5pm, entrance fee) to the west at 23 Yulin Lu. Originally a Buddhist temple garden laid out in 1342 by the monk

LEFT: Garden of Harmony. **BELOW:** ceiling lanterns at the Museum of Opera and Theatre.

Tian Ru in honour of his master, Lion Grove is a poem to the mountain. Encircled by a covered corridor, the garden has piles of rocks and intricate rockeries
– many lion-shaped – weathered by decades in Lake Tai and set among lakes,
pavilions and halls. Last owned by a branch of the architect I.M. Pei's family,
Lion Grove is said to be Emperor Qianlong's inspiration for Yuanmingyuan, the
old Summer Palace on the outskirts of Beijing.

Built in 1960, the **Suzhou Museum** ❻ (Suzhou Bowuguan: daily 8.30am–
4pm; entrance fee) is north of Lion Grove at 204 Dongbei Lu, adjacent to the
former residence of a Taiping Rebellion leader, Li Xiucheng. Its collection of
artefacts from early Suzhou includes a rare pearl stupa, porcelain, funeral relics
unearthed from the mud of Dongshan island, antique maps of Suzhou and the
Grand Canal, and Song art and calligraphy.

Humble by name, magnificent by nature

The name of the Ming-era **Humble Administrator's Garden** ❼ (Zhouzheng
Yuan: daily 7.30am–5pm; entrance fee), just north on Dong Bei Jie, refers to a line
of Jin poetry that says cultivating a garden is the work of a humble man. But this
4-hectare (10-acre) garden, the largest remaining one, is far from a humble undertaking. Laid out by retired Ming imperial censor Wang Xianchen, the three main
areas are thematically linked by water, in pools and ponds of varying sizes. Lined
with a corridor of caged birds, the twists and turns of rock-lined paths burst open
onto a classical landscape: an Olympic-sized pond shivers in the breeze, and
pavilions perch on hillsides and in hollows. The rippling pond is framed to per-
fection within the Ming dynasty contours of the well-named **Hall of Drifting
Fragrance**, where the lingering perfume of the lotuses on the water wafts in.

The 76-metre (250-ft) high mustard-and-vermilion **North Temple Pagoda**
(Bei Si Ta: daily 8am–5pm; entrance fee), on the site of Wu Kingdom ruler
Sun Quan's childhood home, to the west, on the corner of Renmin Lu and Xibei
Jie, dominates the city. It was first built during the 3rd century and completely
rebuilt in the 16th century. A climb to its summit offers spectacular views of the
surrounding area, including the ochre walls of the 17th-century **Nanmu Hall**
(daily 8am–5.30pm; entrance fee), on the grounds.

Across the street, the fascinating **Suzhou Silk Museum** ❶ (Suzhou Sichou
Bowuguan: daily 9am–5.30pm; entrance fee), on Renmin Lu, recounts the
enthralling story of silk in China, beginning with a statue of Lei Zu, the legendary creator of silk (and concubine of Qin Emperor Shi Huangdi). A large bas
relief of camels, laden with bolts of silk, lumber down the Silk Road of antiquity, while rare old silk pieces are displayed and their legends recounted.

By far the museum's best feature is the section devoted to sericulture: one
room features large woven pans holding wriggling silkworms feasting on mulberry leaves, while on another shelf, silk cocoons sit neatly in rows. Weavers
demonstrate how young girls ruined their hands by plunging them into boiling
water to separate the cocoon threads into single strands. Big looms, strung with
jewel-tone silk threads, bob up and down in skilled hands.

A 700-metre (2,300-ft) walkway links four scenic areas of the Ming-era
Garden for Lingering ❷ (Liu Yuan: 7.30am–5pm; entrance fee), at 80 Liuyuan
Lu to the west, outside the city gates. Laid out by Ming minister Xu Taishi, the corridor has inscribed tablets bearing flowery descriptions of the garden by poets and
noted visitors. Outside the **Mandarin Duck Hall** (Yuanyuang) – separate viewing
rooms for men and women remain – stands the garden's pride: the 6.5-metre (21-

Limestone rock formations at the Garden for Lingering.

LEFT: North Temple Pagoda.
BELOW: silk factory.

TIP

The Sheraton Suzhou (Shi Lai Dun Suzhou), at 388 Xin Shi Lu, is built in the style of an ancient Suzhou mansion, with rooms around a classical Chinese garden. You may see costumed actors striding around, as the Sheraton, like all of Suzhou, is a popular setting for period movies.

BELOW:
view from Pan Gate with Ruigang Pagoda in the background (left).

ft), 5,000-kg (11,000-lb) **Cloud Crowned Peak** (Junyun Feng), the largest Lake Tai rock in the Suzhou gardens. West of here is another Xu Xu Taishi work, **West Garden** (Xi Yuan: daily 7.30am–5pm; entrance fee), on Xiyuan Lu.

A visit to Suzhou without seeing **Tiger Hill** Ⓚ (Huqiu Shan: daily 7am–6pm; entrance fee) to the north, would be incomplete, wrote Song poet Su Shi. Less formal and manicured than the others, Tiger Hill contains the tomb of Suzhou's founder He Lu, the Wu king. The garden gets its name from the mythical white tiger that materialised on the 3rd day after his death to guard the grave. Archaeologists suspect it may be that grave, which lies beneath the seven-storey octagonal brick **Cloud Rock Pagoda** (Yunyan Ta) on the hill top, that is causing the tower's severe tilt. Tiger Hill's **Thousand Men Rock** (Qian Ren Shi), at the foot of the hill, is reputedly the gruesome spot where the tomb builders were executed to keep secret the location of the tomb and its treasures, while **Sword Pond** (Jianchi) is said to be where the king's 3,000 swords were buried.

Head back south to climb the well-worn steps of **Five Gate Bridge** (Wumen Qiao) off Nanmen Lu and Suzhou's tallest bridge, for a vista of boats and barges sliding past. **Pan Gate** (Pan Men), the only remaining stretch of Suzhou's 3rd-century city wall, is a short walk away. The climb up the 300 metres (980 ft) of original city wall is rewarded with a view of fishing boats, arched bridges, graceful willows over canals and the 1,000-year-old **Ruigang Pagoda** (Ruigang Ta).

The oldest of the major gardens, **Surging Wave Pavilion** Ⓛ (Canglang Ting: daily 8am–4.30pm; entrance fee), further up Renmin Lu, was laid out in 1044 by poet Su Shunqin. Dominated by a hill, Canglang Ting is uniquely open on its northern border to a canal and this "urban scenery" is one of the garden's highlights. The **Five Hundred Sage Temple** (Wu Bai Ming Xian Si) in the garden's

Maps:
Area 240
City 244

southern reaches, holds ancestral tablets listing Suzhou's ancient luminaries.

The loveliest Suzhou garden is also one of the smallest: the exquisite **Master of the Nets Garden**  (Wangshi Yuan: daily 8am–4.30pm; entrance fee) at 11 Kuotao Xiang. Dating from 1770, its name refers to the ambition of its retired court official owner, who longed to be a fisherman. The intimate garden's charm comes from its delicate, scaled-down features of a traditional garden – courtyards, pavilions and rockeries. In its pavilions are some of Suzhou's most exquisite antique furniture. In fact, the **Peony Study** (Dianchun Yi) has been replicated in New York's Metropolitan Museum of Art's Astor Court and Ming Room. At night, the beautifully-lit pavilions are the setting for traditional performances – opera, music and dance – that transport the viewer to the days of the imperial court (daily shows at 7.30pm). On moonlit nights, enter the moon-gate at the **Moon Watching Pavilion** (Yue Dao Feng Lai Ting) to see the moon thrice over: in the heavens, in the pond reflection, and in a mirror.

The slim towers of **Twin Pagoda** (Shuang Ta: daily 7am–4.30pm) to its north are too flimsy to climb, but its garden is a lovely spot to contemplate this elaborate thank you note from a coterie of successful imperial scholars to their teacher.

Engraved door panel from the Master of the Nets Garden.

Lake Tai: The inspiration of the ages

The scenic beauty of **Lake Tai** ❸ (Tai Hu), one of China's largest freshwater lakes, and inspiration for generations of artists and poets, lies 20 km (12 miles) west of Suzhou. The 2,400-sq km lake (9,270-sq mile) is stocked with fish farms and lotus plants, and dotted with islands and forested hills. Jutting into the lake are the rural idylls of peninsular **Dongshan** and **Xishan** island, 35 km (22 miles) southwest of Suzhou – although modernity is beginning to encroach. Dongshan is the quieter of the two, with small villages and the ancient **Purple Gold Nunnery** (Zijin Shan: daily 7am–5pm; entrance fee). Surrounded by fragrant groves of oranges, the nunnery has a group of 16 painted clay *arhat* (Buddhist saints). There are breathtaking views of the lake, fishing boats and green islands from its summit, **Dragon Head Hill** (Longtou Shan).

BELOW: scenic Lake Tai with Chinese junk boats.

Xishan, which is linked to Suzhou by a causeway and to Dongshan by ferry, is beginning to develop, with more hotels among its Ming-style houses. The **Linwu Caves** (Linwu Dong: daily 8am–5.30pm; entrance fee) are the island's main attraction, along with **Shigong Hill** (Shigong Shan). Both offer spectacular views of the lake.

Lake Tai's most famous site is **Turtle Head Island** (Yuan Tou Zhu: daily 6.30am–5pm; entrance fee), accessible from the town of **Wuxi**, 40 km (25 miles) northwest of Suzhou. Actually a peninsula, the island is renowned for its classic views of the lake with junks sailing past, captured through the **Lake Tai Memorial Archway** (Tai Hu Jia Jue) and from **Perpetual Spring Bridge** (Changqin Qiao), with its cloud of spring cherry blossoms. There is a 360-degree views across the lake from the peninsula's peak, where pavilions and teahouses are sited to take advantage of the views. There is also a ferry to **Three Hills Island** (San Shan Zhu), whose pagoda-topped hill is an excellent point for lake views. ❑

HANGZHOU

The city's legendary beauty rests on the ethereal West Lake and the whimsically named Temple of the Soul's Retreat, where there are 470 rockface stone carvings dating from the 10th century

Maps:
Area 240
City 252

The pleasure place of emperors and governors, **Hangzhou ❹**, the capital of Zhejiang Province, is a classical Chinese beauty. Standing at the city's famous West Lake, where arched bridges span softly shirred waters that melt into a blurred landscape of mountains, is like being inside a Chinese landscape painting. The city was built on wealth, earned by its fortuitous position as the Southern terminus of the Grand Canal, and by royal privilege as China's imperial capital during the Song dynasty. The palace became Hangzhou's greatest patron of the arts, and the weaving of fine silks and intricate brocade was taken to new heights. Despite the inevitable changes of dynasties and capitals, Hangzhou remained a favourite among China's rulers, a place where the noble arts of leisure were cherished among classical gardens and by its famous lake.

Hangzhou continued to thrive, as the Ming rulers widened the Grand Canal to allow larger boats to transport the treasures of Hangzhou to the Forbidden City in Beijing. But the ups and downs of Chinese history affected Hangzhou as well. The Taiping Rebellion razed the city in 1861, followed by its renewed prosperity as a Treaty Port in 1895. The reconstruction of that period was razed again during the Cultural Revolution. However, history repeats itself. The city is growing as a centre for industry and pharmaceuticals, telecommunications and dot-coms in a visible construction boom of plazas, office buildings and shopping malls.

LEFT:
Hangzhou's famous
West Lake at dawn.
BELOW:
boats moored
at West Lake.

The famous West Lake

A city created for leisurely undertakings is not one to be rushed through. Sited 185 km (115 miles) southwest of Shanghai, Hangzhou's beautiful terraced tea landscape, dotted with the occasional pagoda, is best seen on foot, and the natural attractions around West Lake call for slow contemplation – perhaps over a weekend.

Hangzhou's famous **West Lake ❹** (Xi Hu) is first mentioned in Chinese history as the place where the founder of the first Chinese dynasty, the legendary Yu, the tamer of floods, moored his boats. West Lake wasn't yet a lake then and it still wasn't a lake when Qin Emperor Shi Huangdi sailed into the inlet from Hangzhou Bay to moor his boats on what is now the northwest shore. It would not until the 4th century before enough silt would build up to create Zhejiang Province's foremost tourist attraction.

Sitting in a canopied wooden rowboat is an ideal way to see the 5.5-sq km (2.2-sq mile) freshwater lake and its attractions. Past the lake's man-made islands, **Mid-Lake Pavilion** (Huxinting) and **Ruan Yuan's Mound** (Ruangong Dun), disembark at the lake's largest island, **Xiao Ying Island** (Xiao Ying Dao: all daily 8am–6pm; entrance fee). Created in 1607, Xiao Ying is best known as a viewpoint for three 17th-cen-

tury stone pagodas on the lake – **Three Pools Mirroring the Moon** (San Tan Yin Yue), one of the 10 legendary views of West Lake. A lake and a Bridge of Nine Turnings dominates Xiao Ying island, lending credence to the Chinese saying that this is "an island within a lake, a lake within an island".

Sights on Gu Shan island

The 1.5-km (1-mile) **Bai Causeway** (Bai Di), named after Hangzhou poet-governor Bai Juyi, cuts a path around the northern section of the lake connecting Hangzhou's mainland to **Solitary Hill** (Gu Shan), the island on the lake's north-west shore. The causeway runs alongside the island, where an impressive array of sights are found: the **Zhejiang Provincial Museum** **B** (Zhejiang Bowuguan: daily 8.45am–4.45pm; entrance fee), built in 1929 on the grounds of Emperor Qianlong's former imperial palace, has 100,000 cultural relics within its seven halls. It is well-known for its Celadon Hall – Zhejiang was once the main producer of Chinese celadon. The collection includes a rare Five Dynasties *ying*

Pavilions dot the grounds of the Xiling Seal Engraving Society

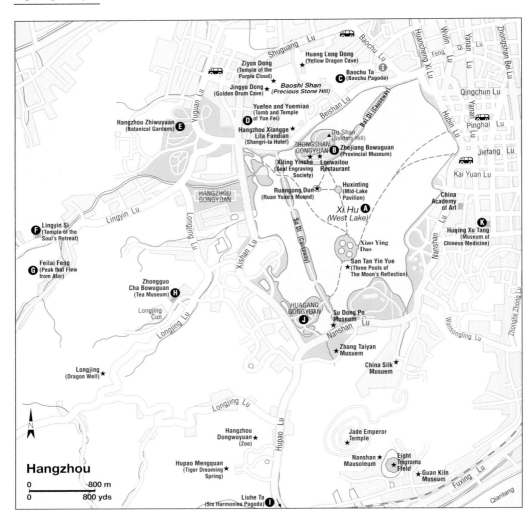

Hangzhou

0   800 m
0   800 yds

Map on page 252

(jar), made in the renowned Yue kilns. Beside the museum is the **Flourishing Literature Pavilion** (Wen Lan), the region's only imperial pavilion library. First built in 1782, it was rebuilt in 1880.

Glance up from here to the northeast for a view of **Precious Stone Hill** (Baoshi Shan) and its slim **Baochu Pagoda** Ⓒ (Baochu Ta), first constructed in the 10th-century Wuyue Kingdom as a talisman to protect the emperor. Rebuilt countless times over the years, the present structure dates from 1933 but cannot be climbed as there is no stairwell.

Back on the island, visit the **Sigillography Museum** (Zhongguo Yingxue Bowuguan: daily 9am–4.30pm; entrance fee), the first Chinese-style building on the left after the bridge, in which the history of the Chinese seal is recounted. Displays range from rough clay shards to tiny carved seals with calligraphy to match. The next Chinese-style house on the causeway, home of ancient Chinese scholar Yu Yue, is an unremarkable one-room exhibition hall, but the back door leads up Solitary Hill. A short walk through pavilions and leafy paths ends on the summit and the 11-storey gloriously unrestored **Pagoda of Avatamsaka Sutra** (Huayanjing Ta), built in 1924. A concession stand sells snacks and a few tables take advantage of the spectacular views over the lake, but otherwise, it is a peaceful spot. The funerary stele of **Sanlao**, Hangzhou's oldest, lies forgotten in a stone pavilion, the steel gates firmly padlocked.

A path leads down the hill from Sanlao to the **Xiling Seal Engraving Society** (Xiling Yinshe: 9am–4.30pm; entrance fee). Founded in 1913, it displays examples of seal engravings on the walls of several pavilions strewn on the hillside. **Louwailou** (Louwailou Caiguan; tel: 0571-8796 9023), Hangzhou's most famous restaurant serves local delicacies in the polished marble-and-glass edifice

LEFT: Hangzhou elder contemplates.
BELOW: Baochu Pagoda.

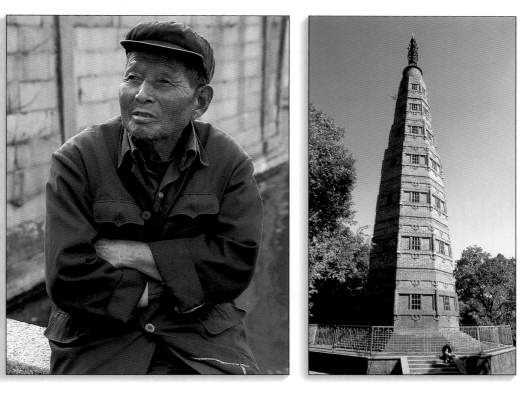

next door. Its Hangzhou specialities such as West Lake sweet-and-sour fish and beggar's chicken (chicken baked in mud, then theatrically broken at the table) are no better than others, but the lakeside view on the roof terrace is unsurpassed. The restaurant, which dates back to 1848, gets its name from a Song dynasty poem.

Next door, a branch of the **Zhejiang Library** (Zhejiang Tushuguan: Mon–Fri 9am–4.30pm) houses 835,000 ancient Chinese books, including rare books copied by Tang scholars. The adjacent **Zhongshan Park** (Zhongshan Gongyuan: daily 6.30am–4.30pm; free) is on the grounds of what was first a Song dynasty imperial palace, later a holiday palace for Emperor Kangxi, and finally, a temple. Today, it has niches with pavilions and twisting bridges and a collection of ornamental rocks from where there are lovely lake views.

North along the causeway is **Autumn Moon on a Calm Lake** (Pinghu Qiuyue), a teahouse and one of the traditional spots from which to view the lake, especially during the full moon night of the Mid-Autumn Festival. Continuing north, past the statue of writer Lu Xun, considered the father of modern Chinese literature, takes one to **Crane Pavilion** (Fanghe Ting), built in 1915 in memory of the Song poet Lin Hejing. He is said to have lived here alone with only a crane for company.

At the end of the causeway lies **Broken Bridge** (Duan Qiao), so called because when winter snow on the bridge melts, it appears as if the bridge has been spilt into two. The bridge is also famous among the Chinese as the setting for the folk tale *Lady White Snake (see margin note on left)*.

The **Su Causeway** (Su Di), running down the length of the lake from north to south, is named after poet-governor Su Dongpo. Much longer than the Bai Causeway, it is lined with weeping willow trees and crosses six arched stone bridges. A small park on the mainland at the causeway's northern end, called

"Lady White Snake", the most famous Hangzhou folk tale, is the story of a white snake who changes herself into a beautiful woman, and falls in love with a young man. They meet for the first time near Broken Bridge.

BELOW:
a teahouse on Solitary Hill island.
RIGHT: pavilion at Temple of Yue Fei.

Lotus in the Breeze at Crooked Courtyard (Quyuan Fenghe: daily 8am–4.30pm; admission fee), is an expanded and restored version of the original courtyard and a favourite spot for viewing lotus flowers.

The lakefront **Shangri-la Hotel Hangzhou** (Hangzhou Xiangge Lila Fandian) on the southwestern shore of the lake and easily the city's premier hotel, was built with the help of Russian advisors as a state guesthouse in 1959 on the site of the Fei Li Temple, demolished for the purpose. Local workers, angered by this desecration, lined the steps on its western side with tombstones to bring ill luck to the Russians. Luminaries Mao Zedong, Zhou Enlai and Richard Nixon have all stayed here. Although updated for 21st-century travellers, it has retained the spacious feel of the old guesthouse.

Yue Fei: A patriot to the end

Next door, the **Tomb and Temple of Yue Fei** (Yuefen and Yuemiao: daily 7.30am–5.30pm; entrance fee) is a popular memorial to the 12th-century Song patriot commander who, despite his success against invaders from the north, was framed, arrested and killed with his son Yueyang on trumped-up charges. He was exonerated and given a proper burial 21 years later in 1163.

Yue Fei's temple was destroyed during the Cultural Revolution in 1966 and rebuilt in 1979. No longer a functioning temple, its main hall is dominated by a Yue Fei statue with a plaque that reads, "Recover our lost territories" (modern-day implications with regard to Taiwan do not go unnoticed). Eight murals in the back tell the story of Yue Fei's life. Laid out as a Song dynasty garden, the temple is connected to the tomb grounds with walkways featuring Yue Fei's own writings in the northern wing and steles with poems about Yue Fei in the southern wing. Iron statues of the four who conspired against Yue Fei kneel shamefacedly before the tombs of Yue Fei and his son. Visitors have smashed them, spat on them, and abused them; locals call them the Song dynasty Gang of Four. Two rows of Ming and Qing stone ceremonial figures, buried during the Cultural Revolution, line the path to the grassy mounds that serve as Yue Fei's tomb.

The back of the temple leads to the **Temple of the Purple Cloud** (Ziyun Dong: daily 6.30am–4pm; entrance fee), the oldest natural cave on the ridge. From here, it's a 30-minute walk to **Yellow Dragon Cave** (Huang Long Dong: daily 6.30am–4pm; entrance fee), past **Golden Drum Cave** (Jingyu Dong). Legend has it that just after the Song dynasty temple was built, a rock at the temple split into the shape of a dragon's mouth, spouting water. The rock is no more today, instead a dragon's head carved into the hill marks the spot where the dragon's mouth was supposed to be.

Hangzhou Botanical Gardens (Hangzhou Zhiwuyuan: 8am–4.30pm; entrance fee), to the west, has 200 hectares (494 acres) of lush greenery, including 120 different kinds of bamboo, 1,200 medicinal herbs in its **Garden of a Hundred Herbs** (Baicao Yuan) and hundreds of varieties of plants, including a redwood planted by Richard Nixon in 1972. The prehistoric metasequioas, which Westerners had thought were extinct till they discovered them in China, grows here.

Map on page 252

"In heaven there is paradise, on earth there are Suzhou and Hangzhou" is an old saying that attests to the legendary beauty of the two cities.

BELOW: statue of Yue Fei at his tomb.

Rock sculpture of the portly Laughing Buddha at the Peak that Flew from Afar.

A short walk south, the **Temple of the Soul's Retreat** **F** (Lingyin Si: daily 7am–4.30pm; entrance fee) is Hangzhou's second biggest attraction, as affirmed by the heaving crowds. **Liugong Pagoda** (Liugong Ta), the ancient hexagonal seven-storey pagoda at the entrance to the temple contains the remains of the Indian monk Huili who built the Temple of the Soul's Retreat in 326.

One of the five famous Chan (Zen) sect Buddhist temples south of the Yangzi during the Southern Song, the temple was spared during the Cultural Revolution, and thus has treasured relics such as 10th-century stone pagodas and sutra pillars in front of the main hall. Inside this **Hall of the Four Heavenly Kings** is an image of the Maitreya (Future) Buddha, protected by an 800-year-old statue of Skanda, the Guardian of Buddhist Law and Order. The **Grand Hall**, accessed through a courtyard, features a 20-metre-tall (65-ft) statue of Sakyamuni Buddha. Carved from 24 blocks of camphor wood in 1956, it is China's largest sitting Buddha and a replica of an original Tang dynasty statue.

The piped-in monks' chanting adds a welcome mystique, especially as the crowds rather rob the temple of any Zen spirit. A hall of 500 *arhat*, (Buddhist saints) on the left, is built in the shape of a swastika, with each *arhat* holding his own symbol. A vegetarian restaurant at the temple serves lunch.

South of the temple is the **Peak That Flew From Afar** **G** (Feilai Feng), The peak, which is actually a cliff, got its name when the Indian monk Huili exclaimed that it looked so much like one in his native India that it must have flown here (indeed, the cliff is smaller than the surrounding peaks, and is the only one made of limestone, not sandstone). The 470 stone carvings on the rockface, mostly intact, date from the 10th to 14th centuries. The oldest ones are the 10th-century Guanyin (Goddess of Mercy) in the **Deep Dragon Cave** (Longhong Dong), the carvings in the **Shot of Gleam Cave** (Shexu Dong), and carvings of Amitabha Buddha and Mahasthamaprapta Bodhisattva. Everyone's favourite is the famous jolly Laughing Buddha, as the Polaroid stand in front of it attests.

BELOW: the so-called Peak that Flew from Afar.

China's most famous tea

This area is tea country, and the **Tea Museum of China** **H** (Zhongguo Cha Bowuguan: daily 8am–4.15pm; entrance fee) does an excellent job documenting the history and culture of tea production in five linked buildings, with delightful recreations of the tea rooms of different ethnic minorities.

Hangzhou's famous tea gets its name from the **Dragon Well** (Longjing) spring, a five-minute drive southwest. This is a small spring in an old temple-turned-teahouse. What is unusual is that the two levels of springs that feed the pond create a line when the water is disturbed, instead of the usual concentric circles. Young girls often splash their faces with the cool water, believing that it will improve their complexions.

The tea itself grows in the terraced tea plantations of **Dragon Well Village** (Longjing Cun), 1.5 km (1 mile) south of the spring. Hikers should seek out the 7-km (4-mile) long path called **Nine Creeks and 18 Gullies** (Jiu Xi Shi Ba Jian) that leads downhill from the Dragon Well. A pleasant walk through tea terraces and across streams, it finally emerges near the **Six**

Harmonies Pagoda ❶ (Liuhe Ta: daily 6.45am–5.30pm; entrance fee) to the southeast, on the northern bank of the Qiantang River.

The pagoda was built in the hope that it might control the river's mighty tidal waves. The seven-storey pagoda was built in 970 and last rebuilt in 1900, but its Song Dynasty structure remains preserved; its interior dates to 1123. The pagoda offers magnificent views over the Qiantang Bridge and is the traditional spot to watch the river's famous tidal bore on the autumn equinox in mid-September *(see margin tip on right)*.

North of the pagoda, **Tiger Dreaming Spring** (Hupao Mengquan: daily 6.30am–5.45pm; entrance fee) is a park renowned for its pure water, which tea connoisseurs say makes it the best place to drink Hangzhou's famous Dragon Well tea. Tea is now sampled in plastic cups at the renovated former temple complex, and the water's high molecular density can be tested by dropping coins into a bowl and watching it rise above the edge without overflowing. Next to the spring is the **Hangzhou Zoo** (Hangzhou Dongwuyuan: daily 9am–4.30pm; entrance fee), with Giant Pandas and Manchurian tigers.

Back at the southern edge of West Lake are the pavilions and fish ponds of **Huagang Park ❶** (Huagang Gongyuan: daily 9am–4.30pm; entrance fee), where one can "view goldfish at flower harbour", as its Chinese name Huagang Guanyu implies, in the former garden of a Song court attendant.

Northwards, to the eastern side of the lake, is Hangzhou city, where a frenzy of construction is creating plazas and shopping malls. Off a newly-constructed "old street" is the **Museum of Chinese Medicine ❻** (Huqing Xu Tang: daily 8am–5.30pm), a working Qing Dynasty courtyard clinic – the oldest in China – at 49 Zhongshan Zhong Lu. ❑

Map on page 252

TIP

The Qiantang River tidal bore caused flooding for years. Today, contained by embankments, it has become a tourist attraction. Hundreds gather in mid-September to watch the wall of water, which can rise as high as 6 metres (20 ft).

LEFT AND BELOW: Longjing tea is considered to be one of China's best.

MOGANSHAN

Explore the mountain's hilly paths, still paved with the stone laid a century ago amid the ubiquitous bamboo, and discover once-grand mansions that were built during the early 1900s

Map on page 240

Hangzhou *(see page 251)* makes a good base for exploring Moganshan; an early start allows a full day of exploration. For travellers coming directly from Shanghai – or those wanting to revel in the ghost-town atmosphere – an overnight option is best. Nestled at the peak of 2,000-metre (6,560-ft) tall Mt Mogan (Moganshan), the resort of **Moganshan** ❺ experienced its prime during the first half of the 20th century, when it was, in the words of Concession-era Shanghai adman Carl Crow, "the favourite summer resort for the Lower Yangzi Valley". Located some 65 km (40 miles) north of Hangzhou and 195 km (120 miles) north of Shanghai, Moganshan's cool evenings and summer temperatures no higher than 27°C (80°F) made it the ideal hill station for foreigners longing for more comfortable climes.

Before the first missionaries came up in the 1890s, there were only Chinese farmers up here, cultivating the bamboo that still grows thickly on Moganshan. Barely ekeing a subsistence living from the soil, they were quite happy to rent their houses to the first foreigners who summered here. While the frugal missionaries only rented houses, they were later joined by wealthier citizens who wanted to replicate their city lifestyles. Some even brought their architects up from Shanghai to construct holiday villas using the grey stone quarried from the nearby hills.

Summer time and the living is easy

By the 1930s, there was a full-fledged summer community on Moganshan, who enjoyed all the amenities of home. There were post offices, telephones, butchers, bakers, a swimming pool, tennis courts, two churches and the all-powerful Moganshan Resort Association, a summer version of the Shanghai Municipal Council. By 1932, the resort had 160 houses, dominated by the Americans with 81, followed by wealthy Chinese – many were in the Kuomintang government – who had 32, and the taipans of the major foreign companies.

Although Moganshan's bamboo forests did inspire Mao to write a poem, the mountain assumed a different character after the Communist victory. In the 1960s, when the Sino-Soviet split raised fears of a nuclear war, the resort was turned into a military garrison. The contingency plan for the Zhejiang Province leadership, based in Hangzhou, was to assemble in Moganshan via secret tunnels leading from the base of the mountain to hillside homes in the event of an attack. Even after the threat had passed, the cadres kept Moganshan to themselves, reopening it to the public only in the 1980s.

Although the tourist maps that come with the entrance ticket to the resort area prefer to focus on Moganshan's "three wonderfuls" (bamboo, clouds

LEFT: Moganshan's lush bamboo groves.
BELOW: bamboo by-products.

and springs), "four excellent things" (freshness, quiet, coolness and greenery), and Communist party connections – no mention of any foreign presence – the resort's great charm lies mostly in its built history, still standing, and wrapped in the mists like a ghost town with palpable spirits.

"In the heart of the Bamboo, 1,800 feet above sea. Beautiful scenery! Swimming Pool! Private Park! Healthy climate! Cool nights!" – from a 1930s Hotel Mokanshan brochure.

Wander along the hilly paths

The temperature begins falling as the mountain is ascended, as one passes bushes of deep green tea growing on terraced fields dotted with simple huts of mud bricks. During Moganshan's heyday, visitors were carried all the way up the mountain on sedan chairs by coolies. Today, taxis and buses transport visitors up to the taxicab yellow bamboo hut at the resort's unmarked **western entrance** (open 24 hours; entrance fee), where silk-covered sedan chairs (carried by strapping country boys) are available on short jaunts for those who want to recreate the past. Winding through the sharp curves on the hills, glimpses of European villas are visible among the bamboo: some have been converted into hotels and restaurants, but most remain untouched.

Moganshan is best explored by wandering along its hilly paths, still paved with the stone laid a century ago, breathing the fresh mountain air and discovering once-grand mansions tucked into the mountain's shanks. Restaurants serve simple Chinese food, always including dishes made with bamboo shoots, Moganshan's main crop.

Just south of the entrance is a small **Bamboo Museum** (Zhuzi Bowuguan: daily 9.30am–3.30pm; entrance fee) that features proud displays of the many uses of bamboo. The grooved mountain road winds northwest to **No. 126**, a grey stone house with curved turrets and Gothic doors and windows that looks at

BELOW: Moganshan countryside.

home in the pine and bamboo forest. Mao stayed in this house built for a foreign capitalist while he was working on China's Constitution in 1954, and he was inspired to pen a poem here as well. No. 126 has a dramatic curved staircase and enclosed porches. It also has a sturdy art deco dining table that comes apart in three pieces, presumably to allow it to be carted up the mountain.

Heading back east, a steep hill above the post office leads to the former **Protestant church**, its rose window boarded up, and now a power station. The parsonage next to it once served as a primary school, but is now abandoned in preparation for a new use. East of the church, thick bamboo pipes lead to the lonely stream-fed swimming pool, almost eerie in the swirling mists. The tennis courts, which once had Chinese pavilions for spectators, are just north of here on the hill, but in rough shape today.

Head back south on the main road, past the Moganshan Management Office, to the **Yellow Temple** (Huang Si), a simple Buddhist temple where locals say gunpowder was stored in the aftermath of the Sino-Soviet split.

By the 1930s, well-heeled Chinese were holidaying at Moganshan, both the Kuomintang leadership and their unofficial guardians, the Green Gang triad, who had a Buddhist retreat up here. Continue south on the main road to the unsurprisingly secluded home of Green Gang boss Du Yusheng, located up a remarkably steep flight of steps. **No. 546** is a full-scale villa housing a shrine to Du's ancestors. This colourful, Chinese-style building stands in stark contrast to **No. 547**, the adjacent drab Western villa in which Du actually lived; this has now been turned into a guesthouse.

From Chiang Kai-shek to backpackers

Further north, the **Dicui Pond** (Dicui Tan), with a classic pavilion, is a favourite beauty spot for local tourists. Just beyond the gate is the far more interesting villa of Kuomintang leader Chiang Kai-shek, now the **Wuling Hotel** (Wuling Fandian).

Although Chiang is reputed to have come to Moganshan on several occasions, including to at least one Green Gang retreat, the exhibition hall in his vacation home counts three visits: his 1927 honeymoon – the same year he and the Green Gang carried out the infamous White Terror massacre of the Communists; during futile peace negotiations with Zhou Enlai; and in 1948, when he tried to launch a new currency to curb the rampant inflation his government had brought.

Chiang called his mansion *Song Yue*, and he called this side of the mountain – which was as far away from the foreigners as it was possible to be – Wuling, after his home village. The mansion's first floor is today a rundown backpackers' hostel, while upstairs, an exhibition room displays photographs of Chiang's colourful life. His wedding photograph, with the fetching Soong May Ling, is on display, as is a picture of Chiang being carried up the mountain in a sedan chair by coolies. Chiang's old bedroom and study, furnished with mahogany Shanghainese art deco pieces, opens out onto a balcony overlooking the house in which his son lived and a scene of the mist-covered hills. ❏

Map on page 240

Anthea Beckett's book "Murder at Mokanshan", is set at the summer resort in 1912. The novel traces the mysterious murder of Robert Felgate, a former missionary and an innkeeper at Moganshan at the time of his death.

BELOW:
Chiang Kai-shek's old villa is now the Wuling Hotel.

NANJING

This old stalwart has many stories to tell: the glorious ancient Ming, modern Kuomintang hopes, scars from the hidden holocaust. Its long and deep past are stored in a wealth of museums and sights

Maps:
Area 240
City 264

apital of the Ming dynasty, the Taiping Heavenly Kingdom and the Republic of China. Site of the Treaty of Nanjing negotiations and the horrific Rape of Nanjing. For a city with such a rich and turbulent past, **Nanjing** , 300 km (186 miles) northwest of Shanghai, is surprisingly sedate. "It has the magic charm of a semi-mediaeval city," wrote chronicler Lin Yutang in *Nanking As I Saw It*, when he visited the then-Kuomintang capital in the early 1930s. Blessed with a fortuitous location protected by mountains and the Yangzi River, Nanjing (meaning "southern capital") has been a magnet for rebels and pretenders to the throne for 5,000 years, and its fortunes have waxed and waned with them. Today, as the capital of Jiangsu Province and lifted by the great Shanghai economic wave, it is experiencing an unusually quiet period of prosperous stability.

Nanjing's vast store of historical treasures and nature spots can take weeks to explore; just its highlights alone will take three days. The city's refinement grew from its two periods as the nation's capital and with its status as a university town – particularly as Nanjing University is one of the nation's most prestigious schools. Its unmistakable confidence arises from its military might; it is the headquarters of the Nanjing Military District, the region responsible for national defence in relation to Taiwan – China's single most important defence issue.

LEFT: posing in front of the Sun Yat-sen Mausoleum.
BELOW: gate leading to Nanjing's Presidential Palace.

World's longest city wall

Ringed by the longest city wall ever built in the world, Nanjing immediately draws visitors into its historical aura. The **Ming City Wall**, parts of which are 600 years old, was built on the ruins of the earlier city walls; a good two-thirds of the 33-km (20-mile) wall have survived. Five provinces supplied the bricks and wealthy families financed the endeavour, which took 200,000 workers and 20 years – from 1366 to 1386. Today, the 12-metre (39-ft) high crenellated walls, punctuated by formidable gates, still dominate the city.

The centre of Nanjing, **Xinjiekou**, is a knot of traffic, office buildings and high-rise hotels. The **Jinling Hotel** (Jinling Fandian) at Hanzhong Lu, modern Nanjing's first five-star hotel, once kept out local Chinese who were not accompanied by a Westerner. To the east, at 292 Changjiang Lu, is the **Presidential Palace** Ⓐ (Zongtong Fu: daily 8am–5pm; entrance fee; last ticket 4.30pm); once through the gates, the street hubbub evaporates. Allow one hour or more in this complex that houses 400 years of Nanjing's turbulent history: Mao's army could not have picked a more symbolic spot from which to liberate Nanjing.

During the early Ming dynasty, the grounds held the palace and **Balmy Garden** (Xu Yuan) of Prince Han. The governor-general of Jiangsu and Anhui took over the premises during the Qing dynasty, adding a replica,

albeit much smaller, of the more famous marble boat in Beijing's Summer Palace, in the garden's lake. Both the boat and the gardens still stand, but the capital's stability proved elusive: in 1853, the Taiping rebels captured Nanjing, and the property became the headquarters of Taiping Heavenly Kingdom leader, Hong Xiuquan. A Christian evangelist who believed himself to be God's other son, Hong built a grandiose, imperial-yellow roofed palace in the style of Beijing's Forbidden City, and called it Palace of the Heavenly Kingdom (Tian Chao Gong).

In 1864, Qing forces crushed the Taiping uprising and recaptured Nanjing, almost destroying the palace in the process. The only palace remnant that still stands is Hong's lavish study and throne room, separated by a courtyard with a bronze statue of the general, which were restored in 2000; the rooms are stocked with rosewood and mother of pearl furnishings, bright red pillars and imperial golden dragons. The image of the man himself, too, has been restored; the exhibition describes Hong, whom historians generally agree was delusional, as the leader of China's largest peasant uprising, and adds Mao's seal of approval.

The site was returned to prominence in 1911 when Sun Yat-sen chose it for the new Republic of China's Kuomintang government buildings. Today, the complex comprises the Presidential Palace, where Sun Yat-sen and later Chiang Kai-shek had lived. Portraits of past residents hang on the walls of the spacious entrance hall that leads to the auditorium where Sun, and later, Chiang were inaugurated into office. Several government offices and reception rooms, fitted with art deco furnishing and original light fixtures, are open to the public in the lovely 1917 neo-classical buildings to the rear. Photographs detail the more recent history of the site, from the excesses of the Kuomintang (Chiang's wife, Soong May Ling, had her own plane, the *May Ling*) to the liberation of the city

Clothes belonging to the legendary Hong Xiuquan on display at the Presidential Palace.

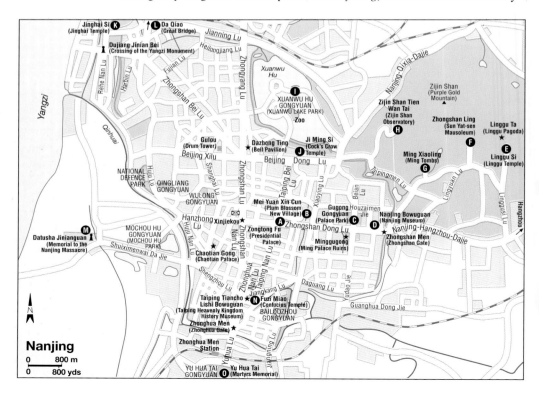

by Communist soldiers atop the archway. Today, the auditorium where Sun was inaugurated is used by the current leadership, the Jiangsu Provincial Committee of the Chinese People's Consultative Congress.

Map on page 264

A tribute to Zhou Enlai

When the Kuomintang occupied the Presidential Palace, the Communist Party offices were a five-minute walk east on Changjiang Lu, in the **Memorial at Plum Blossom New Village** ❽ (Mei Yuan Xin Cun: daily 8am–5pm; entrance fee), now marked with a bronze statue of former Communist Party leader Zhou Enlai. The buildings in the compound include Zhou's former residence and office at No. 30 and the delegation's dormitory and offices at No. 17. An exhibition hall documents the unsuccessful 1946–7 peace talks that were held here between the Kuomintang and the Communists, including a rare photograph of Mao and Chiang chatting amiably together. The **Zhou Enlai Library** (Zhou Enlai Tushuguan: 8am–5pm; entrance fee) in the compound houses a collection of Zhou-related information, his writings and documents. A walk around the neighbourhood, particularly Yongyuan Lane, takes in generous-size 1920s and 1930s Western villas built by the Kuomintang and used today by government officials.

Past the leafy campus of **Nanjing University** (Nanjing Da Sha) to the north, is one of Nanjing's major landmarks, the **Drum Tower** (Gulou: daily 8am–midnight; entrance fee). Built in 1382 on a grassy hill just north of the Beijing Xi Lu traffic circle, the tower is a peaceful respite from the traffic swerving wildly below. Now a teahouse with just one drum, the Drum Tower used to sound the "all's well" signal seven times a day and in emergencies. The two-storey **Bell Pavilion** (Dazhong Ting), to the northeast, dates from 1889. The pavilion

The overthrow of the Beijing University's president by the student body in 1966 marked the start of the Cultural Revolution. Nanjing University followed by unseating its president, Dr Kuang Ya Ming. This gentle scholar spent the Cultural Revolution scrubbing the university's toilets.

BELOW: Presidential Palace gardens with replica Marble Boat.

features a gargantuan bell that was cast in 1388 from iron, silver, gold – and, on the emperor's orders, the blood of virgins.

Past a graceful complex of classical Chinese buildings, the **Second Historical Archives of China** at 309 Zhongshan Dong Lu (closed to the public), head east to **Palace Park ⊙** (Gugong Gongyuan: daily 6am–11pm; entrance fee) on Zhongshan Dong Lu, built by the first Ming Emperor Zhu Yuanzhang. The park, a prototype for Beijing's Forbidden City, was destroyed by the Taipings. What is left are grass lawns and a few palace relics, including the white-marble **Five Dragon Bridges** and the massive five-arched stone gateway, **Wu Gate** (Wu Men), and a sculpture garden of ruined stones from the palace.

A block west, next to the Hilton hotel is the excellent **Nanjing Museum ⊙** (Nanjing Bowuguan: Tues–Sun 9am–5pm; entrance fee) at 321 Zhongshan Dong Lu. Aside from its collection of 440,000 antiques, the museum itself is an attraction, in particular, the History Gallery, a 1947 building by master architect Liang Sicheng. Highlights are interactive exhibitions – visitors can play the bronze serial bells – and displays like the 2,600 squares of jade sewn together to make a 400-kg (880-lb) Han Dynasty jade burial suit, an imperial Qing throne dyed in pig's blood and a bronze deer from the Warring States period.

Zhongshan Gate (Zhongshan Men), Nanjing's eastern gate, casts its dramatic profile a block east. Steep steps lead to the top of the gate, with views of Zhongshan Lu. Early morning exercisers line the crenellations along the top, which gets increasingly overgrown on either side of the gate. East of the museum, veins of deep maroon and dark gold in the rocks give **Purple Gold Mountain** (Zijin Shan), the city's loveliest nature spot, its poetic name. To wander in relative solitude among the tree-shaded avenues, wooded glens and rocky

Nanjing's oppressive summer heat has earned it the title of one of China's "Three Big Furnaces". The other two are Wuhan, in Hubei Province, and Chongqin in Sichuan Province.

BELOW:
Nanjing Museum.

hills is treat enough, but Purple Gold Mountain also contains Nanjing's top three tourist sights: Linggu Temple, Sun Yat-sen Mausoleum and the Ming Tombs.

The **Linggu Temple** ❺ complex (Linggu Si: daily 7.30am–5.30pm; entrance fee) on the mountain's eastern face comprises a number of restored Ming buildings in a forested setting with sweeping views over the countryside. Foremost is the grey-brick **Beamless Hall** (Wuliang Tang), with its vaulted ceiling supported by a quintet of columns, built in 1381 by the first Ming emperor to replace a torn-down temple on the site of his tomb. The largest and oldest of China's beamless halls, it was built to store Buddhist sutras, but has been used in the past as a fortress for the Taipings and a memorial to the Kuomintang martyrs of the 1926–27 White Terror; it is now an exhibition hall.

North of the hall, a grove of evergreen trees surround a teahouse occupying the old Guanyin shrine in the **Pine and Wind Pavilion** (Song Feng Ting). The yellow and red **Linggu Temple** itself, which dates from the 1860s, is a short walk east of the Beamless Hall. An active temple, Linggu has a memorial hall and reliquary to Xuan Zan, the Chinese monk who brought the Buddhist scriptures to China from India. The octagonal 60-metre (197-ft) tall **Linggu Pagoda** (Linggu Ta), north of the temple, evokes Old China, but its white granite and blue glazed tile roof (in Kuomintang colours) give it away as a 1930s memorial to the Kuomintang White Terror martyrs – possibly the only such monument left on the mainland.

Map on page 264

Buddha image at the Linggu Temple.

Top sight: Sun Yat-sen Mausoleum

The Chinese characters for "fraternity" are carved above the archway that leads to the **Sun Yat-sen Mausoleum** ❻ (Zhongshan Ling: daily 7.30am–5.30pm; entrance fee) to the northwest. The dramatic, sweeping monument of white Fujian marble and granite and sea-blue glazed tile, set against forested hills, is Nanjing's most visited tourist site. Dr Sun, whose 1911 revolution overthrew China's imperial system, is deeply revered as the father of the country by both the mainlanders and the Taiwanese.

The mausoleum, designed by Lu Yanzhia, was completed in 1929, five years after Sun's death, and is shaped like an alarm bell to symbolise the patriot's devotion to his cause of awakening the masses. The blue and white colours represent the Kuomintang. A constant flow of visitors stream up and down the 392 steps to the Stele Pavilion and the Memorial Hall, which houses a 5-metre (16-ft) marble seated figure of Sun. The Kuomintang's three principles – Nationalism, Democracy and People's Livelihood – are inscribed on the doors and the "Nation's Construction Outline" in Dr Sun's hand on the east and west walls. The domed Coffin Chamber has a marble likeness of Sun lying atop the coffin with a tiled Kuomintang flag on the ceiling guarding over him for all eternity.

Bypass the Ming Ling Lu entrance to the Ming Tombs, west of Zhongshan Ling, and take a left on Shixiang Lu to the traditional entrance, the S-shaped **Sacred Way** (Shandao: daily 8am–6.30pm; entrance fee). Twelve pairs of life-size stone animals, including camels, elephants, lions and the mythical *xiezhi* beast – the symbol of Nanjing – protect the tomb of Zhu Yuanzhang. Zhu was the first Ming Emperor and the

BELOW: monk from Linggu Temple.

only one of 14 Ming Emperors to be buried in Nanjing (the rest are buried in Beijing's Ming Tombs). Beyond the Sacred Way are the **Ming Tombs** (Ming Xiaoling: daily 7.30am–4pm; entrance fee). As befits a dynastic founder, the tombs were a two-year, 200,000-man undertaking – though they were reduced considerably in the Taiping destruction. The red-walled complex is a peaceful place; its halls, linked by long stone paths along a canal and ancient trees, recount the restorations and excavations at the site. A pine-tree path leads to the **Altar Tower** (Ling Ta), behind which is a hill with the unexcavated tomb of the first emperor, the empress and the 100 court attendants who were buried alive with them.

Astronomical instruments at Zijin Shan Observatory were made by Jesuit priests in the 17th century.

The silver domed roof of the **Zijin Shan Observatory** (Zijin Shan Tien Wan Tai: daily 8am–4.30pm; entrance fee), 3 km (1.8 miles) north of the Ming Tombs, is visible throughout Nanjing. Built in 1929, its sliding roof opens to allow the period telescope beneath to peek out at the sky. Outdoors, there are displays of Ming astronomical instruments, such as the Celestial Globe, the Armillary Sphere and the Horizontal Theodolite, used to measure the celestial bodies. Created by 17th-century Jesuit priests who had come to China to convert the court, they were carted off as war booty by the Allied Powers who quelled the Boxer Rebellion, but were returned in 1919. A small hall documents the history of astronomy in China.

Xuanwu Lake Park (Xuanwu Hu Gongyuan: daily 5am–9pm; entrance fee), west of Purple Gold Mountain, is anchored by the 5-km (3-km) long Lake Xuanwu, which has five islands connected by bridges and is scattered with teahouses, pavilions and restaurants. A popular destination, the park has a full roster of activities – paddle-boating, rowing, swimming – and a theatre and zoo.

BELOW:
a camel statue
at the Ming Tombs.

Just south of Lake Xuanwu is the **Cock's Crow Temple** (Ji Ming Si: daily 8am–5pm; entrance fee), where a temple has sat since 300. The vibrant yellow

buildings date from 1973, as a fire had destroyed the original temple. A newer addition on the temple grounds is the **Yaoshi Pagoda** (Yaoshi Ta), which offers a 360-degree view of the lake and Yangzi River.

Map
on page
264

Nanjing Great Bridge: First Communist project

To the northwest is a little-visited slice of history, the **Jinghai Temple** ❸ (Jinghai Si: daily 8am–4.30pm; entrance fee) which lies at the foot of **Lion Hill** (Shi Shan). Ming Emperor Yongle had the temple built in honour of the 14th-century explorer, Admiral Cheng Ho (Zheng He), the eunuch whose legendary seven voyages took him throughout Asia and to the coast of North Africa. The temple – which houses the **Nanjing Treaty Museum** – was the site of negotiations in 1840 over the Treaty of Nanjing, the document that ceded territorial rights in China to foreign powers. The museum's current incarnation, rebuilt to mark the 1997 Hong Kong handover, has no trace of the Ming original but the halls display a recreation of the signing on the deck of the *Cornwallis*, models of the ship and a Taiping Heavenly Kingdom cannon.

At the peak of Lion Hill stands the 52-metre (171-ft) **Yuejiang Tower** (Yuejiang Ta), built in 2002 to fulfill a 600-year-old dream *(see margin note, right)*. Bright with peacock blue, vermilion and pure gold foil, the tower is little more than a tourist attraction, but the summit of the hill, from which Sun Yat-sen planned his Northern Expeditions, offers lovely views over the Yangzi River.

A 15-minute drive north is the **Nanjing Great Bridge** ❹ (Nanjing Da Qiao), a magnificent 19.5-metre (64-ft) wide double-decker piece of socialist-realist architecture and a source of Chinese pride. This first civil engineering project of the Communists was undertaken when the Russians departed after the Sino-Soviet

Construction on Yuejiang Tower – to mark a battle victory of the first Ming Emperor – was put off 600 years ago when a meteorite struck. In 2002, the tower, at the peak of Lion Hill, was finally completed.

LEFT: Xuanwu Lake Park in autumn.
BELOW: interior detail of the Yuejiang Tower.

The Nanjing Great Bridge, or Da Qiao in Chinese. An elevator from the Great Bridge Park (daily 8am–5pm) allows visitors to take in the view from the bridge's upper deck.

BELOW:
monument at the Memorial to the Nanjing Massacre.

split (some say they took the plans with them) and stands as a symbol of the Chinese people's ability to go it alone. Mao's words on its completion in 1968 – "The people, only the people, are the driving force behind world history" – are inscribed on the bridge with figures of muscled peasants, workers and soldiers. The bridge allowed the completion of the Beijing to Shanghai rail link; trains only take two minutes to cross the lower deck (cars use the upper deck). Before this, trains had to be ferried over the Yangzi, adding two more hours to the journey.

China's hidden holocaust

The **Memorial to the Nanjing Massacre**  (Nanjing Datusha Jinianguan: daily 8am–5pm; entrance fee) lies to the south in a desolate part of town. This depressing place documents the hidden holocaust of World War II that took place in Nanjing, reminding all that "a tragic past should not be forgotten". Tickets to the museum, sited on one of the grounds where the Japanese carried out their mass executions, are purchased from a window resembling a prison cell. A grey concrete forecourt has "300,000" – the number of massacre victims – inscribed over an oversized dismembered head and limb, the body swallowed by the earth.

A barren field of rocks with dead trees has 13 markers commemorating the 13 mass execution sites around the city. A relief describes scenes of the massacre, and the **Crying Wall** is inscribed with the names of those who died, the spaces in-between allowing the greenery of plants to poke through. The underground memorial, with black curtains at the window, is brightened only with cranes made by Japanese schoolchildren. There are displays of skull bones in re-creations of mass execution graves, photographs of pits being unearthed, clinical descriptions of the torture found by pathologists, and chilling pictures of the horror.

THE RAPE OF NANKING

The Japanese Occupation of Nanjing (Nanking) in December 1937 began a systematic pillage and slaughter that wreaked a final death toll of 300,000: more than the immediate deaths of Hiroshima and Nagasaki combined.

About 50,000 Japanese soldiers crashed through the city walls – some scholars theorise that they were ordered to kill all captives lest the city of half a million rise up and revolt. They specialised in mass executions, dumping the bodies into the river or incinerating them with petrol. For weeks, the city's rivers and lakes ran red with blood.

The Japanese fired randomly at civilians and house searches often ended in killing sprees. Victims were half-buried, then ripped apart by German shepherds, made to strip naked and jump into frozen ponds, or burned alive.

One of the worst mass rapes in history brutalised 200,000 women of all ages; soldiers set up "comfort houses", tortured and disembowelled women – and then photographed the scenes.

Fortunately, for some, there was a counter to the soldiers' inhumanity. A handful of foreigners protected by their nationality set up an international safety zone. Untold lives were saved by people like John Rabe, surgeon Dr Robert Wilson and educator Minnie Vautrin – the heroes of Nanjing.

Map
on page
264

Chaotian Palace (Chaotian Gong: daily 9am–11am, 2–5pm; entrance fee includes a court rituals show) to the east, past **Muchou Park**, retains the classical architecture of its Ming temple past. These days, the reconstructed building showcases Ming court dances and rituals. **Taiping Heavenly Kingdom History Museum** (Taiping Tianchao Lishi Bowuguan: daily 7am–5pm; entrance fee), to the south on Zhanyuan Lu, recounts the bizarre tale of the Taiping Peasant Movement, whose laudable goals of ending feudalism and "banning" the evils of alcohol and opium in the name of Christianity were clouded by a bloodbath and the rampant destruction of historical sites.

A temple for scholars since 1034

Lost within a riotous shopping area is the **Confucius Temple**  (Fuzi Miao: daily 8am–9pm; entrance fee), a 10-minute walk east to the intersection of Taiping Nan Lu and Jiankang Lu. Scholars have prayed here since 1034, when the temple was first built as an adjunct to the Jiangnan Examination School. The current Ming-style building dates from the post-Japanese Occupation period. The disciples of China's learned master line the walkway to the temple, which leads to the world's tallest bronze statue of Confucius at 4 metres (13 ft) and weighing 2,500 kg (5,500 lbs). The figure is flanked by a bell and a drum pavilion, both made in 1999, as well as side halls featuring a display of musical instruments. The main temple hall features a collection of 36 jade panels which depict the sage's life.

Most of the supplicants came from the Song-era **Jiangnan Examination School** (Jiangnan Gongyuan: daily 8am–6pm; entrance fee), a short walk east at 1 Jinling Lu. The exhibition displays 40 examination cells, each 1 sq metre (10 sq ft), in which candidates for the rigorous imperial examinations spent the entire nine days of their civil service exam – including bedtime.

Nanjing's southernmost **Zhonghua Gate** (Zhonghua Men), is its most impressive one. The four gargantuan gates, one within the other, was able to hold 3,000 men. Today, they house shops, their crenellated walls decorated with kites and life-sized Ming soldiers.

Nearby, **Rain Flower Terrace** (Yu Hua Tai: daily 7am–10pm) is a massive park with the **Martyrs' Memorial**  (Yu Hua Tai Lieshi Jinnian Guan: daily 8am–5.30pm; entrance fee covers both) as its centrepiece. The park was the home of the 5th-century Buddhist abbot and scholar Yunguang, whose sermons so moved the gods that they showered him with "rainbow pebbles", the multi-coloured stones that are a favourite Nanjing souvenir. In 1927, some 100,000 Communists were massacred here in the Kuomintang's White Terror campaign; an immense 1,300 ton socialist-realist monument, with nine 30-metre (98-ft) tall figures representing the martyrs, stands near the park entrance. North of the park entrance, the Martyrs Memorial is laid out in a long line – uncannily like Washington, DC's Mall and its monuments. The Loyal Souls pavilion leads to the two-storey **Martyrs' Museum** (with exhibitions on the lives of the martyrs and the historic events that led up to the massacre). A rectangular reflecting pool runs north leading up to a flight of steps crowned by a 42-metre (138-ft) obelisk with a muscular statue ripping free from his chains. ❑

Each brick that went into the building of Nanjing's city walls was marked by the names of the workman and overseer, for the sake of quality control.

BELOW: stone Ming soldier at the Zhonghua Gate.

INSIGHT GUIDES
Travel Tips

✵® INSIGHT GUIDES Phonecard

One global card to keep
travellers in touch.
Easy. Convenient. Saves
you time and money.

It's a global phonecard

Save up to 70%* on international calls
from over 55 countries

Free 24 hour global customer service

Recharge your card at any time via customer
service or online

It's a message service

Family and friends can send you voice
messages for free.

Listen to these messages using the phone*
or online

Free email service - you can even listen
to your email over the phone*

It's a travel assistance service

24 hour emergency travel assistance –
if and when you need it.

Store important travel documents online
in your own secure vault

For more information, call rates, and all
Access Numbers in over 55 countries,
(check your destination is covered) go to
www.insightguides.ekit.com or call
Customer Service.

JOIN now and receive
US$ 5 bonus when you
join for US$ 20 or more.

Join today at

www.insightguides.ekit.com

When requested use ref code: **INSAD0103**

OR SIMPLY FREE CALL
24 HOUR CUSTOMER SERVICE

UK	0800 376 1705
USA	1800 706 1333
Canada	1800 808 5773
Australia	1800 11 44 78
South Africa	0800 997 285

THEN PRESS ⓿

For all other countries please go to "Access Numbers" at
www.insightguides.ekit.com

* Retrieval rates apply for listening to messages. Savings based
on using a hotel or payphone and calling to a landline. Correct
at time of printing 01.03

(INS001)

powered by ⊕*ekit*

"The easiest way to make calls and receive messages around the world"

CONTENTS

Getting Acquainted

Area: Shanghai Municipality is about 6,340 sq km (2,448 sq miles), an area that encompasses the 3,924 sq km (1,515 sq miles) of Shanghai City and its 16 districts, plus an additional three counties and 30 islands in the Yangzi River.

Location: Shanghai is on the 31st parallel, 31.4 degrees north of the equator and 25 km (15½ miles) south of the Yangzi River.

Population: Shanghai Municipality has an estimated population of 15 million, a figure that includes the floating population of migrant workers. The population in the city core is about eight million.

Spoken Language: Mandarin Chinese is the official national language of the People's Republic of China, including Shanghai. In China, it is known as *putonghua*, or the common language. Many Shanghainese, however, especially the older people, speak a local dialect called *Shanghai hua*.

Written Language: Written Chinese uses characters based on pictograms, which are pictorial representations of an idea. Since 1958, a standardised Romanisation system called *hanyu pinyin* has been in use *(see page 311 for more details on language)*. This book uses the *pinyin* system for Chinese names and expressions.

Religion: China has five official religions: Buddhist, Taoist, Catholic, Protestant and Islam. Religion may no longer be the opiate of the masses but, predictably, there are controls. For instance, Shanghai's 140,000 Chinese Catholics look to the local Catholic Patriotic Association as their head, not the Pope.

Time Zone: Shanghai (and all of China) is on Beijing time, which is eight hours ahead of Greenwich Mean Time (GMT). There is no daylight savings.

Currency: The Chinese Yuan (CNY), also known as Renminbi (RMB), or "people's money".

Weights and Measures: China uses the Metric system of weights and measures. Traditional Chinese measurements like *jin* (½ kg) and *chi* (1 metre) are commonly used, particularly in the markets and more traditional shops.

Electricity: 220 volts; 50 cycles AC. Chinese-to-foreign conversion accessories – whether it's conversion plugs or voltage converters – are easily available in department stores and hotels.

Dialing Codes: Shanghai's city code is 21; the country code is 86.

Shanghai's northern subtropical monsoon climate is comparable to the southeastern United States, with four distinct seasons. The city's rising damp contributes to Shanghai's humidity: muggy summers, when temperatures hover in the 30°C (86°F) range, chilled-to-the-bone winters with the barometer barely above freezing, and a spring/summer rainy season so damp that mould is a constant.

Although temperatures in Shanghai don't often dip below freezing, the city's location south of the Yangzi means that public buildings, by archaic Chinese law, are not obliged to install heating. Most hotels and international-standard buildings, however, are centrally heated and air-conditioned, depending on the season.

Average temperatures in Shanghai can be misleading, as the city's weather is notoriously capricious. Beautiful crisp spring and autumn days often alternate with extremes of temperatures, while the winter and summer months can be interspersed with milder temperatures.

Shanghai's famous rains fall during the May–September flood season, and are divided into the "spring rains", the "plum rains" (continuous heavy rainfall in mid-June) and the "autumn rains".

July and August, when temperatures hit the high 30s°C are the hottest months, while January, when the mercury sometimes dips below zero, is the coldest. Snow is rare in Shanghai, although there are

Too Many People, Too Few Surnames

When Genghis Khan was asked how he would conquer northern China, it is said that he replied, "I will kill everybody called Wang, Li, Zhang, and Liu. The rest will be no problem."

With over one billion people, it is natural to assume that there would be a surplus of surnames to go around in China. Yet of the 12,000 surnames that once existed in China, only 3,000 remain. Nearly a third of the population shares just five family names. In fact, nearly 90 percent of Chinese use just 100 surnames, with 90 million sharing the name Li, by default, the world's most common surname.

In the United States, by compari-son, there are only 2.4 million people with the name Smith, the most common family name in the English-speaking world.

It is not surprising, then, that literally thousands of people can share the same full name, leading to frustrating cases of mistaken identity.

The possibility of a bureaucratic meltdown over the confusion of a limited number of names is not farfetched. Much of the problem with increasingly fewer surnames began centuries ago when non-Han Chinese, seeking to blend into the dominant culture, abandoned their own surnames and adopted common names of the Han Chinese.

the occasional late December–January flurries. Shanghai's mildest weather is in spring (mid-March to May) and autumn (September to early November).

Government

Shanghai is one of the four municipalities that are directly administered by the central government (the others are Beijing, Chongqing and Tianjin). District and county representatives are elected to its own people's government, the Shanghai People's Congress, which runs the day-to-day affairs of the city. The Shanghai People's Congress in turn elects a mayor to the National People's Congress (NPC), where ultimate authority rests.

The office of the Shanghai mayor is an important stepping stone to Chinese leadership in Beijing. Former prime minister Zhu Rongji and former president Jiang Zemin were ex-mayors of Shanghai. The current incumbent is Han Zheng.

Economy

Shanghai is the economic engine of China. With only one percent of the country's population, the city generates 5 percent of the country's output and 25 percent of its total trade. With a buzzing international financial district called Lujiazui – home to the nation's largest stock exchange, a high-tech development park and export processing zone – the city is well on its way to becoming a global centre of finance and trading.

The nation's principal industrial base is also a major producer of heavy industry (power plants, refineries and China's leading producer of iron and steel). Other major sectors include textiles, electronics and cars – both General Motors and Volkswagen are major players. As China's leading port, Shanghai handles over US$300 million in imports and exports daily, comprising the bulk of the sea trade for the Central China region.

Tourism, both overseas and domestic, is another major sector.

Business Hours

Business hours in Shanghai generally follow international standards, with most offices open from Monday to Friday, 9am to 5pm.

Banks are open Monday to Friday 9am to 4.30pm, and Saturdays until noon while government offices are open Monday to Friday, 9am to 5pm, closed from noon to 2pm.

Post offices are open 7.30am to 5.30pm; the Central Post Office at 276 Suzhou Road (N) is, however, open 24 hours.

Museums are normally open seven days a week from 9am to 5pm. Tickets are sold until 30 minutes before closing time. Most temples and parks are open daily from sunrise to sunset.

Shops and malls generally open between 10am to 10pm daily. Restaurants are often closed between lunch and dinner, although there are exceptions; hotel coffee shops are open 24 hours. Bars and nightclubs stay open until 2 or 3am.

Public Holidays

China has just four public holidays a year, but three of them are a week long. The exception is New Year's Day, January 1. The three long holidays are Spring Festival (Chunjie) or Chinese New Year, in January or February; May Day on May 1; and National Day on October 1.

Schools and government offices work the weekend before or after the holiday. The exact dates of the holiday week and of the working weekend are announced at the beginning of each calendar year.

The seven-day holiday is meant to encourage domestic travel, and as a result, not only is Shanghai packed during the holidays, so is transportation in and out of the city. This is particularly true during Spring Festival, when Shanghai's migrants return to their home village for the festivities.

Planning the Trip

Passports and Visas

Passports should be valid for at least six months before you step out of your home country.

There are several ways of procuring a visa. The easy way is to use the travel agent from whom you buy your air ticket. There will probably be a commission charge on top of the usual visa processing fee paid to the visa office of the Chinese embassy or consulate. If you are part of a group tour, the travel agent will issue a group visa for all the members of the tour party.

Individual travellers may also apply for a visa directly with the Chinese embassy or consulate in their home country. Two passport-size pictures, the completed application form and the application fee are required. There are additional requirements for first-time visa applicants who are foreign-born but of Chinese descent or who were born in China but have migrated overseas.

It takes between seven and 10 working days to process your China visa so make sure you apply for one well before your intended departure.

Application fees vary by country, so check with your country's Chinese embassy or consulate. The fee also depends on the length of stay. The standard tourist visa is a

Visa Forms

The application form for visas may be downloaded from the Chinese Ministry of Foreign Affairs English-language website at www.fmprc.gov.cn/eng.

single-entry 30-day visa. Multiple-entry and 60-day visas are also available at higher cost and may be extended for a further 30 days.

Business and student visas usually allow multiple-entry and come with with three- to six-month validity. However, these require supporting documentation confirming business or student status.

Overseas Chinese embassies

United Kingdom, 49-51 Portland Place, London W1B 1JL, tel: (44-20) 7299 4049; www.chinese-embassy.org.uk.
United States, 2300 Connecticut Avenue NW, Washington DC 20008, USA, tel: (1-202) 328 2500; www.china-embassy.org.
Canada, 515 St Patrick Street, Ottawa, Ontario, Canada KIN 5H3, tel: (1-613) 789 3434; www.chinaembassycanada.org.
Australia, 15 Coronation Drive, Yarralumla, ACT 2600, Canberra, Australia, tel: (61-2) 6273 4780; www.chinaembassy.org.au.
New Zealand, 2-6 Glenmore Street, Wellington, New Zealand, tel: (64-4) 472 1382; www.chinaembassy.org.nz.
Singapore, 150 Tanglin Road, Singapore 247969, tel: (65) 6471 2117; www.chinaembassy.org.sg.

For a complete list of other embassies and consulates, check www.fmprc.gov.cn/eng.

Getting visas in Hong Kong

As many people combine a trip to China with Hong Kong, another option is to get your China visa issued in Hong Kong. Many nationalities only require a valid passport for entry into Hong Kong. Once there, enlist the services of a travel agent or the China Travel Service office (CTS). Obtaining visas in Hong Kong is both inexpensive and speedy – most are issued within two or three working days and same-day service is available, albeit at a premium.
China Travel Service, CTS House, 78-83 Connaught Road, Central, Hong Kong, tel: (852) 2853 3888; fax: (852) 2851 7340; www.chinatravelone.com.

Visa-free transit

Overseas travellers connecting to an onward flight in Shanghai are granted at least 24-hour visa-free transit, with nationals of some countries given 48 hours.

Visa extensions

To extend a business visa, a letter of sponsorship from a Chinese *danwei* (work unit) is required; similarly, student visa extension applications must be accompanied by a letter from the sponsoring school. The process usually takes three business days. Take your application in person to:
Public Security Bureau, 333 Wusong Road (at Kunshan Road), tel: 6321 1997. Mon–Sat 9–11.30am and 1.30–4.30pm.

CUSTOMS

Entry formalities

Officially, China requires tourists to complete a baggage declaration form in duplicate upon entering the country and submit the duplicate upon departure – but, in practice, no customs forms are offered, and baggage spot checks are infrequent. Travellers are asked to go through the red channel when there is something to declare and the green channel otherwise.

Duty free limitations

Visitors may bring in their personal belongings (including food) duty free, as well as two bottles of liquor, two cartons of cigarettes, 50 g of fresh fruit and 72 rolls of still film. Wristwatches, radios, tape recorders, cameras, movie cameras and similar items may be brought in for personal use but must be taken out of China when the visitor departs.

There is no limit to the amount of foreign currency and Chinese Renminbi traveller's cheques that can be brought in; the unspent portion may be taken out.

Gifts for relatives or friends in China, or articles carried on behalf of others, must be declared.

Importing and exporting the following items is prohibited:

● Arms, ammunition and explosives of all kinds.
● Radio transmitters-receivers and their principal parts.
● Chinese Renminbi (Chinese currency) in cash.
● Manuscripts, printed matter, films, photographs, gramophone records, recorded audio tapes and videotapes, etc. which are detrimental to China's politics, economy, culture and ethics.

Also prohibited from import are illegal drugs and pest-infected animals, plants or food products.

Exit formalities

Officially, the rule is that items purchased in China with RMB converted from foreign currencies may be taken out or mailed out of the country after receipts are presented for customs inspection. In practice, this is not monitored or enforced.

In addition to the items mentioned above, it is forbidden to export foreign currency above the amount brought into the country, material that would compromise China's national security, unauthorised and valuable rare books, antiques, animals, plants and seeds, pirated VCDs and CDs, and undeclared precious metals and jewellery. The export of Chinese herbal medicine is limited to the value of RMB 300.

Antiques require a government stamp in order to be exported; most reputable dealers can take care of this.

For an up-to-date list of customs regulations, see www.china.org.cn.

Health and Insurance

Basic health care is perfectly adequate in Shanghai, but complicated health issues are best handled abroad. Ailing travellers are generally treated at one of the city's Western-staffed and managed clinics or at designated foreigners' clinics in local hospitals with English-speaking personnel, but facilities and treatment are limited at both. Other hospitals will treat foreigners, but only in emergencies *(see pages 284–5)*. For more serious and complicated issues, patients are advised to return to their home countries or seek treatment in Hong Kong.

Visitors to Shanghai should therefore have health insurance that includes repatriation (or at least travel to Hongkong for emergency treatment).

Similarly, all the medication you might need – over-the-counter and prescription – should be brought with you, as not all medication can be found in Shanghai.

Vaccines
Other than requiring a yellow fever vaccination certificate from travellers coming from tropical South America or sub-Saharan Africa, Shanghai does not require any immunisations.

The Centre for Disease Control (CDC) in Atlanta, US, recommends the following vaccines for travellers to Shanghai: For more information, check its website: www.cdc.gov.

Be sure to consult your physician at least 4–6 weeks before your trip so that there is sufficient time for the shots to take effect.

Hepatitis A – A food and water-borne viral infection of the liver,

Hepatits A vaccines are not given to children under two years of age.

Hepatitis B – It is estimated that 10 to 15 percent of the Chinese population carry Hepatitis B, which is transmitted through bodily fluids and can lead to chronic liver disease. The vaccine is recommended if you might be exposed to blood (for example, health-care workers), have sexual contact with the local population, stay longer than six months, or be exposed through medical treatment. Hepatitis B vaccine is now recommended for all infants and for children ages 11–12 years who did not receive the series as infants.

Japanese encephalitis – This is only recommended if you plan on visiting rural areas for four weeks or more, except under special circumstances, such as a known outbreak of Japanese encephalitis.

Rabies – Recommended if there is risk of exposure to wild animals.

Booster shots – Booster doses should be given as needed for tetanus, diphtheria and measles, and a one-time dose of polio for adults.

Air and water
Shanghai's air quality has improved dramatically over the years with the

reduction of the use of coal briquettes and the relocation of factories. The city now enjoys 310 days a year of fresh air – according to government statistics. A daily air quality index is available online at www.envir.online.sh.cn.

Tap water must be boiled; bottled water is easily available.

Money Matters

Chinese currency
The Chinese Yuan (CNY) is also known as Renminbi (RMB). One yuan or renminbi (colloquially called *kuai*) is divided into 10 jiao (or *mao*); one jiao is divided into 10 fen. RMB bills are issued by the Bank of China in the following denominations: one, two five, 10, 50 and 100. China's fifth set of new currency was rolled out over several years beginning in the 1990s, with the most recent (and final) addition to the set being the new purple five RMB note and five jiao coin in 2002. Old notes, particularly the fives and 100s (issued in 1999) are still in circulation, so don't be surprised if you receive currency of the same denomination that looks different.

Jiao and fen are issued in bills and coins, although the paper jiao and fen are being phased out in favour of the coins. Coins come in denominations of 1 RMB, 1, 2 and 5 jiao and 1, 2 and 5 fen. These days, fen isn't used much.

Cash machines
If you find yourself short of cash, international credit cards and bank cards (Cirrus, Plus, Visa, Mastercard, American Express) can be used to withdraw local currency from ATMs, which are found throughout the city.

Bank of China will issue credit card cash advances with a 3 percent commission in USD or RMB.

Following are 24-hour ATMs which provide instructions in English.
Bank of China, Hongqiao Airport Arrival Hall; Pudong International Airport Arrival Hall; 139 Ruijin No. 1 Road; and 1377 Nanjing Road.
Bank of Communication, 105 Changle Road.

SARS Alert

China was ground zero for the Severe Acute Respiratory Syndrome (SARS), a potentially fatal respiratory illness which erupted in Guangdong, southern China, in early 2003. Symptoms are flu-like: a fever of over 38°C (100.4°F), followed by a dry cough and breathing difficulties. The disease spreads with epidemic speed, and in the age of jet travel, has spread worldwide.

When news of SARS first made headlines, China came under fire from the international community for covering up the number of actual cases nationwide.

There are as yet no definitive answers on how to prevent the spread of SARS, no vaccine and no real understanding of how to cure

this illness. SARS cases in Shanghai, compared to Beijing, have been very low, and the city acted decisively to prevent the spread of local infections.

By June 2003, SARS seems to be on the wane; with Beijing the last Chinese city to be taken off the list of SARS-affected countries. But there are fears that the illness may flare up again when the winter season starts.

The US Centre for Disease Control in Atlanta recommends frequent hand-washing and avoiding crowded places. Check its informative website at www.cdc.gov.ncidod.sars.

Another reliable information source is the WHO website at www.who.int/csr/sars/en.

Citibank, 19 Zhongshan Road (Peace Hotel); and 100 Yan'an Road, 5/F.
ICBC, 1184 Nanjing Road; Pudong International Airport Arrival Hall; and 960 Huaihai Road.
Hongkong and Shanghai Bank, Ground Floor, West Retail Plaza, Shanghai Centre, 1376 Nanjing Road (W).

Credit cards

China is rapidly moving from a cash economy to a credit one, and international credit cards are now accepted at major hotels and most restaurants – although many Chinese restaurants and hotels only take cash or domestic credit cards. Cash is also king in the markets and most smaller local shops, although department stores do take credit cards.
American Express Hotline: 6279 7183. Open 9am–5.30pm.
Master Card Hotline: 10-800 110 7309.
Visa Hotline: 10-800 110 2911.

Foreign banks

For a comprehensive list of banks in Shanghai, check the Shanghai Banking Association website: www.sbacn.org.
ABN-AMRO Bank, 20 Zhongshan No. 1 Road (E), tel: 6329 9303.
Bank of America, 18th Floor, Lujiazui, 528 Pudong Road (S), tel: 6881 8686.
Bank of America, 18/F South Tower, Stock Exchange Building, 528 Pudong Road (S), tel: 6881 8686.
Banque National de Paris, Room 101, 58 Maoming Road (S), tel: 6472 8762.
Chase Manhattan Bank, 31/F HSBC Tower, 101 Yincheng Road (E), Lujiazui, Pudong, tel: 6841 1848.
Citibank, 101-102 Marine Tower, 1 Pudong Avenue, tel: 5879 1200.
Hongkong & Shanghai Bank, 34/F HSBC Tower, 101 Yincheng Road (E), Lujiazui, Pudong, tel: 6841 1888; and Shanghai Centre, Suite 106, West Retail Plaza, Shanghai Centre, 1376 Nanjing Road (W), tel: 6279 8582.
Standard Chartered Bank, 35/F, China Merchants Tower, 161 Lujiazui Road, Pudong, tel: 5887 1230.

Exchanging money

At the time of press, US$1 was roughly equivalent to RMB 8.3 while £1 bought about RMB 13.

All rates are uniform regardless of whether you exchange money at a bank or hotel. Major currencies can be changed at hotels – but you must be a registered guest – as well as at banks and some department stores. The same applies for traveller's cheques.

Slightly better exchange rates are offered for traveller's cheques as opposed to cash. A black market exists, but is probably not worth the risk.

Convertibility

When you change money, you'll receive a foreign exchange receipt, showing the amount exchanged. Any unused RMB can be changed back into foreign currency at the end of your visit, but you must show the foreign exchange receipt.

In theory, because the Chinese RMB isn't convertible, you won't be able to exchange it back into foreign currency (or vice versa) outside of China. However, in practice, many countries that share borders with China or have business contacts with China will likely have RMB. Check with banks and money exchange outlets in your country.

Emergency money

Western Union, a reliable international money transfer agency, will wire money through the China Courier Service Corp. Identification is required for collection, tel: 6356 6666; or visit the website www.westernunion.com.

Tax

Hotels and restaurants may add service charges of 10–15 percent, but all other taxes are factored into the final bill.

What To Wear/Bring

Shanghai errs on the side of casual, but it is a city of unrelenting style: you'll be forgiven for not wearing a tie, but never for looking like a bumpkin. It always pays to dress well when visiting government offices. Light, breatheable clothes work best in the hot, humid summertime, with a light wrap for the over-air-conditioned restaurants and offices. No Shanghainese would dream of going out without their silk long underwear in the winter, and neither should you: layering is the key to staying warm in Shanghai's winter chill, and the key to managing your temperature when rooms are overheated. Savvy Shanghai travellers always carry a foldable umbrella with them to protect against the frequent sudden showers.

CITS and CTS Abroad

The overseas offices of government travel agencies **China International Travel Service** (CITS) and **China Travel Service** (CTS) all book tours, hotels, flights (international and domestic) and train tickets. It is faster than booking directly with the relevant offices, but you do end up paying higher rates.

You can opt to use these agencies even before you set foot in Shanghai. Alternatively, you can choose to fly to Shanghai and then book your trips locally, either with the CITS or CTS office in Shanghai or one of several privately run travel agencies (see page 290).

Because language makes independent travel in Shanghai more of a challenge than most other cities, tours are a soft option for the less adventurous. Your view of Shanghai will depend a great deal on which tour operator you select. The government agencies, for instance, will give you the government perspective on Shanghai – so you'll miss the chamberpots, charming-but-filthy lanes and much of Shanghai's European history in favour of modern buildings and the much-vaunted successes of the Chinese Communist Party.

Internet Research

The following websites provide a variety of information on travel-related subjects to Shanghai.
General Information
www.china.org.cn
China Foreign Ministry
www.fmprc.gov.cn/eng
Shanghai Government
www.shanghai.gov.cn
Health Matters
www.worldlink-shanghai.com
Air Quality Updates
www.envir.online.sh.cn
Banks in Shanghai
www.sbacn.org
Airport Information
www.shanghaiairport.com
Government Travel Services
www.cits.net; www.ctsho.com;
www.cnto.org; www.cnta.gov.cn
Local Media
http://english.eastday.com
www.chinadaily.com.cn
www.shanghai-star.com.cn
www.english.peopledaily.com
Entertainment and Events
www.cityweekend.com.cn
www.thatsshanghai.com
Hotel Bookings
www.book-a-hotel-in-shanghai.com
www.shanghaihotels.com

Overseas CITS offices

Check www.cits.net for details of the office nearest to you.
CITS Canada: 5635 Cambie Street, BC, Canada V5Z 3A3, tel: (1-604) 267 0033; fax: (1-604) 267 0032; www.citscanada.com.
CITS USA: Los Angeles, 975 East Green Street, Suite 101, Pasadena, CA 91106, USA, tel: (1-626) 568 8993; fax: (1-626) 568 9207; www.citsusa.com; **New York**, 71-01 Austin Street, Suite 204, Forest Hills, NY 11375, USA, tel: (1-718) 261 7329; fax: (1-718) 261 7569; www.citsusa.com.
CITS Australia, 99 King Street, Melbourne 3000, Australia, tel: (61-3) 9621 2198; fax: (61-3) 9621 2919; www.travman.com.au.

Overseas CTS offices

Check www.ctsho.com for details of the office nearest to you.

CTS Hong Kong (Head Office), CTS House, 78-83 Connaught Road, Central, Hong Kong, tel: (852) 2853 3888; fax (852) 2851 7340; www.chinatravelone.com.
CTS USA: San Francisco, 575 Sutter Street, CA 94102, USA, tel: (1-800) 899 8618; fax: (1-415) 352 0399; e-mail: info@chinatravelservice.com; www.chinatravelservice.com;
Los Angeles, 119 S. Atlantic Blvd, Suite 303, Monterey Park, CA 91754, USA, tel: (1-800) 890 8818; fax: (1-626) 457 8955; e-mail: USCTSLA@aol.com.
CTS Canada: Toronto, 438 University Avenue, Suite 306, Ontario, Canada M5G 2K8, tel: (1-416) 979 8993; fax: (1-416) 979 8220; **Vancouver**, 556 West Broadway, BC, Canada V5Z 1E9, tel: (1-604) 872 8787; e-mail chinatl@max-net.com.
CTS United Kingdom, CTS House, 7 Upper Street, Martins Lane, London WC2H 9DL, UK, tel: (44-20) 7836 9911; fax: (44-20) 7836 3121; e-mail cts@ctsuk.com.
CTS Australia, G/F 757-759 George Street, Sydney, NSW 2000, Australia, tel: (61-2) 9211 2633; 9281 7788; e-mail cts@all.com.au.
CTS New Zealand, Level 2, 99 Queen Street, Auckland, New Zealand, tel: (64-9) 309 6458; 309 6459; e-mail cts@chinatravel.co.nz.
CTS Singapore, 1 Park Road, 03-49/52, People's Park Complex, Singapore 059108, tel: (65) 6532-9988, 6532-6367; e-mail cts@singachinatrvl.com.sg.

Speciality Holidays

Abercrombie & Kent
www.abercrombiekent.com.
Shanghai is included in A & K's high-end, in-depth tours of China. Custom-made tours are also available on request. Highly recommended.
Master Tours
www.mastertravel.com.uk.
Small group lecture-study tours focus on specific areas including health, children, society and economics.

Smithsonian Tours
www.smithsonianjourneys.org.
The well-respected Smithsonian study tours offer expert lectures and rich insights into China via tours for individuals, groups and families.
China Rail Travel
www.chinarailtravel.com.
This UK-based tour operator organises insightful tours of China and North Asia by train; tailored packages are available on request.

Tourism Offices Abroad

The **China National Tourist Offices** (CNTO) abroad are useful resources for maps, brochures and travel information. Check its website at www.cnto.org for details.
CNTO Australia, 44 Market Street, 19th floor, Sydney NSW 2000, Australia, tel: (61-2) 9299 4057; fax: (61-2) 9290 1958.
CNTO Canada, 480 University Avenue, Suite 806, Toronto 28013, Canada, tel: (1-416) 599 6636; fax: (1-416) 599 6382.
CNTO Singapore, Suntec Tower 1, Level 12, Unit 02A, 7 Temasek Boulevard, Singapore 038987, tel: (65) 6337 2220.
CNTO UK, 4 Glenworth Street, London NW1, UK, tel: (44-20) 7935 9787; fax: (44-20) 7487 5842.
CNTO USA: Los Angeles, 333 West Broadway, Suite 201, Glendale CA 91204, USA, tel: (1-818) 545 7507; **New York**, 350 Fifth Avenue, Empire State Building, Suite 6413, New York, NY 10118, USA, tel: (1-212) 760 8218.

Getting There

BY AIR

International

All international flights arrive at the futuristic **Pudong International Airport** (abbreviated PVG) in Pudong (tel: 3848 4500 for flight information), located 30 km (18½ miles) from the city centre.

Completed in October 1999, the slick, high-tech facility was designed by French architect Paul Andreu to evoke the image of a seagull in flight, a metaphor for Shanghai soaring. Capable of handling up to 60 million passengers a year, the airport currently handles about 16 million in four connected terminals – departures on the upper level, arrivals below – and 28 runways landscaped around lakes and ponds, a reminder of the fish farms the airport replaced.

Arriving passengers at Pudong airport are whisked through the terminal on travellators and escalators to immigration, before proceeding down one level to baggage claim (carts are free) and customs; those with nothing to declare go through the green channel and those with something to declare go through the red channel.

As you exit customs, hotel information booths are found on the left in the arrival hall, currency exchange facilities are straight ahead, and the Tourist Information Centre (TIC) and China International Travel Service (CITS) counter on the right.

The taxi rank is to the right as you exit the building. *(See page 287 for information on airport-to-city transfers.)*

When departing from the airport, check in and pay departure tax before going through immigration, from where it can be up to a 15-minute walk (albeit aided by travellators and escalators) to your departure gate.

Domestic

All domestic flights arrive at **Hongqiao Airport** (SHA) located 13 km (8 miles) from the city centre (tel: 6268 8918 for flight information). The airport is pushing 40, but thanks to extensive renovations over the years, looks much younger – still, it's just not in the same league as PVG. With a capacity of 9 million passengers and one runway, it is also much smaller.

Arrivals at Hongqiao don't need to go through immigration as this is a domestic airport, but can proceed directly to baggage claim. After clearing customs, hotel reservation

Domestic or Foreign?

Since the handover of Hong Kong and Macau to China, the two former colonies have operated under a "one country, two systems" policy, meaning that they continue to function as before, although now part of China. This policy extends to their being treated as international destinations; travel to both Hong Kong and Macau departs from the international terminal in Pudong and requires an international passport.

Taiwan is even more complicated than the mainland considers it a province of China; Taiwan considers itself a sovereign nation. Flights to Taiwan also depart from the international terminal, and all flights go through Hong Kong or Macau – no direct flights are permitted.

booths are located on the left in the arrival hall. There is a Bank of China and tourist information service in the arrival hall as well. *(See page 287 for information on airport-to-city transfers.)*

Departing passengers must pay the domestic departure tax before proceeding to check-in, customs and immigration.

Departure taxes

International departure tax is RMB 90 per person over 12. Domestic departure tax is RMB 50 per person over 12. Both to be paid at the respective airports.

Airline offices in Shanghai

Air Canada, Suite 702, Central Plaza, 227 Huangpi Road (N), tel: 6375 8899; www.aircanada.com.
Air China, 600 Huashan Road, tel: 6269 2999; www.airchina.com.cn.
Air France, Room 1301, Novel Plaza, 128 Nanjing Road (W), tel: 6360 6688; fax: 6360 6655; www.airfrance.com.
Air Macau, Room 104, Hotel Equatorial, 65 Yan'an Road (W), tel: 6248 1110; fax: 6248 7870; www.airmacau.com.mo.

Air Nippon Airways (ANA), Suite 208, Shanghai Centre East Tower, 1376 Nanjing Road (W), tel: 6279 7000; fax: 6279 7002; www.ana.co.jp.
Asiana Airlines, 2nd Floor, Rainbow Hotel, 2000 Yan'an Road (W), tel: 6219 4000; fax: 6270 3167; www.flyasiana.com.
Austrian Airlines, Suite 1103, Central Plaza, 227 Huangpi Road (N), tel: 6375 9051; fax: 6375 9055; www.aua.com.
China Eastern, 200 Yan'an Road (W), tel: 6247 5953 (domestic); 6247 2255 (international); www.cea.online.sh.cn.
China North West Airlines, 258 Weihai Road, tel: 6267 4233; www.cnwa.com.
Dragonair, Suite 2103-4, Shanghai Plaza, 138 Central Huaihai Road, tel: 6375 6375; fax: 6375 6300; www.dragonair.com.
Eva Airways, Suite 2302, Harbour Ring Plaza, 18 Tibet Road, tel: 5385 2125, 5385 2126; fax: 5385 2127; www.evaair.com.tw.
Japan Airlines, Suite 435, Plaza 66, 1266 Nanjing Road (W), tel: 6472 3000; fax: 6288 2505; www.jal.co.jp.
KLM, Suite 2810, Plaza 66, 1266 Nanjing Road (W), tel: 6884 6884; fax: 810 1855; www.klm.com.
Korean Air, 1st Floor, Yangtze New World, 2099 Yan'an Road (W), tel: 6275 6000, fax: 6275 2777; www.koreanair.com.
Lufthansa, Pu Xiang Plaza, 1600 Century Boulevard, Pudong, tel: 5830 4400; fax: 5830 0616; www.lufthansa.com.
Malaysia Airlines, Suite 209, Shanghai Centre, 1376 Nanjing Road (W), tel: 6279 8579; fax: 6279 8657; www.malaysiaairlines.com.
Northwest Airlines, Suite 2810, Plaza 66, 1266 Nanjing Road (W), tel: 6279 8579; fax: 800 810 1855; www.nwa.com.
Qantas, Suite 203A, West Retail Plaza, Shanghai Centre, 1376 Nanjing Road (W), tel: 6279 8660, 6279 8860; fax: 6279 8650; www.qantas.com.au.
Royal Nepal Airlines, Room C, Zhongsheng Tower, 2067 Yan'an

Road (W), tel: 6270 8352; fax: 6278 4600; www.royalnepal.com.
Shanghai Airlines, 212 Jiangning Road, tel: 6255 0550, 620-8888; www.shanghai-air.com.
Singapore Airlines, Suite 606-608, Kerry Centre, 1515 Nanjing Road (W), tel: 6289 1000; fax: 6289 2000; www.singaporeair.com.
Swissair, Room 2602, Westgate Tower, 1038 Nanjing Road (W), tel: 6218 6810; fax: 6218 6821; www.swissair.com.
Thai Airways, Unit 105, Kerry Centre, 1515 Nanjing Road (W), tel: 5298 5555; fax: 5298 6166; www.thaiairways.com.
Turkish Airlines, Suite 211, Shanghai Centre, 1376 Nanjing Road (W), tel: 3222 0022; fax: 3222 0127; www.thy.com.
United Airlines, Suite 204, Shanghai Centre, 1376 Nanjing Road (W), tel: 6279 8009; www.ual.com.
Virgin Atlantic, Room 221, 12 Zhongshan No. 1 Road (E) (The Bund), tel: 5353 4600; fax: 5353 4601; www.virginatlantic.com.

BY TRAIN

Most travellers use trains for short distance travel within China, but longer distance journeys are also an option. It is certainly possible to follow in the tracks of Paul Theroux, author of *Riding the Iron Rooster*, who travelled from London to China by rail. For high-end China train tours, including tailor-made tours, check the website of China Rail Travel *(see Speciality Holidays, page 279)*.

Most trains arrive and depart from the main **Shanghai Railway Station** (Xin Ke Zhan) at 385 Meiyuan Road, (tel: 6317 9090, 6354 5358) but be sure to check, as some short-distance trains arrive and depart from the **Shanghai South Train Station** at 200 Zhaofeng Road (tel: 6317 9090, 6404 1317).

Tickets
Same-day and next-day train tickets may be purchased at the Shanghai Railway Station's soft seat waiting room (*ruan xi hou che shi*). Hotel

Trains to HK & Beijing

Beijing – The T21/22 is a new deluxe overnight service from Shanghai to Beijing (14 hours) described as a "super-luxury star-rated moving hotel" with ensuite bathrooms, TV sets and Internet access. Trains in both directions depart at 6pm and arrive at 6am the following morning.
Hong Kong – A comfortable train service runs on alternate days from Kowloon's Hung Hom station to Shanghai – if you don't mind the journey time of 25 hours. The K100 departs from Kowloon at 3pm and arrives in Shanghai at 4pm the next day. The K99 departs from Shanghai at 12.25pm and arrives at Kowloon at 1.10pm the next day.

Tickets can be booked through local offices of the CITS, CTS or private travel agents, or check with Hong Kong-based Tiglion Travel at www.train-ticket.net.

concierges and travel agencies, like CITS and CTS, as well as private travel agents, like Crescent Travel, will also book tickets for you *(see Travel Agencies, page 290)*.

Travellers from Hong Kong can book tickets with Tiglion Travel (www.train-ticket.net). For a fee, they will courier tickets to you anywhere in the world.

Train classes
"Hard" and "soft" describe the different classes on the trains ("first" and "second" class is politically incorrect in classless communist China).
Ying Zuo **(Hard seat)** is the classic China train experience, with too many tickets issued for too few spaces (you may end up standing for the duration of the journey), smoke and a constant din. But the overcrowding is made up for by great comraderie, with much sharing of food and conversation.
Ruan Zuo **(Soft seat)** is a less crowded, more Amtrak-style experience. On the double-decker

tourist trains that run to Hangzhou and Suzhou, you can even book hotels at these destinations on board.
Ying Wo **(Hard sleeper)** has two narrow three-tier bunks (six beds in total) to a compartment, no doors – anyone walking by in the corridor gets an eyeful – and no air-conditioning or heating. The lowest bunk is the most expensive. It is also the communal train seat during the day. The top berth is the cheapest and also the stuffiest in the warmer months.
Ruan Wo **(Soft sleeper)** has two bunks (four beds in total) to a closed-door compartment, with air-conditioning.

Comfortable soft-seat tourist trains run between Shanghai and the popular tourist destinations nearby – Hangzhou, Suzhou, Nanjing and Wuxi.

BY BUS

High-speed highways linking Shanghai with its neighbours (Nanjing, Suzhou, Hangzhou, etc.) make buses an efficient budget option for nearby destinations.
Northern Long-distance Bus Station, 80 Gongxing Road, near Baoshan Road and Tianmu Road, tel: 5632 9111. Services Jiading, Anting, Jiangsu, Zhejiang, Shandong, Henan, Hubei, and Fujian.
North Bus Station, 1148 Gonghe Xin Road, at Zhongshan Road (N), tel: 5663 1382, 5653 8064.
New North Bus Station, 258 Hengfeng Road, near Gonghe Road, tel: 5663 0230, 6317 4966. Services Jiangsu, Zhejiang and Anhui provinces.
Private North Bus Station, 783 Hengfeng Road (near Jiaotong Road and Shanghai Railway Station), tel: 6317 4966. Services Zhejiang and Jiangsu provinces. Clean, comfortable buses, with toilets for journeys exceeding two hours.
Western Bus Station, 555 Wuzhong Road, tel: 6438 1285. Services Shanghai suburbs: Xinzhuang, Qingpu, Songjiang and Sheshan, also Zhejiang, Jiangsu, and Anhui.

Xujiahui Bus Station, 111 Hongqiao Road, behind Grand Gateway, tel: 6469 7325. Services Shanghai's southern suburbs, Zhejiang Province, Shaoxing. **Pudong Tangqiao Bus Station**, 40 Pujian Road, tel: 5873 4081. Services Chuansha, Jinshan, Suzhou, Zhejiang and Anhui. **Shanghai Long-Distance Bus Terminal**, near the Shanghai Railway Station in Zhabei. Construction has just started on this new station, which will be completed by 2004. This massive station is expected to handle 1,500 buses and 20,000 passengers a day.

BY BOAT

Cruising down the coastline and amongst river traffic, boats offer an interesting perspective for the adventurous traveller. Local ferries are pretty basic; the overnight boats offer sleeping berths. Luxury cruise liners stop in Shanghai, and there are also luxury ferries to Korea and Japan. There are three piers, all along the Huangpu River.

Ships from Hongkong, Korea and Japan dock at the **International Passenger Terminal** at 1 Waihongqiao Road. Domestic ships and ferries either dock at the **Gongping Road Passenger Terminal** (50 Gongping Road) or at the **Shilipu Passenger Terminal** (111 Zhongshan No. 2 Road).

Tickets can be booked by travel agencies, CTS and CITS *(see page 290)* as well as directly from the ferry booking offices.

Ticket information: tel: 6326 1261. Inquiries (general): tel: 6326 0050.

Practical Tips

Media

Newspapers

There are two major daily English-language newspapers: **Shanghai Daily** (www.shanghaidaily.com or http://english.eastday.com/) published locally with a local perspective on information is the choice for most people; the **China Daily** (www.chinadaily.com.cn) is published out of Beijing. A third paper, the **Shanghai Star** (www.shanghai-star.com.cn) is published on Tuesdays and Fridays with good coverage of the local entertainment and dining scene, and insightful coverage of local issues. The English edition of the Chinese-language **People's Daily** is available on the Internet at www.english.peopledaily.com.

Foreign newspapers and publications are available from four and five-star hotels. One of the best sources is the Portman Ritz-Carlton Shanghai, which carries the *South China Morning Post*, *International Herald Tribune*, *Asian Wall Street Journal* and magazines like *Far Eastern Economic Review*, *Economist*, *Time* and *Newsweek*.

Magazines

Shanghai is awash with free English-language publications of varying quality, most with useful city listings of restaurants, bars and entertainment. The best of the lot is **City Weekend** (www.cityweekend.com.cn) whose articles offer an incisive peek into lifestyles in Shanghai and China. There are several other (like *Shanghai Talk*, *Quo* and *Metrozine*) which are essentially listings magazines, invariably from the perspective of young, on-a-budget native English speakers. Most are available at bars and restaurants around town. Of particular note is **That's Shanghai** (www.thatsshanghai.com).

Shanghai Tatler is a high-quality bilingual publication with beautiful photography and good editorial from a yuppie Shanghainese perspective (www.shanghaitatler.com).

Television

Shanghai Broadcast Network (SBN) has the news in English at 10pm Mon to Sat; Citybeat, a cultural programme in English with garrulous host Gegong airs in that time slot on Sundays.

The news in English is also broadcast on CCTV at 4, 7 and 11pm on weekdays, noon on weekends, while *China This Week* is screened at 2.30pm on Sundays.

Most four and five-star hotels have Star World, CNN, HBO and ESPN.

Radio

BBC World Service is accessible on radio. English language programming is on FM 101.7 and FM 103.7.

Telecommunications

The **country code** for China is 86; the **city code** for Shanghai is 021. When calling Shanghai from **overseas**, drop the prefix zero. When making a **domestic** call from one province to another in China, dial the city code first (including the prefix zero). **Local** calls in Shanghai do not require the city code.

To make an **international direct dial** call from Shanghai, dial the international access code: 00, followed by the country code, the

Useful City Codes

The following are city codes of places covered in the Excursions section of this guidebook

Hangzhou	0571
Moganshan	0572
Nanjing	025
Putuoshan	0580
Suzhou	0512

area code and the local telephone number. The country code for **US** and **Canada** is 1; **UK** 44; **Australia** 61; and **New Zealand** 64.

To save on hefty overseas phone calls, use an international calling card. Following are access codes for US phone card users: **Sprint** (10-813); **MCI** (10-812); and **AT&T** (10-811).

Mobile phones

Most mobile phone users with a roaming facility will be able to hook up with the GSM 900 network that China uses. The exceptions are users from Japan and the North America (unless they have a tri-band phone). Check with your service provider before leaving.

To save on expensive mobile phone charges, consider using a local prepaid phone card. These are available in denominations of RMB 100 and up at magazine stands and convenience stores throughout the city. Note that in China, both incoming and outgoing calls are charged by the minute.

Public telephones

Most public telephones in China use prepaid phone cards, and can be used for local, long distance and international (IDD) calls. Prepaid phone cards are available in amounts of RMB 20, RMB 30, RMB 50 and RMB 100.

Call charges are RMB 0.20 for three minutes, while a call exceeding three minutes is charged RMB 0.10 for every six seconds (or RMB 0.60 for the 4th minute). For some strange reason, it becomes more expensive after the third minute, presumably because the authorities don't want users hogging public phones.

International long-distance call rates vary, but are usually fairly expensive, over RMB 10 a minute. Discounted rates often apply on public holidays.

Internet and e-mail

Most business-class hotels either have rooms with computer ports that allow for high-speed Internet connections or a business centre

where this facilty is available for a fee. A recent crackdown on Internet cafés means that there are far fewer of these around.

The **Shanghai Library** at 1555 Central Huaihai Road (tel: 6445 5555), has several terminals and charges are reasonable. Bring your passport in place of a library card.

Postal Services

Post offices

Shanghai's **main post office** is at 276 Suzhou Road (N) (tel: 6393 6666) and is open 24 hours. Every neighbourhood in Shanghai city has a post office, open 8 to 12 hours a day depending on the area. Post offices in the busiest areas, that is, Sichuan Road, Huaihai Road, Nanjing Road and Xujiahui, are open 14 hours, while the Luwan district post office is open 24 hours.

In addition to mailing and selling stamps, post offices also deliver local courier packages *(see below)* and accept subscriptions for designated magazines and newspapers.

International courier services

DHL-Sinotrans, Shanghai International Trade Centre, 2200 Yan'an Road (W), tel: 6275 3543; and 303 Jinian Road, tel: 6536 2900; www.dhl.com.
UPS, Room 1318, Central Plaza, 318 Central Huaihai Road, tel: 6391 5555; www.ups.com.
Federal Express, 10th Floor, Aetna Building, 107 Zunyi Road, tel: 6275 0808; www.fedex.com.

Local courier services

Express Mail Service (EMS):
Offices at the following locations: 1337 Central Huaihai Road, tel: 6437 4272; 431 Fuxing Road, tel: 6328 3322; 2 Century Boulevard, Pudong, tel: 5047 2288; 146 Gao Qiao Shi Jia Road, Pudong, tel: 5867 5114.

Tipping

Tipping is technically illegal and therefore generally not expected in Shanghai. Many top-end hotels and

restaurants already add service charges of 10–15 percent to their bills. Nonetheless many tip when a service charge has not been added to the bill. In general, tip if you feel that you've received excellent service, or if the staff have been unusually helpful.

Local Tourism Offices

(See also Local Travel Agencies, page 290.)
Shanghai Tourist Information and Service Centre, 303 Moling Road (South Exit of Shanghai Railway Station), tel: 6353 9920; www.tourinfo.sh.cn.

A tourist telephone hotline (tel: 6252 0000) operates daily from 10am to 9pm. Be sure to ask for an operator who speaks English.

There is a Tourist Information and Service Centre at ground level of the Arrival Hall of Pudong International Airport and also in each of Shanghai's districts. Following are some of the more useful ones:
Jingan District Tourist Information & Service Centre, 218 Yuyuan Road (W), tel: 6253 3336.
Luwan District Tourist Information & Service Centre, 127 Chengdu Road (S), tel: 6372 8330, 6318 1882.
Huangpu District Tourist Information & Service Centre, 561 Nanjing Road (E), tel: 5353 1117, 5353 1118.
Yuyuan Tourist Information & Service Centre (north of the gardens), 159 Jiujiaochang Road, tel: 6355 5032, 6355 5033.
Pudong New Area Tourist Information & Service Centre, 541 Dongfang Road, tel: 6875 0593, 5831 8015.

Local Consulates

Australian Consulate, 22/F CITIC Square, 1168 Nanjing Road (W), tel: 5292 5500; fax: 5292 5511; www.dfat.gov.au.
British Consulate, Suite 301, Shanghai Centre, 1376 Nanjing Road (W), tel: 6279 7650; www.britishembassy.org.

Canadian Consulate, Suite 604, Shanghai Centre, 1376 Nanjing Road (W), tel: 6279 8400; www.shanghai.gc.ca.

French Consulate, Rooms 21A, 23B, Qihua Tower, 1375 Central Huaihai Road, tel: 6437 7414; www.consulfrance-shanghai.org.

German Consulate, 181 Yongfu Road, tel: 6433 6953.

New Zealand Consulate, Room 15A, Qihua Tower, 1375 Central Huaihai Road, tel: 6471 1108; fax: 6431 0226; www.mft.govt.nz.

Singapore Consulate, 89 Wanshan Road, tel: 6278 5566; www.mfa.gov.sg/shanghai

United States of America Consulate, 1469 Central Huaihai Road, tel: 6433 6880; fax: 6433 4122; also **American Citizen Services**, 8th Floor, Westgate Mall, 1038 Nanjing Road (W), tel: 3217 4650, after-hours emergencies tel: 6433 3936; www.usembassy-china.org.cn/ shanghai. Open 8.30–11.30am, 1.30–3.30pm.

Business Travellers

As Shanghai is China's economic power house, there is plenty of assistance for those doing business here. The various Chambers of Commerce are an excellent starting point for business information and questions. Another useful source of research is the Shanghai government's business and investment website at www.investment.gov.cn

Chambers of Commerce

The American Chamber of Commerce in Shanghai, 4/F Portman Ritz-Carlton Hotel, 1376 Nanjing Road (W), tel: 6279 7119; www.amcham-shanghai.org.

The Australian Chamber of Commerce, Suite 531, Apollo Building, 1440 Central Yan'an Road, tel: 6248 8301; www.austcham.org.

The British Chamber of Commerce, Rooms 01-02, 17th Floor, Westgate Tower, 1038 Nanjing Road (W), tel: 6218 5022, 6218 5183; fax: 6218 5066, 6218 5193; www.sha.britcham.org.

The Canada China Business Council, Room 1901, Hong Kong Plaza, South Tower, 283 Central Huaihai Road, tel: 6390 6001; fax: 6390 7310; www.ccbc.com.

French Chamber of Commerce, 2/F Eastern Business Building, 586 Pan Yu Road, tel: 6281 3618; fax: 6281 3611; www.ccifc.org.

The German Chamber of Commerce in China-Shanghai, 29/F Pos Plaza, 1600 Century Avenue, Pudong, tel: 5081 2266; fax: 5081 2009; e-mail: office@ahksha.com.cn.

The Shanghai Japan Club of Commerce and Industry, Room 2001, International Trade Building, 2200 Yan'an West Road, tel: 6275 2001; www.cin.or.jp.

Business cards

Business cards – preferably with your name and address in Chinese on the reverse – are a prerequisite to doing business in China. Most hotel business centres will make up new ones for you. For cheaper and just as good quality, copy shops will also print business cards for you. You can either give them one of your existing cards to duplicate, or they can design one for you.

Copy General (24 hrs), 88 Tongren Road, tel: 6279 1694; e-mail: copygsh@mail.uninet.com.cn; and Room 2113, China Merchants Tower, 66 Lujiazui Road, tel: 5879 8238.

Medical Treatment

As noted under Health and Insurance (page 276), basic health care is perfectly adequate in Shanghai, but complicated health issues are best handled abroad. The following are recommended if you need medical treatment.

Clinics

World Link Medical Centre, Unit 30, Mandarine City, 788 Hong Xu Road, Hongqiao, tel: 6405 5788.

World Link Medical Centre – Shanghai Centre Clinic, Suite 203, West Retail Plaza, Shanghai

Centre, 1376 Nanjing Road (W), tel: 6279 7688.

Drs Anderson & Partners, Room 1001, D Block 10th Floor, New Century Plaza, 48 Xing Yi Road, (near Sheraton Grand Taipingyang Hotel), tel: 6270 3263. Mobile: (emergencies) 139 190 1749.

Hospitals

Shanghai Huashan Hospital, Foreigner's Ward: 19th Floor, 12 Central Urumqi Road, tel: 6248 9999 ext. 1900. A mid-sized general hospital which offers most specialities with the exception of obstetrics and gynaecology, and paediatrics.

Shanghai Huadong Hospital, 221 Yan An Road (W), tel: 6248 3180 ext. 3106. A medium-sized teaching hospital, this has a foreigner's clinic in a separate building.

Ruijin Hospital, 197 Ruijin No. 2 Road, tel: (021) 6437 0045 ext. 8101 (outpatients and emergencies only); 6324 0090 ext. 2101 (24-hour house calls). This large teaching hospital offers most specialities. The foreigner's clinic is located in the Guang Ci Hospital, on the grounds.

International Medical Care Centre, Shanghai No. 1 People's Hospital, 585 Jiu Long Road, tel: 6306 9485 (appointments), 6306 9480 (administration). A private health centre attached to a large teaching hospital; offers all specialities including dentistry.

Paediatrics

Paediatric Hospital Shanghai Medical University, Foreigner's Clinic, tel: 6403 7371. House calls can be made before 8.30pm.

Pudong Children's Medical Centre, 1678 Dongfang Road, Pudong, tel: 5873 2020. A large, modern teaching hospital built as a Sino-US joint venture.

Dental

World Link Dental Centre, Unit 30, Mandarine City, 788 Hong Xu Road, tel: 6405 5788.

Shanghai Kosei Dental Hospital, 666 Changle Road, tel: 6247 7000, fax: 6247 6193.

Chinese Medicine

At the core of traditional Chinese medicine is the philosophy that disease is due to an imbalance of *yin* and *yang* in the body. The concept of *yin* and *yang* is that there are polar opposites in the body that must be in balance.

The anatomy of disease is more specifically identified as an interruption of the flow of energy (*qi*) through the channels of the body, channels that are connected by the acupuncture points. Physiology is represented by organ functions, which have both a physical and a mental function. Restoring the body to health requires the correction of this imbalance or disruption through acupuncture and herbal medicines.

Traditional Chinese medicine with English-speaking doctors is available at World Link Medical Centres *(see page 284)*. For more on traditional Chinese medicine, see the Karolinska Institute website, www.mic.ki.se.

Pharmacies

World Link Medical Centres will fill prescriptions *(see page 284)*.
Watson's, 789 Central Huaihai Road, tel: 6474 4775. Open daily 9am–10pm.
Shanghai No. 1 Dispensary, 616 Nanjing Road (E), tel: 6322 4567. Open daily 9am–10pm.
Huashan Yaofang (24 hours), 12 Central Urumqi Road (outside Shanghai Huashan Hospital).

Contraception

Condoms are widely available at the check-out counters in grocery stores, pharmacies, "adult health shops" and, increasingly, at condom vending machines throughout the city. Birth control pills and barrier contraceptives are also available at pharmacies without a prescription.

Children

Fever-reducing medication is easily available, but over-the-counter medication for coughs, colds and other common childhood maladies are less easily available. And while disposable diapers can be easily found in Shanghai (at high prices) this is not so for the rest of China.

Women

Shanghai women prefer sanitary pads to tampons, and while tampons can be found in convenience stores, there is little choice in terms of brands and absorbencies.

Travelling with Kids

Shanghai loves children. This is one of the most child-friendly places on the planet; there is not a museum, a restaurant or a theatre where your child will feel unwelcome. The downside is a loss of privacy: your kids will be touched, stared at, talked to, and photographed – just take a positive attitude about the whole thing (*this* is what it feels like to be a celebrity!) and you'll meet new friends and gain fresh insights.

Hotels are quite relaxed about allowing children to stay with you in a double room at no extra charge. Extra beds are available for a small surcharge. Reliable babysitters, called *ayi* (aunty) are easily available. If you are going to be in Shanghai for any length of time, consider a serviced apartment with kitchen *(see page 295)*. If you have young children, the Shanghai Centre – with its well-equipped playroom, play school, indoor/outdoor pool and host of young families – is an excellent choice.

Disabled Travellers

Shanghai's modern hotels, buildings and museums are all wheelchair accessible, but older buildings and the myriad overpasses and underpasses are not wheelchair accessible. Newer metro stations all have wheelchair ramps, and the older ones are adding them.

Shanghai's wheelchair-bound use motorised wheelchairs to get around, and **Bashi Taxi** (tel: 6431 2788) has several minivans for those who need wheelchairs.

Gay Travellers

Homosexuality is frowned upon in China – it was downgraded from a mental illness only in 2001 – but in liberal Shanghai, the gay scene is an increasingly open, predominantly male one, from cross-dressing singer Coco to well-known gay bars. Nevertheless, discretion prevails, and although foreigners are rarely targeted, China is still basically a conservative society, so flagrant displays are best avoided. Check www.utopia-asia.com/chinshan.htm.

Security and Crime

Shanghai is a relatively safe city, but petty crimes like pickpocketing do happen in crowded areas like train stations, markets and on busy streets. There is very little violent crime against foreigners, but tourists should be aware of scams. One of the better known ones involves locals asking foreign tourists to dinner, in order to "practise their English". After the end of a meal, an extortionate bill arrives, with the local having disappeared, or simply professing that they're "too poor" to pay.

Every neighbourhood has its own police station or post, often labelled in English. This is the place to report any crimes, although you might have to wait for the Public Security Bureau officer in charge of foreigners to handle your case.

Emergency Numbers

Public Security Bureau, 710 Hankou Road, tel: 6321 5380.
Ambulance 120
Fire 119
Police 110
International SOS 6295 0099

Religious Services

To discourage proselytising, Chinese nationals are not allowed by law to attend church services conducted for Shanghai's foreign community. At such services, passports may be required for foreigners.

Catholic

St Peter's Catholic Church, 270 Chongqing Road (S), tel: 6467 8282. English-language Sunday Mass at Shanghai's expatriate's church is at 10.30am; Saturday evening Mass is 5pm.

St Ignatius Cathedral, 158 Puxi Road, Xujiahui Qu, tel: 6469 0930. 7 and 10.30am and 6pm Sunday mass in Shanghainese; foreigners may attend.

Fu Jia Rose Church, 1115 Pudong Dadao, Pudong. Call 5885 3172 for Mass times.

Dongjiadu Cathedral, 175 Dongjiadu Road, tel: 6377 5665. Chinese Sunday Mass only at 7.30am.

Protestant

Shanghai Community Church, 53 Hengshan Road, tel: 6437 6576. English-language service for foreigners is at 4pm on Sunday.

Jewish

The Shanghai Jewish Centre, Shang-Mira Garden Villa No. 2, 1720 Hongqiao Road, tel: 6278 0225. For times of Shabbat services and to make reservations for Shabbat meals, check its website at www.chinajewish.org.

Muslim

Xiaotaoyuan Mosque, 52 Xiaotaoyuan Street (off Fuxing Road (E) at Henan Road), tel: 6377 5443. Open 8am–7pm.

Buddhist/Taoist

Jing An Temple, 1686 Nanjing Road (W). Open daily 7.30am–4pm.
Jade Buddha Temple, 170 Anyuan Road (at Jiangning Road). Open daily 8am–12pm, 1–5pm.

Etiquette

Bear in mind the following rules:
  Shoes should be removed when entering homes; often slippers will be provided.
  Use both hands to present business cards at meetings.
  Tea should be offered when someone visits you, whether at home or in a business setting.

If you invite someone for dinner, you are expected to pay for the entire meal – Shanghainese do not go Dutch. Nevertheless, the Shanghainese are very forgiving of foreigners when it comes to local rules of etiquette, so you will be excused of most gaffes.

  The most serious breaches of etiquette, though, tend to involve politics rather than manners: although the atmosphere is far more open now, it is still wise to stay away from political discussions, especially ones involving ultra-sensitive topics like Taiwan and Tibet.

Watch Your Step

Shanghai has a list of "Seven Nos" that it would like its citizens to observe, one of which is spitting. Chinese believe that excess phlegm must be cleared as it causes ill health. At least these days they generally don't spit indoors, and the more socially aware – given the recent SARS scare – discreetly spit into tissues or trash cans.

Photography

Shanghai is a compelling photographic subject, whether it's the space-age new buildings and highways, the graceful old architecture and its people or the collision of the old and the new. Generally, people are quite happy to be photographed, and as photography is quite popular among the ever-hip Shanghainese, you may find yourself at the other end of the camera as well. Shanghai is surprisingly lax when it comes to photography in museums; so far it is only forbidden in the Shanghai Museum and at Jade Buddha Temple.

  The one area of photographic sensitivity are government buildings, military installations and airports: snapping photos of government buildings and restricted areas will get you hauled to the local Public Security Bureau for a potentially long interrogation, and your film will be confiscated.

Getting Around

Orientation

The Huangpu River separates Pudong district, literally "east of the Huangpu", from the rest of Shanghai, or Puxi, "west of the Huangpu". Suzhou Creek divides the thriving midsection of Puxi from its quieter northern suburbs.

  There are places to stay and things to do all over the city, but travellers will find the highest concentration of sights, restaurants, entertainment and hotels in the Nanjing Road corridor in Puxi, anchored by the Portman Ritz-Carlton Hotel and continuing east to the Westin, just blocks away from the Bund. This is where the majority of shopping, museums and attractions lie. Travellers with business in Pudong have a wide range of hotels to choose from as well, from five-star properties like the Grand Hyatt and the St Regis to four-star business hotels like Courtyard by Marriott.

  Streets run north to south and east to west in gridlike fashion, except for oval-shaped Nanshi and the old racetrack contours that ring People's Square. The major streets run the length of the city and have directional tags: for example, Huaihai West, Huaihai Central or Huaihai East. Buildings are usually sequentially numbered, odd numbers on one side of the street and even numbers on the other. To find an address, you should know its cross-street, such as, Huaihai Road near (kaojing) Gao'an Road.

  The city is bisected from east to west by the Yan'an Road Elevated Highway and from north to south by Chongqing Road Elevated Highway.

  Buses cover most of the city but are packed during peak hours and have Chinese-only information. The sleek subway system, however, is an easy way to get around; the lines are still being extended and is linked to a new elevated light railway system, the Pearl Line. Taxis are an inexpensive and usually plentiful option.

From the Airport

Pudong International Airport
This is located about 30 km (18½ miles) from the city, so use one of the following modes of transport.

Taxis: There is a well-marked and very organised taxi line outside the arrival hall; taxis to the city centre in Puxi cost approximately RMB 180 and take about an hour, depending on traffic conditions.

Airport Buses: There are six routes from the airport to different points in the city (cost ranges from RMB 15–20); the pick-up point is between Doors 7 and 15 in the arrival hall. Tickets for Route 1, Hongqiao Airport and Route 2, Shanghai Exhibition Centre, may be purchased at the airport bus ticket counter in the arrival hall. Tickets for other routes may be purchased on the bus. The buses run from 6am–7pm and take about 75 minutes to reach the city centre.

Hotel Shuttles: The major hotels all have booths at the airport; private cars and shuttle buses can be arranged here, although it's usually best to do this in advance.

Maglev: The high-speed Maglev (short for magnetic levitation) train runs from the airport to Pudong's Longyang subway station. The 30-km (19-mile) journey takes only eight minutes. Tickets are priced at RMB 50 each. If you don't have much luggage, change to the subway (Metro Line 2) to get to your final destination in the city (15 minutes to downtown Pudong and 30 minutes to Puxi). Otherwise take a taxi from Longyang station (20–30 minutes to downtown Pudong and 45 minutes to Puxi).

Instead of conventional steel wheels on rails, the Maglev uses electro-magnetic technology to hover and glide above the guide rails at speeds of up to 430 km (267 miles) an hour. The Shanghai line, which cost a whopping US$1.2 billion to build, began daily operations in September 2003.

Inter-airport: (see Hongqiao Airport below).

Hongqiao Airport
This airport is strictly for domestic flights. To get to the city, 13 km (8 miles) away, use one of the following modes of transport.

Taxi: There are two taxi lines outside the airport; one for short-distance journeys and the other to Pudong. Taxis to the city centre in Puxi cost approximately RMB 60 for the 30–45 minute ride plus the RMB 15 toll. Avoid the taxi touts who hang around the arrival hall and who invariably charge much more.

Airport Bus: Hongqiao Airport's shuttle bus runs from the airport (lower level) to the Shanghai Exhibition Centre, directly across from the Shanghai Centre. The cost is RMB 5–7 and journey time is about 45 minutes.

Inter-airport: The 40-km (25-mile) distance between Pudong and Hongqiao airports is one of the longest journeys in Shanghai, so take note if you have to make a connection from an international flight to a domestic one (or vice versa). There are regular airport shuttle buses between the two costing RMB 20 while a taxi (one-hour) will set you back by at least RMB 200. Meanwhile, airport authorities are working on

New Street Names

As part of its bold new bid to become an international tourist and convention destination, Shanghai recently changed all its romanised *pinyin* street names into English. The Chinese characters still remain, but Nanjing Xi Lu is now known as Nanjing Road (W). Unfortunately, taxi drivers and most people you would ask for directions on the streets are more likely to understand the Chinese names.

Still, you should not have too much trouble as long as you take note of the following translations. Most of the actual street names have not changed (Nanjing, Fuzhou, etc.), just the *pinyin* name for street or road; direction, ie North, South, East or West; and the number 1 or 2.

English	Chinese	English	Chinese
Road	Lu	South	Nan
Street	Jie	East	Dong
Avenue	Da Dao, Da Jie	West	Xi
Central	Zhong	One	Yi
North	Bei	Two	Er

In a few cases, Chinese names have been translated into English:

English	Chinese
Urumqi Road	Wulumuqi Lu
Tibet Road	Xizang Lu
People's Avenue	Renmin Da Dao
Century Boulevard	Shiji Da Dao
People's Square	Renmin Guangchang

Here are a few sample translations of roads:

English	Chinese
Zhongshan No. 1 Road (E)	Zhongshan Dong Yi Lu
Ruijin No. 2 Road	Ruijin Er Lu
Henan Road (N)	Henan Bei Lu
Henan Road (S)	Henan Nan Lu
Nanjing Road (E)	Nanjing Dong Lu
Nanjing Road (W)	Nanjing Xi Lu
Central Henan Road	Henan Zhong Lu

connecting the two airports more efficiently. By 2005, Metro Line 2 will link to Hongqiao Airport, enabling travel between the two airports by a combination of subway and Maglev.

Taxis

Taxis are one of Shanghai's great deals: inexpensive and usually plentiful (6–7pm dinner time and rainy days are exceptions). The city's cab drivers are also generally a reliable and honest lot – to the point that they will tell you if they don't know your destination. Shanghai has begun a campaign to teach taxi drivers English, but for the average taxi driver, this is limited to "Hello" and "Stop here?" It's best to have the name and address of the destination written out in Chinese, and, failing that, the name of the street and the cross-street in Chinese.

Taxis are metered and drivers turn it on as a matter of course. Fares cost RMB 10 for the first 2 km (1¼ miles), and RMB 2 per additional km after that. Expect to pay a 30 percent surcharge for trips after 11pm. Tips are not expected.

Payment is either by cash or by stored-value cards (which can also be used on the metro and buses) sold at subway stations; cards can be topped up at convenience stores like Lawsons and 21. Cards cost RMB 100, with RMB 70 available for use (RMB 30 is the deposit for the card, which is returned when the card is surrendered).

Always ask for a printed receipt (*fa piao* in Chinese) which records the taxi number and the taxi company's telephone number; this will help in the event you leave something behind in a taxi. With the exception of mobile phones, things are usually returned promptly. The

Figuring it Out

No. 24 on a licence means that a driver is brand new. Otherwise, the lower the number, the longer the driver has been driving. The laminated licences in the taxis also feature stars, which reflect how the driver scored on his driving test – five stars and you have a winner!

receipt also includes the number for complaints, which is prominently displayed in the taxi as well.

Most taxis can be hired for the whole day, and can also be booked in advance for a surcharge.

Dazhong Taxi	800 620 1688
Bashi Taxi	6431 2788
Qiangsheng	6258 0000
Qian Wei Red Flag	5683 2029
Jin Jiang Tourism Taxi	6464 7777
Taxi Complaints	6323 2150

How to get to Places of Interest Outside Shanghai

Train tickets can be booked at the Shanghai Railway Station at 385 Meiyuan Road, tel: 6317 9090. Confirm all train schedules at: www.expatsh.com/railwaytimetable.htm. You could also arrange for a private car hire with driver or use a travel agent *(see page 290)*. Many of the places below are part of standard package tours; if not ask for one to be tailor-made for you.

Chongming Island

By Ferry: Until the river crossing from Waigaiqiao in Pudong is completed, taking a ferry from Shanghai's northeastern ports is the best way to get to Chongming. The fastest is from Baoyang in Shanghai to Nanmen on Chongming, which takes 30–40 minutes. Take a taxi from Nanmen to your hotel or final destination.
Baoyang to Nanmen ferries run 13 times a day, with an additional trip on the weekends. Ferries run from 7.10am–5pm, tel: 5612 2081.
Nanmen to Baoyang ferries run from 6.30am–4.30pm, tel: 6961 2710, 6961 2711.

Putuoshan

By Ferry: Ferry tickets can be purchased from travel agents or directly from the Shilipu Passenger Terminal (111 Zhongshan No. 2 Road). Arrive at Shilipu by 8am for the two-hour bus ride to either Jinshan or Luchao. From here, the fast ferry takes three hours to get to Putuoshan. The return ferry from Putuoshan leaves at 4 and 5pm. An overnight ferry also leaves Shanghai at 6pm daily, arriving in Putuoshan at 6am.
By Air: Visitors can fly into Shen Jia Men on the neighbouring island of Zhoushan and then take a 10-minute ferry ride to Putuoshan.

Suzhou

By Train: The double-decker tourist train goes through the countryside, a comfortable, scenic way to travel to Suzhou. There are trains every hour from 3am–6pm departing Shanghai; the journey takes about 90 minutes.
By Car: If you avoid leaving during the rush hour, the new high-speed highway is the fastest way to travel

to Suzhou, getting you there in just over an hour.

Hangzhou

By Train: There are regular departures from 6am–5pm daily on the double-decker tourist train from Shanghai to Hangzhou; the journey takes a little over two hours.
By Car: The car trip to Hangzhou takes approximately the same time, depending on the traffic.

Moganshan

By Car: Moganshan is best done as a sidetrip from Hangzhou. From there, get a hired car or taxi. The journey takes about an hour.

Nanjing

By Train: The double-decker tourist train from Shanghai makes several departures for Nanjing between 3am and 5pm. The journey takes about five hours.
By Car: The Shanghai-Nanjing high-speed highway has cut travel time considerably; the journey is about three hours if you avoid rush hour.

Metro

Shanghai's slick subway system (*di tie*) is an efficient way to get around the city and avoid traffic jams, although the subway during rush hour has human jams of its own. Subway signs are all in English, making it easy to navigate.

There are three lines currently in operation: **Metro Line 1** runs north-to-south from the Shanghai Railway Station to Xinzhuang in the southern suburbs. **Metro Line 2** runs an east-west axis from Zhangjiang to Zhongshan Park. Both lines converge at People's Square.

The third line called the **Pearl Line**, short for the Pearl Mass Transit Light Rail, is a mostly elevated 36-km (22-mile) line that runs from north to south via the Shanghai Railway Station.

The city plans to complete 11 subway lines and 10 light rail lines by 2025, and construction is already underway on some of these.

Single-journey subway tickets may be purchased at ticket machines or counters at the metro stations. Trains operate from 6am to midnight. Fares are RMB 1–4 depending on the distance. Stored-value cards, called *jiaotong* cards, may be purchased at all metro station counters and can be used for taxis and buses as well. Cards cost RMB 100, but the stored value is RMB 70 – RMB 30 is a deposit which you will get back when the card is returned.
Metro Hotline 6318 9000.

Car Rental

Tourists are no longer expressly prohibited from driving in Shanghai, but neither are they encouraged. Since taxis are so easy to come by in Shanghai, inexpensive – even for day and weekend trips – and the challenge of asking for directions in Chinese so daunting, they are the preferred alternative.

Most car rental agencies offer private car hire with drivers. Expect to pay RMB 600–800 a day. Petrol cost is usually included in the rates.

Cars rental companies
Shanghai Anji Car Rental, 1387 Changning Road, tel: 6268 0862.
Dazhong, 98 Guohuo Road, tel: 6318 5666.
Hertz Car Rental, Suite 306, 1088 Yan'an Road, tel: 6252 2200.
Shanghai Yongda Automotive Rent Co Ltd, 2757 Zhangyang Road, tel: 5860 7079.

Bus

Buses tend to be crowded and difficult to figure out without some rudimentary knowledge of Chinese, and some of the older ones don't have air-conditioning. Most buses run from 6am to midnight while some special services operate 24 hours. Fares cost from RMB 1–2 and tickets are sold on board by a conductor.

If you are feeling adventurous, consider doing some of the routes recommended in the text box on page 290. Try and avoid buses during peak hours and keep a firm grip on your valuables.

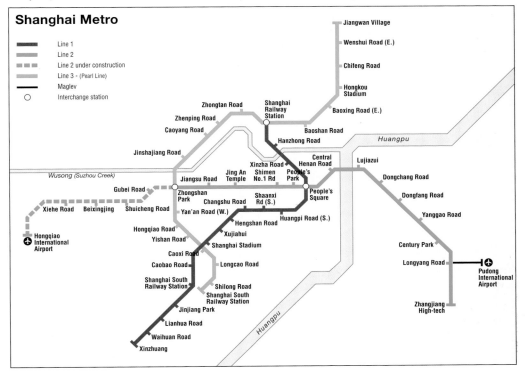

Shanghai Metro

Useful Bus Routes

No. 2 Central Huaihai Road and Hengshan Road to Xujiahui.
No. 11 Runs the perimeter of the Old City around People's Road and Zhonghua Road.
No. 20 From Zhongshan Park to Yuyuan Road, Nanjing Road (W), People's Square and Jiujang Road (near the Bund).
No. 42 From the Bund at Guangdong Road to Renmin Road by Yu Garden and Bazaar in the Old City, along Central Huaihai Road and Xiangyang Park through Xujiahui to Shanghai Stadium.
No 518 People's Square to Pudong Road (S).
No 911 Zhonghua Road (near Central Fuxing Road) near the Old City through Huaihai Road to Hongqiao Road and the zoo.
No 930 People's Square to Tibet Road (S) to Dongtai Market and Renmin Road in the Old City.

Local Travel Agencies

The local offices of government travel agencies, China International Travel Service (CITS), China Travel Service (CTS) and China Youth Travel Service (CYTS), can all book tours, hotels, flights (international and domestic) and train tickets. In addition, there are a handful of private travel agents.
Shanghai China Travel Service (SCTS), 881 Central Yan'an Road, tel: 6247 8888; fax: 6247 5878; e-mail: webmaster@scts.com.
Shanghai China Youth Travel Service (CYTS), 2 Hengshan Road, tel: 6433 1826; fax: 6445 5396; e-mail: cyts@public.sta.net.cn.
Shanghai China International Travel Service (CITS), 1277 Beijing Road (W) (main office), tel: 6289 8899; fax: 6289 4928; 146 Huangpi Road (S), tel: 6387 4988; 66 Nanjing Road (E), tel: 6323 4067; 2 Jinling Road (E), tel: 6323 8770; www.scits.com.
Shanghai Jinjiang Tours, 191 Changle Road, tel: 6466 2828; fax: 6466 2297; www.jjtravel.com. Part of the state-owned Jinjiang Group

(which owns some of Shanghai's best historic properties, including the Peace Hotel) this reputable agent offers package tours of major Chinese cities, including Shanghai. In Shanghai, its "optional tours" include city tours and tours to Zhouzhuang and Tong Li water villages as well as day trips and overnight excursions to Suzhou and Hangzhou. It can also customise tours to Nanjing and places further afield, but you'll need to arrange this beforehand.
Crescent Travel, 511 Weihai Road, Suite 1010, Shanghai Shen Shi, tel: 6272 3718, 6272 7199.
This small and customer-friendly private travel agency provides booking services for airline, train and boat tickets, and can also create custom-made itineraries. Unlike the canned package tours run by the big state-owned companies, this agency is better geared for the more independent traveller. Owner Helen Gong speaks good English, and will organise trips for you in Shanghai and throughout China even at short notice.

River Cruises

Huangpu River Cruises runs cruises that offer spectacular vistas of the Bund and Pudong skyline, as well as close-up views of the cable bridges that span the river. Unless you're particularly interested in the developments in the Pudong area, the one-hour cruise will suffice.
Boats leave on the half-hour between 9am and 9pm and have a counter selling snacks and drinks on board; some evening cruises offer dinner as well. Be sure to opt for the more expensive tickets as these have the best views.
The one-hour cruise to the Yangpu Bridge costs RMB 25–35; the two-hour cruise to Yangpu and Nanpu bridges costs RMB 35–70 while the full three-and-a-half-hour cruise is priced between RMB 50–100. This trip goes to as far as Wusong Kou, the entrance to the Yangzi River, and back. Watch for the castle-like Yangshupu Power Plant, near the Yangpu Bridge, Fuxing Island (from which Chiang

Kai-Shek beat his retreat from the Communist army) and Wusong Kou, site of Opium War battles.
Tickets can be booked from the office at **219-239 Zhongshan No. 2 Road (E)** or at the **Shanghai Ferry Travelling Bus Company** at 127 Zhongshan No. 1 Road (E), tel: 6374 4461.

Speciality Tours

Jewish Shanghai
Israeli writer and photographer Dvir Bar-Gal conducts tours of Shanghai's Jewish heritage, in Hebrew, if requested.
Dvir Bar-Gal, tel: (052) 518 855 in Israel; tel: 6283 5629 in Shanghai; e-mail: dbargal@hotmail.com.

Historic Shanghai
The Shanghai Historic House Association (SHHA) conducts tours of historic sites, covering architecture, history, Jewish history, Chinese Shanghai and religious Shanghai, and will customise tours for those with specific interests. The SHHA also holds a semi-annual house tour featuring private historic homes. For more information check www.historic-shanghai.com; e-mail: Info@historic-shanghai.com.

Jinjiang City Tour Bus

These hop-on and hop-off sightseeing buses are an ideal way of taking in Shanghai's major city attractions. Departing every 45 minutes from just outside the Okura Garden Hotel (58 Maoming Road (S) at Changle Road), the buses stop at tourist destinations around Shanghai including the Bund, Yu Garden and Bazaar, People's Square and the Oriental Pearl Tower. Passengers can get off at any destination and take the next bus with the same ticket. Tickets priced at RMB 18 are valid for the whole day. A complete loop of the city takes 1¾ hours. Tickets may be bought from the conductor on board or at **Shanghai Jinjiang Tours**, 191 Changle Road, tel: 6466 2828; fax: 6466 2297.

Where to Stay

Choosing a Hotel

Shanghai is bursting with hotels which fit virtually every budget and taste – from top-of-the-line luxury hotels to long-stay serviced apartments, boutique historic guesthouses and simple backpacker haunts. The slick international-chain hotels rival their Western counterparts – they're newer, bigger and have more amenities, but there is also a solid number of mid-range offerings.

A recent entrant has been good quality Chinese hotels, which offer accommodation similar to four-star international chains, but without the facilities and at deeply discounted prices. Travellers on a budget should note that several of the city's budget and mid-priced hotels are located in one-time grand historic hotels.

Autumn and spring, when the weather is nicest, is high season – with rates following suit. Rates also spiral when there are big conferences or events in town.

Compare hotel rates online at www.book-a-hotel-in-shanghai.com or www.shanghaihotels.com.

Note: Prices are quoted in USD because it is the accepted practice at most international hotels in Shanghai.

BUND AREA

Westin Shanghai (Waitan Zhong Xin)
88 Henan Road
Tel: 6335 1888; Fax: 6335 2888
www.starwood.com
Located just two blocks from the Bund, the Westin is the only international hotel in the Bund area. The generously sized rooms in this impressive luxury hotel offer in-

room broadband connection, sweeping views of Pudong and the Huangpu River, and excellent restaurants. The Westin has all the facilities you'd expect from a five-star – pool, fitness centre, business centre and the added bonus of the Banyan Tree Spa on site. $$$$

Peace Hotel (Heping Fandian)
20 Nanjing Road (E)
Tel: 6321 6888; Fax: 6329 0300
www.shanghaipeacehotel.com
Shanghai's most famous historic hotel – where Noel Coward wrote *Private Lives* and Shanghai society danced on the rooftop while Communism knocked – retains its old-world charm in the public areas and restaurants. With the exception of the 10 national suites (Indian, Chinese, American, British, Spanish, French, etc), some of which date from the 1930s, the regular rooms have been renovated and chopped up into characterless boxes. The service is spotty, cuisine average, and the much-touted Jazz Band pretty awful. The 8th-floor rooftop bar has fabulous views over the river and Bund. No swimming pool, even though it's listed as a five-star. $$$

Hotel Price Guide

$$$$	USD 150 and up
$$$	USD 100–150
$$	USD 50–100
$	less than USD 50

Sofitel Hyland Hotel (Hailun Bin'guan)
505 Nanjing Road (E)
Tel: 6351 5888; Fax: 6351 4088
www.accorhotels-asia.com
This four-star has an excellent location along the Nanjing Road walking street, close to both Nanjing Road shopping and Bund sightseeing. The Sofitel has a very standard-issue feel to it, but the higher floors have excellent views over Nanjing Road and the Huangpu River. $$$

Ocean Hotel (Yuanyang Fandian)
1171 Dong Da Ming Road
Tel: 6545 8888; Fax: 6545 8993
A modern, Chinese-managed four-star

hotel, the Ocean Hotel is a tour group favourite located about 10 minutes from the Bund overlooking the Huangpu River. Its Hongkou location makes it ideal for explorations of the Jewish quarter, which often begin or end at the hotel's revolving restaurant overlooking Hongkou. $$

Shanghai Mansions (Shanghai Da Sha)
20 Suzhou Road (N)
Tel: 6324 6260; Fax: 6306 5147
www.broadwaymansions.com
This 22-storey, 1930s building (former site of the Foreign Correspondents Club) is showing its age, but the four-star hotel still offers comfortable accommodation and an ideal location – just across the Suzhou Creek from the Bund – for forays to the Bund, Pudong and the Jewish quarter. Foreign journalists watched the Communists march into Shanghai from this hotel, and American officers were billeted here after the war. The rooftop terrace has fabulous views of Pudong and the Bund – be sure to ask for a room with Bund views. $$

Pujiang Hotel (Pujiang Fandian)
15 Huangpu Road
Tel: 6324 6388; Fax: 6324 3179
Just minutes from the Bund, the Pujiang is a backpacker favourite that was built as the grand Astor House Hotel, where ballerina Margot Fonteyn once stayed. The impressive Victorian interior has hardly been touched, giving the dorms and doubles a sense of high-style and plenty of history. $

NANJING ROAD (W) AREA

Four Seasons Hotel Shanghai (Si Ji Dajiudian)
500 Weihai Road
Tel: 6256 8888; Fax: 6256 6678
www.fourseasons.com/shanghai
Opened in 2002, the characteristic luxury and service of the Four Seasons chain has made it a favourite of business and upscale tourists, despite a slightly out of the way location. Pool, spa services, rooftop lounge. $$$$

Hotel Equatorial (Guidu Jiudian)
65 Yan'an Road (W)
Tel: 6248 1688; Fax: 6248 1773
www.equatorial.com
The Equatorial is a second-tier
business hotel whose consistent
service and prime location, next to
the Hilton, has won it a loyal
following. Facilities include a small
gym, indoor pool overlooking the
Children's Palace and a business
centre. **$$$$**

JC Mandarin
(Shanghai Jinwen Hua Dajiudian)
1225 Nanjing Road (W)
Tel: 6279 1888; Fax: 6279 1822
www.jcmandarin.com
Renovated in 2003 and located
across the street from the Shanghai
Centre (and the more expensive
Portman Ritz-Carlton) and right next
to the Shanghai Exhibition Centre,
the five-star JC Mandarin's
Mandarin Club Executive Floor often
wins kudos from business
travellers. Facilities include a
business centre, indoor pool,
squash and tennis courts. **$$$$**

J.W. Marriott Hotel
(Shanghai Mingtian Guangchang)
399 Nanjing Road (W)
Tel: 6360 0503; Fax: 6360 0510
www.marriotthotels.com
Marriott's first premium "J.W."
branded hotel in China is part of the
multi-use Tomorrow Square complex,
which includes the Marriott serviced
apartments and retail space in Puxi's
tallest building. Opened in late-2003,
the luxury five-star hotel's facilities
include a swimming pool, health
club, salon and extensive in-room
amenities as well as a great location
near the People's Square museums
and the Grand Theatre. **$$$$**

Portman Ritz-Carlton
(Boteman Dajiudian)
1376 Nanjing Road (W)
Tel: 6279 8888; Fax: 6279 8887
www.ritz-carlton.com
Anchoring the Shanghai Centre and
winner of Bloomberg's Best Business
Hotel, the Portman Ritz-Carlton is a
favourite of business travellers and
state visitors, including presidents
Clinton and Bush. The five-star hotel
has a full complement of facilities
like a fitness centre, tennis courts,
indoor-outdoor pool and the gourmet

Italian restaurant Palladio. Ask about
the Chinese herbal bubble baths and
the Presidential Bike Pack, a ride
through Shanghai on the General
Manager's classic motorcycle. **$$$$**

Heng Shan Moller Villa (Hengshan
Ma Lie Bie Shu Fandian)
30 Shanxi Road (S)
Tel: 6247 8881; Fax: 6289 1020
www.mollervilla.com
A landmark Gothic fantasy
dominated by steeples and spires,
and built by a Norwegian shipping
magnate in 1936, Moller House
was refurbished and converted into
a charming small hotel in 2002.
The historic older building is often
booked by government dignitaries
and rooms may not be open to the
public, however. **$$$**

Hilton Hotel (Xierdun Fandian)
250 Huashan Road
Tel: 6248 0000; Fax: 6248 3848
www.hiltonshanghai.com.cn
A Shanghai institution, the five-star
Hilton runs smoothly and continual
refurbishments keep it looking
young. Broadband in the rooms,
indoor pool, gym, business centre, a
swish spa and the best doormen in
Shanghai. Centrally located between
the main shopping streets of
Central Huaihai Road and Nanjing
Road, the hotel is a five-minute walk
from the Julu Road bar strip. **$$$**

Jing An Hotel (Jing An Bin'guan)
370 Huashan Road
Tel: 6248 1888; Fax: 6248 2657
Right next door to the Hilton, the
main building of this locally
managed four-star hotel was built in
the Spanish style in 1935. Guests
rooms have been renovated, but
several of the function rooms retain
their vintage glamour – notably the
ninth-floor banqueting room and the
first floor San Diego Room, where a
weekly Sunday chamber music
recital is held. An adjacent
Japanese-style building was added
in 1985. Centrally located between
Huaihai Road and Nanjing Road,
there is only the basics in terms of
facilities, but the sprawling garden
compensates. **$$$**

Pacific Hotel (Jinmen Dajiudian)
108 Nanjing Road (W)
Tel: 6327 6226; Fax: 6372 3634
A three-star hotel managed by the

local Jinjiang Group, the Pacific is a
no-frills hotel located in the historic
Union Insurance Building. There is
very little in the way of facilities, but
its central location across from
People's Square makes it an
excellent location for Shanghai
Museum and Grand Theatre visits. **$$**

Park Hotel (Guoji Fandian)
170 Nanjing Road (W)
Tel: 6327 5225; Fax: 6327 6958
www.parkhotel.com
Once Shanghai's tallest hotel and
the building that inspired a young
I.M. Pei to study architecture,
renovations in 1999 removed the
historic interior in favour of a slick
modern one. The rooms are
international-standard and
comfortable and the historic Ladislau
Hudec-designed art deco exterior
remains a Nanjing Road landmark.
Located across from People's
Square, the hotel is ideally situated
for People's Square museums and
Grand Theatre visits. **$$**

Hotel Price Guide

$$$$	USD 150 and up
$$$	USD 100–150
$$	USD 50–100
$	less than USD 50

HUAIHAI/HENGSHAN AREA

Okura Garden Hotel
(Hua Yuan Fandian)
58 Maoming Road (S)
Tel: 6415 1111; Fax: 64715 8866
www.gardenhotelshanghai.com
A five-star managed by Japan's
Okura Group, the public areas of
the hotel occupy the renovated
Cercle Sportif Français (French
Club), with much of the historic
detail still intact. Guest rooms,
located in the modern hotel tower
to the rear, offer all the modern
amenities, including an indoor
swimming pool, health club and
business centre. The sprawling
gardens of the French Club are one
of the great perks of this centrally
located hotel, just around the
corner from the major department
stores on Huaihai Road. **$$$$**

**Jinjiang Hotel and Grosvenor House
(Jinjiang Fandian, Guibin Lou)**
59 Maoming Road (S)
Tel: 6258 2582; Fax: 6472 5588
www.jinjianghotelshanghai.com
This pair of five-star hotels, now
managed by the local Jinjiang Group,
was built by old Shanghai tycoon
Victor Sassoon as the Cathay
Mansions and Grosvenor House.
Recent renovations have created
anonymous standard hotel interiors
(although details like fireplaces and
old moulding remain), but the 26
suites are furnished with antiques.
Excellent health club, with swimming
pool, new fitness centre and bowling
alley. An international restaurant row
is located on the grounds. US
President Nixon and Chinese
Premier Zhou En-lai signed the
Shanghai Communique here in
1972. Centrally located just off
Huaihai Road. **$$$**
Jinjiang Tower (Jinjiang Dajiudian)
161 Changle Road
Tel: 6415 1188; Fax: 6415 0045
www.jjtcn.com
The five-star flagship of the Jinjiang
Group dominates this neighbourhood
with its 43-storey circular hotel
tower. Modern, international-style
rooms have views of the city.
Facilities include an outdoor pool,
two gardens, a business centre and
shopping arcade. **$$$**

Old World Charm

**Xingguo Guest House
(Xingguo Bin'guan)**
Managed by the Radisson Plaza
(contact details same as above)
and occupying prime position on
the former grounds of Butterfield
& Swire, these historic buildings
are anchored by an enormous
Gatsby-esque lawn and old trees.
Whenever he was in town,
Chairman Mao enjoyed staying at
Building Number One, with its
dramatic, sweeping staircase and
stately Ionic columns. Guests
may use the Radisson facilities.
Note: the guesthouse is owned
by the state, and may be closed
to guests for security reasons if
state visitors are staying here. **$$**

**Radisson Plaza Xingguo Hotel
(Shanghai Xingguo Bin'guan)**
78 Xingguo Road
Tel: 6212 9998; Fax: 6212 9996
www.radisson.com
Completed at the end of 2001, this
contemporary high-rise sits at the
edge of the former Butterfield &
Swire compound, taking full
advantage of the vast green lawns.
Out of the urban hustle but just
minutes from Huaihai Road by taxi,
the Radisson's facilities include an
excellent indoor pool, spa and
health club, squash and bowling
facilities, as well as a business
centre. Rooms are of ample size
and tastefully furnished. **$$$**
**Regal International East Asia Hotel
(Fuhao Huan Qiu Dong Ya Jiudian)**
516 Hengshan Road
Tel: 6415 5588; Fax: 6445 8899
www.regal-eastasia.com
This slick modern five-star is
located in the diplomatic district,
just outside Xujiahui and a 10-
minute drive from Huaihai Road.
The hotel's well maintained tennis
centre is among the best in the city
– many top Shanghai government
officials play here – as is the hotel
gym and pool. Hengshan Park and
Xujiahui Park are across the street,
and the Hengshan Road strip of
bars and restaurants is a block
away. **$$$**
**Ruijin Guesthouese
(Ruijin Bin'guan)**
118 Ruijin No. 2 Road
Tel: 6472 5222; Fax: 6472 2277
Five renovated historic villas set in
seven hectares on the former
Morriss Estate, with the luxury of
sprawling grounds dotted with
fountains and pavilions. Located
right in the heart of the French
Concession. The excellent Face bar,
Hazara Indian restaurant and La Na
Thai restaurant are in Building No.
4 on the grounds, Huaihai Road
shopping is close by and the bars
and nightlife of Maoming Road are
at the Ruijin's doorstep. Owned by
the state, the Ruijin may be closed
to guests for security reasons if
state visitors are staying here. **$$$**
Taiyuan Villa (Taiyuan Bie Shu)
160 Taiyuan Road
Tel: 6471 6688; Fax: 6471 2618

One of the loveliest mansions in the
French Concession and dating back
to the 1920s, Taiyuan Villa is the
former Marshall House, where
General George Marshall tried to
negotiate a truce between the
Kuomintang and the Communists
and, which later, was also a
favourite residence of Madam Mao.
Refurbished using 1930s Shanghai
furniture, rooms overlook the villa's
lawn. Owned by the state, it may be
closed to guests for security
reasons if state visitors are staying
here. **$$$**
**Hengshan Hotel
(Hengshan Bin'guan)**
534 Hengshan Road
Tel: 6437 2929; Fax: 6433 5732
Built in 1936 as the former Picardie
Apartments, the Hengshan Hotel
lost much of its historic charm after
a 2002 refurbishment that
modernised and updated rooms
and added a decidedly gilded touch
to public areas. A convenient
location in the diplomatic district on
the edge of Xujiahui, the Hengshan
is convenient to both Huaihai Road
and Xujiahui Park areas. **$$**

HONGQIAO

**Marriott Hongqiao
(Wanhou Hongqiao Dajuidian)**
2270 Hongqiao Road
Tel: 6237 6000; Fax: 6237 6222
www.marriott.com
A business hotel with a resort
atmosphere – from the low-rise
building to the palms in the lobby
and the outdoor pool – the Marriott
is eight minutes from Hongqiao
Airport and next door to the
exhibition centre, right in the heart
of expat suburbia. Its sports bar,
Champions, is the neighbourhood
pub for Shanghai expats, while
facilities include a pool, health club,
tennis and squash. **$$$$**
**Sheraton Grand Taipingyang
(Xilaidun Haoda Taipinyang
Fandian)**
5 Zunyi Road (S)
Tel: 6275 8888; Fax: 6275 5459
www.sheratongrand-shanghai.com
The former Westin Tai Ping Yang has
been re-branded as the more

luxurious five-star Sheraton Grand, but the European-style individuality, flair and service remain. A business traveller's favourite, the Sheraton has a great location next to the INTEX Convention centre and close to the Shanghai Everbright Convention and Exhibition Centre, Hongqiao Airport, and a reputation for having one of the city's best Italian restaurants (Giovanni's) and deli. Indoor pool, health club, business centre. **$$$$**

Xijiao State Guest House (Xijiao Bin'guan)
1921 Hongqiao Road
Tel: 6219 8800; Fax: 6433 6641
www.sh-xijiaoguesthouse.com
Emperor Akihito and Queen Elizabeth II once stayed here – the latter in the Presidential Suite in Building No. 7 – but what really sets this place apart is its setting in an 80 hectare woodland park. Villas are dotted throughout, and there are seasonal flowers and plants as well as walkways by the river. The location is convenient to Hongqiao area and the Hongqiao Airport but is a good 20 minutes away from the city centre. Health club, tennis and squash courts. **$$$$**

Hongqiao State Guest House (Hongqiao Ying Bin'guan)
1591 Hongqiao Road
Tel: 6219 8855; Fax: 6275 3903
A collection of vintage villas in a range of Western architectural styles set in beautifully landscaped rolling grounds. The former guesthouse No. 415 of the General Office of the Party Committee of Shanghai is now open to the public, but if state officials stay here, the guest house may be closed for the duration to foreigners. Gym, outdoor pool. **$$$**

Renaissance Yangtze (Yangzi Jiang Dajiudian)
2099 Yan'an Road (W)
Tel: 6275 0000; Fax: 6275 0750
www.marriott.com
Refurbished in 2002 to a much more luxurious style, the Renaissance's great asset (if you are in Shanghai for business) is its location in the midst of all the convention centres – SITC, INTEX and Shanghai Mart. Its facilities include an indoor pool, health club and spa. **$$$**

Shanghai Worldfield Convention Hotel (Shanghai Shibo Huiyi Dajiudian)
2106 Hongqiao Road
Tel: 6270 3388; Fax: 6270 4554
Less slick than the Marriott next door, this massive four-star hotel is a comfortable, less expensive alternative – although the staff don't speak much English. Facilities include a pool, gym, business centre and beauty salon. Located next to the Convention Centre, the hotel is 3 km (2 miles) from the domestic Hongqiao airport. **$$$**

Cypress Hotel (Longbai Fandian)
2419 Hongqiao Road
Tel: 6268 8868; Fax: 6268 1878
www.cypresshotel.com
The hotel itself is modern but is set in a historic location in the rambling grounds of old Shanghai tycoon Victor Sassoon's former estate, allowing strolls through rambling woods. Facilities include tennis and squash courts, an indoor pool, jogging track and a fitness centre. A five-minute walk to the zoo. **$$**

Hotel Price Guide

$$$$	USD 150 and up
$$$	USD 100–150
$$	USD 50–100
$	less than USD 50

PUDONG

Grand Hyatt Shanghai (Jinmao Kaiyue Dajiudian)
88 Century Boulevard,
Jin Mao Tower
Tel: 5830 3338; Fax: 5830 8838
www.shanghai.hyatt.com
The highest hotel in the world is a high-design beauty located between the 54th and 88th floors of China's tallest building, the 21st-century art deco pagoda, the Jin Mao Tower. Situated in the heart of Pudong's Lujiazui financial district, this is where high-tech meets Shanghai style, with plenty of "world's highest" experiences, from bars to bubble baths and swimming pools. meeting and conference facilities; for after-hours, the popular nightclub Pu-J's is in the basement. **$$$$**

Pudong Shangri-la (Xianggelia Dajiudian)
33 Fucheng Road
Tel: 6882 6888; Fax: 6882 0160
www.shangri-la.com
This elegant riverside hotel has eye-to-eye views of the Bund, just across the river, and some of the most generously sized rooms and suites in the city. Located in Pudong's Lujiazui financial district, it is a key Pudong business hotel, with the requisite meeting and conference facilities. Fitness centre, indoor pool, tennis court. B.A.T.S., the basement bar and entertainment zone with live music, has become a Shanghai institution. **$$$$**

St Regis (Ruiji Hongta Dajiudian)
889 Dong Fang Road
Tel: 6875 9888; Fax: 5830 3608
www.starwood.com/stregis
The jewel of Dong Fang Road, the St Regis design was impressive enough to make it to the pages of *Architectural Digest*. One of the most luxurious hotels in the city, the St Regis has a host of perks like 24-hour butler service, ergonomic desk chairs and high-end Bose CD players in the rooms, plus an in-house spa in addition to the more standard facilities. Restaurants include the gourmet Italian outlet Danieli's, which, along with the rooms, offer views of Pudong. **$$$$**

Intercontinental Shanghai (Xinya Tangchen Dajiudian)
777 Zhangyang Road
Tel: 5831 8888; Fax: 5831 7777
www.pudong.china.intercontinental.com
Formerly the New Asia Thomson, the hotel's morph into the Intercontinental included a refurbishment that freshened it up considerably. The hotel is located near the Next Age department store in a somewhat uninspiring Pudong heartland neighbourhood, but Lujiazui business district is a short drive away. The hotel has an indoor pool and health club. **$$$**

Oriental Riverside Hotel (Dongfang Binjiang Dajiudian)
2727 Binjiang Dadao
Tel: 5879 2727; Fax: 5887 9707
www.shicc.net

Kid-Friendly Hotels

These short-stay serviced apartments with kitchen facilities are ideal for those with children, or even those who just want more elbow room.

Ascott Pudong
3 Pudong Avenue, Pudong
Tel: 6886 0088; Fax: 6886 0001
www.the-ascott.com

The Shanghai Centre
Suite 742, 1376 Nanjing Road (W)
Tel: 6279 8600; Fax: 6279 8610
www.shanghaicentre.com

Somerset Grand Shanghai
8 Jinan Road, Luwan District
Tel: 6385 6888; Fax: 6384 8988
www.the-ascott.com

Somerset Xuhui Shanghai
888 Shanxi Road (S),
Xu Hui District
Tel: 6466 0888; Fax: 6466 4646
www.the-ascott.com

Pudong's only "five-star convention hotel" lacks the gloss of brand-name five-stars, but makes up for it with an unbeatable location for conference goers: directly next to the International Conference Centre in the heart of the Lujiazui financial district. Good meeting facilities; ask for a room with a river view. **$$$**

**Courtyard by Marriott
(Lu Wan Yi Dajiudian)**
838 Dong Fang Road
Tel: 6886 7886; Fax: 6886 7889
www.marriott.com
Comfortable four-star geared for the business traveller with an eye on the balance sheet. Rooms have generously sized work desks, two phones with dataports and the full range of business amenities including meeting facilities. Located close to Lujiazui, across the street from the St Regis. **$$**

**Hotel Nikko Pudong
(Zhongyou Rihang Dajiudian)**
969 Dongfang Road
Tel: 6875 8888; Fax: 6875 8688
www.nikkohotels.com
An out-of-the-way 1997 hotel that looks a little dated, but is otherwise perfectly comfortable. The hotel describes itself as "American-style", but that only refers to the

contemporary décor: the restaurants are Cantonese, Shanghainese and Japanese. Business centre, indoor pool, health club and a bowling alley. **$$**

**Novotel Atlantis Shanghai
(Haishen Nuofute Dajiudian)**
728 Pudong Avenue
Tel: 5036 6666; Fax: 5036 6677
www.accorhotels-asia.com
The city's most elegant four-star. The rooms are smallish, but the entire hotel has a European sense of style. Restaurants include the revolving ART50, an art gallery-eatery, a cigar bar and pub. **$$**

CHONGMING ISLAND

**Bao Dao Resort
(Bao Dao Du Jia Cun)**
Chongming Island
Tel: 5933 9479
www.bao-dao.com
Startlingly modern hotel at the edge of the forest park, with bowling, tennis and swimming pool **$$**

Senlin Resort (Senlin Du Jia Cun)
Chongming Island
Tel: 5933 8453
The Senlin provides more basic rooms in rustic cabins. **$**

PUTUOSHAN

**Putuoshan Hotel
(Putuoshan Fandian)**
No. 93 Meicen Lu
Tel: (580) 609 2828
Fax: (580) 609 1818
A modern hotel; clean, comfortable, but not especially atmospheric. Situated close to Puji Temple. **$$**

**Ronglai Yuan Guest House
(Ronglai Bin'guan)**
Xiang Hua Jie (next to Puji Temple)
Tel: (580) 609 1262
A converted monastery with ancient trees in the courtyard and simple accommodations. **$**

SUZHOU

**Gloria Plaza Hotel Suzhou
(Kailai Da Jiu An)**
535 Gan Jiang Dong Lu

Tel: (512) 6521 8855
Fax: (512) 6521 8533
www.gloriahotels.com
This well-appointed business hotel is located close to the Singapore Industrial Park but is also convenient to the gardens. Facilities include a business centre and health club. **$$$**

**Sheraton Suzhou Hotel and Towers
(Xi Lai Tun Suzhou Jiudian)**
388 Xin Shi Lu
Tel: (512) 6510 3388
Fax: (512) 6510 0888
www.sheraton-suzhou.com
Suzhou's best hotel, this low-rise resort hotel is designed in traditional Chinese style around a beautifully laid out classical garden. The design compensates for its location, which is not especially near any of the major gardens. Indoor pool, gym, business centre. **$$$**

Nanlin Hotel (Nanlin Fandian)
20 Gun Xiu Fang Lu
Tel: (512) 522 4641
Popular with tour groups, the Nanlin is laid out over 3.5 hectares (8½ acres) in southeast Suzhou. Amenities include a swimming pool, fitness centre, business centre and shopping arcade. **$$**

HANGZHOU

**Hangzhou Shangri-la
(Hangzhou Xiangge Lila Fandian)**
78 Beishan Lu
Tel: (571) 8797 7951
Fax: (571) 8707 3545
www.shangri-la.com
Hangzhou's best hotel is ideally situated overlooking West Lake. A former state guesthouse that has hosted Richard Nixon, Mao Zedong and Zhou En-lai, the hotel's old wing was renovated in 2000 in the grandiose Shangri-la style, but the spacious rooms and lake views remain. The hotel is set in sprawling wooded grounds. Health club, indoor swimming pool. **$$$$**

**Hyatt Regency Hangzhou
(Hangzhou Kaiyue Jiudian)**
28 Hu Bin Lu
Tel: (571) 8779 1234
Fax: (571) 8779 1818

www.hangzhou.regency.hyatt.com
Opened in mid-2003, the Hyatt is
part of a lakefront development that
includes residential apartments and
a department store. This luxury hotel
caters to business guests as well as
holidaymakers, with broadband in
the rooms, a day spa and Camp
Hyatt for children under 12. **$$$$**

**Ramada Hangzhou Haihua
(Haihua Dajiudian)**
298 Qingchun Lu
Tel: (571) 8721 5888
www.ramadahangzhou.com
A stylish four-star modern high-rise
on the northeastern shore of West
Lake in the heart of the business
district. Business centre, indoor
pool, and 10 minutes from the train
station. **$$**

Huagang Hotel (Huagang Fandian)
4 Xishan Lu
Tel: (571) 771 324
Lovely gardens are the main
attraction of this budget hotel,
which is set on the western side of
West Lake. Gym, restaurant. **$**

MOGANSHAN

Wuling (Wuling Fandian)
Tel: (052) 803 3132
www.mogan-mountain.com
Chiang Kai-Shek's old villa is now a
backpacker flophouse. The rooms
are shabby and the service
indifferent, but the high ceilings and
wooden floors are intact, and the
grounds are lovely. **$**

NANJING

**Sheraton Nanjing Kingsley Hotel
& Towers
(Nanjing Jin Si Li Xi Lai Tun
Jiudian)**
169 Hanzhong Lu
Tel: (25) 666 8888
Fax: (25) 666 9999
www.starwood.com
Popular business hotel close to the
Confucius Temple (Fuzi Miao) area,
the Sheraton is busy on weekdays.
Weekends are quieter and rates are
likely to be lower. Swimming pool,
gym, tennis courts and shopping
arcade. **$$$**

**Hilton Nanjing
(Nanjing Xierdun Fandian)**
319 Zhongshan Dong Lu
Tel: (25) 4808 888
Fax: (25) 4809 999
www.hilton.com
Located just off the Shanghai-
Nanjing highway in the eastern part
of the city, by the old city wall and
gate, next to the new Nanjing
Museum, and at the foot of Purple
Mountain. The 40-storey hotel has
an indoor pool, gym and bowling
alley. **$$**

Hotel Price Guide

$$$$	USD 150 and up
$$$	USD 100–150
$$	USD 50–100
$	less than USD 50

**Shangri-la Dingshan, Nanjing
(Xiangge Lila Dingshan, Nanjing)**
90 Cha Er Lu
Tel: (25) 880 2888
Fax: (25) 882 1729
www.shangri-la.com
Located in a complex with luxury
serviced apartments, the hotel has
a distinctive Chinese pavilion roof
perched on a modern high-rise.
Rooms offer broadband and views
of the Yangzi and the surrounding
greenery. Facilities include an
outdoor pool, fitness centre, tennis
courts and a golf driving range. **$$**

**Shuang Men Lou Nanjing
(Shuang Men Lou Fandian)**
185 Huju Bei Lu
Tel: (25) 805 961
A no-frills hotel just south of
Zhongshan Road, the Shuang Men
Lou doesn't have much by the way
of facilities beyond television sets
in the rooms, and a restaurant on
site, but it is set in a lovely garden.
$

Where to Eat

Restaurants

Shanghai's restaurant scene,
always rich in local eating places,
has blossomed to include a medley
of international cuisines in addition
to a new breed of elegant Chinese
eateries serving many of the
country's regional cuisines. There is
also a vibrant street food scene.

Price, in Shanghai, is not
necessarily an indication of quality.
While many of Shanghai's finest
restaurants are expensive, with
beautiful decor to match, just as
many excellent eateries cost only a
little more than street stalls, with
food served in homey surroundings.

Most restaurants have a fairly
casual dress code. The
Shanghainese are unfailingly stylish,
however, and people do dress up for
the top restaurants in town – but
you probably won't be turned away if
you're underdressed. When in
doubt, err on the side of casual-chic.

To stay current with what's new
in town, check the local English
language magazines: *That's
Shanghai* and *City Weekend* have
the best restaurant listings and
review new restaurants monthly.

Note: Chinese restaurant prices
will vary widely depending on what
you order. Delicacies – hairy crab in
season, raw crab roe, shark's fin
soup – can push your bill well into
four and even five figures (RMB) as
can wine and several rounds of
drinks. Always check the prices of
what you order. It's generally not
wise to allow a restaurant staff
member to order for you.

Unless otherwise noted, restau-
rants are open daily from 11am–3pm
for lunch and 6–11pm for dinner.
*See also pages 79–85 of the
Features section.*

What to Eat

SHANGHAINESE

1221 (Yi Er Er Yi)
1221 Yan'an Road (W)
(at Panyu Road)
Tel: 6213 6585, 6213 2441
Serves all the classics of Shanghai cuisine (plus specials from throughout China) in a very Western, contemporary-chic setting – with English-speaking staff and bilingual menus – making it very accessible to foreigners. Although the dishes are not remarkable in any way, they do offer a taste of authentic homestyle Shanghainese food. Tea is poured from a long-spout "dragon" teapot, a Sichuan tradition that is a little gimmicky, but fun. An institution in the expatriate community. **$**

1931 (Hao Gu Meishi Fang)
112 Maoming Road (S)
(at Nanchang Road)
Tel: 6472 5264
Nostalgic, romantic ambience that takes its cue from Shanghai, circa 1931. The hearty, homestyle Shanghainese and regional Chinese specialities are quite simple, but presented with flair. *Qipao*-clad waitresses and a nice collection of vintage collectibles, from the gramophone by the bar to the 1930s Shanghai girl posters. Lunch set menus are a good deal. Favourite hangout for Shanghai's small lesbian community. **$**

Baoluo
271 Fumin Road (at Changle Road)
Tel: 5403 7239
This popular Shanghai restaurant specialises in seafood, but there is a full menu of meat and vegetable dishes as well. Don't despair at the long lines that snake down the street: the small façade conceals a rambling restaurant. This is a typical Chinese restaurant: smoky, crowded, noisy, and not especially clean, but the food is spectacular. Drunken crab, fish-flavoured eggplant and "Swiss steak" – cubes of meat in a sweet, yellow sauce – are house specialities.
Reservations after 7pm are essential so call ahead to book. **$**

Big Fan (Da Feng Che)
1440 Hongqiao Road
(at Yan'an Road (W))
Tel: 6219 7514
Located in the historic Spanish-style Granada villas, the Big Fan serves all the standard Shanghai favourites – fish-flavoured eggplant, red-cooked pork – in an old-Shanghai setting. Its location near the antique shops of Hongqiao makes it an excellent spot for a breather between bouts of shopping. **$**

Club Jin Mao (Jin Mao Julebu)
88th floor, Jin Mao Tower (in the Grand Hyatt) 88 Century Boulevard
Tel: 5049 1234 ext. 8688
Originally a private club, Club Jin Mao is now open to the public, serving haute Shanghainese food in the Hyatt's characteristic high-style east-west ambience. **$$$**

Restaurant Price Guide

Price range for a meal for two (Asian or Western), excluding drinks:
  $$$$ RMB 800 and above
   $$$ RMB 500–800
    $$ RMB 250–500
     $ less than RMB 250

Gap (Jinting)
8 Zunyi Road (near the Hong Qiao Friendship Store)
Tel: 6278 2900
8 Hengshan Road (at Urumqi Road)
Tel: 6473 4828
The name and logo may be borrowed from an American clothing store, but the Gap's huge menu covers strictly Chinese food with an emphasis on Shanghainese dishes. It's a mass market sort of place, with enormous, noisy dining rooms and dancing girls. **$$**

Grape (Putaoyuan Jiujia)
55 Xinle Road
Tel: 5404 0486; and
2606 Yan'an Road (W)
Tel: 6295 2518
The very first Shanghai restaurant to cater to the foreign community back in the 1980s, the Grape serves homestyle Shanghainese cuisine in a casual, friendly atmosphere. Classic Shanghai

dishes share menu space with exotica like snake and dog. English menu and English-speaking manager. **$**

Green Wave Pavilion (Lubolang)
115 Yuyuan Road
Tel: 6328 0602
In addition to the standard Shanghai restaurant menu, Lubolang is famous for its collection of Shanghai snacks in this eatery that has hosted Queen Elizabeth II and President Clinton. Lubolang is an expensive tourist restaurant – these snacks are also available at the stalls in Yu Garden Bazaar – but you don't have to stand in line, there is seating, and there are English menus. Open from 7am onwards till dinner. **$$**

Henry (Hengli Canting)
8 Xinle Road (at Shaanxi Road)
Tel: 5403 3448
Homestyle Shanghainese cuisine and regional specialities are served in a retro art nouveau setting that recalls the French Concession in the 1930s, when this was Rue Henri. Henry's lemon chicken is a big favourite. English menu, but the staff speak very little English. **$**

Meilongzhen (Meilongzhen Jiu Jia)
Lane 1081, 22 Nanjing Road (W)
(at Shanxi Road)
Tel: 6253 5353
Meilongzhen's beautiful, dilapidated old mansion once hosted a meeting of the Communist Party of China, thus ensuring its survival in the midst of the building boom in this section of Nanjing Road (W). Inside, the décor is Victorian-meets-Chinese with seven different dining halls (Beautiful Plum Blossom, Dragon-Phoenix etc), each decorated accordingly. The cuisine is Shanghainese-Sichuan, with house specialities that include "twice-cooked" pork with pancakes, Meilongzhen special chicken and beancurd with crab roe. **$$**

Old Shanghai Restaurant (Shanghai Lao Fandian)
242 Fuyou Road
Tel: 6328 9850
Dating back a century, the Shanghai Lao Fandian, in the Old City, claims to be the city's first Shanghainese restaurant. The chefs have certainly

perfected their cuisine, the dishes here – particularly the seafood – are fresh and expertly cooked. House specialities include "eight-jewelled duck", "squirrel-shaped fish" and "pork ribs in prickly ash and salt". **$$$**
Shanghai Uncle (Hai Shang Ah Shu)
211 Tianyaoqiao Road
Tel: 6464 6430
Owned by Li Zhonghang, son of famed Chinese chef Virginia Lee (author, with Craig Claiborne, of the classic *Chinese Cookbook*), this is the restaurant that homesick older Shanghainese go to when they want the real stuff. Classics like red-cooked pork are served along with Li's family tales of the rich and famous in old Shanghai, making this a memorable experience all round. **$$$**
The 7 (Qi Hao Ju Le Bu)
7 Donghu Road
(at Central Huaihai Road)
Tel: 6415 7777
The 7's setting, in an almost perfectly preserved manor house with a porch and manicured lawn, would alone make it worth a visit, but it also serves excellent, well-prepared Shanghainese food, as well as some regional specialities. A live jazz band performs at the bar downstairs on weekends. **$$$**
Wang Baohe Restaurant (Wang Baohe Jiujia)
603 Fuzhou Road
Tel: 6320 7609
"King of crabs and ancestor of wine", Wang Baohe is a Shanghai institution that started out as a liquor store but has been serving Shanghai hairy crab feasts since the 1920s – everything you can imagine is made from the hairy crab, from dumplings to soup to the fried noodles. "Chrysanthemum" crab feasts are a speciality during autumn crab season. **$$$**
Yang's Kitchen (Yang Jia Chu Fang)
No. 3 Lane 9 Hengshan Road
(at Dongping Road)
Tel: 6445 8418
A stylishly renovated vintage French Concession villa with a courtyard for al fresco dining in warm weather, Yang's Kitchen serves a refined version of homestyle Shanghai

cooking. Yang's classics include shrimp with garlic, drunken chicken, Mandarin fish and eggplant casserole. **$**
Ye Shanghai
338 Huangpi Road (S) House 6, Xintiandi
Tel: 6311 2323
Beautifully prepared and presented Shanghainese snack food, noodles and dessert served with gourmet panache and fusion twists in a refurbished *shikumen* house that is itself a design fusion. Business set lunches on weekdays. **$$**

Join the Queue

Local food aficionados generally agree that the best *xiao long bao* (steamed pork dumplings filled with soup) are found at Nanxiang Steamed Bun Restaurant (Nanxiang Mantou Dian) at Yu Garden (85 Yuyuan Road, tel: 6355 4206). Because there are a number of such places clustered at Yu Garden and all sport similar names, head for the one with the longest queue – always a surefire sign of quality offerings.

OTHER CHINESE

Cantonese
Be There or Be Square (Bu Jian Bu San)
139 Wujiang Road
(at Shi Men No. 1 Road)
Tel: 6272 5217, 6272 2369
This Cantonese restaurant, which gets its name from a popular Chinese movie, serves tasty, authentic *dian xin* (dim sum) in a nice environment. The mostly Cantonese main dishes include hotpots. Set lunches are also served. **$**
Xian Yue Xuan
849 Huashan Road
Tel: 6251 1166
This gourmet Cantonese restaurant is set in a gorgeous garden setting in historic Ding Xiang (Clove) Garden, the love nest of reformer Li Hongzhang and his favourite concubine, Clove. Refined, high-quality Cantonese cuisine and

Sunday *dian xin* (dim sum) is served overlooking the garden. Specialities include shark's fin soup, drunken prawns and Cantonese goose. **$$$**
Xing Hua Lou
343 Fuzhou Road
(at Shandong Road)
Tel: 6355 3777
This Cantonese restaurant, which dates back to the reign of Emperor Xianfeng in the mid-1800s, is famous for its bakery in general and its mooncakes in particular. The restaurant upstairs serves generous (if sometimes greasy) portions of Cantonese favourites in a tasteful setting, while downstairs, lines form for the *dian xin* (dim sum) and baked goods. **$$**

Beijing and Northern
Chang An Dumpling (Chang An Jiaozi Lou)
1586 Pudong Avenue
(at Min Sheng Road)
Tel: 5885 8416; and
8 Yunnan Road
(at Yan'an Road E)
Tel: 6328 5156
Homesick northerners, who eat a far greater variety of dumplings than the Shanghainese, come here for the 108 different kinds of dumplings with fillings. **$**
Quanjude Peking Duck (Quanjude Kaoya Dian)
4/F 786 Central Huaihai Road
(at Ruijin Road)
Tel: 5404 5799
www.shanghaiquanjude.com
This is a branch of Beijing's most famous Peking Duck restaurant, which has several branches in the capital (and through which, it seems, all tour groups must pass). Quanjude serves every bit of the duck; the crispy skin is especially delicious. Watching the chefs carve up the duck is a real treat, but it does tend to be greasy. Branches in Pudong and elsewhere; call for more information. **$$**

Hangzhou
Louwailou
2260 Hongqiao Road
(at Hong Mei Road)
Tel: 6262 6789

A branch of Hangzhou's famous lakeside restaurant serving the same classic specialities that made it a favourite of luminaries like Lu Xun and Zhou Enlai – although the setting here is not quite as spectacular (the only hint of a lake are the pictures of West Lake on the walls). House specialities include Louwailou's trademark Beggar's Chicken (whole chicken, stuffed with pork, marinated with Shaoxing wine, and covered with mud and baked – then dramatically split open at the table), West Lake vinegar fish and *dongpo rou* (pork slices). **$$**

Sichuan
China Moon (Haishang Mingyue)
No. 316/F CITC Square,
1168 Nanjing Road (W)
Tel: 3218 1379
This elegant eatery at an elegant address serves the classics of Sichuan's spicy cuisine: *mapo tofu* (minced pork and soft tofu in spicy bean sauce) spicy chicken with chili peppers, *dan dan mien* (spicy noodles) and fried long beans. This is the kind of place to go if you have a business expense account. **$$$**

Xinjiang
Afunti (Afanti Shichang)
B/F Tianshan Hotel,
775 Quyang Road
(at Zhongshan No. 1 Road N)
Tel: 6555 9604
A branch of the original Afunti in Beijing – which has become legendary – Shanghai's Afunti serves the same authentic Xinjiang cuisine in an upscale environment. Hand-pulled noodles, kebabs, *ququ* (mutton-stuffed dumplings) and a roasted lamb that melts in your mouth. A lively atmosphere. Open from 7.30am till dinner daily. **$$**

WESTERN

American
Hard Rock Café (Yingshi Canting)
Shanghai Centre Retail Plaza,
1376 Nanjing Road (W)
Tel: 6279 8888
The franchised Hard Rock

Restaurant Price Guide
Price range for a meal for two (Asian or Western), excluding drinks:
$$$$ RMB 800 and above
$$$ RMB 500–800
$$ RMB 250–500
$ less than RMB 250

experience, from rock memorabilia to the burgers, fries, cokes and sandwiches (but also an authentic Hainan Chicken Rice) to the T-shirts. Populated mostly by homesick Americans, yuppie Chinese and families (Hard Rock, with its kids menu, balloons and colouring book, is very child-friendly). A Filipino band plays covers most nights after 8pm. **$$$**

KABB (Kai Bo)
Unit 1, House 5, North Block Xintiandi, Lane 181 Taicang Road (at Madang Road)
Tel: 3307 0798
A renovated *shikumen* house in Xintiandi is the setting for this American bistro. Hot dogs, burgers, thick deli-style sandwiches and burritos, plus a great weekend brunch. **$$**

TGIF (Xing Qi Wu Canting)
10 Hengshan Road
Tel: 6473 4502
Vintage American signs line the walls of this cookie-cutter US franchise, which serves mostly glamourised fast food, from oversized sandwiches to burgers, ribs and pasta. Big screen TV broadcasts sports and movies; creative cocktails. Set lunch specials and a kid's menu. **$$**

Tony Roma's (Duo Li Loma)
Suite 109, Shanghai Centre Retail Plaza, 1376 Nanjing Road (W)
Tel: 6279 7129
The US franchise "famous for ribs" specialises in ribs with different combinations of sauces and sizes, as well as burgers, salad and pasta. During the warmer months, diners can eat outside at the outdoor plaza with a view of Nanjing Road (W). **$$**

Continental
Dublin Exchange (Du Bo Lin)
2/F HSBC Tower 101,
Yin Cheng Road (E)
Tel: 6841 2052
With chefs from Ireland's famed Ballymaloe Cookery School, Dublin Exchange serves gourmet Irish food in a beautiful banker's style pub in the heart of Pudong. Beef and Guinness pie, Irish black pudding, Irish stew and trifle, plus Guinness on tap, of course. **$$**

Kathleen's Fifth
5/F 325 Nanjing Road (W) (in the Shanghai Art Museum building; entrance in the rear next to Grand Theatre)
Tel: 6327 0004
One of the city's most remarkable spaces, Kathleen's Fifth is located on the roof, just under the clock tower, of the Shanghai Art Museum – the former Racing Club. It's set in the heart of People's Square, with spectacular views and two rooms actually in the clock tower. Modernist décor is the backdrop for Continental cuisine crafted by an American chef. **$$$**

Luna
Nos 15, 16, Lane 25,
169 Taicang Road, Xintiandi (at Madang Road)
Tel: 6336 1717
A laid-back, stylish bistro in the style of a European café, Luna's creative menu includes offerings from North Africa and Spain as well as the more standard menu items. **$$**

M on the Bund (Mishi Xi Canting)
No. 5 The Bund,
7/F corner Guangdong Road
Tel: 6350 9988
The only Shanghai restaurant that *Conde Nast Traveler* hailed as one of the world's best 50 restaurants, M on the Bund combines an updated 1930s interior with a creative menu of Western food and the city's best view of the Bund. M's classics include Mandarin Beluga caviar, slow baked salt-encased lamb and a divine Pavlova for dessert. Also serves Sunday lunch and afternoon tea. Closed for lunch on Monday. **$$$$**

**Paulaner Brauhaus
(Bao Laina Xi Canting)**
150 Fenyang Road (at Taiyang Road)
Tel: 6474 5700; and House 19-20,
North Block Xintiandi, Lane 181
Taicang Road (at Madang Road)
Tel: 6320 3925
This very popular German chain of
microbreweries serves Bavarian
meat-potatoes-and-sauerkraut in a
rustic beer hall atmosphere,
complete with antique German
wooden benches, long wooden
tables and stained glass. Smooth
microbrewed beers and a lively,
convivial atmosphere. The Fenyang
Road outlet, in a lovely three-storey
French Concession villa, is packed
every night. **$$$**

The Grill (Shao Kao)
56th Floor, Grand Hyatt Shanghai,
Jin Mao Tower, 88 Century Boulevard
Tel: 5047 1234 ext. 8908/09
Deservedly reputed for some of the
freshest meat and seafood in town,
with awe-inspiring views of the city.
Highlights include quality cuts of
meat from Atlanta's Meta Company,
blue swimmer crab cakes, beef
short ribs marinated in soy sauce,
ginger, garlic and sesame, and
grilled Norwegian salmon. Open for
dinner only. **$$$$**

Italian

AD Domus (Aidi Duomusi)
200 Yan'an Road (W)
(at Urumqi Road N)
Tel: 6248 8499
Authentically Italian menu in an
upscale, authentically Italian setting
created by the chef who made
Giovanni's (at the Sheraton Grand
Taipinyang) reputation. Venetian
stucco walls, Renaissance-style
paintings, mosaics, vaulted ceilings
and arched windows are the
backdrop for a regional Italian menu
with a focus on the south of the
country. Imported fish and meat
plus extensive Italian wine list. **$$$**

Baci (Bei Xi)
2A Gaolan Road (at Sinan Road),
Fuxing Park
Tel: 5383 2328
A branch of Hong Kong's Lan Kwai
Fong Group's restaurant of the
same name, Baci is set in Fuxing
Park and serves honest, homestyle

Italian cuisine in a stylish, retro
setting. **$$**

Giovanni's (Jifan Nisi)
27/F, Sheraton Grand Taipinyang
Hotel, 5 Zunyi Road (S)
Tel: 6275 8888
With over a decade to perfect its
craft, Shanghai's first gourmet
Italian restaurant serves some of
the city's best Italian food in a
27th-floor eatery overlooking
Hongqiao. Freshly made pasta, beef
carpaccio, chicken supreme and the
tiramisu are Giovanni classics. **$$$**

Palladio (Palan Duo Yidali Canting)
Portman Ritz-Carlton Shanghai,
1376 Nanjing Road (W)
Tel: 6279 8888 ext. 5177
Sophistication reigns, from the
contemporary décor to the haute
cuisine menu and one of the city's
finest collections of Italian wines.
Menu highlights include the antipasti,
saffron risotto and the molten hot
chocolate pudding. Outdoor seating
in the piazza by the pond is available
during the warm months. **$$$$**

Va Bene (Hua Wan Yi Canting)
House 7, North Block Xintiandi,
Lane 181 Taicang Road
(at Madang Road)
Tel: 6311 2211
Grandeur reigns at Va Bene: crystal
chandeliers, fine china, high ceilings,
and a contemporary Italian haute
cuisine menu. Highlights include beef
carpaccio with black olive pate and
fresh mushrooms, lobster-stuffed
tortellini, imported fish and meat
plus an impressive wine list with
emphasis on Italian wines. **$$$$**

French

Ashanti Dome (Axiangti Canting)
16 Gaolan Road (at Sinan Road)
Tel: 5306 6777
Well-prepared haute French cuisine,
in an old Russian Orthodox church.
The place to dine is on the second
floor, under the murals of the dome.
The owner's wines from his South
African vineyard are served. Open
for dinner daily and lunch on Sat
and Sun only. **$$$**

C'est la Vie (San Le Wei Canting)
207 Maoming Road
Tel: 6415 9567
In terms of cuisine, this is perhaps
Shanghai's most sophisticated

French restaurant. C'est la Vie's
specialities change with the
seasons, and may include the
"trilogy of goose" (foie gras prepared
three ways), veal with coffee sauce,
chocolate profiteroles, and an
impressive wine list. Open for dinner
only; closed Sun. **$$$$**

Restaurant Price Guide

Price range for a meal for two
(Asian or Western), excluding
drinks:
$$$$ RMB 800 and above
$$$ RMB 500–800
$$ RMB 250–500
$ less than RMB 250

Fusion

Art 50 (Xuan Gong Wu Shi Xuan Zhuan Canting)
Novotel Atlantis Hotel, 728 Pudong
Avenue (at Juye Road)
Tel: 5036 6666 ext. 1442
Creatively presented Australasian
fusion cuisine in a revolving
restaurant that doubles as an art
gallery. The art exhibits, from
ShanghART, change monthly, and
diners enjoy revolving art exhibits
as well as a spectacular panorama
of Pudong. **$$**

Lapis Lazuli (Zang Long Fang)
9 Dongping Road (at Hengshan Road)
Tel: 6473 1021
A sophisticated Chinese-style
interior using plenty of natural fibres
and materials, Lapis Lazuli serves
Continental and Japanese cuisines,
the former somewhat bland. An
especially good coffee and tea
menu (with delicacies like lavender
tea) served on glazed Balinese
pottery. **$$$**

La Villa Rouge (Xiao Hong Lou)
811 Hengshan Road, in Xujiahui Park
Tel: 6431 6639
A beautiful old mansion, once the
EMI recording studio, set in Xujiahui
Park. Japanese chef prepares four
different *prix fixe* menus (four, five,
eight or nine courses) each week,
blending French, Italian and
Japanese cuisine in elegant
surroundings. Outdoor seating
available in the warmer months
only. **$$$$**

Nobu
Three on the Bund, 3 Zhongshan
No. 1 Road (E) (at Guangdong Road)
Tel: 6323 3355
www.threeonthebund.com
Scheduled to open Jan 2004 and
located in a historic Bund building
redesigned by Michael Graves, this
is the legendary Japanese fusion
master's first venture into China.

Sasha's (Sasha Canting)
House 11, 9 Dongping Road
(at Hengshan Road)
Tel: 6474 6166
French cuisine in the country club
setting of the Soong family
compound. The Roger Verges-
inspired kitchen serves seasonal
fusion meals on the second floor of
this restored mansion. **$$$**

T8 Restaurant & Bar (Ti Hu)
Unit 8, North Block Xintiandi,
Lane 181 Taicang Road
(at Madang Road)
Tel: 6355 8999
One of Shanghai's most beautiful
restaurants, T8's interior is a
serene and distinctly Shanghainese
oasis, located in an old Shanghai
shikumen house. An adventurous
fusion menu filters Asian classics
through a French prism. Closed for
lunch on Tuesdays. **$$$$**

TMSK (Tou Ming Si Kao)
Unit 2, House 11, North Block
Xintiandi, Lane 181 Taicang Road
(at Madang Road)
Tel: 6326 2227
The owners of the crystal shop
Liulichang, China's version of
Lalique, have created a magical
crystal restaurant at TMSK, from the
vaulted ceilings honeycombed with
crystal to the red crystal barstools
and crystal bathroom sinks. The
fusion menu includes classics like
caviar and salmon tartare as well
as contemporary spins on old
favourites like Peking duck and
roast chicken. Open for dinner only;
closed on Monday. **$$$$**

Vong
Three on the Bund, 3 Zhongshan
No. 1 Road (E) (at Guangdong Road)
Tel: 6323 3355
www.threeonthebund.com
Scheduled to open Jan 2004,
celebrity chef Jean-Georges
Vongerichten's stylish restaurant is
located in a restored Bund building-
turned-upscale complex.

Mexican
Mexico Lindo
Villa 1, 3911 Hongmei Road
Tel: 6262 2797
Shanghai's most authentic Mexican
eatery, with all the usual Mexican
standards (enchiladas,
chimichangas, nachos) plus family
recipes from chef Eduardo's
Mexican mama. Tropical-style
outdoor dining and killer margaritas,
too. **$$**

OTHER ASIAN

Japanese
Ambrosia (Xian Zhi Xuan)
150 Fenyang Road (at Fuxing Road)
Tel: 6431 3935
Japanese cuisine served in a
fabulous Concession-era mansion.
Open for dinner daily and lunch on
Sat and Sun only. **$$$**

Southeast Asian
Bali Laguna (Hong Ya Can Yin)
189 Huashan Road
(inside Jing An Park)
Tel: 6248 6970
Despite its name, Bali Laguna
serves Southeast Asian rather than
Balinese cuisine, but both the décor
and the setting (at the edge of a lily
pond surrounded by a lush green
landscape) is the closest thing in
Shanghai to Bali. Menu highlights
include satay, grilled fishcake
wrapped in banana leaf, beef
rendang (a dry spicy curry) and
laksa (rice noodles in spicy coconut
gravy). **$$**

Vietnamese
Cochin China (Ou Yuen Nian Dai)
889 Julu Road
Tel: 6445 6797
A colonial Vietnam ambience in a
refurbished French Concession villa,
Cochin China has an impressive
range of selections, but the food is
a little heavy on the oil. Highlights
include the green papaya salad,
crab in sour tamarind sauce and
Vietnamese chicken curry served
with a baguette. **$$**

Thai
La Na Thai (La Na Canting)
Building 4, 118 Ruijin No. 2 Road,
Upstairs, part of FACE restaurant
Ruijin Bingguan
Tel: 6466 4238
An old manor house decorated with a
restrained Southeast Asian aesthetic
is the setting for La Na Thai. The
Thai chef focuses on Thailand's
northern La Na region, with house
specials like deep-fried prawn cakes
with dipping sauce, green papaya
salad, pomfret with sweet basil
sauce and Thai coconut milk ice
cream. Open for dinner only. **$$$**

Irene's Thai (Tai Shi Canting)
263 Tongren Road
Tel: 6247 3579
Thai chefs serve genuine Thai
cuisine in a meticulously authentic
Thai-style interior embellished with
Buddha images, silk brocade and
quaint spirit houses. Chicken in
pandan leaves, Mandarin fish with
Thai spices and tom yam soup are
Irene classics. **$$$**

Simply Thai (Tian Tai Canting)
5C Dongping Road
(at Hengshan Road)
Tel: 6445 9551
Minimalist Thai elegance is the
setting for Thai cuisine so authentic
that the restaurant caters for Thai
royalty when they're in town. A team
of Thai chefs mans the kitchens,
creating favourites like Thai fish
cakes, green chicken curry and Thai
"red rubies" dessert. Dining outside
on the deck overlooking the gardens
of the Music Conservatory is one of
Shanghai's great pleasures. **$**

Indian
Hazara (Hazara Canting)
Building 4, 118 Ruijin No. 2 Road,
Downstairs, part of FACE restaurant
Ruijin Bingguan
Tel: 6466 4238
Hazara's tented interior is located
in the same manor house as La Na
Thai *(see above)*, this time with a
minimalist Indian décor. The cuisine
is Indian frontier food, with
specialities that include *raan e
hazara*, a leg of baby lamb
marinated in Indian spices, *dhaal*
(black lentils), *navrathan khorma*
(nine-curried vegetables) and *gulab*

jamun (caramelised dumplings) for dessert. Open for dinner only. **$$$$**

Indian Kitchen (Yindu Xiao Chu)
572 Yong Jia Road (between Yue Yang and Urumqi roads)
Tel: 6473 1517
South Indian cuisine is the speciality at this casual and unpretentious neighbourhood restaurant. Samosas, chicken curry, and the breads are all winners. **$**

Tandoor Indian Restaurant (Yindu Canting)
South Bldg Jinjiang Hotel,
59 Maoming Road (S)
Tel: 6472 5494
Outstanding interpretations of northern Indian cuisine against a romantic Silk Road-inspired décor. Tandoori is the speciality of the house, along with excellent kebabs, curries and breads. **$$$$**

Chinese vegetarian

Gongdelin
445 Nanjing Road (W)
Tel: 6327 0218
Shanghai's most famous vegetarian restaurant has been in business since 1922. Gongdelin serves vegetarian versions of favourite Chinese dishes – everything from chicken to fish. **$**

Jue Lin Restaurant (Jue Lin Canting)
250 Jinling Road (E)
Tel: 6326 0115
Jue Lin serves mock meat dishes, all made with gluten and tofu, and almost identical in taste and texture to the real thing, and all decorated with elaborate vegetable carvings. **$**

TEAHOUSES AND CAFÉS

Bonomi Café (Bonuomi Kafedian)
Room 226, Pudong Development Bank Building, 12 Zhongshan No. 1 Road (E)
Tel: 6329 7506
Coffee, tea and snacks in the old Hong Kong and Shanghai Bank building on the Bund. Open Mon–Fri 8.30am–6pm, Sat 10am–4pm. **$**

Coffee Bean and Tea Leaf (Xiang Tei Bin)
Unit 140-141, Shanghai City Centre, 100 Zunyi Road
Tel: 6237 1458

LA-based franchise serves iced mochas and other coffee speciality drinks along with sandwiches, desserts and snacks. **$**

Coffee Club (Xiang Fei Ge)
8 Jinan Road
Tel: 5382 8370
Stylish branch of this Singapore café serves different varieties of coffee, sandwiches and snacks in a Moroccan-inspired setting. **$**

Harn Sheh (Han She Paomo Hong Cha Fang)
10 Hengshan Road
(at Taojiang Road)
Tel: 6474 6547
Contemporary Chinese teahouse, serving teas and snacks. **$**

Huxinting Teahouse (Hu Xin Ting)
Jiu Qu Bridge, Yu Garden
Tel: 6373 6950
Shanghai's most famous teahouse, the lovely Huxinting was said to be the model for the Blue Willow plate design. Early morning is best; after 10am it gets tourist-heavy. Open daily 8.30am–9.30pm. **$**

Keven Café (Kai-wen)
525 Hengshan Road
(at Wuxing Road)
Tel: 6433 5564
Shanghai's version of a diner, manned by a former Hilton chef and serving good wholesome food that ranges all over the map (from a mean version of Indonesian fried rice to homestyle tuna sandwiches and great breakfasts. Open daily 7.30–2am. **$**

Old China Hand Reading Room (Hanyuan Shuwa)
27 Shaoxing Road
Tel: 6473 2526
Photographer Deke Erh's bookshop café lined with antiques, books on Shanghai and the photographers' works on old Shanghai. Coffee, tea, juice and beer as well as finger food. Open daily, 9.30am–midnight. **$**

Restaurant Price Guide

Price range for a meal for two (Asian or Western), excluding drinks:

$$$$	RMB 800 and above
$$$	RMB 500–800
$$	RMB 250–500
$	less than RMB 250

Culture

Beijing may be the centre of Chinese culture, but Shanghai, with its state-of-the-art Grand Theatre, is a likely candidate as the future centre of international culture. With an Oriental Arts Centre specialising in Chinese arts opening in the near future, Shanghai is set to take on the mantle of China's most cultured city. The Grand Theatre offers highbrow culture, with names like Pavarotti, Yitzhak Perlman and top symphonies. Foreign ballet companies, musicals (*Cats*) and Western operas (*Aida, La Traviatta*) all visit on a regular basis.

Local talent is on tap with two local symphonies – as the home of the Shanghai Conservatory, the city has a long and proud musical tradition – the Shanghai Ballet and several Peking opera companies.

Increasingly, there is more popular fare as well. Although the SARS outbreak cancelled the Rolling Stones 2003 Asia Tour, British bands Suede and Morcheeba made it to Shanghai.

The Grand Theatre hosts both Western and Chinese opera, but the centre for Peking opera is the Yifu Theatre. Fans of Chinese opera should try to get in a performance of local Kunju opera, perhaps best known for their performance of the *Peony Pavilion*. Chinese theatre, much of it avant-garde, is performed at the Shanghai Drama Arts Centre and the Shanghai Theatre Academy. English captions make it accessible to foreign audiences.

Shanghai's famous acrobatics troupes hold regular performances at the Shanghai Centre Theatre and the Great World Theatre.

The annual Shanghai International Arts Festival sees a

month of international arts performances, most of which are world-class, held around town.

Currently, authorities only permit 12 international films (read: Hollywood blockbuster movies) each year, but that should change with WTO regulations. There is an annual Film Festival; the Alliance Francaise has regular screenings of French films; and the Canadian Consulate holds a monthly movie night. Maria's Choice Film Club shows contemporary Chinese films with English subtitles.

See also pages 63–69 of the Features section.

Buying Tickets

Tickets for all arts performances can be purchased from the Shanghai Cultural Information and Booking Centre, 272 Fengxian Road, tel: 6217 2426. Movie tickets are available at the cinemas. Grand Theatre tickets are available at the theatre booking office at 200 People's Road.

For up-to-the-minute entertainment information, check www.thatsshanghai.com or www.cityweekend.com.cn.

Performance Venues

Shanghai Grand Theatre, 300 People's Avenue, tel: 6372 8701, 6372 8702. The premier venue for highbrow culture – theatre, dance, music and opera.
Majestic Theatre, 66 Jiang Ning Road, tel: 6217 4409. This art deco theatre started life as a movie theatre, but today hosts primarily ballets and plays.
Shanghai Centre Theatre, 1376 Nanjing Road (W), tel: 6279 8663, 6279 7132. Shanghai Acrobatic troupe holds regular performances here; shows at 7.30–9pm, but to be sure, call for schedule.
Shanghai Circus World, 2266 Gong He Xin Road (at Da Ning Road), tel: 5665 3646, 6652 7750. Performances Sat–Sun 7.30–9pm; call for other performance times.
Shanghai Grand Stage, 1111 Cao Xi Road (N) (inside the Shanghai

Easy Tickets

Like the original designer gear that shows up in Shanghai's clothing markets, no one asks where the scalper gets his tickets from and how he is able to sell them so cheaply – and indeed, why the major entertainment venues tolerate him. Many of Shanghai's upstanding citizens use them regularly; some have their own personal scalper they call when tickets are needed. Transactions are simple: show up about half an hour before showtime, pick a scalper, give him your order, check that the seating on the tickets is acceptable, and pay. Be warned, however, that tickets are sometimes no cheaper than box office tickets, and it is often difficult to get seats together.

Stadium), tel: 6438 5200, 6438 4952 ext 2567. The appropriately named Shanghai Grand Stage is used for mega-events, like cultural shows for the launching of the Tourism Festival, and rock concerts.
Shanghai Music Conservatory, 20 Fenyang Road, tel: 6437 0137. This is a music school, not an orchestra, but students do perform regular concerts for the public. Call and ask if there are scheduled performances.
Shanghai Stadium, 1111 Cao Xi Road (N), tel: 6438 5200, 6438 4952 ext. 2567. Mainly rock concerts, including headliners from Hong Kong.
Shanghai Theatre Academy, 630 Huashan Road, tel: 6248 2920 ext. 3040. Chinese-language modern theatre.
Great World Theatre, 1 Tibet Road (S), tel: 6326-3760, 6326-6703. The atrium courtyard of this grand old entertainment complex features acrobatic performances, while upstairs, Peking opera is performed in a smaller theatre.
Yifu Theatre, 701 Fuzhou Road, tel: 6351 4668. Peking opera performances on Saturday and Sunday.

Art House Cinema

Canadian Consulate Films, Room 804, Tenant Activity Room, Shanghai Centre, 1376 Nanjing Road (W). Canadian films shown on the last Wednesday of every month; no bookings.
Cine-Club de l'Alliance, 6/F Alliance Francaise de Shanghai, 297 Wu Song Road, tel: 6357 5388. French films with Chinese subtitles, Fridays at 6.30pm.
Maria's Choice – Send e-mail to MariasChoice-subscribe@topica.com to receive regular e-mails on screenings of contemporary Chinese movies with English subtitles.
Shanghai Film Art Centre, 160 Xinhua Road, tel: 6280 4088. The main centre for the Shanghai International Film Festival.

Art Galleries

In addition to the performing arts, Shanghai is also home to a growing number of art galleries specialising in Chinese contemporary art and sculpture *(see pages 71–75)*. For some background on Chinese art, visit the Shanghai Museum and the Shanghai Art Museum, which are excellent showcases of both the legacy of Chinese art and culture and its contemporary work.

Art galleries are concentrated in several areas: Taikang Road, just south of Maoming Road and Fuxing Park, is a government-approved art street where galleries are located in spiffed-up old warehouses. Nearby, the Fuxing Park and Shaoxing Road area also has clusters of galleries. For yet more options, head to Suzhou Creek's early 20th century warehouses, which are now home to both artists and art galleries.

Shanghai's big artfest comes in even years, when the **Shanghai Biennale** brings top international and domestic artists to the city.

Taikang Road
Bai Sui Zi Gallery, 45 Taikang Road, tel: 5465 2413. Open daily 10am–6pm.

Hands in Clay Pottery Studio, No. 1 Lane 210 Taikang Road, tel: 5465 4042. Open Mon–Sat 9am–5.30pm.

Jenny Art Studio, 200 Taikang Road, tel: 5466 2600. Open daily 10am–5pm.

Shanghai Centre for Decentralised Arts, Unit 1, Suite 105, 190 Taikang Road, tel: 5465 1504. Open daily 10am–6pm.

Shanghai Deke Erh Centre, Bldg 3, Lane 210 Taikang Road, tel: 6415 0675. Photographer Deke Erh's 800 square metre space is used for exhibitions, concerts, and even book readings.

Taikang Art Centre, No. 9 Lane 210 Taikang Road, tel: 6467 2275. Open daily 10am–6pm.

The Pottery Workshop, 2/F 220 Taikang Road, tel: 6445 0902. Open Mon–Sat 10am–6pm.

Yi Dian Gallery, 25B Taikang Road, tel: 5465 1645/8. Open daily 10am–10pm.

Shaoxing Road

Angle Gallery, 40-42 Shaoxing Road, tel: 6433 2128. Open daily noon–10pm.

Classic Art Gallery, 108 Shaoxing Road, tel: 6433 1939.

Future Attitude Art Gallery, 37 Shaoxing Road, tel: 6466 5184; e-mail: futureview@sohu.com.

Old China Hand Reading Room, 27 Shaoxing Road, tel: 6473 2256. Open daily 12pm–12am.

Ton Hall Gallery, 19C Shaoxing Road, tel: 6473 7319. Open daily 10am–7pm.

Fuxing Park

Art Scene China, No. 8 Lane 37 Fuxing Road (W), tel: 6437 0631; www.artscenechina.com. Open daily 10.30am–8.30pm.

Madame Mao's Dowry, 70 Fuxing Road (at Yong Fu Road), tel: 6437 1255. Contemporary art and Cultural Revolution-era prints.

ShanghART, 2A Gaolan Road in Fuxing Park, tel: 6359 3923; www.shanghart.com.

Suzhou Creek

Eastlink, 5/F Building 6, 50 Moganshan Road, tel: 6276 9932.

Contemporary Chinese art, often edgy.

ShanghART Warehouse, 50 Moganshan Road, tel: 6359 3923. The granddaddy of Shanghai contemporary art galleries, with a good selection of artists and monthly exhibitions.

Art Scene China Warehouse, 50 Moganshan Road, tel: 6437 0631. High quality contemporary Chinese art and sculpture exhibitions.

Elsewhere in Puxi

BizArt, 3/F Building 5, 758 Julu Road, tel: 6247 0484; www.biz-art.com. Open Mon–Fri 2–7pm, Sat–Sun 2–8pm.

Elegant Art Gallery, 5 Anfu Road, tel: 5403 9942.

Liu Hai Siu Art Centre, 1660 Hongqiao Road, tel: 6270 1018.

Propaganda Poster Art Centre, Room BOC, 868 Huashan Road. For opening times and information call 6211 1845, mobile 130 0327 2117 (Yang Peiming).

Shanghai Grand Theatre Gallery, 286 Huangpi Road, tel: 6386 8686 ext. 3214. Open Tues–Sun 10am–6pm.

The Room with a View, 12/F 479 Nanjing Road (W), tel: 6352 0256; www.wuliang.net.

Xintiandi Gallery, 338 Huangpi Road, tel: 5382 9898. Open 9am–5pm.

Yi Bo Gallery, 198 Huayuan Shiqiao Road, Pudong, tel: 5888 0111. Open daily 10am–5pm.

Shanghai Contemporary, The Bund Centre, 88 Central Henan Road, tel: 6335 1358; www.shanghai-contemporary.com. Open Tues–Sat 12am–8pm.

Pudong

ART50, 728 Pudong Avenue, Novotel Atlantis, tel: 5036 6666 ext. 1688. A fusion restaurant with regular exhibitions from ShanghART. Open daily 11am–11pm.

Painters Village, No. 3 Building, 2970 Pudong Avenue, tel: 5850 0290. Artist's community where painters live and exhibit.

Nightlife

When the sun goes down, the neon comes up in "the city that doesn't sleep". The disco-madness of the mid-1990s has faded, leaving a thriving bar and nightclub scene which runs the gamut from seedy to stylish, and includes its fair share of drugs and ladies of the evening. Shanghai's main bar-hopping streets are Hengshan Road, Maoming Road (S) and Julu Road; the first is slightly more upscale and begins earlier; the latter two are more late-night.

The club scene attracts brand name DJs like Paul Oakenfeld as well as DJs from the surrounding region, and while the live music scene is not as vibrant as Beijing's, there are nevertheless several enclaves of good live music, both local and imported.

See also pages 93–99 of the Features section.

Sources of Info

Shanghai's listings magazines provide pages of every bar in the city, as well as highlights of the new ones. The most reliable are: *That's Shanghai* www.thatsshanghai.com; and *City Weekend* www.cityweekend.com.cn

MAOMING ROAD (S) AREA

Bars and nightclubs

Blue Frog, 207-23 Maoming Road (S) (at Central Fuxing Road), tel: 6445 6634. Cosy pub with jazz as its mainstay that has become a Maoming Road favourite. Open Mon–Fri 11am–2am, Sat–Sun 4pm–2am.

Buddha Bar/Buddha Lounge, 172 Maoming Road (at Yong Jia Road), tel: 6415 2668. Music and dance rule at the clubbing hotspot upstairs; downstairs it's the chill-out lounge. Open daily 9pm–2am, till 7am on weekends.

California Club (Lan Kwai Fong at Park 97), 2A Gaolan Road (in Fuxing Park), tel: 5383 2328. Jam-packed hotspot playing house and techno; popular with the young, rich and wannabe famous crowd. Expect to queue on weekends. Open Sun–Thur 7pm–2am, Fri–Sat 9pm till late.

Face Bar, Building 4, Ruijin Guest House, 118 Ruijin No. 2 Road (at Yong Jia Road), tel: 6466 4328. An upscale bar with a beautiful chic, minimalist Southeast Asian ambience, good drinks list and outdoor seating overlooking the lawn. Open daily 2pm–2am.

Judy's Too, 176 Maoming Road (S) (at Nanchang Road), tel: 6473 1417. The grand old lady of Maoming, Judy's Too is a sleazy late-night favourite for dancing (downstairs) and dining (upstairs). Open daily 7pm–2am.

Manhattan, 207 Maoming Road (S) (at Fuxing Road W), tel: 6467 0284. Formerly located on Julu Road, the new Manhattan is still smoky, crowded and lined with hungry-eyed ladies. Open daily 7pm till late.

Live music
House of Blues & Jazz, 158 Maoming Road (S) (at Nanchang Road), tel: 6437 5280. Live blues and jazz as well as jazz selections from the CD player in one of the most authentic retro settings in Shanghai. Open daily 5.30pm–1.30am.

HENGSHAN ROAD AREA

Bars and nightclubs
The Blarney Stone, 5A Dong Ping Road (at Yue Yang Road), tel: 6415 7496. Shanghai's most authentic Irish pub, down to the brogue of the bartenders. Live music too. Open daily 11–2am.

Bourbon Street, 191 Hengshan Road (at Gao'an Road), tel: 6445 7556. New Orleans French Quarter décor with live music after 9.30pm. Open daily 7pm–2am.

Maya, 4/F Yunhai Building, 1333 Central Huaihai Road (at Baoqing Road), tel: 6415 2218. A house band alternates with a DJ at this club catering to the thirtysomething crowd. Open daily 8pm–2am.

Real Love, 10 Hengshan Road (at Gao'an Road), tel: 6474 6830. Crowded disco that's popular with college students and twentysomethings. Open daily 8.30pm–2am.

Sasha's, House 11, 9 Dongping Road (at Hengshan Road), tel: 6474 6166. The stylish, wood-panelled bar in this Soong family mansion gets smoky, noisy and crowded after 8pm. Open daily 10–2am.

O'Malley's Irish Pub, 42 Taojiang Road, tel: 6474 4533. An Irish Pub Company franchise, O'Malley's looks as if it were lifted from the Emerald Isle, from the light fixtures to the antique signs on the walls. Located in a French Concession villa with a lovely garden, the Guinness and home-brewed O'Malley's ale is popular with the city's expatriates. Open daily 11–2am.

Paulaner Brauhaus (see restaurant listings page 300).

Live music
Cotton Club, 1428 Central Huaihai Road (at Fuxing Road), tel: 6437 7110. Wynton Marsalis jammed here when he was in town – you'll hear some of the city's best jazz here. Open Sun–Thur 9.30pm–12.30am, Fri–Sat 10pm–1.30am.

JULU ROAD AREA

Bars and nightclubs
Caribe, 877 Julu Road (at Chang Shu Road), tel: 6249 5512. A Caribbean-Cuban theme with a treehouse (for the DJ), live Cuban rhythms and a thick menu of tropical cocktails (to go with the décor). Open daily 6pm–2am.

Goodfellas, 907 Julu Road (at Changshu Road), tel: 6467 0775. Known as a place for serious drinkers and pushy prostitutes, Goodfellas also has a small dance floor, darts and a DJ who spins classic rock. Open daily 7pm–2am.

Apocalypse Now, 3/F Yaxin Guangchang, 401 Changshou Road (at Changde Road), tel: 6276 6855. There are drinks, of course, but the main thing at Apocalypse Now is the dancing. Open daily 5pm–2am.

XINTIANDI AREA

Bars and nightclubs
Bonne Sante, 1/F East Tower, 8 Jinan Road (at Chong De Road), tel: 6384 2906. Shanghai's first wine bar is a stylish minimalist place. Wine tastings on Wednesdays and occasional live music. Open daily 6pm–2am.

Tou Ming Si Kao (TMSK), Unit 2, House 11, North Block Xintiandi, Lane 181 Taicang Road (at Madang Road), tel: 6326 2227. Coloured glass sculpture is its theme – from the bar to the barstools to the artsy wine glasses. Open daily 11.30–1am.

Paulaner Brauhaus, (see restaurant listings page 300).

Star East Shanghai, Unit 1, House 7, North Block Xintiandi, Lane 181 Taicang Road (at Madang Road), tel: 6311 4991. A Hong Kong version of Planet Hollywood with investors like Jackie Chan and friends, this is a glitzy, buzzing spot. Open daily, 11–2am.

Live music
Ark Live House, 15 Xintiandi Road (N), Lane 181 Taicang Road (at Madang Road), tel: 6326 8008. Currently Shanghai's premier contemporary live music venue, this popular Japanese-invested place hosts creative musicians from around the world. Open daily 5.30pm–2am; check magazine listings for concerts and events.

CJW, Unit 4, House 2, Lane 123 Xing Ye Road (at Madang Road), tel: 6385 6677. This New York-style jazz joint has three smoky floors featuring cigars, live jazz and wine. Open daily 11.30–2am.

BUND AREA

Bars and nightclubs
Fest Beer House, 11 Hankou Road (at Zhongshan No. 1 Road E), tel: 6321 8447. Microbrewed fresh beer (both dark and light) brewed in the copper stills that dominate the bar is the highlight at Fest, located just steps away from the Bund. Open daily 11–1am.
Brauhaus 505, Hotel Sofitel Hyland, 505 Nanjing Road (W) (at Shanxi Road), tel: 6351 5888. Microbrewed beer and live music in a beer hall atmosphere. Open daily 11–1.30am.

Live music
Niche Bar, 2/F The Westin Shanghai, 88 Central Henan Road (at Yan'an Road E), tel: 6335 1888 ext 7342. Jazz musicians from the US play at this contemporary bar. Open Sun–Thur 5pm–2am; Fri–Sat and eve of public holiday 5pm–3am.
Peace Hotel Old Jazz Bar, 20 Nanjing Road (W), tel: 6321 6888 ext 6210. The aging group of Dixieland jazz players didn't play at the Peace Hotel in the old days (although some of them did play in old Shanghai), and they're not especially good, but they do play the oldies in the beautiful old-world Peace Hotel. Open daily 8pm–1.30am.
The Glamour Bar, (at M on the Bund) 7/F 20 Guangdong Road (at Zhongshan No. 1 Road), tel: 6350 9988. Glamorous spot for jazz, vocals and classical, call for performance information or check www.m-theglamourbar.com. This 21st century impression of a Hollywood movie set with its stunning views of the Bund is an atmospheric setting for martinis and classic cocktails. Open 6–10.30pm.
Tropicana, 8-9/F, 261 Sichuan Road (at Hankou Road), tel: 6329 2472. Lively Cuban themed-bar/restaurant in a Concession-era bank building just off the Bund, this has

Russian dancing girls, a Cuban band and a packed dance floor with salsa-ing Shanghainese. Open daily 11.30–2.30pm and 6.30pm till late.

PUDONG

B.A.T.S., B/F Pudong Shangri-la Hotel, 30 Fucheng Road, tel: 6882 8888 ext. 6425. The Shangri-la's upscale rathskeller is a popular weekend stop for clubbers (and a favourite of Shanghai's ladies of the evening) with a good selection of drinks as well as cigars. Open Tues–Sun 6pm–1am.
Dublin Exchange, 2/F HSBC Tower 101, Yincheng Road (E), Lujiazui, Pudong, tel: 6841 2052. Stylish banker's pub serving Guinness on tap and some of the best bar snacks in Shanghai. Open Mon–Fri 10am–11pm, Sat 5–11pm.
PU-Js, Grand Hyatt Hotel, Jin Mao Tower, 88 Century Boulevard, Pudong, tel: 5409 1234 ext. 8732. Music Room, Tapas Bar, Dance Zone and KTV. Jazz singer Coco often croons here. Open Sun–Thur 7pm–1am, Fri–Sat 7pm–2am.

NANJING ROAD

Club La Belle, 2/F, 333 Tong Ren Road (at Beijing Road), tel: 6247 9666; www.labelle-shanghai.com. European DJs now spin in the Green House, old Shanghai architect Ladislau Hudec's residential masterpiece. Open daily 10.30pm–2am.
Long Bar, Shanghai Centre, 1376 Nanjing Road (W), tel: 6279 8268. A Shanghai legend and one of the longest-lasting bars in the city, the Long Bar's retro Shanghai environment and Shanghai Centre location attracts the business community – or perhaps it's the dancing girls? Open daily 10–3am.
Malone's American Café, 255 Tongren Road (at Nanjing Road W), tel: 6247 2400. A sports bar with big screen TV and live rock, six nights a week. Open 11–2am.

ELSEWHERE IN PUXI

Goya, 357 Xinhua Road (at Dingxi Road), tel: 6280 1256. A Manhattan-style martini bar in an intimate, candlelit lounge dotted with comfy couches and plush armchairs. Open Sun–Thur 7pm–2am; Fri–Sat 7pm–4am.
Mei, 200 Taikang Road (at Sinan Road), tel: 6415 0710. Art bar on trendy art street Taikang Road, Mei is effortlessly chic. Art videos, DJs.
Rojam, 4/F Hong Kong Plaza, 283 Central Huaihai Road (at Song Shan Road), tel: 6390 7181. Young crowd, including American School teenagers in this huge space. Monday Ladies Night is a Shanghai institution.
Shanghai Sally's, 4 Xiangshan Road (at Sinan Road), tel: 5382 0738. One of Shanghai's oldest English-style pubs, Shanghai Sally's upstairs is the home of the Hash House Harriers, while downstairs hosts China Comedy Club events. Open Tues–Sat 4pm till late, Sun 11am till late.

Gay Venues

Asia Blue, 5F 679 Dingxi Road (at Yan'an Road W), tel: 6294 1202. Open 6pm–2am.
Home, 18 Gaolan Road (at Sinan Road), tel: 5382 0373. Open 6pm–2am.
Saladan Eighty Percent, 1/F, 375 Xin Feng Road (at Chang Ping Road), tel: 6266 1917. Open daily 7.30pm–2am.

Sport

Urban Shanghai has its share of city sports – mostly of the indoor variety – and surprisingly good spectator sports. The major sports teams, the Shanghai Sharks basketball team and the Shanghai Shenhua football team, are worth watching. The Sharks sent its star player, Yao Ming, to the NBA and Shanghai Shenhua's football team members helped China qualify for the World Cup. International tournaments include the Heineken Tennis Open, which usually brings top names in the tennis world to town and the Volvo Open, which does the same for golf.

Spectator Sports

Shanghai Shenhua football – Hongkou Stadium, 715 Dong Ti Yu Hui Road. Call for ticket information: tel: 6553 2388.
Shanghai Sharks basketball – Luwan Stadium, 128 Zhao Jia Bang Road. Call for ticket information: tel: 6467-5358. China's basketball pride, Yao Ming (now of the Houston Rockets), previously played for the Sharks.
Heineken Tennis Open, www.heinekenopenshanghai.com. Held every September, it attracts big names like Michael Chang and Andre Agassi.

Participant Sports

GOLF

Most of the upper-end hotels will arrange for tee times at nearby golf courses. Located on the outskirts of the city, most courses are between 30 minutes to an hour from the city centre.

Shanghai Binhai Golf, Binhai, Nahui, Pudong, tel: 5805 8888.
Shanghai Golf Club, 3765 Jiahang Gong Road, Jiading District, tel: 5995 0111.
Shanghai Grand City Club, 9988 Zhongchun Road, Qi Bao Town, tel: 6419 3676.
Shanghai International Golf Country Club, Xinyang Cun, Zhujiajiao Zhen, Qingpu District, tel: 5972 8111.
Shanghai Silport Golf & Country Club, 1 Xubao Road, Dianshan Lake, Kunshan, tel: (0520) 748 1970; fax: (0520) 748 2544. Local golfers say that this is the best course in Shanghai. Home of the professional tournament, the Volvo.
Shanghai Links Golf & Country Club, 1600 Lingbai Gonglu, Pudong, tel: 5897 5899; fax: 5897 4607. Members only, but worth a visit if you have connections.
Shanghai Grasslands Golf Club, 1366 Huqingping Highway, Xujing, Qingpu County, tel: 5976 6666; fax: 5976 7676.
Shanghai Hongqiao Golf Course, 567 Hongxu Road, tel: 6406 5606; fax: 6406 3502.
Shanghai Riviera Golf Resort, 277 Yangzi Road, Jiading County, tel: 5912 6888 ext. 129; fax: 5912 9712.
Shanghai Sun Island International Club, 2588 Shentai Road, Qingpu County, tel: 5983 0888; fax: 5983 1625.
Suzhou Sunrise Golf Club, tel: (0512) 549 1883, or 6469 7829 in Shanghai. This lovely Japanese-managed, Nicklaus-designed course comes highly recommended. Just a little more than an hour from downtown Shanghai, the facilities at this well-maintained course are among the best to be found in China.
Shanghai Tianma Country Club, 1 Tianmashan Zhen, Songjiang County, tel: 6268 5500; fax: 6268 2525.
Shanghai Tomson Golf Club, 1 Longdong Road, Pudong, tel: 5833 8888; fax: 5933 9698. It is not easy to get on these lovely links, which is surrounds the Tomson Villas residential development, but

worth the effort as it is among the most conveniently located courses in the Shanghai area. You'll have to locate a member or a resident of the villas in order to make tee time.

DRIVING RANGE

Shanghai Lujiazui Golf Club, 501 Central Yin Cheng Road, Pudong, tel: 5882 9028. Conveniently located near the Grand Hyatt in Pudong.

RUNNING

Hash House Harriers. A local running fraternity mostly made up of expatriates. Organises runs on Sundays, 4pm in summer and 3pm in winter. Check its website www.shanghaihhh.com for more details.

RUGBY

Shanghai Football Club, tel: 3423 0521; www.shanghaifootballclub.com. Contact Mark Tomas for more details.

TENNIS/SQUASH

Many hotels have tennis and squash courts.
Shanghai International Tennis Centre, 516 Hengshan Road, tel: 6415 5588 ext. 82.
Shanghai Racquet Club, Lane 555 Jinfeng Road, Hucao Town, Minhang District, tel: 2201 0088.

Shopping

Shanghai's shopping runs the gamut from mega-mall department stores to streetside tailors, and it all seems to converge at the sprawling Xiangyang Fashion Market *(see text box page 309)*, where virtually everything imaginable is on sale. Some of Shanghai's best buys are special to Shanghai: lifestyle boutiques with Shanghai fusion stuff; antiques from the Concession era; propaganda posters from the 1960s; and custom-designed clothes, jewellery and furniture.

Most large malls and department stores are open daily from 9–10am to 9–10pm daily. Smaller shops may operate shorter hours so call first. *See also pages 87–91 of the Features section.*

Shopping Malls/Stores

NANJING ROAD AREA

Plaza 66, 1266 Nanjing Road (W), tel: 6279 0910.
No. 1 Department Store, 830 Nanjing Road (E), tel: 6322 3344.
CITIC Square, 1168 Nanjing Road (W), tel: 6218 0180.
D-Mall, 221 People's Avenue (at Nanjing Road, under People's

Bargain Buys

Adventurous bargain hunters will enjoy the tiny shops along Shanxi Road (S). They don't look like much, but this is where you'll find made-for-export brands (like Nike, Reebok, North Face) and original designer labels (like Talbots, Ann Taylor, Nordstrom's). Needless to say, the stock changes constantly, so if you see something you like, snap it up immediately!

Square), tel: 6358 2245.
Isetan, Westgate Mall, 1038 Nanjing Road (W), tel: 6272 1111.
Itokin, 592 Nanjing Road (E), tel: 6852 3668.
Westgate Mall, 1038 Nanjing Road (W), tel: 6218 7878.

HUAIHAI ROAD

Isetan, 523 Central Huaihai Road, tel: 5306 1111.
Parksons, 918 Central Huaihai Road, tel: 6415 6384.
Shanghai Square, 138 Central Huaihai Road, tel: 6359 2659, 6359 8459.
Taipingyang, 333 Central Huaihai Road, tel: 5306 8888.
Times Square, 149 Central Huaihai Road, tel: 6327 5566.

Clothing Sizes

Made-in-Shanghai clothes are exported around the world, and in Shanghai, you are likely to find them in American sizes as much as British or Japanese ones.

XUJIAHUI

Grand Gateway Mall, 1 Hongqiao Road, tel: 6407 6622.
Oriental Shopping Centre, 8 Caoxi Road (N), tel: 6487 0000.
Taipingyang, 932 Hengshan Road, tel: 6407 8888.

PUDONG

Super Brand Mall, 168 Lujiazui Road, tel: 6887 7888.
Next Age Department Store, 501 Zhangyang Road, Pudong, tel: 5830 1111.

Antiques

There are two kinds of antiques shoppers: the kind for whom sifting through junk and unrestored pieces is part of the joy of antiquing, and the kind who just wants the finished, polished piece.

Fortunately, many of the Hongqiao

area antique shops offer both experiences at their warehouses and showrooms.Sifting is *de rigeur* at the antiques markets, mainly concentrated in the Old City area.

HONGQIAO

Alex's Antique Shop, 1970 Hongqiao Road, tel: 6242 8734.
China Antique Link, 1888 Wuzhong Road, tel: 6419 9908.
Fei Feng Furniture Co, 1750 Wuzhong Road, tel: 5458 0640.
Henry Antique, 8 Hongzhong Road, tel: 6401 0831.
Hu & Hu Antiques, 1685 Wuzhong Road, tel: 6405 1212.
Kang-Da Antique Furniture Factory, 1245 Wuzhong Road, tel: 6401 2563.
Zhong Zhong Jia Yuan Antique, 28 Hongxu Road, tel: 6406 4066.

DOWNTOWN

Changjiang Tang Antiques Co, 50 Dongtai Road, tel: 5306 2033.
Duo Yun Xuan Art Studio, F1-2, 422 Nanjing Road, tel: 6360 6475.
Shanxi Old Ware Store, 324 Changle Road, tel: 6318 4620.
Cang Bao Building, 459 Fangbang Road. Open daily 5am–5pm.
Hua Bao Building, 265 Fangbang Road. Open daily 9am–7pm.

Books

Because of government controls, foreign publications are generally available only through state distributors: Foreign Languages Bookstore, Book City, Shanghai Book Traders and some hotel outlets.
Foreign Languages Bookstore, 390 Fuzhou Road, tel: 6322 3200. The city's best selection of English language books, from best-sellers to business, fiction, travel guides, cookbooks, classics, children's books and a small selection of magazines.
Shanghai Book City, 465 Fuzhou Road, tel: 6352 2222. Its small English-language section is on the 6th floor.

Markets and Bazaars

Yu Garden Bazaar, with its maze of speciality arts and crafts and souvenir shops (bordered by Anren Street, Fuyou Road, Jiujiaotang Road and Fangbang Road) is a must-do on every tourist's itinerary. For other interesting shopping options, head for the open-air markets that specialise in a single theme.

- **Xiangyang Fashion Market**. Central Huaihai Road (at Xiangyang Road). Daily 10am–7pm. This market offers an immense selection of knock-off and genuine designer branded clothes, accessories and outerwear, along with home décor and gift items, in a crazy bazaar-like atmosphere.
- **Dongjiadu Fabric Market**. Dongjiadu Road (at Zhongshan Road). Daily 9am–5pm. All types of fabric, including traditional Chinese silk, Thai silk, cotton, upholstery fabrics etc. Bargaining hard is de rigeur. Many stalls have tailors on hand at very reasonable prices.
- **Dongtai Antiques Market**. Dongtai Road (at Liuhekou Road). Daily 9am–5pm. As Shanghai's largest antiques market, the outdoor stalls and shops carry an array of antiques – some fake, some real – from the Qing Dynasty to the Cultural Revolution, with plenty of treasures from Shanghai's Concession era as well.

Confucius Temple Book Market, Wenmiao Road (at Zhonghua Road, in the temple courtyard). Quite a few foreign language books are scattered amongst the used and vintage books at this market. Open Sunday mornings only.
Shanghai Foreign Languages Used Bookshop, 89 Shang Ze Road (at Ruijin Road). Used magazines as well as an interesting selection of foreign language books, some of it quite rare.
Shanghai Book Traders Bookstore, 50 Hongqiao Road, tel: 6487 3787. Also at airports and hotels.

Home Accessories

Chine Concept, 74 Wu Yuan Road, tel: 5404 1216. Hemp cushions, incense, scented oils, vases and silk tablecloths from all over the region sold in an elegant courtyard home.
Simply Life, 1-2 and 5 Xintiandi, 123 Xingye Road, tel: 6387 5100 (flagship store). Also branches at 9 Dongping Road (at Huashan Road), tel: 3406 0509; One Xintiandi, 181 Taicang Road (at Madang Road), tel: 3307 0178; and in Maison Mode, 1312 Central Huaihai Road (at Changshu Road), tel: 6431 0100, ext. 022. Contemporary designs with an Asian touch for tableware, ceramics, linens and glassware.
Shanghai Trio, 181 Taicang Road (at Madang Road), tel: 6466 6884. Innovative Chinese-inspired designs for linens, shawls, trendy gifts and souvenirs. Open daily 10am–7pm.

Fabrics

Golden Dragon Cloth Shop, 858 Central Huaihai Road, tel: 5404 0159. Silk brocades, blue calico, linens and other fabrics.
Fabric Depot, 1269 Wuzhong Road, tel: 6405 6890. Four floors of top-of-the-line upholstery and curtain fabric at wholesale prices. Tailors can make up curtains, cushions, sofa covers, etc.
Lan-lan Chinese Hand-painted Silk Nankeen, Building 24, Lane 637 Changle Road (at Changshu Road), tel: 4717 9471.
Shanghai Blue Printed Cloth Monopoly, 384 Changle Road (at Maoming Road), tel: 6256 3686.
Silk King (Zhen Si Shang Sha). This state-owned chain of silk stores has a wide selection of silks and provides a tailoring service as well. Various locations around town: 139 Tianping Road, tel: 6282 1533; 66 Nanjing Road (E), tel: 6321 2193; 819 Nanjing Road (W), tel: 6215 3114; 550 Central Huaihai Road, tel: 6327 5566 ext. 6103; and 1371 Sichuan Road (N), tel: 6324 0790.

Jewellery

PEARLS

Inexpensive pearls are available at the shops in Yu Garden and Bazaar, but for more sophisticated designs and better quality, visit the shops below:
Pearls by Amy, 1445 Gubei Road, tel: 6275 3954; and 110 No. 1F CIMIC Tower, 1090 Century Boulevard, Pudong; www.amy-pearl.com
Fang Hua Pearls and Jewellery, Suite 111, West Retail Plaza, Shanghai Centre, 1376 Nanjing Road (W), tel 6279 8958.
Angel Pearls & Gems, Suite 605, Shanghai Centre, 1376 Nanjing Road (W), tel: 6279 8287.

GOLD JEWELLERY

Spanish Gift Present Company, 1207 Nanjing Road (W), tel: 6279 1030.
Lao Feng Xian, 432 Nanjing Road (E), tel: 6356 8036.
Jinya Gold and Jewellery Shop, 1006 Central Huaihai Road, tel: 6467 2712.

SILVER AND TIBETAN

Passepartout, 106 Changshu Road, tel: 6248 3889.
Made in Heaven, Building 1, Lane 116 Changshu Road, tel: 6249 5882.
Arabian Nights, 110 Changshu Road, tel: 6248 1487.
Nirvana, Shanghai Old Street, 445 Central Fangbang Road, tel: 6278 916 or (136) 0183 1496.

Arts & Crafts

Arts and Crafts Museum, 79 Fenyang Road, tel: 6437 2509.
Shanghai Jingdezhen Porcelain Artware Shop, 1175 Nanjing Road (W), tel: 6437 2509.
Friendship Store, 6 Zunyi Road (S), Hongqiao, tel: 6270 0000; and 40 Beijing Road (E), tel: 5308 0600.
For Art Galleries, see page 303.

Children

General

China's one-child policy has created a generation of parents eager to offer their "Little Emperors" plenty of diversions. So in addition to being a child-friendly place, Shanghai also offers a host of entertainment for kids.

Shanghai Acrobats, Shanghai Centre Theatre, 1376 Nanjing Road (W), tel: 6279 8663, 6279 7132. The Shanghai Acrobatic troupe holds regular performances here; 7.30–9pm daily.

Shanghai Circus World, 2266 Gong He Xin Road (at Da Ning Road), tel: 5665 3646, 6652 7750. Performances Sat–Sun 7.30–9pm, call for other performance times.

Shanghai Zoo, 2382 Hongqiao Road, tel: 6268 7775. Daily 7.30am–5pm. It's not the perfect zoo, but Shanghai Zoo is one of China's better zoos and its sprawling grounds allow kids to run off steam. Kids especially enjoy feeding the pigeons, ducks and giraffes; watching the pandas go down their slide; and the seal show. There are also bumper cars, an incredibly spooky ghost train, a giant ferris wheel, and a Little Tykes indoor playground.

Indoor Play, 780 Changning Road (in Zhongshan Park), tel: 6210 7388. Fun Dazzle, an indoor playground with ball pits, tunnels and slides is a great place for a rainy day.

Shanghai Wild Animal Park, Nanhui County, Pudong. As the name suggests, this is Shanghai's own safari, with walk-through and drive-through areas. Daily 8am–5pm.

Great World (Da Shi Jie), 1 Tibet Road (S) (by Yan'an Road E), tel: 6326 3760 ext. 40 or 57, or tel: 6374 6703. Decadent old Shanghai gambled and partied here, but it's a great place for kids in new Shanghai. Old-fashioned Fun House mirrors welcome you at the entrance; there are acrobat shows all day long in the open-air atrium; video games; a ghost train; and an indoor play space on the top floor. Day shows 9am–9.30pm. Night shows 7.30–9.30pm.

Amusement Parks

Dino Water Park, Ming Heng District, 78 Xinzhen Road, tel: 6478 3333. Large wave pool, slides and rafting maze, but it does get very crowded in the summer. Daily 9am–9pm during summer.

Jinjiang Amusement Park, 201 Hongmei Road, tel: 8436 4956, 8468 0844. Classic amusement park, with bumper cars, rides, haunted house, roller coasters, log rides, carousels and a great Pirates of the Caribbean-type ride. Daily 8.30am–5pm.

Traffic Park, 101 Zunyi Road (by the Westin Hotel), tel: 6259 9446. Kids drive electric cars and bikes around the streets of a miniature Shanghai, complete with mini-Oriental Pearl Tower. Daily 6am–5.30pm.

Aquariums

Aquaria 21, Gate 4, Changfeng Park, 451 Dadu He Road (by Jinsha Jiang Road), tel: 5281 8888 ext. 6838. Beautiful aquarium, each area themed, plus a great shark tunnel. Also access to scuba equipment and facilities. Daily 9am–5pm.

Shanghai Ocean Aquarium, 158 Yincheng Road (N) (next to the Oriental Pearl Tower), tel: 5877 9988. Shanghai's state of the art aquarium, opened in 2002, with 8 zones and 28 themed areas, including the world's longest shark tunnel. Open daily 9am–9pm.

Parks and Gardens

Most parks have great playgrounds, with trampolines, slides and sometimes paddle boats and rides.

Fuxing Park, Fuxing Road at Chongqing Road, tel: 6372 0662. Playground, remote-control boats, roller coaster, carousel, bumper cars. Open daily 6am–6pm.

Gongqing Forest Park, Yangpu District, 2000 Jungong Road, tel: 6574 0586. Lots of flowers and trees, BBQ area, fishing, horseback riding, boating. Open daily 6am–5pm.

Jing An Park, 1649 Nanjing Road (W), tel: 6248 3238. Children's playground and amusement area.

Lu Xun Park, 146 Dongjiang Wan Road, tel: 6540 0009. Big entertainment section for children.

Shanghai Botanical Garden Park, 1111 Longwu Road, south of Longhua Road, tel: 6451 3369. Paddle boats for rent on their duck-shaped lake. Picnic BBQ area. Open daily 7am–5pm.

Xiangyang Park, 1008 Central Huaihai Road (at Xiangyang Road, across from Xiangyang Market), tel: 5404 2208. Playground with battery-operated cars, rides, and trampolines. Open daily 6am–6pm.

Zhongshan Park, 780 Changning Road (at end of Dingxi Road), tel: 6226 4149. Recently re-landscaped, this is more than just a park: boating on the lake, kite-flying, bird and fish worlds, and the indoor Fun Dazzle play area. Open daily 6am–6pm.

Museums

Shanghai Science & Technology Museum, 2000 Century Boulevard, tel: 6862 2000. IMAX theatres, children's interactive museum with science and technology exhibits, indoor rainforest. Tues–Sun 9am–5pm.

Shanghai Natural Wild Insect Kingdom, 1 Fenghe Road, Lujiazui, Pudong, tel: 5840 5921. Live insects in terrariums, and an animal show every 30 minutes during school and public holidays with bugs and other creepy crawlies (trainers take the creatures around for kids to touch). Kids can go fishing in the indoor pond and take home what they catch. Daily 9am–9pm.

Language

Mandarin

People in China (including Shanghai) speak *putonghua*, or common language, known in the West as Mandarin. *Putonghua* is promoted as the standard language across the country, though most Chinese people also speak a local dialect. Many Shanghainese for instance prefer speaking their own dialect, *Shanghai hua (see box below)*.

Shanghai Dialect

Most Shanghainese prefer speaking their own dialect, *Shanghai hua*, and it may be the only language of older Shanghainese. A lilting dialect that sounds almost Japanese, Shanghainese is unintelligible to Mandarin speakers and to speakers of most other dialects. It is derived from the Wu region south of the Yangzi river.

Romanised Chinese

Since 1958, the *hanyu pinyin* system has been used to represent Chinese characters phonetically in the Latin alphabet. *Pinyin* has become internationally accepted, so that Peking today is written as Beijing and Mao Tsetung as Mao Zedong.

Although the street signage in Shanghai was recently changed to English, it is still helpful to learn the basic rules of the *pinyin* system. When asking for a place or street name, you need to know how it is pronounced, otherwise you won't be understood.

Most modern dictionaries use the *pinyin* system. This transcription may at first appear confusing if one doesn't see the words as they are pronounced. The city of Qingdao, for example, is pronounced *chingdow*.

Chinese characters

Written Chinese uses thousands of characters, many of which are based on ancient pictograms, or picture-like symbols. Some characters used today go back more than 3,000 years. There are strict rules in the method of writing, as the stroke order affects the overall appearance of the characters. Some 6,000–8,000 characters are in regular use; 3,000 characters are sufficient for reading a newspaper.

Mainland China has reformed written Chinese several times since 1949, and simplified characters are now used. In Hong Kong and Taiwan, the old characters remain standard.

Tones

It is sometimes said that Chinese is a monosyllabic language. At first sight, this seems to be true, since each character represents a single syllable that generally indicates a specific concept. However, in modern Chinese, most words are made up of two or three syllables, sometimes more. In the Western sense, spoken Chinese has only 420 single-syllable root words, but tones are used to differentiate these basic sounds.

Tones make it difficult for foreigners to learn Chinese, since different tones give the same syllable a completely different meaning. For instance, *mai* with a falling fourth tone (*mài*) means to sell; if it is pronounced with a falling-rising third tone (*mǎi*), it means to buy. If you pay attention to these tones, you can soon tell the difference, though correct pronunciation requires much practice. Taking another example, the four tones of the syllable ma: first tone, *mā* means mother; second tone, *má* means hemp; third tone, *mǎ* means horse; and fourth tone *mà* means to complain.

The first tone is pitched high and even, the second rising, the third falling and then rising, and the fourth falling. There is also a fifth, "neutral" tone.

There are a standard set of diacritical marks to indicate which of the four tones is used:
mā = high and even tone
má = rising tone
mǎ = falling then rising tone
mà = falling tone

Pronunciation

The pronunciation of the consonants is similar to those in English: b, p, d, t, g, k are all voiceless; p, t, k are aspirated; b, d, g are not aspirated. The i after the consonants ch, c, r, sh, s, z, zh is not pronounced; it indicates that the preceding sound is lengthened.

Pinyin/Phonetic/Sound
a/a/f**a**r
an /un/r**un**
ang/ung /l**ung**
ao/ou/l**oud**
b/b/**b**ath
c/ts/ra**ts**
ch/ch/**ch**ange
d/d/**d**ay
e/er/d**ir**t
e (after i,u,y)/a/tr**a**m
ei/ay/m**ay**
en/en/wh**en**
eng/eong/**ng** has a nasal sound
er/or/h**o**nour
f/f/**f**ast
g/g/**g**o
h/ch/lo**ch**
i/ee/k**ee**n
j/j/**j**eep
k/k/ca**k**e
l/l/**l**ittle
m/m/**m**onth
n/n/**n**ame
o/o/b**o**nd
p/p/tra**pp**ed
q/ch/**ch**eer
r/r/**r**ight
s/s/me**ss**
sh/sh/**sh**ade
t/t/**t**on
u/oo/sh**oo**t
u (after j,q,x,y)/as German
u+/mu+**de**
w/w/**w**ater
x/sh/as in **sh**eep
y/y/**y**ogi
z/ds/re**ds**
zh/dj/**j**ungle

GREETINGS

English	Pinyin	Chinese
Hello	Nǐ hǎo	你好
How are you?	Nǐ hǎo ma?	你好吗?
Thank you	Xièxie	谢谢
Goodbye	Zài jiàn	再见
My name is...	Wǒ jiào...	我叫...
My last name is...	Wǒ xìng...	我姓...
What is your name?	Nín jiào shénme míngzi?	您叫什么名字?
What is your last name?	Nín guìxìng?	您贵姓?
I am very happy...	Wǒ hěn gāoxìng...	我很高兴...
All right	Hǎo	好
Not all right	Bù hǎo	不好
Can you speak English?	Nín huì shuō Yīngyǔ ma?	您会说英语吗?
Can you speak Chinese?	Nín huì shuō Hànyǔ ma?	您会说汉语吗?
I cannot speak Chinese	Wǒ bù huì Hànyǔ	我不会汉语
I do not understand	Wǒ bù dǒng	我不懂
Do you understand?	Nín dǒng ma?	您懂吗?
Please speak a little slower	Qǐng nín shuō màn yìdiǎn	请您说慢一点儿
What is this called?	Zhège jiào shénme?	这个叫什么?
How do you say...	Zěnme shuō?	...怎么说?
Please	Qǐng	请/谢谢
Never mind	Méi guānxì	没关系
Sorry	Duìbùqǐ	对不起

PRONOUNS

English	Pinyin	Chinese
Who/who is it?	Shéi?	谁?
My/mine	Wǒ/wǒde	我/我的
You/yours (singular)	Nǐ/nǐde	你/你的
He/his	Tā/tāde	他/他的
She/hers	Tā/tāde	她/她的
We/ours	Wǒmen/wǒmende	我们/我们的
You/yours (plural)	Nǐmen/nǐmende	你们/你们的
They/theirs	Tāmen/tāmende	他们/他们的
You/yours (respectful)	Nín/nínde	您/您的

TRAVEL

English	Pinyin	Chinese
Where is it?	zài nǎr?	...在哪儿?
Do you have it here?	Zhèr... yǒu ma?	这儿有... 吗?
No/it's not here/there aren't any	Méi yǒu	没有
Hotel	Fàndiàn/bīnguǎn	饭店/宾馆
Restaurant	Fànguǎn	饭馆
Bank	Yínháng	银行
Post Office	Yóujú	邮局
Toilet	Cèsuǒ	厕所
Railway station	Huǒchē zhàn	火车站
Bus station	Qìchē zhàn	汽车站
Embassy	Dàshíguǎn	大使馆
Consulate	Lǐngshìguǎn	领事馆
Passport	Hùzhào	护照
Visa	Qiānzhèng	签证
Pharmacy	Yàodiàn	药店
Hospital	Yīyuàn	医院
Doctor	Dàifu/yīshēng	大夫/医生
Translate	Fānyì	翻译
Bar	Jiǔbā	酒吧
Do you have...?	Nín yǒu... ma?	您有... 吗?
I want/I would like	Wǒ yào/wǒ xiǎng yào	我要/我想要
I want to buy...	Wǒ xiǎng mǎi...	我想买...
Where can I buy it?	Nǎr néng mǎi... ma?	哪儿能买吗?

This/that	Zhège/nèige	这个/那个
Green tea/black tea	Lúchá/hóngchá	绿茶/红茶
Coffee	Kāfēi	咖啡
Cigarette	Xiāngyān	香烟
Film (for camera)	Jiāojuǎn	胶卷儿
Ticket	Piào	票
Postcard	Míngxìnpiàn	明信片
Letter	Yì fēng xìn	一封信
Air mail	Hángkōng xìn	航空信
Postage stamp	Yóupiào	邮票

SHOPPING

How much?	Duōshǎo?	多少
How much does it cost?	Zhège duōshǎo qián?	这个多少钱?
Too expensive, thank you	Tài guì le, xièxie	太贵了，谢谢
Very expensive	Hěn guì	很贵
A little (bit)	Yìdiǎn	一点儿
Too much/too many	Tài duō le	太多了
A lot	Duō	多
Few	Shǎo	少

MONEY MATTERS, HOTELS, TRANSPORT, COMMUNICATIONS

Money	Qián	钱
Chinese currency	Rénmínbì	人民币
One yuan/one kuai (10 jiao)	Yì yuán/yì kuài	一元/一块
One jiao/one mao (10 fen)	Yì jiāo/yì máo	一角/一毛
One fen	Yì fēn	一分
Traveller's cheque	Lǚxíng zhīpiào	旅行支票
Credit card	Xìnyòngkǎ	信用卡
Foreign currency	Wàihuìquàn	外汇券
Where can I change money?	Zài nǎr kěyǐ huàn qián?	在哪儿可以换钱?
I want to change money	Wǒ xiǎng huàn qián	我想换钱
What is the exchange rate?	Bǐjià shì duōshǎo?	比价是多少?
We want to stay for one (two/three) nights	Wǒmen xiǎng zhù yì (liǎng/sān) tiān	我们想住一(两，三)天
How much is the room per day?	Fángjiān duōshǎo qián yì tiān?	房间多少钱一天?
Room number	Fángjiān hàomǎ	房间号码
Single room	Dānrén fángjiān	单人房间
Double room	Shuāngrén fángjiān	双人房间
Reception	Qiāntai/fúwùtai	前台/服务台
Key	Yàoshi	钥匙
Clothes	Yīfu	衣服
Luggage	Xíngli	行李
Airport	Fēijīchǎng	飞机场
Bus	Gōnggòng qìchē	公共汽车
Taxi	Chūzū qìchē	出租汽车
Bicycle	Zìxíngchē	自行车
Telephone	Diànhuà	电话
Long-distance call	Chángtú diànhuà	长途电话
International call	Guójì diànhuà	国际电话
Telephone number	Diànhuà hàomǎ	电话号码
Telegram	Diànbào	电报
Computer	Diàn nǎo/jìsuànjī	电脑/计算机
Check e-mail	Chá diànxìn	查电信
Use the internet	Shàng wǎng	上网

TIME

When?	Shénme shíhou?	什么时候?
What time is it now?	Xiànzài jídiǎn zhōng?	现在几点种?
How long?	Duōcháng shíjiān?	多长时间?

One/two/three o'clock	Yì diǎn/liǎng diǎn/sān diǎn zhōng	一点/两点/三点种
Early morning/morning	Zǎoshang/shàngwǔ	早上/上午
Midday/afternoon/evening	Zhōngwǔ/xiàwǔ/wǎnshang	中午/下午/晚上
Monday	Xīngqīyī	星期一
Tuesday	Xīngqīèr	星期二
Wednesday	Xīngqīsān	星期三
Thursday	Xīngqīsì	星期四
Friday	Xīngqīwǔ	星期五
Saturday	Xīngqīliù	星期六
Sunday	Xīngqītiān/xīngqīrì	星期天/星期日
Weekend	Zhōumò	周末
Yesterday/today/tomorrow	Zuótiān/jīntiān/míngtiān	昨天/今天/明天
This week/last week/ next week	Zhègexīngqī/shàngxīngqī/ xiàxīngqī	这个星期/上星期/ 下星期
Hour/day/week/month	Xiǎoshí/tiān/xīngqī/yuè	小时/天/星期/月
January/February/March	Yīyuè/èryuè/sānyuè	一月/二月/三月
April/May/June	Sìyuè/wǔyuè/liùyuè	四月/五月/六月
July/August/September	Qīyuè/bāyuè/jiǔyuè	七月/八月/九月
October/November/December	Shíyuè/shíyīyuè/shíèryuè	十月/十一月/十二月

EATING OUT

Restaurant	Cāntīng/fànguǎn	餐厅/饭馆儿
Attendant/waiter	Fúwùyuán	服务员
Waitress	Xiǎojiě	小姐
Eat	Chī fàn	吃饭
Breakfast	Zǎofàn	早饭
Lunch	Wǔfàn	午饭
Dinner	Wǎnfàn	晚饭
Menu	Càidān	菜单
Chopsticks	Kuàizi	筷子
Knife	Dāozi	刀子
Fork	Chāzi	叉子
Spoon	Sháozi	勺子
Cup/glass	Bēizi/bōlíbēi	杯子/玻璃杯
Bowl	Wǎn	碗
Plate	Pán	盘
Paper napkin	Cānjīn zhǐ	餐巾纸
I want...	Wǒ yào...	我要
I do not want...	Wǒ bú yào...	我不要
I did not order this	Zhège wǒ méi diǎn	这个我没点
I am a vegetarian	Wǒ shì chī sù de rén	我是吃素的人
I do not eat any meat	Wǒ suǒyǒude ròu dōu bù chī	我所有的肉都不
I do not eat any meat or fish	Wǒ suǒyǒude ròu hé yú, dōu bù chī	我所有的肉和鱼都不吃
Please fry it in vegetable oil	Qīng yòng zhíwù yóu chǎo chǎo	请用植物油炒炒吃
Beer	Píjiǔ	啤酒
Red/white wine	Hóng/bái pútaojiǔ	红/白葡萄酒
Liquor	Bái jiǔ	白酒
Mineral water	Kuàngquánshuǐ	矿泉水
Soft drinks	Yǐnliào	饮料
Cola	Kělè	可乐
Tea	Cháshuǐ	茶水
Fruit	Shuǐguǒ	水果
Bread	Miànbāo	面包
Toast	Kǎomiànbāo	烤面包
Yoghurt	Suān nǎi	酸奶
Fried/boiled egg	Chǎo/zhǔ jīdàn	炒/煮鸡蛋
Rice	Mǐfàn	米饭
Soup	Tāng	汤
Stir-fried dishes	Chǎo cài	炒菜

Beef/pork/lamb/chicken	Niú/zhū/yáng/jī ròu	牛肉/猪肉/羊肉/鸡肉
Fish	Yú	鱼
Vegetables	Shūcài	蔬菜
Spicy/sweet/sour/salty	Là/tián/suān/xián	辣/甜/酸/咸
Hot/cold	Rè/liáng	热/凉
Can we have the bill, please	Qǐng jié zhàng/mǎidān	请结帐/买单

Specialities

Peking Duck	Běijīng kǎoyā	北京烤鸭
Hotpot	Huǒ guō	火锅
Phoenix in the Nest	Fèng zài wōlǐ	凤在窝里
Mandarin fish	Tángcù guìyú	糖醋鳜鱼
Thousand layer cake	Qiān céng bǐng	千层饼
Lotus prawns	Ôu piànn'r xiārén	藕片儿虾仁
Homestyle cooking	Jiā cháng cài	家常菜

Appetizers

Deep-fried peanuts	Zhá huāshēngmǐ	炸花生米
Boiled peanuts	Zhǔ huāshēngmǐ	煮花生米
Soft beancurd	Bàn dòufu	拌豆腐
"Hairy" green beans	Máo dòu	毛豆
Mashed cucumber	Pái huāngguā	排黄瓜
Pressed beancurd strips	Dòufu sī	豆腐丝
Thousand Year-Old Eggs	Sōnghuā dàn	松花蛋
Smoked beancurd with celery	Qíncài dòufu gān'r	芹菜豆腐干儿

Meat dishes

Aubergine/eggplant fritters stuffed with minced pork	Qié hé	茄盒
Spicy chicken with chillies	Làzi jīdīng	辣子鸡丁
Spicy chicken with peanuts	Gōngbào jīdīng	宫爆鸡丁
Pork with egg and "tree ear" fungus	Mùxū ròu	木须肉
Shredded pork with bamboo shoots	Dōngsǔn ròusī	冬笋肉丝
Beef in brown sauce	Hóngshāo niúròu	红烧牛肉
Sizzling "iron plate" beef	Tiěbǎn niúròu	铁板牛肉
Beef with potatoes	Tǔdòu niúròu	土豆牛肉

Seafood

Prawns with cashew nuts	Yāoguǒ xiārén	腰果虾仁
Carp in brown sauce	Hóngshāo lǐyú	红烧鲤鱼
Boiled prawns	Shuǐzhǔ xiārén	水煮虾仁
Stir-fried prawns	Qīngchǎo xiārén	清炒虾仁
Sweet and sour mandarin fish	Tángcù guìyú	糖醋鳜鱼
Hot and sour squid	Suānlà yóuyú juàn	酸辣鱿鱼卷

Vegetable dishes

Sweetcorn with pine kernels	Sōngrén yùmǐ	松仁玉米
Mange tout/snowpeas	Hélán dòu	荷兰豆
Spicy "dry" green beans	Gānbiān biǎndòu	干煸扁豆
Spicy "fish flavour" aubergine	Yúxiāng qiézi	鱼香茄子
Greens with dried mushrooms	Xiānggū yóucài	香菇油菜
Spicy beancurd with chilli	Málà dòufu	麻辣豆腐
Stir-fried egg and tomato	Xīhóngshì chǎo jīdàn	西红柿炒鸡蛋
Fried shredded potato	Tǔdòu sī	土豆丝
Clay pot with beancurd soup	Shāguō dòufu	沙锅豆腐
Sour cabbage with "glass" noodles	Suāncài fěnsī	酸菜粉丝
Potato, aubergine and green pepper	Dì sān xiān	地三鲜

Staple food

Steamed bread	Mántou	馒头
Cornbread	Wōtou	窝头
Fried rice	Dàn chǎo fàn	蛋炒饭
Plain rice	Bái fàn	白饭
Sizzling rice crust	Guōbā	锅巴
Noodles	Miàntiáo	面条
Pancakes	Bǐng	饼

Soups

Hot and sour soup	Suānlà tāng	酸辣汤
Egg and tomato soup	Xīhóngshì jīdàn tāng	西红柿鸡蛋汤
Beancurd soup	Dòufu tāng	豆腐汤
Lamb and marrow soup	Yángròu dōngguā tāng	羊肉冬瓜汤
Fish-head soup	Yútóu tāng	鱼头汤

Fast food

Noodles	Miàntiáo	面条
Stuffed pasta parcels	Jiǎozi	饺子
with meat/vegetable filling	ròu xiàn/sù xiàn	肉馅/素馅
Steamed meat buns	Bāozi	包子
"Pot stickers" (fried jiaozi)	Guōtiē	锅贴
Egg pancake	Jiān bǐng	煎饼
Wonton soup	Húndùn	混沌
Soy milk	Dòu jiāng	豆浆
Deep-fried dough sticks	Yóutiáo	油条

NUMBERS

One	Yī	一
Two	Èr	二
Three	Sān	三
Four	Sì	四
Five	Wǔ	五
Six	Liù	六
Seven	Qī	七
Eight	Bā	八
Nine	Jiǔ	九
Ten	Shí	十
Eleven	Shíyī	十一
Twelve	Shíèr	十二
Twenty	Èrshí	二十
Thirty	Sānshí	三十
Forty	Sìshí	四十
Fifty	Wǔshí	五十
Sixty	Liùshí	六十
Seventy	Qīshí	七十
Eighty	Bāshí	八十
Ninety	Jiǔshí	九十
One hundred	Yībǎi	一百
One hundred and one	Yībǎi língyī	一百零一
Two hundred	Liǎng bǎi	两百
Three hundred	Sān bǎi	三百
Four hundred	Sì bǎi	四百
Five hundred	Wǔ bǎi	五百
One thousand	Yīqiān	一千

The Bund

外滩

Meteorological Signal Tower	气象信号塔
M on the Bund	米氏西餐厅
Shanghai Pudong Development Bank	上海浦东发展银行
Customs House	海关大楼
American International Assurance Building	友邦大楼
Peace Palace Hotel	和平饭店南楼
Peace Hotel	和平饭店北楼
Bank of China	中国银行大楼
Shanghai Foreign Trade Building	外贸大楼
Huangpu Park	黄埔公园
Monument to the People's Heroes	人民英雄纪念碑
Bund History Museum	外滩历史博物馆
Nanjing Road (E)	南京东路
No. 1 Department Store	上海第一百货商店
Red Temple	红庙
Yong An Road Market	永安路市场
St Joseph's Church	天主教若瑟堂
Shanghai Museum of Natural History	上海自然博物馆

People's Square

人民广场

Shanghai Art Museum	上海美术馆
Old Shanghai Art Museum	上海美术馆老馆
Tomorrow Square	明日广场
Shanghai Grand Theatre	上海大剧院
Shanghai Museum	上海博物馆
Shanghai Urban Planning Centre	上海城市规划展示馆
Mu'en Church	沐恩堂
Yifu Theatre	逸夫舞台
Great World	大世界
Park Hotel	国际饭店

Nanshi

南市

Yu Garden Bazaar	豫园小商品市场
Yu Garden	豫园
Mid-Lake Pavilion Teahouse	湖心亭茶楼
Cang Bao Building	藏宝楼
Shanghai Old Street	上海老街
Peach Orchard Mosque	小桃园清真寺
Confucius Temple	孔庙
Dongtai Road Antiques Market	东台路古玩市场
Shanghai Wan Shang Flower and Bird Market	上海万商花鸟市场
Dajing Tower	大镜塔
Dongjiadu Cathedral	董家渡天主堂
Dongjiadu Fabric Market	董家渡布料批发市场
Museum of Folk Art	上海民间收藏陈列馆

Fuxing Park

复兴公园

Site of the First National Congress of the Communist Party of China	中国"一大"会址
Xintiandi	新天地
Ashanti Dome	阿香蒂餐厅
Sun Yat-sen's Former Residence	孙中山故居
Zhou Enlai's Former Residence	周恩来故居
Ruijin Guesthouse	瑞金宾馆
Maoming Road (S)	茂名南路

Jingwen Flower Market	精文花市
Central Huaihai Road	淮海中路
Xiangyang Fashion Market	襄阳路服饰市场
Okura Garden Hotel	花园饭店
Old Jinjiang Complex	老锦江饭店
Shanghai Arts and Crafts Museum	上海工艺美术博物馆
Taiyuan Villa	太原别墅
Taikang Road	泰康路
Shanghai Public Security Museum	上海公安博物馆

Huaihai and Hengshan 淮海路和衡山路

French Consul-General's Residence	法国总领事官邸
US Consulate-General	美国领事馆
Shanghai Library	上海图书馆
Soong Ching Ling's Former Residence	宋庆龄故居
Jiao Tong University	交通大学
C.Y. Tung Maritime Museum	海军上海博物馆
Xujiahui Park	徐家汇公园
La Villa Rouge	小红楼
Community Church	国际礼拜堂
Shanghai Conservatory of Music Middle School	上海音乐学院附中

Jing An 静安

Moller Villa	马勒别墅
Ohel Rachel Synagogue	拉西尔会堂
Meilongzhen	梅龙镇
Shanghai Exhibition Centre	上海展览中心
Shanghai Centre	上海商城
Jing An Park	静安公园
Jing An Temple	静安寺
Municipal Children's Palace	上海市少年宫
Julu Road	巨鹿路
Chinese Printed Blue Nankeen Exhibition Hall	中国蓝印花布馆

Changning 长宁

Xingguo Guesthouse	兴国宾馆
No. 3 Middle School for Girls	上海市第三女子中学
Hua Xia Sex Culture Museum	华夏文化博物馆
Changning District Revolutionary Historical Relic Exhibition Hall and Editorial Offices of the Bolshevik	长宁区革命历史文物陈列馆
Changning District Children's Palace	长宁区少年宫
Zhongshan Park	中山公园
East China Institute of Politics and Law	华东政法学院
Changfeng Park	长风公园
Aquaria 21	大洋海底世界
Jingdezhen Ceramics Art Centre	景德镇瓷器上海艺术中心

Hongqiao & Gubei 虹桥和古北

Soong Ching Ling Mausoleum	宋庆龄陵园
Friendship Shopping Centre	友谊商店
Carrefour	家乐福
Gubei Flower and Bird Market	古北花鸟市场
Wuzhong Road	吴中路
Hongqiao State Guesthouse	虹桥迎宾馆
Xijiao Guesthouse	西郊宾馆

Shanghai Zoo	上海动物园
Cypress Hotel	龙柏宾馆

Xujiahui & Longhua

徐家汇和龙华

Xujiahui Cathedral	徐家汇天主堂
Statue of Paul Xu	徐光启像
Shanghai Stadium	上海体育场
Longhua Pagoda	龙华塔
Longhua Temple	龙华寺
Longhua Cemetery of Martyrs	龙华烈士陵园
Shanghai Botanical Gardens	上海植物园
Jinjiang Amusement Park	锦江游乐场
Dino Beach	热带风暴水上乐园

Hongkou & Zhabei

虹口和闸北

Waibaidu Bridge	外白渡桥
Russian Consulate	俄罗斯领事馆
Shanghai Post Office	上海邮政总局大楼
Gongping Forest Park	共青森林公园
Ohel Moishe Synagogue	摩西会堂
Duolun Road Cultural Celebrities Street	多伦路文化街
League of Left Wing Writers Museum	左翼作家联盟博物馆
Lu Xun's Former Residence	鲁迅故居
Lu Xun Park	鲁迅公园
Tomb of Lu Xun	鲁迅墓
Hongkou Football Ground	虹口足球场
Suhe Art Galleries	苏州河艺术画廊
Jade Buddha Temple	玉佛寺

Pudong

浦东

Bund Tourist Tunnel	外滩人行观光隧道
Jin Mao Tower	金茂大厦
Lujiazui	陆家嘴
Lujiazui Development Showroom	陆家嘴发展陈列馆
Oriental Pearl Tower	东方明珠电视塔
Natural Wild Insect Kingdom	上海自然野生昆虫馆
Shanghai Stock Exchange Building	上海证券大厦
Science and Technology Museum	上海科技馆
Century Park	世纪公园
Shanghai Wild Animal Park	上海野生动物园
Pudong International Airport	浦东国际机场

Western Suburbs

西郊

Nanxiang	南翔
Jiading	嘉定
Sheshan	佘山
Songjiang	松江
Zhujiajiao	朱家角
Heritage Village for Arts and Culture	上海民族文化村
Grand View Garden	大观园
Zhouzhuang	周庄
Jinshan	金山

Further Reading

Pre-1949

A Short History of Shanghai by F. Hawks-Potts. Kelly & Walsh, 1928 (reprint) An indepth history of the Concessions and Settlements up to 1928 by a former headmaster of St John's, Shanghai's Harvard.

Gangsters in Paradise by Lynn Pan. Heinemann, 1985. Brilliant portrait of Shanghai's underworld in its heyday by one of Shanghai's foremost authors. Out of print in the West, available in Shanghai.

Shanghai Remembrance by Frank T. Leo. Noble House, 2000. Lovely memoir of an upper class Shanghai boy growing up during the 1930s and 40s, filled with rich details on wealthy Chinese of the period.

Shanghai by Harriet Sergeant. Trafalgar Square, 1998. One of the best social histories of old Shanghai.

China to Me by Emily Hahn. E-reads, 1999. An American expatriate's memoir of her nine years in China and Hong Kong.

The Soong Dynasty by Sterling Seagrave. HarperCollins, 1986. A well-researched, eminently readable book-that-reads-like-a-novel about Shanghai's First Family.

Shanghai 37 by Vicky Baum. Oxford University Press reprint, 1986. A novel that captures Shanghai in its heyday, quirks and all.

Bound Feet and Western Dress: A Memoir by Pang-mei Natasha Chang. Anchor Books, 1997. The biographical story of Pang's great-aunt, Yu-i, who bucked old Shanghai tradition by divorcing her husband and became the first president of Shanghai's Women's Bank.

Tracing it Home: Journeys around a Chinese Family by Lynn Pan. Secker & Warburg, London 1992. Pan's beautifully written auto-biographical story of connecting her Shanghai-born family's disparate threads; a keen insight into one of old Shanghai's great families.

Post-1949

Empire of the Sun, by JG Ballard. Buccaneer Books, 1997. The remarkable autobiographical story of a young boy growing up in the prison camps of Shanghai. Made into a movie of the same name by Steven Spielberg.

The Fall of Shanghai – The Communist Takeover in 1949 by Noel Barber. Macmillian, 1979. A journalist's keen-eyed view of the events and machinations leading up to the Communist victory of 1949.

Secret War in Shanghai by Bernard Wasserstein. Houghton-Mifflin, 1999. Brilliant account of Shanghai on the eve of World War II, with well-drawn portraits of all the players.

Life and Death in Shanghai by Nien Cheng. Penguin, 1988. Beautifully written account of a privileged woman's ordeal during the Cultural Revolution in Shanghai.

Red Azalea by Anchee Min. Berkeley Publishing Group, 1995. An honest account of growing up during the Cultural Revolution in Shanghai, chronicling the various injustices and torments through the eyes of a teenage girl. Winner of the Carl Sandburg Literary Award.

Jewish Shanghai

Ghetto Shanghai by Emily Pike Rubin. Shengold Publishers, 1993. A personal, autobiographical account of a young girl's experience in Shanghai's Jewish ghetto.

Strangers Always: A Jewish Family in Wartime Shanghai by Rena Krasno. Pacific View Press, 1992. The best of the autobiographical Jewish ghetto books, Krasno writes from the perspective of a Shanghailander – she was born in Shanghai – and with an eye for detail that brings the book alive.

Modern Shanghai

Shanghai: Rocky Rebirth of a Legendary City by Pamela Yatsko. John Wiley & Sons, 2000. The first book to chronicle modern Shanghai's rise, by a former Far Eastern Economic Review correspondent.

Riding the Iron Rooster by Paul Theroux. Ivy Books, 1990. First published in the 1980s, the book is rather charmingly dated, with its talk of "FECs" and Friendship Stores, but Theroux is a first-class travel writer and brings to life the China of 20 years ago, showing how very different everything was.

Riding the Dragon by Kathleen Lau. Shanghai Book Traders, 2003. A guide for expatriates moving to Shanghai by the founder of That's magazines. A treasure trove of information and good advice on how to deal with modern Shanghai, plus plenty of insider's tips.

Shanghai Baby by Wei Hui. Pocket Books, 2001. Banned in China for its mild sexuality, Shanghai Baby is not particularly well-written, but its value lies in its insights into the minds and lives of Shanghai's cutting-edge younger generation.

Architecture

A Last Look: Western Architecture in Old Shanghai by Tess Johnston and Deke Erh. Old China Hand Press, 2003. Shanghai historian Johnston and photographer Erh team up to capture Shanghai's legacy of Western architecture in photographs and with Johnston's delicious details of old Shanghai life.

Frenchtown by Tess Johnston and Deke Erh, Old China Hand Press, 2000. Their best book to date captures the essence of the French Concession, with evocative photographs, old memorabilia, and profiles of key places and figures.

Food

That's Shanghai Restaurant Guide. China Intercontinental Press, 2003. Comprehensive listing of Shanghai's restaurants – Chinese, Western and everything else.

Shanghai's 50 Best International Restaurants by Tina Kanagaratnam. Shanghai Book Traders, 2002. Reviews of the 50 best non-Chinese restaurants in the city.

ART & PHOTO CREDITS

Every effort has been made to trace copyright holders, and we apologise in advance for any unintentional omissions.

AKG Photo 18, 24, 28
Bettmann/Corbis 35
Bill Wassman 4R, 90, 126, 131M, 133, 138M, 156, 156M, 176, 202, 245R, 245M, 250, 253L
Bill Wassman/APA front flap bottom, back flap bottom, back cover centre top, back cover centre bottom, spine, 1, 5, 93, 96, 112, 113, 129M, 130, 132R, 132M, 134R, 136M, 143, 152M, 153, 159, 160M, 162, 163M, 167, 181R, 193, 194L, 199, 201M, 202M, 203, 207M, 210M, 212, 215, 217M, 227, 228, 229, 247M, 256M, 257R
Blaine Harrington 134L, 135, 136, 151R, 170, 182M
Bob Krist 6/7
Chris Stowers 129, 169, 216R
David Henley/CPA 3, 4L, 33, 41, 79, 111, 144, 149, 151M, 154,

205, 219M, 222, 234/235, 236, 242, 245L, 247L, 248, 249M, 251, 253R, 254L/R, 255, 262, 267, 267M, 268, 271
Dr. Feng Shan Ho Family Collection 213
Document China back flap top, 10/11, 12, 40, 43, 44, 45, 46, 53, 58, 63, 66R, 92, 98, 108, 120/121, 132L, 137, 160, 191, 201, 207R, 211, 220
Francis Dorai/APA 103, 151L, 243, 246, 247R
Grand Hyatt Shanghai 84
History Archives 20, 23, 26, 27, 30, 31, 32L/R, 34, 127
Imaginechina back cover right, 2/3, 4/5, 8/9, 14/15, 17, 42, 47, 48/49, 50/51, 52, 54, 55, 56, 57L/R, 59, 64, 65, 66L, 67, 68, 69, 70, 71, 72, 73, 74, 75, 76/77, 78, 81, 82, 83, 85, 86, 87, 88, 89, 91, 94, 95, 97, 100, 101, 102, 104, 105, 109, 110, 114/115, 116/117, 118/119, 122, 138, 140, 142, 143M, 145, 146, 146M, 147, 148, 152, 154M, 155, 157, 158, 161, 164, 165,

165M, 166, 168, 168M, 172, 173, 174, 175, 175M, 177, 178, 179, 180M, 181L, 182, 183, 184, 185, 186, 187, 189L/R, 190, 191M, 192, 194R, 194M, 196, 197, 198, 200, 204, 207L, 208, 209, 210, 214, 216L, 218, 219, 221, 223, 224, 225M, 226, 227M, 230, 231, 238, 239, 240M, 241, 249, 252M, 256, 257L, 258, 259, 260, 261, 263, 264M, 265, 266, 268M, 269L/R, 270, 270M
Luca Tettoni Photography 80
Michael Koeppel/APA 131
Patrick Cranley 99, 139, 141, 171, 196M, 225
Paul Beiboer 272
Shanghai Municipal Library 16, 19, 21, 22, 25, 29L/R, 36, 37, 38, 39, 173M
Stephanie Berger 60/61, 62
VPA Images front flap top, back cover left, 106/107, 232/233

Map Production Dave Priestley
© 2003 Apa Publications GmbH & Co.
Verlag KG (Singapore branch)

INSIGHT GUIDE Shanghai

Cartographic Editor **Zoë Goodwin**
Production **Caroline Low**
Design Consultants
Carlotta Junger, Graham Mitchener
Picture Research **Hilary Genin, Britta Jaschinski**

Index

sk

A
B
C
E
F
G
H
I
J
a
b
c
d
e
f
g
i
j
k
l

Insight FlexiMaps

Maps in Insight Guides are tailored to complement the text. But when you're on the road you sometimes need the big picture that only a large-scale map can provide. This new range of durable Insight Fleximaps has been designed to meet just that need.

Detailed, clear cartography
makes the comprehensive route and city maps easy to follow, highlights all the major tourist sites and provides valuable motoring information plus a full index.

Informative and easy to use
with additional text and photographs covering a destination's top 10 essential sites, plus useful addresses, facts about the destination and handy tips on getting around.

Laminated finish
allows you to mark your route on the map using a non-permanent marker pen, and wipe it off. It makes the maps more durable and easier to fold than traditional maps.

The world's most popular destinations
are covered by the 133 titles in the series – and new destinations are being added all the time. They include Alaska, Amsterdam, Bangkok, Barbados, Beijing, Brussels, Dallas/Fort Worth, Florence, Hong Kong, Ireland, Madrid, New York, Orlando, Peru, Prague, Rio, Rome, San Francisco, Sydney, Thailand, Turkey, Venice, and Vienna.

INSIGHT GUIDES
The world's largest collection of visual travel guides

INSIGHT GUIDES

The classic series that puts you in the picture

Alaska
Amazon Wildlife
American Southwest
Amsterdam
Argentina
Arizona & Grand Canyon
Asia's Best Hotels
  & Resorts
Asia, East
Asia, Southeast
Australia
Austria
Bahamas
Bali
Baltic States
Bangkok
Barbados
Barcelona
Beijing
Belgium
Belize
Berlin
Bermuda
Boston
Brazil
Brittany
Brussels
Buenos Aires
Burgundy
Burma (Myanmar)
Cairo
California
California, Southern
Canada
Caribbean
Caribbean Cruises
Channel Islands
Chicago
Chile
China
Continental Europe
Corsica
Costa Rica
Crete
Croatia
Cuba
Cyprus
Czech & Slovak Republic
Delhi, Jaipur & Agra

Denmark
Dominican Rep. & Haiti
Dublin
East African Wildlife
Eastern Europe
Ecuador
Edinburgh
Egypt
England
Finland
Florence
Florida
France
France, Southwest
French Riviera
Gambia & Senegal
Germany
Glasgow
Gran Canaria
Great Britain
Great Gardens of Britain
  & Ireland
Great Railway Journeys
  of Europe
Greece
Greek Islands
Guatemala, Belize
  & Yucatán
Hawaii
Hong Kong
Hungary
Iceland
India
India, South
Indonesia
Ireland
Israel
Istanbul
Italy
Italy, Northern
Italy, Southern
Jamaica
Japan
Jerusalem
Jordan
Kenya
Korea
Laos & Cambodia
Las Vegas

Lisbon
London
Los Angeles
Madeira
Madrid
Malaysia
Mallorca & Ibiza
Malta
Mauritius Réunion
  & Seychelles
Melbourne
Mexico
Miami
Montreal
Morocco
Moscow
Namibia
Nepal
Netherlands
New England
New Orleans
New York City
New York State
New Zealand
Nile
Normandy
Norway
Oman & The UAE
Oxford
Pacific Northwest
Pakistan
Paris
Peru
Philadelphia
Philippines
Poland
Portugal
Prague
Provence
Puerto Rico
Rajasthan
Rio de Janeiro

Rome
Russia
St Petersburg
San Francisco
Sardinia
Scandinavia
Scotland
Seattle
Shanghai
Sicily
Singapore
South Africa
South America
Spain
Spain, Northern
Spain, Southern
Sri Lanka
Sweden
Switzerland
Sydney
Syria & Lebanon
Taiwan
Tanzania & Zanzibar
Tenerife
Texas
Thailand
Tokyo
Trinidad & Tobago
Tunisia
Turkey
Tuscany
Umbria
USA: On The Road
USA: Western States
US National Parks: West
Venezuela
Venice
Vienna
Vietnam
Wales
Walt Disney World/Orlando

The world's largest collection of visual travel guides & maps